Shakespeare's Histories

Shakespeare's Histories

Edited by Emma Smith

Blackwell
Publishing

350 Main Street, Malden, MA 02148-5020, USA
108 Cowley Road, Oxford OX4 1JF, UK
550 Swanston Street, Carlton, Victoria 3053, Australia

First published 2004 by Blackwell Publishing Ltd

Library of Congress Cataloging-in-Publication Data

Shakespeare's histories / edited by Emma Smith.
    p. cm. – (Blackwell guides to criticism)
  Includes bibliographical references (p.) and index.
  ISBN 0-631-22007-0 (alk. paper) – ISBN 0-631-22008-9 (pbk. : alk. paper)
    1. Shakespeare, William, 1564–1616 – Histories. 2. Historical drama,
English – History and criticism. 3. Great Britain – History – 1066–1687 –
Historiography. 4. Literature and history – Great Britain. 5. Kings and rulers
in literature. 6. Middle Ages in literature. I. Smith, Emma, 1970– II. Series.

PR2982.S493 2004
822.3'3–dc21   2003051818

A catalogue record for this title is available from the British Library.

Typeset in 10/12.5pt Caslon
by Kolam Information Services Pvt Ltd, Pondicherry, India
Printed and bound in the United Kingdom
by MPG Books Ltd, Bodmin, Cornwall

For further information on
Blackwell Publishing, visit our website:
http://www.blackwellpublishing.com

Contents

Preface   vii

Acknowledgements   viii

1   The Development of Criticism of Shakespeare's Histories   **1**

2   Genre   **34**

Richard III and the Shape of History
Marjorie Garber   42

The Instability of History in the *Henry IV* Sequence
Paola Pugliatti   66

3   Language   **97**

Psychoanalysing the Shakespeare Text
Harry Berger   103

Value and Metaphor in the Lancastrian Tetralogy
Sandra K. Fischer   123

4   Gender and Sexuality   **143**

Elizabeth
Leah S. Marcus   147

King John
Jean E. Howard and Phyllis Rackin   182

5   History and Politics   **196**
Shakespeare's Irish History
Andrew Murphy   203

Shakespeare and National Identities
Graham Holderness   225

6   Performance   **246**
In the Context of English History
Margaret Shewring   253

Stagecraft and Imagery in Shakespeare's *Henry VI*
Alan C. Dessen   272

Index   289

Preface

This *Guide to Criticism* has two purposes. First, it offers a narrative overview of pre-twentieth-century responses to Shakespeare's history plays, including generous extracts from major commentators. It then presents twentieth-century criticism, divided into thematic sections: 'Genre', 'Language', 'Gender and Sexuality', 'History and Politics' and 'Performance'. Each of these sections includes a short overview of criticism in the area, and then reprints in full two significant recent studies. Thus the *Guide* stands as a substantial critical history and collection of recent criticism, reprinted in a single volume for ease of reference. Secondly, through the overview introductions to each section, and through the extensive bibliographies, the *Guide* also offers those readers who have access to further critical reading some suggestions about how to navigate the great sea of secondary literature on Shakespeare, by indicating key debates or interventions in the critical history. Some of the editorial material is not specific to the histories, and therefore overlaps with the companion volumes, *Shakespeare's Tragedies* and *Shakespeare's Comedies*.

The *Guide* is not, nor could it be, definitive or exhaustive, nor is it intended to canonize those authors and arguments included; rather, it is intended to be indicative of the range and vitality of Shakespearian criticism over four hundred years, from the earliest sixteenth-century responses to the new playwright up to the end of the twentieth century.

Editorial references to Shakespeare's plays use the Oxford edition, *William Shakespeare: The Complete Works*, ed. Stanley W. Wells and Gary Taylor (Oxford: Clarendon Press, 1986).

Acknowledgements

The editor and publisher wish to thank the following for permission to use copyright material:

Harry Berger, 'Psychoanalyzing the Shakespeare Text: The First Three Scenes of the "Henriad"', in *Making Trifles of Terrors: Redistributing Complicities in Shakespeare* (1997), pp. 148–67, Stanford University Press.

Alan C. Dessen, 'Stagecraft and Imagery in Shakespeare's *Henry VI*', in *The Yearbook of English Studies*, 23 (1993), pp. 65–79, Modern Humanities Research Association.

Sandra K. Fischer, '"He means to pay": Value and Metaphor in the Lancastrian Tetralogy', *Shakespeare Quarterly*, 40: 2 (1989), pp. 149–64, Folger Shakespeare Library. © Folger Shakespeare Library. Reprinted with permission of The Johns Hopkins University Press.

Marjorie Garber, 'Descanting on Deformity: Richard III and the Shape of History', in *Shakespeare's Ghost Writers: Literature as Uncanny Causality* (1987), pp. 28–51, Methuen and Co. Copyright © 1987 from *Shakespeare's Ghost Writers* by Marjorie Garber. Reproduced by permission of Routledge, Inc., part of the Taylor and Francis Group.

Graham Holderness, '"What ish my nation?": Shakespeare and National Identities', *Textual Practice*, 5 (1991), pp. 74–93, Methuen. Reprinted with permission of Taylor and Francis Ltd (http://www.tandf.co.uk/journals). The chapter also appears in Graham Holderness, *Cultural Shakespeare: Essays in the Shakespeare Myth* (Hatfield: University of Hertfordshire Press, 2001).

Jean E. Howard and Phyllis Rackin, 'King John', in *Engendering a Nation: A Feminist Account of Shakespeare's English Histories* (1997), pp. 119–33, Routledge.

Leah S. Marcus, 'Elizabeth', in *Puzzling Shakespeare: Local Reading and its Discontents* (1988), pp. 51–83, University of California Press.

Andrew Murphy, 'Shakespeare's Irish History', *Literature and History*, 5 (1996), pp. 38–59, Manchester University Press, Manchester, UK.

Paola Pugliatti, 'Time, Space and the Instability of History in the *Henry IV* Sequence', in *Shakespeare the Historian* (1996), pp. 102–31, Macmillan. Reproduced with permission of Palgrave Macmillan.

Margaret Shewring, 'In the Context of English History', in *King Richard II* (Shakespeare in Performance) (1996), pp. 91–116, Manchester University Press, Manchester, UK.

Every effort has been made to trace copyright holders and to obtain their permission for the use of copyright material. The editor and publisher will gladly receive any information enabling them to rectify in subsequent editions any error or omission.

1

The Development of Criticism of Shakespeare's Histories

1590–1660: Early Assessments

Contemporary mentions of Shakespeare are thin on the ground. It is striking – and salutary – for an historical account of early Shakespearian criticism to have its starting-point in Robert Greene's disparaging remark about the young playwright as 'an upstart Crow, beautified with our feathers, that with his *tiger's heart wrapped in a player's hide* supposes he is as well able to bombast out a blank verse as the best of you' (1592, in Schoenbaum, 1975: 115) – the reference is to the Duke of York's description of Queen Margaret in *3 Henry VI* as 'O tiger's heart wrapped in a woman's hide' (I. iv. 138). Perhaps Greene's animosity was prompted by emerging jealousy of the newcomer's literary powers since, by the time Shakespeare's narrative poems *Venus and Adonis* (1593) and *The Rape of Lucrece* (1594) were published, their author was routinely included in lists of eminent Elizabethan authors. Thomas Nashe refers to the affective power of *1 Henry VI* in his *Pierce Penniless his Supplication to the Divell* (1592):

> How would it have joyed brave Talbot (the terror of the French) to think that after he had lain two hundred years in his tomb, he should triumph again in the stage, and have his bones new embalmed with the tears of ten thousand spectators at least at several times, who, in the tragedian that represents his person, imagine they behold him fresh bleeding. (Schoenbaum, 1975: 120)

The *Shakspere Allusion Book* lists a number of other scattered references and echoes, particularly relating to Falstaff. Francis Meres's commonplace book *Palladis Tamia* (1598) praises Shakespeare's generic versatility:

> As *Plautus* and *Seneca* are accounted the best for Comedy and Tragedy among the Latins so Shakespeare among the English is the most excellent

in both kinds for the stage; for comedy witness his *Gentlemen of Verona*, his *Errors*, his *Loves Labours Lost*, his *Loves Labours Won*, his *Midsummer Night's Dream* and his *Merchant of Venice*: for tragedy his *Richard the 2. Richard the 3. Henry the 4, King John, Titus Andronicus* and his *Romeo and Juliet*. (Meres, 1598: 282)

Here, as in early printed texts of the plays, some of the titles later designated 'histories' are noted as 'tragedies'. Ben Jonson seems to be aiming at Shakespeare's history plays, among others, when he sneers at playwrights who 'with three rusty swords / And help of some few foot-and-half-foot words / Fight over York and Lancaster's long jars' in the Prologue to *Every Man in his Humour* (performed in 1598, with Shakespeare in the cast).

The first substantial act of memorializing and of shaping Shakespeare's critical reputation was the publication in 1623 of a substantial folio volume collecting together thirty-six plays as *Mr William Shakespeares Comedies, Histories and Tragedies* (often known as the First Folio, or abbreviated to F). The title of the work reveals one of its most significant critical legacies: in dividing the plays into three genres in its catalogue, the First Folio established the critical categories still in use today: 'comedies', 'histories' and 'tragedies'. The catalogue also, importantly, confined the genre of history to plays dealing with English, rather than classical, history. Thus the plays listed as histories in 1623 are, in their order, *The Life and Death of King John, The Life & death of Richard the second, The First part of King Henry the fourth, The Second part of K. Henry the fourth, The Life of King Henry the Fift, The First part of King Henry the Sixt, The Second part of King Hen. the Sixt, The Third part of King Henry the Sixt, The Life & Death of Richard the Third*, and *The Life of King Henry the Eight*. The organizing principle here seems to be historical chronology rather than date of composition or performance.

John Heminges and Henry Condell, Shakespeare's fellow-actors and the men responsible for the publishing of his collected plays, addressed their prefatory epistle 'To the Great Variety of Readers':

It had been a thing, we confess, worthy to have been wished, that the Author himself had lived to have set forth, and overseen his own writings; But since it hath been ordained otherwise, and he by death departed from that right, we pray you do not envy his Friends, the office of their care, and pain, to have collected and published them; and so to have published them, as where (before) you were abused with diverse stolen, and surreptitious copies, maimed, and deformed by the frauds and stealths of injurious impostors, that exposed them: even those, are now offered to your view cured, and perfect of their limbs; and all the rest, absolute in their numbers, as he conceived them. Who, as he was a happy imitator of Nature, was a most gentle expresser of it.

His mind and hand went together: And what he thought, he uttered with that easiness, that we have scarce received from him a blot in his papers. But it is not our province, who only gather his works, and give them you, to praise him. It is yours that read him. And there we hope, to your diverse capacities, you will find enough, both to draw, and hold you: for his wit can no more lie hid, then it could be lost. Read him, therefore; and again, and again: And if then you do not like him, surely you are in some manifest danger, not to understand him. And so we leave you to other of his Friends, whom if you need, can be your guides: if you need them not, you can lead yourselves, and others. And such Readers we wish him. (Wells and Taylor, 1986: xlv)

The playwright Ben Jonson contributed an elegy:

> Thou art a monument, without a tomb,
> And art alive still, while thy book doth live,
> And we have wits to read, and praise to give.
> That I not mix thee so, my brain excuses;
> I mean with great, but disproportioned Muses:
> For, if I thought my judgement were of years,
> I should commit thee surely with thy peers,
> And tell, how far thou didst our Lyly out-shine,
> Or sporting Kyd, or Marlowe's mighty line.
> And though thou hadst small Latin, and less Greek,
> From thence to honour thee, I would not seek
> For names; but call forth thundering Aeschylus,
> Euripides, and Sophocles to us,
> Paccuvius, Accius, him of Cordova dead,
> To life again, to hear thy buskin tread,
> And shake a stage: Or, when thy socks were on,
> Leave thee alone, for the comparison
> Of all, that insolent Greece, or haughty Rome
> Sent forth, or since did from their ashes come.
> Triumph, my Britain, thou hast one to show,
> To whom all Scenes of Europe homage owe.
> He was not of an age, but for all time!
> And all the Muses still were in their prime,
> When like Apollo he came forth to warm
> Our ears, or like a Mercury to charm!
> Nature herself was proud of his designs,
> And joyed to wear the dressing of his lines!
>   (Wells and Taylor, 1986: xlv)

In his *Timber, or Discoveries*, first published in 1640, Jonson again addressed Shakespeare's reputation, referring back to Heminges and Condell's 'To the Great Variety of Readers':

I remember the players have often mentioned it as an honour to Shakespeare, that in his writing, whatsoever to be penned, he never blotted out line. My answer hath been, 'Would he had blotted a thousand'; which they thought a malevolent speech. I had not told posterity this but for their ignorance, who choose that circumstance to commend their friend by wherein he most faulted; and to justify mine own candour: for I loved the man, and do honour his memory, on this side idolatry, as much as any. He was, indeed, honest, and of an open and free nature; had an excellent fantasy, brave notions, and gentle expressions; wherein he flowed with that facility that sometime it was necessary he should be stopped. '*Sufflaminandus erat*' ['Sometimes he needed the brake'], as Augustus said of Haterius. His wit was in his own power, would the rule of it had been so too. Many times he fell into those things, could not escape laughter: as when he said in the person of Caesar, one speaking to him, 'Caesar, thou dost me wrong'; he replied 'Caesar did never wrong, but with just cause'; and such like: which were ridiculous. But he redeemed his vices with his virtues. There was ever more in him to be praised than to be pardoned. (Donaldson, 1985: 539–40)

1660–1720: Texts in Print and on Stage

It is to post-Restoration culture that we need to look to see the establishment of many now-familiar preoccupations and approaches to Shakespeare. As Michael Dobson notes, in his study of the 'extensive cultural work that went into the installation of Shakespeare as England's National Poet' between 1660 and 1769:

so many of the conceptions of Shakespeare we inherit date not from the Renaissance but from the Enlightenment. It was this period, after all, which initiated many of the practices which modern spectators and readers of Shakespeare would generally regard as normal or even natural: the performance of his female roles by women instead of men (instigated at a revival of *Othello* in 1660); the reproduction of his works in scholarly editions, with critical apparatus (pioneered by Rowe's edition of 1709 and the volume of commentary appended to it by Charles Gildon the following year); the publication of critical monographs devoted entirely to the analysis of his works (an industry founded by John Dennis's *An Essay upon the Writings and Genius of Shakespeare*, 1712); the promulgation of the plays in secondary education (the earliest known instance of which is the production of *Julius Caesar* mounted in 1728 'by the young Noblemen of the Westminster School'), and in higher education (first carried out in the lectures on Shakespeare given by William Hawkins at Oxford in the early 1750s); the erection of monuments to Shakespeare in nationally symbolic public places (initiated by Peter Sheemaker's statue in Poets' Corner, Westminster Abbey, unveiled in 1741); and the promotion of Stratford-upon-Avon as a site of secular pilgrimage (ratified at Garrick's jubilee in 1769). (Dobson, 1992: 3)

Ben Jonson's half-praise, half-sneer in his elegy about Shakespeare's classical knowledge – 'small Latin, and less Greek' – was an early suggestion of one of the obstacles to Shakespeare appreciation in post-Restoration culture. The Restoration aesthetics of neoclassicism favoured poetry as imitation of classical, especially Roman, authors, and the idea of the writer as educated craftsman following ancient generic rules. This led, inevitably, to a stress on Shakespeare's attempts at the classically sanctioned genres of tragedy and comedy, rather than the vernacular sixteenth-century genre of chronicle history play. Thus Thomas Fuller identifies Shakespeare among *The Worthies of England* in 1662, but is preoccupied with his subject's education, or lack of it:

> *Plautus,* who was an exact Comaedian, yet never any Scholar, as our Shakespeare (if alive) would confess himself. Add to all these, that though his Genius generally was *jocular,* and inclining him to *festivity,* yet he could, (when so disposed), be *solemn* and *serious,* as appears by his Tragedies, so that *Heraclitus* himself (I mean if secret and unseen) might afford to smile at his Comedies, they were so *merry,* and *Democritus* scarce forbear to sigh at his Tragedies they were so *mournful.* He was an eminent instance of the truth of that Rule, *Poeta non fit, sed nascitur,* one is not *made* but *born* a Poet. Indeed his Learning was very little, so that as *Cornish diamonds* are not polished by any Lapidary, but are pointed and smoothed even as they are taken out of the Earth, so *nature* it self was all the *art* that was used upon him. (Fuller, 1662: 126)

The introduction of nature as a term of cultural valorization to balance against art is key to the recuperation of Shakespeare in this period. When, for example, Margaret Cavendish defends Shakespeare in one of her *Sociable Letters* of 1664, she argues that Shakespeare transforms his historical materials through the vitality of his characters:

> So well he hath expressed in his plays all sorts of persons, as one would think he had been transformed into every one of those persons he hath described; and as sometimes one would think he was really himself the clown or jester he feigns, so one would think, he was also the King and Privy Counsellor...who would not think he had been such a man as his Sir *John* Falstaff? and who would not think he had been *Harry* the Fifth?...Shakespear's wit and eloquence was general, for, and upon all subjects, he rather wanted subjects for his wit and eloquence to work on, for which he was forced to take some of his plots out of history, where he only took the bare designs, the wit and language being all his own. (Thompson and Roberts, 1997: 12–13)

Early in this process of recuperating Shakespeare is John Dryden's important statement of neoclassical aesthetics, his essay *Of Dramatic Poesie* (1668). Dryden's essay takes the form of a discussion between four interlocutors: Eugenius, Crites, Lisedeius and Neander, generally believed to represent Dryden himself. While others of the conversationalists praise Ben Jonson as 'the greatest man of the last age' because of his adherence to classical rules, particularly the unities of time, place and action (Dryden, 1969: 14), Neander favours Shakespeare for his untutored but instinctive, intuitive expression. Shakespeare is to be praised for his natural learning, despite his flaws:

> he was the man who of all Modern, and perhaps Ancient Poets, had the largest and most comprehensive soul. All the Images of Nature were still present to him, and he drew them not laboriously but luckily: when he describes anything, you more than see it, you feel it too. Those who accuse him to have wanted learning, give him the greater commendation: he was naturally learn'd; he needed not the spectacles of Books to read Nature; he look'd inwards, and found her there. (Dryden, 1969: 47)

In his history plays, Shakespeare is criticized for disregarding the unities of time:

> they are rather so many chronicles of kings, or the business many times of thirty or forty years, crampt into a representation of two hours and a half, which is not to imitate or paint nature, but rather to draw her in miniature, to take her in little; to look upon her through the wrong end of a perspective, and receive her images not only much less, but infinitely more imperfect than the life. (Dryden, 1969: 29)

In the comparison with Ben Jonson, which was to be the touchstone for the nascent literary criticism of Shakespeare in the Restoration period, however, Neander's emotional loyalties were clear. Comparing Falstaff – 'the best of comical characters' (1969: 51) – to Morose from Jonson's *Epicoene, or The Silent Woman*, Neander sees Shakespeare's character as a 'miscellany of humours or images, drawn from so many several men . . . the very sight of such an unwieldy old debauch'd fellow is a Comedy alone' (1969: 51–2): 'If I would compare [Jonson] with *Shakespeare*, I must acknowledge him the more correct Poet, but *Shakespeare* the greater wit. *Shakespeare* was the *Homer*, or Father of our Dramatick Poets; *Johnson* was the *Virgil*, the pattern of elaborate writing; I admire him, but I love *Shakespeare*' (1969: 50).

In his preface to the first scholarly edition of Shakespeare's works (1709–10), the poet laureate and tragedian Nicholas Rowe advocates a more historically informed appreciation of Shakespeare's apparent divergence from classical precepts:

> If one undertook to examine the greatest part of these [Shakespeare's tragedies] by those rules which are established by Aristotle, and taken from the model of

the Grecian stage, it would be no very hard task to find a great many faults: but as Shakespear lived under a kind of mere light of nature, and had never been made acquainted with the regularity of those written precepts, so it would be hard to judge him by a law he knew nothing of. We are to consider him as a man that lived in a state of almost universal license and ignorance: there was no established judge, but every one took the liberty to write according to the dictates of his own fancy. (Rowe, 1709–10: xxvi)

Rowe argues that writing outside the constraints of literary tradition allows Shakespeare's imagination free rein:

I believe we are better pleased with those thoughts, altogether new and uncommon, which his own imagination supplied him so abundantly with, than if he had given us the most beautiful passages out of the Greek and Latin poets, and that in the most agreeable manner that it was possible for a master of the English language to deliver them. (1709–10: iv)

He also recognizes the generic hybridity of many, even the majority, of Shakespeare's plays, arguing that the history plays might be re-categorized as tragedies: 'His plays are properly to be distinguished only into comedies and tragedies. Those which are called histories, and even some of his comedies, are really tragedies, with a run or mixture of comedy amongst them' (1709–10: xvii). Chief among this 'run' of comedy in the history plays was the character of Falstaff, 'allowed by every body to be a Master-piece':

the character is always well-sustained, though drawn out into the length of three plays; and even the account of his death, given by his old landlady Mrs Quickly, in the first Act of *Henry V*, though it be extremely natural, is yet as diverting as any part of his life. If there be any fault in the draught he has made of this lewd old fellow, it is, that though he has made him a thief, lying, cowardly, vainglorious, and in short every way vicious, yet he has given him so much Wit as to make him almost too agreeable; and I don't know whether some people have not, in remembrance of the diversion he had formerly afforded them, been sorry to see his friend Hal use him so scurvily, when he comes to the crown in the end of the *Second Part of Henry the Fourth*. (1709–10: xvii–xviii)

Rowe praises Shakespeare for his historical accuracy:

For those plays which he has taken from the English or Roman history, let any man compare them, and he will find the character as exact in the poet as the historian. He seems indeed so far from proposing to himself any one action for a subject, that the title very often tells you, 'tis *The Life of King John, King Richard*, &c. What can be more agreeable to the idea our historians give of Henry the Sixth, than the picture Shakespear has drawn of him! His Manners are every where exactly the same with the story; one finds him still described with simplicity, passive sanctity, want of courage, weakness of mind, and easy submission to the governance of an imperious wife, or prevailing faction: though at the same time the poet does justice to his good qualities, and moves the pity of his audience for him, by showing him pious, disinterested, a condemner of the things of this world, and wholly resigned to the severest dispensations of God's providence. (1709–10: xxvii–xxix)

A final, seventh volume appended to Rowe's edition in 1710 added a more extensive critique of the dramatic qualities of the plays in 'An Essay on the Art, Rise and Progress of the Stage in Greece, Rome and England' by Charles Gildon. Gildon's assessment of Shakespeare's art is according to classical precedent, and thus he condemns the plays' contravention of the unities. By definition, Gildon argues, life does not follow these generic rules, and therefore plays based on historical events are likely to fall short of classical standards:

I would therefore recommend to the poet the entire invention of his own fable, there being very few actions in history, that are capable of being made general and allegoric, which is the beauty and essential of both an epic, and dramatic action. Not but the poet may take incidents from history and matter of fact, but then they must have that probability and verisimilitude, that art requires. (1709–10: xliii)

Since Gildon followed Rowe in asserting that the history plays follow their sources closely, they were not likely to achieve this dramatic unity:

since these Plays are Histories, there can be no Manner of Fable or Design in them. I shall not therefore give the Plot but refer the Reader to those Historians where he may find the Stories at large, and by them judge how near Shakespear has kept to the Character, History has given us of them. (1709–10: 338)

Shakespeare, he argues, already knew and pre-empted this criticism, apologizing for his failings in the choruses to *Henry V*:

The Prologue to this play is as remarkable as any thing in Shakespear, and is a proof, that he was extremely sensible of the absurdity, which then possessed the stage in bringing in whole kingdoms, and lives, and various actions in one piece; for he apologizes for it, and desires the audience to persuade their imaginations to help him out and promises a Chorus to help their imagination. (1709–10: 346–7)

In the end, Gildon's view of Shakespeare is mixed:

Shakespear is indeed stored with a great many beauties, but they are in a heap of rubbish; and as in the ruins of a magnificent pile we are pleased with the capitals of pillars, the Basso-relievos and the like as we meet with them, yet how infinitely more beautiful, and charming must it be to behold them in their proper places in the standing building, where every thing answers the other, and one harmony of all the parts heightens the excellence even of those parts. (1709–10: 425)

Gildon expanded this view in his book *The Complete Art of Poetry* (1718), in which the final chapter offers 'Shakespeariana: or Select Moral Reflections, Topicks, Similies and Descriptions from Shakespear' – the first book of Shakespearian quotations.

It is easy to see how the idea of a Shakespeare good in parts also reflects contemporary stage practice. What Gildon is attempting critically – the sifting of worthy from unworthy elements of the plays – scores of stage-plays attempted dramatically, in adapting, rewriting and recombining Shakespeare's works to suit the tastes of new audiences. These adaptations are themselves works of criticism; often, in prefatory material and epilogues, explicitly so. Many have a definite contemporary political agenda, and many implicitly endorse prevailing neoclassical ideas about generic decorum by disciplining the mixed generic structure of many of Shakespeare's history plays and identifying them more closely as comedies or tragedies.

In 1680 Nahum Tate's version of *Richard II* seemed to suggest parallels between the play's depiction of deposition and the Exclusion Crisis, although Tate disingenuously denied any implied commentary: 'to form any resemblance between the times here written of, and the present, had been unpardonable presumption in me. If the prohibitors [censors] conceive any such notion I am not accountable for that' (Vickers, 1974: I, 321–2). Tate alters the characterization of Richard from Shakespeare's, painted 'in the worst colours of history, dissolute, unadviseable, devoted to ease and luxury' (1974: I, 322); instead, he endows his king 'with the language of an active, prudent prince, preferring the good of his subjects to his own private pleasure' (I, 323).

Also with an opportunistic eye to political parallels was John Crowne's *Henry the Sixth, the First Part with the Murder of Humphrey Duke of Gloucester* (1681), presented in its dedicatory epistle as 'no indifferent satire upon the most pompous and potent folly that ever reigned in the minds of men, called popery' (Crowne, 1681: [A2]). Crowne also adapted parts 1 and 2 of *Henry VI* as *The Misery of Civil War* (1680), with a prologue describing it as a 'rod / To whip us for a fault, we too much love / And have for ages liv'd, call'd civil strife' (Crowne, 1680: A2). In 1700 Thomas Betterton adapted Shakespeare as *King Henry IV, with the Humours of Sir John Falstaff*, and in the same year, Colley Cibber's influential version of *Richard III*, which was theatrically the most popular of all Shakespearian adaptations in this period, had its first performances. Cibber drew on *3 Henry VI* as well as others of the history plays to create a theatrical vehicle for the actor playing Richard, whose part was amplified with several new soliloquies. Many of the enduring qualities of this adaptation have been preserved in Laurence Olivier's 1955 film, which uses a number of Cibber's innovations. In 1720 Charles Molloy's version of *Henry V* was performed as the comedy *The Half-pay Officers*, and Theophilus Cibber presented *King Henry VI: A Tragedy* as a warning against civil strife. Aaron Hill adapted *Henry V* in 1723: his *King Henry the Fifth* offers a 'breeches role' for Harriet, the king's sweetheart who follows him to France dressed as a boy. In the same year, Ambrose Philips's *Humfrey, Duke of Gloucester: A Tragedy* (an adaptation of *2 Henry VI*) presented itself as the story of Humfrey, 'a free-born hero' for whom 'destruction is the patriot's doom, / When Kings are only ministers of Rome' (Philips, 1723: A4). Francis Gentleman's adaptation of *Richard II* was performed in 1755.

1720–1765: Editions and Editors

Contemporaneous with the process of adaptation and rewriting for the stage was the attempt to establish a 'correct' text for the study. Alexander Pope's edition of 1723 described itself on its title page as 'Collated and Corrected by the former Editions'. Pope's 'Preface of the Editor' evades the task of the critic in favour of that of the new, humanist textual scholar, the editor. Rather than entering 'into a Criticism upon this Author', Pope sets out to 'give an account of the fate of his Works, and the disadvantages under which they have been transmitted to us. We shall hereby extenuate many faults which are his, and clear him from the imputation of many which are not' (Pope, 1723: I, i–ii). Pope acquits Shakespeare of the charges that neoclassical critics had laid at his door: 'To judge therefore of Shakespear by Aristotle's rules, is like trying a man by the Laws of one Country, who acted under those of another' (1723: I, vi). Rather, Pope repeats the critical orthodoxy that Shakespeare 'is not so much an Imitator, as an Instrument, of Nature; and 'tis not so just to say that he speaks from her, as that she speaks through him' (I, ii), and makes a particular feature of Shakespeare's characterization:

> His Characters are so much Nature her self, that 'tis a sort of injury to call them by so distant a name as Copies of her... Every single character in Shakespear is as much an Individual, as those in Life itself; it is as impossible to find any two alike; and such as from their relation or affinity in any respect appear most to be Twins, will upon comparison be found remarkably distinct. To this life and variety of Character, we must add the wonderful Preservation of it; which is such throughout his plays, that had all the Speeches been printed without the very names of the Persons, I believe one might have apply'd them with certainty to every speaker. (1723: I, ii–iii)

Pope praises Shakespeare's 'Power over our Passions' (I, iii), and also his intellectual control of 'the coolness of Reflection and Reasoning' (I, iv).

Many of Shakespeare's perceived faults are in fact, Pope proposes, errors of the printing and publication process. He surmises that Shakespeare did not authorize or check those of the plays that were published in quarto editions during his lifetime, and that therefore:

> how many low and vicious parts and passages might no longer reflect upon this great Genius, but appear unworthily charged upon him? And even in those which are really his, how many faults may have been unjustly laid to his account from arbitrary Additions, Expunctions, Transpositions of scenes and lines, confusion of Characters and Persons, wrong application of Speeches, corruptions of innumerable Passages by the Ignorance, and wrong Corrections of 'em again by the Impertinence, of his first Editors? (I, xxi)

In 1726, a volume appeared with the descriptive title *Shakespeare Restored: or, a Specimen of Many Errors, as well Committed, and Unamended, by Mr Pope in his Late Edition of this Poet*. Its author, Lewis Theobald, proposed numerous new readings and emendations, many of which were plagiarized by Pope for his second edition which appeared in 1728. Pope pilloried Theobald in the first edition of his mock-epic poem the *Dunciad* published a few months later, mocking his pedantry in footnotes wondering whether 'Dunciad' should be spelt 'Dunceiad' and pitying 'hapless Shakespear, yet of Tibbald sore, / Wish'd he had blotted for himself before'. Theobald's riposte was his own Shakespeare edition of 1733, *The Works of Shakespeare in Seven Volumes. Collated with the Oldest Copies, and Corrected; With notes, Explanatory and Critical.*

Theobald's style is effusive:

> No Age, perhaps, can produce an Author more various from himself, than Shakespeare has been universally acknowledg'd to be. The Diversity in Stile, and other Parts of Composition, so obvious in him, is as variously to be accounted for. His Education, we find, was at best but begun: and he started early into a Science from the Force of Genius, unequally assisted by acquir'd Improvements. His Fire, Spirit, and Exuberance of Imagination gave an Impetuosity to his Pen: His Ideas flow'd from him in a Stream rapid, but not turbulent; copious, but not ever overbearing its Shores. The Ease and Sweetness of his Temper might not a little contribute to his Facility in Writing: as his Employment, as a Player, gave him an Advantage and Habit of fancying himself the very Character he meant to delineate. (Theobald, 1733: I, xv)

His view of his predecessor and literary rival Pope, and of Thomas Rymer, a critic disgusted by *Othello* (see the companion volume *Shakespeare's Tragedies*, pp. 10–11), is clear; Shakespeare studies has its first real personality clash:

He has acted with regard to our Author, as an Editor, whom Lipsius mentions, did with regard to Martial; *Inventus est nescio quis Popa, qui non vitia ejus, sed ipsum, excidit.* He has attack'd him like an unhandy Slaughterman; and not lopp'd off the Errors, but the Poet.

Praise sometimes an Injury. When this is found to be the Fact, how absurd must appear the Praises of such an Editor? It seems a moot Point, whether Mr Pope has done most Injury to Shakespeare as his Editor and Encomiast; or Mr Rymer done him Service as his Rival and Censurer. Were it every where the true Text, which That Editor in his late pompous Edition gave us, the Poet deserv'd not the large Encomiums bestow'd by him: nor, in that Case, is Rymer's Censure of the Barbarity of his Thoughts, and the Impropriety of his Expressions, groundless. They have Both shewn themselves in an equal Impuissance of suspecting or amending the corrupted Passages: and tho' it be neither Prudence to censure, or commend, what one does not understand; yet if a Man must do one when he plays the Critick, the latter is the more ridiculous Office. And by That Shakespeare suffers most. (1733: I, xxxv–xxxvi)

Theobald's is not, however, the last word in this particular bibliographic and personal spat. In 1747 Pope, together with his collaborator William Warburton, brought out an edition to trump Theobald: *The Works of Shakespear in Eight Volumes. The Genuine Text (collated with all the former Editions, and then corrected and emended) is here settled: Being restored from the Blunders of the first Editors, and the Interpolations of the two Last: with A Comment and Notes, Critical and Explanatory.*

Theobald's edition establishes and promulgates his own theory of the editor's task. This covers three activities: 'the Emendation of corrupt Passages; the Explanation of obscure and difficult ones; and an Inquiry into the Beauties and Defects of Composition' (1733: I, xl). He elaborates on his editorial principles:

Where-ever the Author's Sense is clear and discoverable, (tho', perchance, low and trivial;) I have not by any Innovation tamper'd with his Text; out of an Ostentation of endeavouring to make him speak better than the old Copies have done.

Where, thro' all the former Editions, a Passage has labour'd under flat Nonsense and invincible Darkness, if, by the Addition or Alteration of a Letter or two, I have restored to Him both Sense and Sentiment, such Corrections, I am persuaded, will need no Indulgence.

And whenever I have taken a greater Latitude and Liberty in amending, I have constantly endeavoured to support my Corrections and Conjectures by parallel Passages and Authorities from himself, the surest Means of expounding any Author whatsoever... Some Remarks are spent in explaining Passages, where the Wit or Satire depends on an obscure Point of History: Others, where Allusions are to Divinity, Philosophy, or other Branches of Science. Some are added to shew, where there is a Suspicion of our Author having borrow'd from the Antients: Others, to shew where he is rallying his Contemporaries; or where He himself is rallied by them. And some are necessarily thrown in, to explain an obscure and obsolete Term, Phrase, or Idea. (1733: I, xliii–xliv)

Theobald echoed Rowe's sense of Shakespeare's fidelity to historical sources: 'he was a close and accurate Copier wherever his fable was founded on History' (I, xlii). Further editions, including those by Thomas Hanmer (1743) and Edward Capell (1767), appeared throughout the eighteenth century as each editor claimed to be improving on the text of his predecessors.

Shakespeare's most significant and influential eighteenth-century mediator was editor and critic Samuel Johnson, whose annotated edition appeared in 1765. Johnson sets out 'to inquire, by what peculiarities of excellence *Shakespeare* has gained and kept the favour of his countrymen' (Johnson, 1765: I, viii). The answer, for Johnson is that:

> *Shakespeare* is above all writers ... the poet of nature; the poet that holds up to his readers a faithful mirrour of manners and of life. His characters are not modified by the customs of particular places, unpractised by the rest of the world; by the peculiarities of studies or professions, which can operate but upon small numbers; or by the accidents of transient fashions or temporary opinions: they are the genuine progeny of common humanity, such as the world will always supply, and observation will always find. His persons act and speak by the influence of those general passions and principles by which all minds are agitated, and the whole system of life is continued in motion. (1765: I, viii–ix)

For Johnson, Shakespeare is a philosopher and teacher, filled with 'practical axioms and domestick wisdom', but he argues strongly against the recent tendency to find Shakespeare's greatness in particular passages: 'he that tries to recommend him by select quotations, will succeed like the pedant in *Hierocles*, who, when he offered his house to sale, carried a brick in his pocket as a specimen' (I, ix). Verisimilitude, the quality of creating recognizable individuals, dialogue and scenarios, is key to Johnson's appraisal of Shakespeare's work. Thus '*Shakespeare* has no heroes; his scenes are occupied only by men, who act and speak as the reader thinks that he should himself have spoken or acted on the same occasion', he 'approximates the remote, and familiarizes the wonderful', and his reader can benefit from 'reading human sentiments in human language' (I, xi–xii). This is evident in Shakespeare's history plays, which are to be judged as depictions of humanity rather than of politics or hierarchy: '*Shakespeare* always makes nature predominate over accident; and if he preserves the essential character, is not very careful of distinctions superinduced and adventitious. His story requires Romans or kings, but he thinks only on men' (I, xii). Johnson also dismisses classical generic precedent as inapplicable to the history plays, thereby disallowing neoclassical objections:

His histories, being neither tragedies nor comedies, are not subject to any of their laws; nothing more is necessary to all the praise which they expect, than that the changes of action be so prepared as to be understood, that the incidents be various and affecting, and the characters consistent, natural and distinct. No other unity is intended, and therefore none is to be sought. (I, xxiv)

He uses *Henry V* as an example in his argument about how 'Imitations produce pain or pleasure, not because they are mistaken for realities, but because they bring realities to mind':

When the imagination is recreated by a painted landscape, the trees are not supposed capable to give us shade, or the fountains coolness; but we consider, how we should be pleased with such fountains playing beside us, and such woods waving over us. We are agitated in reading the history of *Henry* the Fifth, yet no man takes his book for the field of *Agencourt*. (I, xxix)

Johnson criticizes Shakespeare for loose and sometimes careless plotting, and for a tendency to tail off in the latter part of his plays, so that 'his catastrophe is improbably produced or imperfectly represented' (I, xx), and elsewhere Shakespeare is rebuked for the violation of chronology and his use of anachronisms, and for occasionally strained or wearisome rhetoric. Johnson reserves his most lengthy, and famous, censure for Shakespeare's wordplay:

A quibble is to *Shakespeare*, what luminous vapours are to the traveller; he follows it at all adventures; it is sure to lead him out of his way, and sure to engulf him in the mire. It has some malignant power over his mind, and its fascinations are irresistible. Whatever be the dignity or profundity of his disquisition, whether he be enlarging knowledge or exalting affection, whether he be amusing attention with incidents, or enchaining it in suspense, let but a quibble spring up before him, and he leaves his work unfinished. A quibble is the golden apple for which he will always turn aside from his career, or stoop from his elevation. A quibble, poor and barren as it is, gave him such delight, that he was content to purchase it, by the sacrifice of reason, propriety and truth. A quibble was to him the fatal *Cleopatra* for which he lost the world, and was content to lose it. (I, xxiii–xxiv)

Like previous commentators, Johnson allows for a mixture of good and bad qualities in Shakespeare's work: 'he has scenes of undoubted and perpetual excellence, but perhaps not one play which, if it were now exhibited as the work of a contemporary writer, would be heard to its conclusion.' Rather, Johnson argues, 'it must be at last confessed, that as we owe everything to him, he owes something to us; that, if much of his praise is paid by perception and judgement, much is likewise given by custom and veneration' (I, xlvi).

1765–1800: Texts on Page and Stage

Johnson's interest in the texts of the plays did not extend to an interest in their theatrical performance. Sandra Clark describes the eighteenth century's preference for adapted Shakespeare on the stage as a 'paradox whereby Shakespeare's works achieved the status of "classics" in the study while for a long period on the stage the divine Bard (as he came to be called) was often represented by plays only a small proportion of which he actually wrote' (Clark, 1997: xliii). Shakespeare's position in the theatre during the eighteenth century was largely dependent on his tragedies (see Hogan, 1952: vol. II). Bell's Acting Edition of 1774, dedicated to David Garrick, 'the best illustrator of, and the best living comment on, Shakespeare' (Bell, 1969: I, 3), presents itself as 'a companion to the theatre' (I, 8) rather than a critical edition. It prints the texts with the standard performance cuts and emendations, proposing that these changes allow 'the noble monuments he has left us, of unrivalled ability, [to] be restored to due proportion and natural lustre, by sweeping off those cobwebs, and that dust of depraved opinion, which Shakespeare was unfortunately forced to throw on them' (I, 6). Bell's edition also presents itself as an alternative to the increasingly scholarly and specialized writing on Shakespeare, as a forerunner to self-consciously pedagogic or introductory volumes popular in the twentieth century:

> it has been our peculiar endeavour to render what we call the essence of Shakespeare, more instructive and intelligible; especially to the ladies and to youth; glaring indecencies being removed, and intricate passages explained; and lastly, we have striven to supply plainer ideas of criticism, both in public and private, than we have hitherto met with.
>
> A general view of each play is given, by way of introduction.
>
> Though this is not an edition meant for the profoundly learned, nor the deeply studious, who love to find out, and chace their own critical game; yet we flatter ourselves both parties may perceive fresh ideas started for speculation and reflection. (Bell, 1969: I, 9–10)

Unlike previous editors, who had praised Shakespeare's fidelity to historical source, Bell's particular stress on theatrical representation finds dramatic success an alternative locus of tribute. Thus the introductory remarks to *Richard III* argue:

> whatever doubts may arise as to the real character and figure of our Third Richard, Shakespeare was most undoubtedly right to make him a confirmed, uniform villain: nothing in the medium way would have been half so striking on the stage, and it was equally prudent to present him deformed in figure, as well as in mind; though the unities are grossly, yet they are almost imperceptibly,

broken, in this play; the events appear so admirably connected with, and consequential to, each other: nature speaks in all the characters with plain, intelligible dignity; no bombast swells upon the ear, no improbability intrudes on belief; upon the whole it must always read well, but act better. (1969: III, 3)

Of *1 Henry IV*, the edition notes that 'against our critical relish, he has mingled mirth, and some very low of its kind, with sadness. However, Falstaff's luxuriance, and the Prince of Wales's pleasantry, are excellent: all the Tragic parts, particularly Hotspur's, are very well written; it is more regular than most of Shakespear's pieces, but does not, nor never will, please the Ladies' (IV, 3); *Henry V*, despite some 'low quibbling comedy', shows Shakespeare 'summon[ing] all his powers, to do the hero justice' (IV, 3); *1 Henry VI* does not meet with approval, since 'National transactions, however important they may be in their nature and consequences, are not likely to have a very popular effect, as they tend chiefly to indulge political reflection, but have very little to gratify taste. Such pieces as this are also very barren of female characters and affecting circumstances, without which the Drama is too defective' (VII, 89).

While Shakespeare criticism looks to be a male preserve, women were also increasingly involved, although the assumption in Bell's edition that history plays had little to offer women readers and audiences may be borne out in their limited commentary on this genre. Elizabeth Montagu's *An Essay on the Writings and Genius of Shakespear, compared with the Greek and French Dramatic Poets* (1769) was extensively reprinted and translated, and focuses largely on the tragedies in response to Voltaire's attack. Montagu scorned as narrow-minded critics who criticized Shakespeare's learning:

> For copying nature he found it in the busy walks of human life, he drew from an original, with which the literati are seldom well acquainted. They perceive his portraits are not of the Grecian or of the Roman school: after finding them unlike to the celebrated forms preserved in learned museums they do not deign to enquire whether they resemble the living persons they were intended to represent. (Montagu, 1970: 17)

History allows Shakespeare to break down 'the barriers that had before confined the dramatic writers to the regions of comedy, or tragedy. He perceived the fertility of the subjects that lay between the two extremes' (1970: 66). Since 'those dramas of Shakespeare, which he distinguishes by the name of his histories, being of an original kind and peculiar construction, cannot come within any rules which are prior to their existence' (1970: 55), it is rather Shakespeare's facility in drawing recognizable characters that Montagu most admires: his 'dramatis personae are men, frail by constitution, hurt by ill habits, faulty and unequal. But they speak with human voices, are actuated by human passions, and are engaged in the common affairs of human life' (1970: 81). History is a genre more suited to moral reflection than is tragedy: 'the various interests and characters in these historical plays, and the mixture of the comic, weaken the operations of pity and terror, but introduce various opportunities of conveying moral instruction, as occasion is given to a variety of reflections and observations, more useful in common life than those drawn from the conditions of kings and heroes, and persons greatly superior to us by nature or fortune' (1970: 62). Montagu pays particular attention to the two parts of *Henry IV*, praising their characterization, and plotting, and drawing favourable comparisons with Euripides.

Elizabeth Griffith, in her *The Morality of Shakespeare's Drama Illustrated* (1775), described Shakespeare as a 'Philosopher' whose 'anatomy of the human heart is delineated from *nature*, not from *metaphysics*; referring immediately to our intuitive sense and not wandering with the schoolmen' (Griffith, 1971: ix), and thus, perhaps, uniquely accessible and applicable to contemporary women largely denied a classical education. Like Montagu, Griffith is able to claim authority to write on Shakespeare by wresting him from the enervating grasp of the scholar and reinstating him as the poet of everyday life. At times, in her extensive commentary, Griffith speaks consciously as a female reader of Shakespeare, as when she discusses parallels between Hotspur and Prince Hal in their bravery: 'women are apt to esteem the ancient virtue of courage at a higher rate than men in general are' (1971: 226).

Character study was to be the dominant theme of Romantic criticism of Shakespeare, and it had one of its earliest exemplars in Maurice Morgann's *An Essay on the Dramatic Character of Sir John Falstaff* (1777): 'an Essay professing to treat of the courage of *Falstaff*, but extending itself to his whole character; to the arts and genius of his Poetic-Maker, Shakespeare; and thro' him sometimes, with ambitious aim, even to the principles of human nature itself' (Morgann, 1972: 283). Morgann's defence of his subject from the charge of cowardice was written more in 'the character and tone of an advocate than an inquirer' (Smith, 1963: 203). He attempts to derive a vocabulary with which effects of character can be discussed, differentiating between 'mental impressions' and 'understanding': 'the understanding seems for the most part to take cognizance of *actions* only, and from these to infer *motives* and *character*; but the sense we have been speaking of proceeds in a contrary course; and determines of *actions* from certain *first principles of character*, which seem wholly out of the reach of the understanding' (Smith, 1963: 207). Morgann argues that 'no part whatever of his character seems to be fully settled in our minds . . . it must be a strange art in Shakespeare which can draw our liking and good will towards so offensive an object' (Smith, 1963: 209). This close analysis of a single aspect of a play was something new – and also expounded a controversial proposition. James Boswell records Samuel Johnson's retort: 'Why sir, we shall have the man come forth again, and as he has proved Falstaff to be no coward, he may prove Iago to be a very good character' (quoted in Morgann, 1972: 12n).

Other character studies by William Richardson (1784), on *Richard III* among others, and by Thomas Whately (1785), comparing *Macbeth* and *Richard III*, set the scene for work by Coleridge and Hazlitt. There were, however, other critical strands also emerging. In 1794 Walter Whiter published *A Specimen of a Commentary on Shakspeare. Containing I. Notes on As You Like It. II. An Attempt to Explain and Illustrate various passages on a new principle of criticism, derived from Mr Locke's doctrine of The Association of Ideas.* Whiter explained John Locke's idea of 'association' as 'the combination of those ideas, which have no natural alliance or relation to each other' (Whiter, 1972: 65). Whiter argued that critics had hitherto been preoccupied by discovering:

> the *direct*, though sometimes perhaps obscure allusions, which the poet has *intentionally* made to the customs of his own age, and to the various vices, follies, passions and prejudices, which are the pointed objects of his satire or his praise. But the commentators have not marked those *indirect* and *tacit* references, which are produced by the writer with *no* intentional allusion; or rather they have not unfolded those trains of thought, alike pregnant with the materials *peculiar* to his age, which often prompt the combinations of the poet in the wildest exertions of his fancy, and which conduct him, unconscious of the effect, to the various *peculiarities* of his imagery or his language. (1972: 71–2)

As an example of his method of disinterring connotations and connections between particular words through extensive and densely referenced analogues, his explication of the phrase 'purple testament of bleeding war' in *Richard II* (III. iii. 93) takes in references to editors and critics, the anonymous play *The First Part of Jeronimo*, analogue metaphors of books and binding from *The Winter's Tale* and *Romeo and Juliet*, the 'unbookish jealousy' of Othello (IV. i. 100) and scores of other linguistic correlations (1972: 95–107). Whiter's is an early, painstaking example of the close verbal analysis developed by twentieth-century critics as diverse as Caroline Spurgeon, Frank Kermode and Patricia Parker (see Chapter 3 on Language).

1800–1840: Romantic Appropriations by Schlegel, Coleridge and Hazlitt

This stress on the language of the plays was implicitly continued by Romantic readers. In his *Shakespeare und kein Ende* (translated as 'Shakespeare ad Infinitum') of 1815, Johann Wolfgang von Goethe claimed that 'Shakespeare belongs by necessity in the annals of poetry; in the annals of theatre he appears only by accident' (quoted in Bate, 1992: 76). For Goethe, Shakespeare's power is in language: 'there is no higher or purer pleasure than to sit with closed eyes and hear a naturally expressive voice recite, not declaim, a play of Shakespeare's' (Bate, 1992: 70). For Goethe, as for many critics of the period, Shakespeare is a Romantic thinker, 'a decidedly modern poet' (1992: 72), drawing his character from 'England, the sea-encircled and mist-covered country, whose enterprise reaches all parts of the earth' (1992: 70). There are, however, moments of high dramatic and visual symbolism; for example, the moment in which 'the son and heir in *Henry IV* takes the crown from the side of the slumbering king, who lies sick unto death – takes the crown and marches proudly away with it. But these are only moments, scattered jewels, separated by much that is untheatrical' (1992: 77).

Whereas one major current in eighteenth-century Shakespeare criticism was to sift the plays for such 'scattered jewels' and to point out their weaknesses, Romantic critics such as August von Schlegel argued for their 'organic unity', a structural organization intrinsic to the literary work which 'unfolds itself from within' and is not imposed by a framework of rigid classical aesthetics. As Bate (1992) argues, the continuing influence of this method, taken up by I. A. Richards (1929) as 'practical criticism', can still be seen in the many educational contexts in which close reading aimed at uncovering organic form is taught and examined (Bate, 1992: 5). In his lectures, translated into English in 1846, Schlegel identifies characterization as one of Shakespeare's most dominant qualities:

> Never, perhaps, was there so comprehensive a talent for characterization as Shakspeare. It...grasps every diversity of range, age and sex, down to the lispings of infancy...the king and the beggar, the hero and the pickpocket, the sage and the idiot, speak and act with equal truthfulness; not only does he transport himself to distant ages and foreign nations...He gives us the history of minds; he lays open to us, in a single word, a whole series of their anterior states. (Schlegel, 1846: 363–4)

The English history plays form 'one of the most valuable of Shakespeare's works...I say advisedly *one* of his works, for the poet evidently intended them to form one great whole. It is, as it were, an historical heroic poem in the dramatic form, of which the separate plays constitute the rhapsodies' (1846: 419). Schlegel argues for the fidelity of Shakespeare to his sources such that 'we may attain from them a knowledge of history in all its truth', but more significantly the history plays furnish 'examples of the political course of the world, applicable to all times':

> This mirror of kings should be the manual of young princes; from it they may learn the intrinsic dignity of their hereditary vocation, but they will also learn

from it the difficulties of their situation, the dangers of usurpation, the inevitable fall of tyranny, which buries itself under its attempts to obtain a firmer foundation; lastly, the ruinous consequences of the weaknesses, errors, and crimes of kings, for whole nations and many subsequent generations. (1846: 419–20)

Schlegel argues for the careful crafting of the sequence into a whole, with *King John* and *Henry VIII* as 'the Prologue and Epilogue to the other eight' (1846: 422).

Discussing the plays in turn, Schlegel enjoys the role of Prince Arthur in *King John*, who becomes a 'sacrifice of unprincipled ambition: his fate excites the warmest sympathy' (1846: 423). He discusses *Richard II* as a tragedy: 'Shakspeare exhibits a noble, kingly nature, at first obscured by levity and the errors of an unbridled youth, and afterwards purified by misfortune, and rendered by it more highly and splendidly illustrious' (1846: 424). Falstaff is praised as 'the crown of Shakspeare's comic invention' (1846: 426). Schlegel argues that *Henry V* posed certain structural and dramatic challenges which Shakespeare met with the addition of the choruses, 'which unite epic pomp and solemnity with lyrical sublimity' (1846: 430), but the question of stage realism remains, with an eye to the increasing pageantry and spectacle of nineteenth-century productions:

It is certainly laughable enough that a handful of awkward warriors in mock armour, by means of two or three swords…should decide the fate of mighty kingdoms. But the opposite extreme is still much worse. If we in reality succeed in exhibiting the tumult of a great battle, the storming of a fort, and the like, in a manner any way calculated to deceive the eye, the power of these sensible impressions is so great that they render the spectator incapable of bestowing that attention which a poetical work of art demands; and thus the essential is sacrificed to the accessory. (1846: 431)

In *Richard III*, Schlegel is sensible of Richard's attractiveness:

Richard is the soul or rather the daemon, of the whole tragedy…Notwithstanding the uniform aversion with which he inspires us, he still engages us in the greatest variety of ways by his profound skill in dissimulation, his wit, his prudence, his presence of mind, his quick activity, and his valour. He fights at last against Richmond like a desperado, and dies the honourable death of a hero on the field of battle. Shakspeare could not change this historical issue, yet it is by no means satisfactory to our moral feelings. (1846: 437)

Samuel Taylor Coleridge's important observations on Shakespeare are scattered through his papers and the extant accounts of his lectures. He himself had once planned 'a historical drama of King Stephen, on the plan of Shakespeare's historical dramas' (Hawkes, 1969: 242). Coleridge discusses the genre of history as 'the transitional state between the epic and the drama' (quoted in Hawkes, 1969: 243), and differentiates between *Richard II*, a '*purely* historical drama', and *Henry IV*, '*mixed* drama' (Hawkes, 1969: 243): 'this distinction does not depend upon the quantity of historical events compared with the fictions, for there is as much *history* in *Macbeth* as in *Richard*, but in the relation of the history to the plot. In the purely historical plays, the history *informs* the plot; in the mixed it *directs* it; in the rest, as *Macbeth, Hamlet, Cymbeline, Lear*, it subserves it' (quoted in Hawkes, 1969: 243). His lecture on *Richard II* begins with a definition of the genres of history and of tragedy:

> Fully to comprehend the nature of the Historic Drama, the difference should be understood between the epic and tragic muse. The latter recognises and is grounded upon the free-will of man; the former is under the control of destiny, or, among Christians, an overruling Providence... In the tragic, the free-will of man is the first cause, and accidents are never introduced; if they are, it is considered a great fault. To cause the death of a hero by accident, such as slipping off a plank into the sea, would be beneath the tragic muse, as it would arise from no mental action. (quoted in Hawkes, 1969: 277–8)

Writing on the history plays, Coleridge proposed that 'in order that a drama may be properly historical, it is necessary that it should be the history of the people to whom it is addressed':

> In the composition, care must be taken that there appear no dramatic improbability, as the reality is taken for granted. It must, likewise, be poetical; – that only, I mean, must be taken which is the permanent in our nature, which is common and therefore deeply interesting to all ages. The events themselves are immaterial otherwise than as the clothing and manifestation of the spirit that is working within. (quoted in Hawkes, 1969: 214)

It follows from this that the history plays are predominantly patriotic: 'one great object of his historic plays... was to make his countrymen more patriotic; to make Englishmen proud of being Englishmen' (1969: 261).

William Hazlitt's *Characters of Shakespear's Plays* published in 1817 sets out to extend Schlegel's analysis and to illustrate Pope's remarks on Shakespeare's distinctive characterization: 'every single character in Shakespear, is as much an individual as those in life itself' (Hazlitt, 1998: I, 85). Of *Richard II*, Hazlitt argues that 'the weakness of the king leaves us leisure to take a greater interest in the misfortunes of the man' (1998: I, 181); he echoes the praise of Falstaff as 'the most substantial comic character that ever was invented' (1998: I, 186) and thus 'we could never forgive the Prince's treatment of Falstaff; though perhaps Shakespear knew what was best, according to the history, the nature of the times, and of the man' (1998: I, 193). Perhaps because of this, Hazlitt was unusually critical of the character of Henry V, as 'careless, dissolute and ambitious', with 'no idea of any rule of right or wrong, but brute force, glossed over with a little religious hypocrisy and archiepiscopal advice' (1998: I, 194). However:

> We like him in the play. There he is a very amiable monster, a very splendid pageant. As we like to gaze at a panther or a young lion in their cages in the Tower, and catch a pleasing horror from their glistening eyes, their velvet paws and dreadless roar, so we take our very romantic, heroic, patriotic, and poetical delight in the boasts and feats of our younger Harry, as they appear on the stage and are confined to lines of ten syllables; where no blood follows the stroke that wounds our ears, where no harvest bends beneath horses' hoofs, no city flames, no little child is butchered, no dead men's bodies are found piled on heaps and festering the next morning – in the orchestra! (1998: I, 195)

Hazlitt considered the *Henry VI* plays inferior to the other histories in their depiction of the 'bear-garden' of civil war (1998: I, 200), but he argues that Shakespeare's distinctive characterization is evident in the differences between Richard II and Henry VI despite their external similarities:

> They are kept quite distinct in Shakespear. Both were kings, and both unfortunate. Both lost their crowns owing to their mismanagement and imbecility; the one from a thoughtless, wilful abuse of power, the other from an indifference to it ... Richard bewails the loss of the kingly power only as it was the means of gratifying his pride and luxury; Henry regards it only as a means of doing right, and is less desirous of the advantages to be derived from possessing it than afraid of exercising it wrong. (1998: I, 202)

Hazlitt deplored the adaptations that passed for Shakespeare on the stage, arguing, in the context of Cibber's *Richard III* (see pp. 9–10), that 'the only rule, indeed, for altering Shakespear is to retrench certain passages which may be considered either as superfluous or obsolete, but not to add or transpose any thing' (1998: I, 208). *Richard III* is dominated by its central figure – 'that mixture of intellectual vigour with moral depravity' – which 'is almost every where predominant, and marks its lurid track throughout' (1998: I, 208). By contrast, Hazlitt sees that King John 'is kept pretty much in the background', although there are 'few characters on the stage that excite more disgust and loathing': only the 'beauties of language' and 'richness of the imagination' 'relieve the painfulness of the subject' (1998: I, 214).

Hazlitt's dramatic criticism also influenced his writing. As Goethe's sense that the stage was no 'worthy field for [Shakespeare's] genius' (Bate, 1992: 77) suggests, the general tenor of Romantic criticism was disdainful of the plays, particularly the tragedies, in performance. A famous essay of Charles Lamb in 1811 asserted that 'the plays of Shakspeare are less calculated for performance on a stage, than those of almost any other dramatist whatever' (Lamb and Lamb, 1903: 115). Alongside this prevailing view there was also, however, a significant strand of theatre reviewing as practised by Leigh Hunt and Hazlitt. Many of Hazlitt's most realized conceptions of Shakespearian characters draw from his experiences in the theatre. Edmund Kean's portrayal of Richard III, while it 'should have more solidity, depth, sustained and impassioned feeling, with somewhat less brilliancy, with fewer glancing lights, pointed transitions and pantomimic evolutions', had some particularly memorable aspects:

> The courtship scene with Lady Anne [I. ii] is an admirable exhibition of smooth and smiling villainy. The progress of wily adulation, of encroaching humility, is finely marked by his action, voice and eye. He seems, like the first Tempter, to approach his prey, secure of the event, and as if success had smoothed his way before him . . . Richard should woo less as a lover than as an actor – to shew his mental superiority, and power of making others the playthings of his purposes. Mr Kean's attitude in leaning against the side of the stage before he comes forward to address Lady Anne, is one of the most graceful and striking ever witnessed on the stage. (Hazlitt, 1998: I, 207)

In his collected dramatic criticism, published as *A View of the English Stage* (1818), Hazlitt develops the interest in character evinced in his Shakespeare monograph, often reusing the same material. He offers additional reviews of Kean's Richard III, and comments that Kean's Richard II was mistakenly active: 'Mr Kean made it a character of *passion*, that is, of feeling combined with energy; whereas it is a character of *pathos*, that is to say, of feeling combined with weakness' (Hazlitt, 1998: III, 53). Hazlitt also sees a disappointing Falstaff performed by Stephen Kemble, and discusses Kemble's brother John in a lacklustre *King John*.

Also concerned with characterization is Anna Jameson's *Characteristics of Women, Moral, Poetical, and Historical* (1832), although, as the title of her book suggests, its aims extend beyond Shakespeare criticism. Jameson's discussions of female characters in the histories are limited, and she tends to use historical material not included in the plays as an implicit part of Shakespeare's characterization. She investigates the background of Constance (*King John*) and 'the result of a life of strange vicissitude; the picture of a tameless will, and high passions, for ever struggling in vain against a superior power; – and the real situation of women in those chivalrous times, are placed before us in a few noble scenes' (Jameson, 1832: II, 192). Of Margaret of Anjou, Jameson is sure that 'she is not one of Shakspeare's women': 'he who knew so well in what true greatness of spirit consisted – who could excite our respect and sympathy even for a Lady Macbeth, would never have given us a heroine without a touch of heroism...he would have redeemed her from unmingled detestation; he would have breathed into her some of his own sweet spirit – he would have given the woman a soul' (1832: II, 248–9). Perhaps Jameson's limited engagement with the plays is gendered, as pre-empted by Elizabeth Inchbald, actress and writer, in her *The British Theatre* (1808). Inchbald's remarks on *1 Henry IV* are trenchant:

> This is a play which all men admire, and which most women dislike. Many revolting expressions in the comic parts, much boisterous courage in some of the graver scenes, together with Falstaff's unwieldy person, offend every female auditor; and whilst a facetious Prince of Wales is employed in taking purses on the highway, a lady would rather see him stealing hearts at a ball, though the event might produce more fatal consequences.
>
> The great Percy, they confess, pays some attention to his wife, but still more to his horse: and, as the king was a rebel before he mounted the throne, and all women are naturally loyal, they shudder at a crowned head leagued with a traitor's heart. (quoted in Bate, 1992: 353)

1840–1880: Hero-worship and the New Shakspere Society

The worship of Shakespeare's powers which George Bernard Shaw would later dub 'Bardolatry' had its most famous mid-century expression in Thomas Carlyle's 'The Hero as Poet', a chapter in his influential *On Heroes, Hero-worship, and the Heroic in History* (1840): 'here, I say, is an English King, whom no time or chance, Parliament or combination of Parliaments, can dethrone! This King Shakspeare, does not he shine, in crowned sovereignty, over us all, as the noblest, gentlest, yet strongest of rallying-signs; indestructible' (Carlyle, 1993: 97). Like his Romantic predecessors, Carlyle stresses Shakespearian characterization, but he also has something to say about the particular effects of the histories which, like Schlegel, he sees as an epic sequence:

> That battle of Agincourt strikes me as one of the most perfect things, in its sort, we anywhere have of Shakspeare's. The description of the two hosts: the worn-out, jaded English; the dread hour, big with destiny, when the battle shall begin; and then that deathless valour: 'Ye good yeomen, whose limbs were made in England!' [III. i. 24–5] There is a noble Patriotism in it, – far other than the 'indifference' you sometimes hear ascribed to Shakspeare. A true English heart breathes, calm and strong, through the whole business; not boisterous, protrusive; all the better for that. There is a sound in it like the ring of steel. (Carlyle, 1993: 93)

Carlyle saw in Shakespeare the enduring and 'articulate voice' of the nation (1993: 97).

In 1844, Matthew Arnold wrote in his sonnet 'Shakespeare': 'Others abide our question. Thou art free./We stand and ask – Thou smilest and art still,/Out-topping knowledge.' As the Victorian period continued, there were different attempts to escape Arnold's sense of the ultimate unknowability of Shakespeare, and instead to explicate aspects of his writing. Many of these were influenced by the new quasi-scientific methods of bibliographic scholarship expounded by the New Shakspere Society, founded in 1874. The society's aims were set out by its director, F. J. Furnivall, in the prospectus:

> To do honour to Shakspere [Footnote: This spelling of our great Poet's name is taken from the only unquestionably genuine signatures of his that we possess...Though it has hitherto been too much to ask people to suppose that Shakspere knew how to spell his own name, I hope the demand may not prove too great for the imagination of the Members of the new Society], to mark out the succession of his plays, and thereby the growth of his mind and art; to promote the intelligent study of him, and to print Texts illustrating his works and his times, this *New Shakspere Society* is founded. (Furnivall, 1874: n. p.)

Furnivall made explicit the connections between this new branch of literary criticism and the scientific temper of the age:

> Dramatic poet though Shakspere is, bound to lose himself in his wondrous and manifold creations; taciturn 'as the secrets of Nature' though he be; yet in this Victorian time, when our geniuses of Science are so wresting her secrets from Nature as to make our days memorable for ever, the faithful student of Shakspere need not fear that he will be unable to pierce through the crowds of forms that exhibit Shakspere's mind, to the mind itself, the man himself, and see him as he was...(Furnivall, 1874: n.p.)

One attempt to classify and develop Shakespearian study can be seen in a new edition of the plays, introduced by Furnivall: *The Leopold Shakspere. The Poet's Works in Chronological Order. From the Text of Professor Delius* (Delius, 1879). Furnivall's introduction stressed the scientific investigation of Shakespeare's development and the importance of studying his whole oeuvre 'as parts of a whole, and in relation to the other parts, as well as singly' (1879: cxvii). Of the history plays, Furnivall wrote that Shakespeare was here engaging with 'the great political questions which were stirring his countrymen in his own time'; in particular, 'the disputed succession of Elizabeth and her title to the Crown, her government by favourites, the continual conspiracies against her, either home-grown or supported by foreign aid' (1879: xxxvi).

Furnivall also wrote an introduction to an influential account translated from the German of G. G. Gervinus, *Shakespeare Commentaries* (1877).

Gervinus's commentaries covered all the plays. He proposed that the history plays show a Shakespeare shifting his focus from 'private life and personal existence' in the comedies towards 'the wide outward sphere of public life' (1877: 248). They are patriotic plays influenced by their age: 'How the political heart throbs through them, how repeatedly in Shakespeare is that Themistocles' counsel advanced, which enjoins on England to place all her power and confidence on her coast and her vessels, a counsel which has been repeated numberless times by orators in Parliament, with Shakespearian quotations' (1877: 250). The politics of the histories is ultimately conservative: 'For the historical plays teach history to those who cannot read it in the Chronicles; these plays are written with this aim, to teach subjects obedience, to represent the untimely ends of such as have moved insurrections, and the flourishing estate of such as prove themselves faithful and keep clear of traitorous stratagems' (1877: 251).

Gervinus praises Shakespeare for his approach to his historical source material: 'Shakespeare has had but one law in using each and all his sources, a law which he applied equally to the driest historical chronicle as to the most fantastic novel – he sought after nature and inner truth' (1877: 252). Shakespeare subscribes to 'a double authority, that of poetry and of history combined':

> The more freely and boldly he does this, as Shakespeare has done in Richard III, the more poetically interesting will his treatment of the history become, but the more will it lose its historical value; the more truly and closely he adheres to reality, as in Richard II, the more will his poetry gain in historical meaning and forfeit in poetic splendour. (1877: 253)

Gervinus argues that the histories possess 'a boundless *comprehensiveness* and a *wider* value' than the non-historical drama: 'it is this widespread responsibility, this extensive agency of the political actor, which has compelled the acceptance of another moral law and another moral standard for history than that relating to private life' (1877: 256). He sees the grouping of the plays into series as an inevitable consequence of this extended scope:

> The representation of ideas that step beyond the domestic circle, of characters whose moral development requires just as much breadth as the passionate nature of tragic characters demands depth, or actions incapable of compression into one catastrophe, and requiring rather epic fulness, all this has been accomplished by Shakespeare in his histories, and he has thus enriched dramatic poetry with a new species. (1877: 257–8)

As the Victorian period advanced, such commentaries on Shakespeare multiplied, and the task of accounting for and explicating not just individual plays but their progress and place in the author's career became more pressing. Following Gervinus's commentaries, a number of book-length studies of Shakespeare's work appeared, of which Edward Dowden's influential *Shakspere: A Critical Study of his Mind and Art* (1875) was pre-eminent. Eschewing the scientific methodologies advocated by Furnivall and later by Moulton (1885), Dowden states his intention: 'To approach Shakspere on the human side is the object of this book' (Dowden, 1875: vi). The human side is that of Shakespeare himself, as the study is concerned 'to connect the study of Shakspere's works with an inquiry after the personality of the writer, and to observe, as far as is possible, in its several stages the growth of his intellect and character from youth to full maturity' (1875: v), and also of his characters. Dowden's study stressed a Shakespeare who prompts questions rather than providing easy or comfortable answers. He cannot be co-opted to orthodox beliefs because of the time in which he wrote:

> Poetry in this Elizabethan period is put upon a purely human basis. No Fate broods over the actions of men and the history of families; the only fatality is the fatality of character. Luck, an outstanding element, helping to determine the lives of mortals, and not reducible to known law, luck good and bad Shakspere readily admits; but luck is strictly a thing in the course of nature. The divinity which shapes our ends works efficiently, but secretly...If we recognise in the moral order of the world a divine presence, then the divine presence is never absent from the Shaksperian world. (1875: 24)

The history plays are most interesting to Dowden for their illumination of Shakespeare himself:

> That Shakspere should have accomplished so great an achievement towards the interpreting of history is much, – that he should have grasped in thought the national life of England during a century and upwards, in her periods of disaster and collapse, or civil embroilment, and of heroic union and exaltation, – this is much. But that by his study of history Shakspere should have built up his own moral nature, and have fortified himself for the conduct of life, was, we may surmise, to Shakspere the chief outcome of his toil. (1875: 163)

Whereas many earlier critics had considered the history plays as distinct because of their presumed proximity to chronicle sources, Dowden's interpretation stressed their Shakespearian qualities: 'even Shakspere cannot transcend himself' (1875: 164). History plays are more concerned with *doing* than *being*: 'the question in this case is not, What has been the life of your soul, what have you thought and suffered and enjoyed? The question is, What have you done?' The histories 'deal with the finite issues of failure or success in the achieving of practical ends; and the feeling which they leave with us is that of a wholesome, mundane pity and terror, or a sane and strong mundane satisfaction' (1875: 166). Unlike the tragedies' depiction of 'the mystery of evil...before which we stand appalled', the histories show us 'wrong-doing, which is followed by inevitable retribution' (1875: 167).

Dowden divided the history plays into two groups dealing with 'kingly strength' – Henry IV, Henry V and Richard III – and 'kingly weakness' – King John, Richard II and Henry VI (1875: 168). He likens Richard III to a Marlovian protagonist 'distinguished by a few strongly marked and inordinately developed qualities. There is in the characterization no mystery, but much of a daemonic intensity' (1875: 180–1), and observes interestingly that 'mere verisimilitude in the play...becomes at times subordinate to effects of symphonic orchestration, or of statuesque composition' (1875: 181). Whereas King John is 'a dastardly criminal', 'we cannot refrain from yielding a certain tribute of admiration to the bolder malefactor, who ventures on the daring experiment of choosing evil for his good' (1875: 189). Of Richard II, Dowden notes:

> Life is to Richard a show, a succession of images; and to put himself into accord with the aesthetic requirements of his position is Richard's first necessity. He is equal to playing any part gracefully which he is called upon by circumstances to enact. But when he has exhausted the aesthetic satisfaction to be derived from the situations of life, he is left with nothing further to do. He is an amateur in living; not an artist. (1875: 195)

By contrast, Bolingbroke is a practical, self-controlled and powerful figure.

> There is nothing infinite in the character of Henry, but his is a strong finite character. When he has attained the object of his ambition he is still aspiring, but he does not aspire towards anything higher and further than that which he had set before him; his ambition is now to hold firmly that which he has energetically grasped. (1875: 206)

Of *1 Henry IV*, Dowden is sympathetic to Hal, arguing, despite his soliloquy at the end of Act I, scene 2, that 'we must not suppose that Henry formed a deliberate plan for concealing the strength and splendour of his character in order afterwards to flash forth upon men's sight and overwhelm and dazzle them' (1875: 211). In *Henry V* the character reaches its apogee, having surrendered 'ease and strength and self ... on behalf of England' (1875: 219). Something of the popularity of Dowden's account can be traced in its frequent reissuing, going through a dozen editions by the end of the nineteenth century.

Dowden's rival for this market was the poet A. C. Swinburne, whose *A Study of Shakespeare* was first published in 1880. Swinburne had his own division of Shakespeare's writing, into a first period, 'lyric and fantastic', a second period, 'comic and historic' and a third, 'tragic and romantic'. Swinburne elaborates that 'it is not, so to speak, the literal but the spiritual order which I have studied to observe and to indicate: the periods which I seek to define belong not to chronology but to art' (Swinburne, 1880: 16). He argued against the New Shakspere Society's preferred scientific metrical analysis as the approach of the 'horny eye and the callous finger of a pedant' (1880: 7). Swinburne's criticism was concerned with the change of Shakespeare's language, the growth and development of his verse and tone, but these were modulations that 'can only be traced by ear and not by finger' (1880: 16). 'The consummation and the crown' of the history plays are judged to be *Henry IV* and *V*: 'of all Shakespeare's plays they are the most rhetorical; there is more talk than song in them, less poetry than oratory; more finish than form, less movement than incident' (1880: 68–9).

Swinburne holds Arthur in *King John* in particular affection as, with Cordelia in *King Lear*, 'chapels in the cathedral of man's highest art' (1880: 75). He also wishes for 'some reasonable and acceptable theory as to the play of *King Henry VIII*' (1880: 82). Generic considerations lead to an interesting double perspective on *King John*: 'we might say that the English hero [Faulconbridge] becomes the central figure of the poem as seen from its historic side, while John remains the central figure of the poem as seen from its tragic side' (1880: 98). Swinburne views *Henry V* as a continuing patriotic epic: 'In the mightiest chorus of *King Henry V* we hear the pealing ring of the same great English trumpet that was yet to sound over the battle of the Baltic, and again in our later day over a sea-fight of Shakespeare's own . . . His typical English hero or historic protagonist is a man of their type who founded and built up the empire of England in India; a hero after the future pattern of Hastings and of Clive' (1880: 114–15).

1880–1914: Patriotism and Serial Performance

By the turn of the century, the tradition of seeing the plays performed in historical sequence became more common: W. B. Yeats described seeing the plays in Stratford-upon-Avon 'in their right order, with all the links that bind play to play unbroken; and partly because of a spirit in that place, and partly because of the way play supports play, the theatre moved me as it has never done before' (Yeats, 1961: 97). Yeats was sympathetic to Richard II, seeing Shakespeare's depiction as conveying 'the defeat that awaits all, whether they be artist or saint, who find themselves where men ask of them a rough energy and have nothing to give but some contemplative virtue', while 'Merry England was fading' (1961: 106). This is an existential rather than a political world:

> Shakespeare cared little for the State, the source of all our judgments, apart from its shows and splendours, its turmoils and battles, its flamings-out of the

uncivilised heart. He did indeed think it wrong to overturn a king, and thereby to swamp peace in civil war, and the historical plays from *Henry IV* to *Richard III*, that monstrous birth and last sign of the wrath of Heaven, are a fulfilment of the prophecy of the Bishop of Carlisle... He mediated as Solomon, not as Bentham meditated, upon blind ambitions, untoward accidents, and capricious passions, and the world was almost as empty in his eyes as it must be in the eyes of God. (Yeats, 1969: 106–7)

More usual Victorian and Edwardian reactions to the history plays tended, following Schlegel, Coleridge and Swinburne, to stress their patriotism. Sidney Lee argued that 'the Shakespearean drama enjoins those who love their country wisely to neglect no advantage that nature offers in the way of resisting unjust demands upon it... the dramatist's doctrine of patriotism has lost little of its pristine vitality, and is relevant to current affairs' (Lee, 1906: 187). This is not to say that they celebrate England's glory, rather that they explain 'why kingly glory is in its essence brittle rather than brilliant... we are brought to a study of the causes of the brittleness of national glory' (1906: 180). Writing of *Henry V* in a programme note for Lewis Waller's heroic production in 1900 against the background of the Boer War, Lee proposed a topical emendation for the lines referring to Essex's hoped-for victory in Ireland which is part of the fifth chorus. 'We feel instinctively that the change of a single word ("Afric" for "Ireland") would carry a step further Shakespeare's method of vivifying the past by associating it with the present, and would give this sentence an application even more immediate to our own contemporary history' (Lee, 1900: 11).

There were dissenting voices, however. Writing in 1896, Shaw could not 'forgive Shakespear quite for the worldly phase in which he tried to thrust such a Jingo hero as his Harry V down our throats. The combination of conventional propriety and brute masterfulness in his public capacity with a lowlived blackguardism in his private tastes is not a pleasant one' (quoted in Wilson, 1969: 117). In his preface to his *Saint Joan* (1924), Shaw criticizes Shakespeare's apparent surrender to English patriotism in depicting Joan so scurrilously in *1 Henry VI* (Wilson, 1969: 124). Reviewing Henry Irving as Richard III in 1896 in typically robust terms, Shaw echoes Dowden and delights in the comedic aspects of the play as the best of Punch and Judy entertainment:

It has abundant devilry, humor and character, presented with a luxuriant energy of diction in the simplest form of blank verse. Shakespear revels in it with just the sort of artistic unconscionableness that fits the theme. Richard is the prince of Punches: he delights Man by provoking God, and dies unrepentant and game to the last. His incongruous conventional appendages, such as the Punch hump, the conscience, the fear of ghosts, all impart a spice of outrageousness which leaves nothing lacking to the fun of the entertainment, except the solemnity of those spectators who feel bound to take the affair as a profound and subtle historical study. (quoted in Wilson, 1969: 176)

Reviewing, grandly, the scope of Shakespeare's plays and his characterization, Shaw concludes that 'only one man in them all who believes in life, enjoys life, thinks life worth living, and has a sincere, unrhetorical tear dropped over his death-bed; and that man – Falstaff!' (quoted in Wilson, 1969: 238).

Also on the side of Falstaff was A. C. Bradley's influential essay 'The Rejection of Falstaff', published in his *Oxford Lectures on Poetry* (1909). Bradley develops the warm feelings towards Falstaff evinced by previous critics including Rowe, Morgann and Hazlitt, suggesting that his banishment from the newly crowned Henry V in Act V, scene 4 of *2 Henry IV* causes us 'pain and some resentment' (Bradley, 1909: 251). This Bradley sees as 'one of our methods of conventionalising Shakespeare': 'his readers expect him to mark in some distinct way his approval or disapproval of that which he represents . . . but the truth is that he shows the fact and leaves the judgment to them.' Another example is furnished from the history plays in which 'we are always trying to turn him into a partisan': 'He shows us that Richard II was unworthy to be king, and we at once conclude that he thought Bolingbroke's usurpation justified; whereas he shows merely, what under the conditions was bound to exist, an inextricable tangle of right and unright' (1909: 255). Bradley argues that it is to mistake Shakespeare's intention to feel that the play ends on a negative note, but that our disbelief at Henry's treatment of Falstaff registers that here the dramatist 'overshot his mark': 'he created so extraordinary a being, and fixed him so firmly on his intellectual throne, that when he sought to dethrone him he could not' (1909: 259).

A companion volume on *Shakespeare's Tragedies* ends the section on pre-twentieth-century criticism with A. C. Bradley's monumental *Shakespearean Tragedy* (1904). In an account of criticism of the tragedies this work provides a natural and cumulative chronological point. In the case of the histories, with the increasing sense of their political engagement and their appropriation to continuing political contexts, it seems appropriate that a political and military event, the outbreak of war in 1914, should form the end of a critical era.

References and Further Reading

Bate, Jonathan (1989) *Shakespearean Constitutions: Politics, Theatre, Criticism 1730–1830*. Oxford: Clarendon Press.

——(1992) *The Romantics on Shakespeare*. New Penguin Shakespeare Library. London: Penguin.

Bell, John (1969) *Bell's Edition of Shakespeare's Plays* (1774), 8 vols. London: Corn-market Press.

Betterton, Thomas (1700) *King Henry IV, with the Humours of Sir John Falstaff, A Tragi-comedy.* London.

Bradley, A. C. (1909) *Oxford Lectures on Poetry.* London: Macmillan.

Capell, Edward (1767) *Mr William Shakespeare his Comedies, Histories, and Tragedies.* London.

Carlyle, Thomas (1993) *On Heroes, Hero-worship, and the Heroic in History* (1840). Berkeley, CA: University of California Press.

Cibber, Colley (1700) *The Tragical History of King Richard III.* London.

Cibber, Theophilus (1720) *King Henry VI: A Tragedy.* London.

Clark, Sandra (1997) *Shakespeare Made Fit: Restoration Adaptations of Shakespeare.* London: Dent.

Crowne, John (1680) *The Misery of Civil War: A Tragedy.* London.

——(1681) *Henry the Sixth, the First Part.* London.

Delius, Nikolaus (ed.) (1879) *The Leopold Shakspere: The Poet's Works in Chronological Order*, intro. F. J. Furnivall. London: Cassell, Petter and Galpin.

Dennis, John (1712) *An Essay on the Genius and Writings of Shakespear.* London.

Dobson, Michael (1992) *The Making of the National Poet: Shakespeare, Adaptation and Authorship, 1660–1769.* Oxford: Clarendon Press.

Donaldson, Ian (ed.) (1985) *Ben Jonson.* Oxford: Oxford University Press.

Dowden, Edward (1875) *Shakspere: A Critical Study of his Mind and Art.* London.

Dryden, John (1969) *Of Dramatic Poesie* (1668). Menston: Scolar Press.

Fuller, Thomas (1662) *The History of the Worthies of England.* London.

Furnivall, F. J. (1874) 'New Shakspere Society prospectus', *Transactions of the New Shakspere Society*, 1.

Gervinus, G. G. (1877) *Shakespeare Commentaries*, trans. F. E. Bunnett, new rev. edn. London: Smith Elder and Co.

Gildon, Charles (1718) *The Complete Art of Poetry*, 2 vols. London.

Griffith, Elizabeth (1971) *The Morality of Shakespeare's Drama Illustrated* (1775). London: Frank Cass.

Hanmer, Thomas (1743) *The Works of Shakespear.* Oxford.

Hawkes, Terence (ed.) (1969) *Coleridge on Shakespeare.* Harmondsworth: Penguin.

Hazlitt, William (1998) *The Selected Writings of William Hazlitt*, 9 vols, ed. Duncan Wu. London: Pickering and Chatto.

Hill, Aaron (1723) *King Henry the Fifth; or, The Conquest of France by the English. A Tragedy.* London.

Hogan, Charles Beecher (1952) *Shakespeare in the Theatre, 1701–1800*, 2 vols. Oxford: Clarendon Press.

Jameson, Anna Brownell (1832) *Characteristics of Women, Moral, Poetical and Historical*, 2 vols. London.

Johnson, Samuel (ed.) (1765) *The Plays of William Shakespeare*, 10 vols. London.

Lamb, Charles and Lamb, Mary (1903) *The Works of Charles and Mary Lamb*, ed. E. V. Lucas. London: Methuen.

Lee, Sidney (1900) *Shakespeare's Henry V: An Account and an Estimate.* London: Smith Elder.

—— (1906) *Shakespeare and the Modern Stage, with Other Essays*. London.

LeWinter, Oswald (1970) *Shakespeare in Europe*. Penguin Shakespeare Library. Harmondsworth: Penguin.

Meres, Francis (1598) *Palladis Tamia. Wits Treasury: The Second Part of Wits Commonwealth*. London.

Molloy, Charles (1720) *The Half-pay Officers: A Comedy*. London.

Montagu, Elizabeth Robinson (1970) *An Essay on the Writings and Genius of Shakespear* (1769). London: Frank Cass.

Morgann, Maurice (1972) *Shakespearian Criticism: Comprising An Essay on the Dramatic Character of Sir John Falstaff* (1777), ed. D. Fineman. Oxford: Clarendon Press.

Moulton, Richard Green (1885) *Shakespeare as a Dramatic Artist: A Popular Illustration of the Principles of Scientific Criticism*. Oxford: Clarendon Press.

Philips, Ambrose (1723) *Humfrey, Duke of Gloucester: A Tragedy*. London.

Pope, Alexander (1723) *The Works of Shakespear*. London.

—— and Warburton, William (1747) *The Works of Shakespear in Eight Volumes*. London.

Richards, I. A. (1929) *Practical Criticism*. London: Kegan Paul.

Richardson, William (1784) *Essays on Shakespeare's Dramatic Characters of Richard the Third, King Lear, and Timon of Athens*. London: John Murray.

Rowe, Nicholas (1709–10) *The Works of Mr William Shakespear: Revis'd and Corrected, with an Account of the Life and Writings of the Author*, 7 vols. London.

Schlegel, August Wilhelm von (1846) *A Course of Lectures on Dramatic Art and Literature*, ed. John Black and A. J. W. Morrison. London: H. G. Bohn.

Schoenbaum, Samuel (1975) *William Shakespeare: A Documentary Life*. Oxford: Clarendon Press in association with Scolar Press.

Smith, David Nichol (1963) *Eighteenth Century Essays on Shakespeare*. Oxford: Clarendon Press.

Swinburne, Algernon Charles (1880) *A Study of Shakespeare*. London: Chatto and Windus.

Taylor, Gary (1989) *Reinventing Shakespeare: A Cultural History from the Restoration to the Present*. London: Viking.

Theobald, Lewis (1726) *Shakespeare Restored: or, a Specimen of Many Errors, as well Committed, and Unamended, by Mr Pope in his Late Edition of this Poet*. London.

—— (1733) *The Works of Shakespeare in Seven Volumes*. London.

Thompson, Ann and Roberts, Sasha (1997) *Women Reading Shakespeare, 1660–1900: An Anthology of Criticism*. Manchester: Manchester University Press.

Vickers, Brian (1974) *Shakespeare: The Critical Heritage*, 6 vols. London: Routledge and Kegan Paul.

Wells, Stanley W. and Taylor, Gary (1986) *William Shakespeare: The Complete Works*. Oxford: Clarendon Press.

Whately, Thomas (1785) *Remarks on Some of the Characters of Shakespeare*. London.

Whiter, Walter (1972) *A Specimen of a Commentary on Shakespeare* (1794). Menston: Scolar Press.

Wilson, Edwin (1969) *Shaw on Shakespeare*. Harmondsworth: Penguin.

Woudhuysen, H. R. (1989) *Samuel Johnson on Shakespeare*. New Penguin Shakespeare Library. London: Penguin.

Yeats, W. B. (1961) *Essays and Introductions*. London: Macmillan.

2

Genre

Whereas Shakespeare's comedies and tragedies can draw on classical models for their generic validation, the question of genre in relation to the history plays has been rather more up for critical grabs. The issue of whether these plays should be considered individually or as parts of a greater sequential whole, their relation to other genres and their defining thematic and structural characteristics have been discussed by a range of critics.

Almost all criticism of the history plays since the mid-twentieth century has had to take account of E. M. W. Tillyard's *Shakespeare's History Plays* (1944, rev. edn 1969). Tillyard's influential critique argues for a sequential reading of the plays as embodying a 'whole contemporary pattern of culture' (1969: 11), 'the Elizabethan world order' (1969: 18): the Elizabethans believed that 'the universe was a unity, in which everything had its place, and it was the perfect work of God. Any imperfection was the work not of God but of man... when Shakespeare deals with the concrete facts of English history he never forgets the principle of order behind all the terrible manifestations of disorder' (1969: 19, 25). The history plays also conform to contemporary political pressures, in particular the 'Tudor Myth', defined as the narrative told by the shaky Tudor dynasty from Henry VII onwards that 'the union of the two houses of York and Lancaster through his marriage with the York heiress was the providential and happy ending of an organic piece of history' (1969: 36). Tillyard discusses the influence of Machiavelli, Montaigne, Holinshed and other chroniclers in an extensive contextualization of this dominant cultural doctrine.

The second part of Tillyard's book takes the plays individually as meditations on the theme of order. Thus *Richard III* is seen to 'display the working out of God's plan to restore England to prosperity' (1969: 205); 'Shakespeare conceived his second tetralogy as one great unit' (1969: 240) and this 'epic' run of plays must therefore be treated as 'a single organism' (1969: 242); and

'*Richard II* does its work in proclaiming the great theme of the whole cycle of Shakespeare's History Plays: the beginning in prosperity, the distortion of prosperity by a crime, civil war, and ultimate renewal of prosperity' (1969: 267). Tillyard sees *Henry IV* crowded 'with pictures of life as it was lived in the age of Elizabeth ... through them [Shakespeare] expresses his own feelings about his fatherland' (1969: 304). But the liveliness of Hal's depiction in *Henry IV* causes problems for his characterization as king in *Henry V*: 'it would have been too risky to allow him to remain the ironist after he had come to the throne', and so Shakespeare jettisons his own character creation and substitutes 'one which, though lacking all consistency, satisfied the requirements both of the chroniclers and of popular tradition. No wonder if the play constructed round him shows a great falling off in quality' (1969: 311). Lily Campbell's *Shakespeare's 'Histories': Mirrors of Elizabethan Policy* (1947) also stresses Shakespeare as 'a man among men, a man who can be understood only against the background of his own time' (1947: 6). Her concept of 'Shakespeare's political use of history' (1947: 117) is discussed in the section 'History and Politics', as are Graham Holderness's reading of the plays as 'a type of Renaissance historiography' in his *Shakespeare Recycled: The Making of Historical Drama* (1992: 1) and Phyllis Rackin's historicized investigation of theories of causality, performance and representation in her *Stages of History: Shakespeare's English Chronicles* (1990).

Derek Traversi, in *Shakespeare from Richard II to Henry V* (1957), argues against excessive historical contextualization as a risk of 'obscuring their true individuality, the personal contribution by which they live as works of art' (1957: 1). Traversi sees the tetralogy as closely thematically integrated, with the history of Prince Hal as its central motif: 'The question we come increasingly to ask ourselves, as we follow the various stages of the Prince's career, is one which, because it stands in evident relationship to realities in the moral order, has several dramatic possibilities: What are the personal, as distinct from the political, qualities that go to the making of a king?' (Traversi, 1957: 4). His study goes on to develop readings of the individual plays which exemplify this process of education and self-development.

John Wilders's *The Lost Garden* (1978) discusses the ways in which 'in the minds of Shakespeare's historical characters, personal and political motives are so combined and confused as to be inseparable' (1978: 2), and argues that it is in the personal that Shakespeare locates the forces of historical agency:

> The causes of national unity, of division, of prosperity or decline are, in Shakespeare's view, to be found not, as some of the fifteenth century chroniclers had believed, in the providential power of God, nor, as we are now inclined to think, in social and economic conditions, but in the temperaments of national leaders and their reactions towards one another. To understand the course of history we must understand these men. (Wilders, 1978: 2)

Wilders proposes that 'since most of the tragedies are based on historical events, they are in this sense histories, though not all the history plays are tragedies' (1978: 5). One difference between histories and tragedies for Wilders is that 'whereas the death of a tragic hero conveys a sense of an ending, the impression created by a history play is that the life of a nation has neither beginning nor ending' (1978: 6). The dramatic qualities of the histories are of more significance than any putative political moral or exemplum, argues Wilders: 'Shakespeare portrays history as a struggle by succeeding generations of men to establish ideal worlds which are beyond their powers to create' (1978: 9), hence the 'lost garden' of his study's title.

Like Wilders, Paul N. Siegel's *The Gathering Storm*, subtitled 'a Marxist analysis', stresses Shakespeare's interest in 'the history that human beings make, the consequences of their actions' (Siegel, 1992: 51). He argues that Elizabethan audiences 'did not have to be persuaded about the need for order and obedience; they had to be made to feel with every fibre of their beings what they already accepted', and observes that 'although Shakespeare's history plays are shaped by the dominant ideology of the age, this does not mean that they merely teach a simple lesson' (Siegel, 1992: 55). Henry Kelly's *Divine Providence in the England of Shakespeare's Histories* (1970) studies contemporary doctrine to counter claims that the history plays dramatize patterns of sin and retribution across the generations and points out that all providential attributions in the plays themselves are part of the characterization of their speakers rather than an ideology to which the plays subscribe. Shakespeare's greatest contribution to historical writing was 'to unsynthesize the syntheses of his contemporaries and to unmoralize their moralizations' (Kelly, 1970: 304), leaving open the question 'as to how God would distribute praise and blame and sanctions for good and evil in these instances' (1970: 306).

Larry Champion's chapter titles in his account of the history plays trace a development from 'the search for dramatic form' in the *Henry VI* plays, through 'a maturity of perspective' in the later plays towards a 'celebration of history' in *Henry VIII* (Champion, 1980). The earlier plays show a writer 'conscious of the necessity for a breadth of vision which, by forcing the spectators to observe the action from a multiplicity of angles, accommodates a focus larger than the fortunes and misfortunes of any single individual' (1980: 185). Shakespeare goes on to develop 'a powerfully ambivalent historical perspective' in *King John*, where he makes the issues 'assume an ambivalence that provides a genuine human dimension for the play', and in *Henry IV*, where seeing the principals in different contexts generates 'a mixed response' (1980: 186). A similar effect is created in *Henry V* through 'the consistent interweaving of thematically related episodes which suspend the spectators between allegorical abstraction and absorption in character analysis' (1980: 187).

Irving Ribner's account of *The English History Play in the Age of Shakespeare* (1965) discusses the limited critical work on the definition of a history play and places Shakespeare's contribution alongside that of contemporary writers. He analyses the three parts of *Henry VI* as 'a unified trilogy' (Ribner, 1965: 95) in which characters are 'drawn firmly, but as political, not private, figures' (1965: 96):

> Implicit in the *Henry VI* plays is a philosophy of history which was medieval in origin, but still much a part of the intellectual life of Elizabethan England. Its keystone is the concept of divine providence as the ruling force in a well-ordered universe, in which each element is designed to serve its proper function. The events of history are never arbitrary or capricious; they are always in accordance with God's beneficent and harmonious plan. (Ribner, 1965: 103).

The later history plays are also seen as 'a unified tetralogy devoted to the triumph of the House of Lancaster' (1965: 151). The plays respond to the contemporary question of the succession, and 'in Richard and Bolingbroke, Shakespeare saw two directly antithetical royal types, and by objectively comparing them he could formulate his notions of what a king should and should not be' (1965: 157). The history plays 'are not political propaganda; they are the expression of a profoundly moral view of human relations which does not differ essentially from that which he expressed in his non-historical plays' (1965: 158). Robert Ornstein's *A Kingdom for a Stage: The Achievement of Shakespeare's History Plays* focuses on 'what is original' about the plays (1972: 2), in response to criticism concerned to show their topicality or contemporary orthodoxy. He considers each tetralogy to have 'a distinctive architectural unity' through which Shakespeare reaches 'beyond politics and history to the universal themes and concerns of his maturest art' (1972: 31).

A number of critics look at the intersections between the history plays and other adjacent genres: Charles Forker discusses 'Shakespeare's Chronicle Plays as Historical-Pastoral' (1965); S. L. Bethell looks at 'The Comic Element in Shakespeare's Histories', focusing especially on 'the use of wit in the dialogue to express comically a leading serious theme' (Bethell, 1952–3: 89); Nicholas Brooke considers *Richard III* in his *Shakespeare's Early Tragedies* (1968). Alexander Leggatt groups English and Roman histories together in his *Shakespeare's Political Drama* (1988). In his *Anatomy of Criticism* (1957), Northrop Frye proposes that 'history merges so gradually into tragedy that we often cannot be sure when communion has turned into catharsis ... there seems to be a far less direct connection between history and comedy: the comic scenes in the histories are, so to speak, subversive' (Frye, 1957: 284). H. B. Charlton's careful analysis in *Shakespeare, Politics and Politicians* (1929) argues that 'comedy and tragedy are concerned with the eternal or ephemeral fate of individual man. The history-play is concerned with communities of men, and primarily with nations. The real hero of the English history-play is England' (Charlton, 1929: 11).

A collection of essays edited by John Velz as *Shakespeare's English Histories: A Quest for Form and Genre* (1996) includes A. Elizabeth Ross on 'Hand-me-down-heroics: Shakespeare's Retrospective of Popular Elizabethan Heroical Drama in *Henry V*' and Charles Forker's discussion of Shakespeare's early histories and Marlowe's *Edward II*. G. K. Hunter's 'Afterword: Notes on the Genre of the History Play' argues that the history plays offer 'a confirmation of the political values that the monarchical government of the time required' as well as 'a much grander pattern of fall and recovery, given its most pervasive presence in the Christian story of paradise lost in Eden and paradise regained in the second coming' (Velz, 1996: 230–1). Characters in the history plays look

> beyond the supporters and opponents they have to deal with to a vision of a future in which things can be made different. Such expectations are perpetually disappointed, the ideals are postponed, but we recognize the necessary truth of the engagement with time that such hope involves, the psychological need to believe that the ideal is connected to an external and provable reality. (Velz, 1996: 240)

Donald Watson confines himself to *Shakespeare's Early History Plays* (1990), analysing them as theatre and as, like Tudor ideology and the institution of the stage, 'products of the same highly stylised and formalised culture which tended to translate the political into the aesthetic' (Watson, 1990: 33). John Dover Wilson's *The Fortunes of Falstaff* (1943) argues for the two parts of *Henry IV* as a single coherent whole. Alvin Kernan coins the term 'Henriad' for the four plays *Richard II* to *Henry V* in his essay in *Modern Shakespearean Criticism* (Kernan, 1970: 245). Across this epic sweep he traces the 'passage from the Middle Ages to the Renaissance and the modern world'; 'the movement from feudalism and hierarchy to the national state and individualism'; 'a passage from a situation in which man knows with certainty who he is to an existential condition in which any identity is only a temporary role'; 'from a garden world to a fallen world'; and 'from ceremony and ritual to history' (1970: 245–6). In his *The Drama of Power*, Moody Prior stresses the 'impression of interrelatedness and coherence which the plays seem to convey' (Prior, 1973: 6), but suggests that 'the idea of two tetralogies locks the plays into two compartments which may have been simply an unpremeditated result of the order of composition' (1973: 7), the result of critical, rather than authorial, principles of organization.

> The record of the years from Richard II to Richard III became for Shakespeare what the Galapagos Islands were for Darwin. It was a well-documented story of a nation in crisis and on trial, a proving ground for institutions, theories of government, and the characters of the men whose destinies cast them in principal roles in these great affairs of state. (Prior, 1973: 12)

Taken together, the histories offer 'a panoramic spectacle of political man in action' (1973: 13). Like Tillyard, Prior feels that the sequence is anti-climactic, with *Henry V* 'a theatrically handsome fulfilment of an obligation, performed with skill but without deep conviction' (1973: 341).

Kristian Smidt's *Unconformities in Shakespeare's History Plays* (1982) has companion volumes on tragedies and comedies. She argues that plot and character discrepancies develop 'gaps between expectation and fulfilment' (1982: 3), and interrogates these as indications of Shakespeare's sometimes flawed or imperfectly achieved intentions or working processes. The 'general reader', Smidt argues with the faintest of echoes of Falstaff on honour, is 'better served by an assurance that a tangle is a tangle, a fracture a fracture, than with verbal sophistications and dubious casebooks purporting to explain the mental processes of imaginary characters' (Smidt, 1982: 9). On questions of genre she is equally brisk: 'Shakespeare's history play was neither a dramatised epic nor an adapted morality, even if it absorbed features from both epic and morality play. It had no identity to cut it off from tragedy and it had some affinities with comedy' (1982: 16), and diversity is seen as the keynote of this loose generic grouping. Later chapters identify the integrity of individual plays, as well as their particular role in relation to a paired play or mini-sequence.

James Calderwood sees the second tetralogy not as a political or moral sequence but as 'a relatively contained metadrama in which the playwright subjects the nature and materials of his art to radical scrutiny' (Calderwood, 1979: 1), and focuses particularly on the role of language in the plays (see p. 99). David Scott Kastan's *Shakespeare and the Shapes of Time* (1982) draws a different analogy: 'the drama is able to attempt a mimesis of the process, or at least the putative process, of history itself [providing] an analogy to and an experience of the flow of history' (Kastan, 1982: 3–4). Kastan considers two types of historical time at work in the history plays: the providential and linear, and the classical and cyclical. Shakespeare's histories are seen as characteristically 'open-ended structures' (1982: 51), which force us to 'confront our fragile existence as "time's subjects" (*2 Henry IV*, I. iii. 120) released into a world of contingency and flux' (1982: 55). A chapter on *Henry V* stresses the unremediable inexorability of time: the words of the Epilogue 'powerfully declare this bond and declare the failure – even as they establish the appeal – of his heroic effort to deny the moral and chronological loss that existence in time demands' (1982: 76).

Tom Driver's comparative study *The Sense of History in Greek and Shakespearean Drama* (1960) also develops theories of time and the parallels between dramatist and historian, through a sequence of paired analyses of Shakespearian and classical plays. In *Time and the Artist in Shakespeare's English Histories* (1983), John Blanpied argues that 'the plays show us that Shakespeare was profoundly concerned with the *idea* of history – that is, as a category of experience with a distinctive nature, simultaneously implacable and ghostly, undeniable and elusive, and that he was determined to find the dramatic form that most truly expressed this special kind of reality' (Blanpied, 1983: 12): the figure of the king as artist, machiavel, performer and antic forms the locus for the plays' dramatic and historical energies. The 'fundamental motive of the histories was the need to make a future', but 'futility sits deep in the bone of the histories – most poignantly when it seizes those figures who are most fiercely and complexly committed to the justification of their lives in time' as, for example, Henry V (1983: 246–7). The history plays' remembered relation to a lost past is the central theme of Robert Jones's *These Valiant Dead: Renewing the Past in Shakespeare's Histories* (1991).

A. P. Rossiter's important essay 'Ambivalence: The Dialectic of the Histories', in his *Angel with Horns* (1961), argues with a flourish of capital letters that the histories are characterized by a 'Doubleness':

> in the conflicting values set by the Greatness (the Triumph) of the National Destiny, and the Frustration, the inadequacy, of the Individual (the frail Man within the robe) – there is nothing complex in the 'Doubleness'. It falls just short of the tragic; where Man's greatness is asserted in his destruction. That falling-short is characteristic of the Histories. (Rossiter, 1961: 42)

Part of this duality is an ironization of concepts of order proposed by Tillyard and others:

> the Tudor myth of Order...was too doctrinaire and narrowly moral for Shakespeare's mind: it falsified his fuller experience of men. Consequently, while employing it as frame, he had to undermine it, to qualify it with equivocations: to vex its applications with sly or subtle ambiguities: to cast doubt on its ultimate human validity, even in situations where its principles seemed most completely applicable. (Rossiter, 1961: 59)

Paola Pugliatti's argument in her *Shakespeare the Historian* is also for the ideological and structural importance of Shakespeare's cross-examination of history and historical representation, rather than his endorsement of particular positions (see her chapter on *Henry IV* reprinted below). Like Norman Rabkin, whose influential application of the *gestalt* optical illusion that is simultaneously a rabbit and a duck to the 'irreducible complexity of things' in *Henry V* (Rabkin, 1981: 61) stresses a simultaneity of divergent perspectives rather than a single correct reading, Pugliatti stresses the 'multiplicity of histories': 'history as possibility' (Pugliatti, 1996: 72).

References and Further Reading

Bethell, S. L. (1952–3) 'The comic element in Shakespeare's histories', *Anglia*, 71: 82–101.

Blanpied, John W. (1983) *Time and the Artist in Shakespeare's English Histories.* Newark: University of Delaware Press.

Brooke, Nicholas (1968) *Shakespeare's Early Tragedies.* London: Methuen.

Calderwood, James L. (1979) *Metadrama in Shakespeare's Henriad: Richard II to Henry V.* Berkeley, CA: University of California Press.

Campbell, Lily Bess (1947) *Shakespeare's 'Histories': Mirrors of Elizabethan Policy.* Huntington Library Publications. San Marino, CA: Huntington Library.

Champion, Larry S. (1980) *Perspective in Shakespeare's English Histories.* Athens: University of Georgia Press.

Charlton, H. B. (1929) *Shakespeare, Politics and Politicians.* Oxford: The English Association.

Driver, Tom Faw (1960) *The Sense of History in Greek and Shakespearean Drama.* New York: Columbia University Press.

Forker, Charles (1965) 'Shakespeare's chronicle plays as historical-pastoral', *Shakespeare Studies*, 1: 84–104.

Frye, Northrop (1957) *Anatomy of Criticism: Four Essays.* Princeton, NJ: Princeton University Press.

Holderness, Graham (1992) *Shakespeare Recycled: The Making of Historical Drama.* London: Harvester Wheatsheaf.

Jones, Robert C. (1991) *These Valiant Dead: Renewing the Past in Shakespeare's Histories.* Iowa City: University of Iowa Press.

Kastan, David Scott (1982) *Shakespeare and the Shapes of Time.* London: Macmillan.

Kelly, Henry Ansgar (1970) *Divine Providence in the England of Shakespeare's Histories.* Cambridge, MA: Harvard University Press.

Kernan, Alvin B. (1970) *Modern Shakespearean Criticism: Essays on Style, Dramaturgy, and the Major Plays.* New York: Harcourt Brace and World.

Leggatt, Alexander (1988) *Shakespeare's Political Drama: The History Plays and the Roman Plays.* London: Routledge.

Ornstein, Robert (1972) *A Kingdom for a Stage: The Achievement of Shakespeare's History Plays.* Cambridge, MA: Harvard University Press.

Prior, Moody E. (1973) *The Drama of Power: Studies in Shakespeare's History Plays.* Evanston, IL: Northwestern University Press.

Pugliatti, Paola (1996) *Shakespeare the Historian.* Basingstoke: Macmillan.

Rabkin, Norman (1981) *Shakespeare and the Problem of Meaning.* Chicago: University of Chicago Press.

Rackin, Phyllis (1990) *Stages of History: Shakespeare's English Chronicles.* Ithaca, NY: Cornell University Press.

Ribner, Irving (1965) *The English History Play in the Age of Shakespeare*, rev. edn. London: Methuen.

Rossiter, A. P. (1961) *Angel with Horns: And Other Shakespeare Lectures*, ed. Graham Storey. London: Longman.

Siegel, Paul N. (1992) *The Gathering Storm: Shakespeare's English and Roman History Plays. A Marxist Analysis.* London: RedWords.

Smidt, Kristian (1982) *Unconformities in Shakespeare's History Plays.* Atlantic Highlands, NJ: Humanities Press.

Tillyard, E. M. W. (1944) *Shakespeare's History Plays.* London: Chatto and Windus (rev. edn, 1969).

Traversi, Derek (1957) *Shakespeare from Richard II to Henry V.* Stanford, CA: Stanford University Press.

Velz, John W. (ed.) (1996) *Shakespeare's English Histories: A Quest for Form and Genre.* Binghamton, NY: Medieval and Renaissance Texts and Studies.

Watson, Donald G. (1990) *Shakespeare's Early History Plays: Politics at Play on the Elizabethan Stage.* London: Macmillan.

Wilders John (1978) *The Lost Garden: A View of Shakespeare's English and Roman History Plays.* London: Macmillan.

Wilson John Dover (1943) *The Fortunes of Falstaff.* Cambridge: Cambridge University Press.

Richard III and the Shape of History

Marjorie Garber

In this ingenious essay Garber uses Richard's physical deformity as an image for Shakespeare's warping of his historical material, and therefore as a meta-historical trope for the writing of history itself. Seen in this light, the play is self-consciously mediating its own deformation of history and historiography. Garber's own histories, taking in Freud as well as Tillyard, Lacan as well as Bacon, show something of the exciting breadth of critical matrices that can be brought into collision with the Shakespearian text.

Marjorie Garber, 'Descanting on Deformity: Richard III and the Shape of History', in *Shakespeare's Ghost Writers: Literature as Uncanny Causality* (London: Methuen, 1987), pp. 28–51.

And thus having resoued all the doubts, so farre as I can imagine, may be moued against this Treatise; it onely rests to pray thee (charitable Reader) to interprete fauorably this birth of mine, according to the integritie of the author, and not looking for perfection in the worke it selfe. As for my part, I onely glory thereof in this point, that I trust no sort of vertue is condemned, nor any degree of vice allowed in it: and that (though it not be perhaps so gorgeously decked, and richly attired as it ought to be) it is at the least rightly proportioned in all the members, without any monstrous deformitie in any of them.

James I, *Basilikon Doron*

Upon a time when Burbidge played Richard III there was a citizen grew so far in liking with him that, before she went from the play, she appointed him to come that night unto her by the name of Richard the Third. Shakespeare, overhearing their conclusion, went before, was entertained and at his game ere Burbidge came. Then, message being brought that Richard the Third was at the door, Shakespeare caused return to be made that William the Conqueror was before Richard the Third.

John Manningham's *Diary* (13 March 1601)

I

How does the logic of ghostly authorship inform – or deform – not only the writing of literature but also the writing of history? As a way of approaching this question, I begin with a passage from *The Comedy of Errors*:

> O! grief hath chang'd me since you saw me last,
> And careful hours with time's deformed hand
> Have written strange defeatures in my face:
> But tell me yet, dost thou not know my voice?
> (V. i. 298–301)[1]

A complex interrelationship between time and deformation is clearly outlined in Egeon's plea for recognition. For time's hand is already deformed as well as deforming, and it is, explicitly, a writing hand. Between the 'deformed hand' and the still recognizable speaking voice comes, as always, the shadow. Hand/voice; written/spoken. Here, though, that which is *written* is deformed, twisted out of shape, imbued with 'strange defeatures.' The wonderful word *defeature* means both 'undoing, ruin' and 'disfigurement; defacement; marring of features' (*OED*). In *The Comedy of Errors* it is twice used to describe the change of appearance wrought by age upon the face, both in Egeon's speech given above, and in Adriana's lament for her lost beauty, its loss hastened, she thinks, by her husband's neglect: 'Then is he the ground / Of my defeatures' (II. i. 97–8). It is unfortunate that 'defeature' has become, as the *OED* points out, 'obsolete,' 'archaic,' 'now chiefly an echo of the Shakespearean use' because it offers a superbly concrete picture of the *effects* of ruin, the visible, readable consequences of being – or coming – undone.

I would like to arrive, in this chapter, at a consideration of the way in which 'time's deformed hand' writes, and thus defaces, history. The concept of 'defeature' is a useful place to start from, since the visible marks of political defeat are often written, or characterized, in what one age will call history-writing and another, propaganda. My subject, the 'defeatured' player in this exemplum, will be Richard III, an especially interesting case not only because of the fascination that history has exercised on both admirers and detractors, but also because, like Oxford and Bacon in the Shakespeare authorship controversy, Richard III has been the occasion for more amateur detective work, and for the foundation of both English and American societies to clear his name. The Richard III Society, originally known as the Fellowship of the White Boar, was founded in England in 1924; the Friends of Richard III Incorporated, the Society's American counterpart, included among its founding members the actresses Helen Hayes and Tallulah Bankhead.

The most recent full-length study of Richard, by Charles Ross,[2] while in most ways apparently an extremely careful and balanced account, shows the usual pique at this 'amateur' espousal of Richard's cause, which has led in turn to the unwelcome development of amateurs writing history: 'an Oxford professor of English law, a headmaster at Eton, several peers of the realm and a number of historical novelists and writers of detective stories,' prominent among them women. Ross cites Josephine Tey, Rosemary Hawley Jarman, and 'a number of others, nearly all women writers, for whom the rehabilitation of the reputation of a long-dead king holds a strange and unexplained fascination.'[3] By implication these women are following the self-deluded path of the Lady Anne, whose 'strange and unexplained' capitulation to Richard's suit in Shakespeare's play demonstrates female folly and a slightly sentimental belief that a bad man can be reformed or redeemed by the love of a good woman.

Ross's view of Richard is fact-oriented, balanced but binary. He concludes that Richard 'does not appear to have been a complex man,' and that 'any contrarity of "character" of Richard III stems not from what we know about him but from what we do not know about him.'[4] It is the historian's job to discover the facts, and thus to dispel mystery, fantasy, undecidability. With this decidedly 'professional,'[5] male, and hegemonic view of the use and abuse of history-writing, set forth in an introductory chapter that is designed to articulate 'The Historical Reputation of Richard III: Fact and Fiction,' we may begin our consideration of a dramatic character who is self-described as both deformed and defeatured, himself compact of fact *and* fiction: 'Cheated of feature ... Deformed, unfinished ... scarce half made up' (*Richard III*, I. i. 19–21).

Shakespeare's use and abuse of history in the *Henry VI* plays, and particularly in *Richard III*, is often viewed as a consequence, deliberate or adventitious, of the move by Tudor historians to classify Richard III as self-evidently a villain, his deformed body a readable text. Shakespeare, in such interpretations, emerges as either an unwitting dupe of More, Hall, and Holinshed, or as a co-conspirator, complicit in their design, seizing the opportunity to present the Plantagenet king defeated by Elizabeth's grandfather as unworthy of the throne, as unhandsome in person as in personality.

Either the dramatist was himself shaping the facts for political purposes, or he was taken in by the Tudor revisionist desire to inscribe a Richard 'shap'd' and 'stamp'd' for villainy.

In either case, the persuasive power of the portrait has endured. As recently as 1984, for example, René Girard could assert confidently that 'When Shakespeare wrote the play, the king's identity as a "villain" was well-established. The dramatist goes along with the popular view, especially at the beginning. Richard's deformed body is a mirror for the self-confessed ugliness in his soul.'[6]

It is clear, however, that no account of Shakespeare's literary or political motivations in foregrounding his protagonist's deformity is adequate to explain the power and seductiveness of Richard's presence in the plays. Indeed, the very fascination exerted by the historical Richard III seems to grow in direct proportion to an increase in emphasis on his deformity.

It may be useful here to document briefly the ways in which the vagaries of transmission, like a game of historical telephone, succeeded in instating Richard's deformity as the party line. The story of Richard's prolonged gestation, 'held for two years in his mother's womb, emerging with teeth, and with hair down to his shoulders,' like the picture of the hunchback, 'small of stature, having a short figure, uneven shoulders, the right being higher than the left,' is first told in the *Historia Regium Angliae* of Warwickshire antiquary John Rous, who died in 1491.[7] Polydore Vergil, Henry VII's Italian humanist historian, situated Richard in the scheme of providential history as the antagonist of Tudor ascendancy. Thomas More's *History of Richard III* established the enduring popular image of the villainous king as monster, in an account that artfully ascribes some of the more lurid details to rumor while passing them on:

> Richarde the third sonne, of whom we nowe entreate, was in witte and courage egall with either of them, in bodye and prowesse farre vnder them bothe, little of stature, ill fetured of limmes, croke backed, his left shoulder much higher then his right, hard fauoured of visage, and suche as in states called warlye, in other menne other wise. He was malicious, wrathfull, enuious, and from afore his birth, euer frowarde. It is for trouth reported, that the Duches his mother had so muche a doe in her trauaile, that shee coulde not bee deliuered of hym uncutte: and that hee came into the worlde with the feete forwarde, as menne bee borne outwarde, and (as the fame runneth) also not vntothed, whither menne of hatred reporte aboue the trouthe, or elles that nature chaunged her course in hys beginninge, whiche in the course of his lyfe many thinges vnnaturallye committed.[8]

More's account was borrowed by both Hall and Holinshed, and survives substantially unchanged in Shakespeare's *Richard III*. We might note that there is already a disparity between Rous's 'history' and More's. Rous describes Richard's right shoulder as being higher than his left. More, with equal particularity, asserts that 'his left shoulder [was] much higher then his right.' The augmentation *much* puts a spin on the reversal; More grounds his own authority in rhetorical emphasis, and in doing so further distorts the figure of Richard – and the rhetorical figure for which he will come to stand. Both the change of shoulder – toward the sinister – and the emphasis implied by *much* suggest the pattern of amplification and embellishment characteristic of the Richard story throughout its own history.[9]

In the first tetralogy, unusual stress is placed on Richard's physical deformity, which is repeatedly anatomized and catalogued. King Henry calls him 'an indigested and deformed lump' (*3 Henry VI*, V. vi. 51), Clifford a 'foul indigested lump, / As crooked in thy manners as thy shape!' (*2 Henry VI*, V. i. 157–8), and the Lady Anne a 'lump of foul deformity' (*Richard III*, I. ii. 57). Significantly, he is at once 'misshap'd,' unshaped, and preshaped. Born in a sense prematurely ('sent before my time'), feet first, and with teeth already in his mouth, to the wonderment of the midwife and waiting women (*3 Henry VI*, V. vi. 52, 75–6), he is disproportioned and deformed, but also at the same time unfinished, incomplete, as his own testimony makes plain. Nature, he says in *3 Henry VI*, conspired with love

> To shrink mine arm up like a wither'd shrub,
> To make an envious mountain on my back
> Where sits deformity to mock my body;
> To shape my legs of an unequal size,
> To disproportion me in every part,
> Like to a chaos, or an unlick's bear-whelp
> That carries no impression like the dam.
>   (III. ii. 156–62)

In the opening soliloquy of *Richard III*, he recurs to this description, again placing the blame on nature and love:

> I, that am rudely stamp'd, and want love's majesty
> To strut before a wanton ambling nymph;
> I, that am curtail'd of this fair proportion,
> Cheated of feature by dissembling nature,
> Deformed, unfinished, sent before my time
> Into the breathing world scarce half made up,
> And that so lamely and unfashionable
> That dogs bark at me as I halt by them –
> Why I, in this weak piping time of peace,
> Have no delight to pass away the time,
> Unless to spy my shadow in the sun,
> And descant on mine own deformity.
>   (I. i. 16–27)

Generations of readers have been strongly affected by this relation between the deformity and the moral or psychological character of Richard. One such reader was Sigmund Freud, who turned to the example of Richard's deformity to characterize patients who think of themselves as 'exceptions' to normal rules. Such patients, Freud says, claim that 'they have renounced enough and suffered enough, and have a claim to be spared any further exactions; they will submit no longer to disagreeable necessity, for they are *exceptions* and intend to remain so too.'[10] This claim seems apt enough for Richard's opening soliloquy, which Freud goes on to quote: 'that figure in the creative work of the greatest of poets in whose character the claim to be an exception is closely bound up with and motivated by the circumstance of congenital injury.'[11] But when Freud comes to discuss the passage, he finds it to signify not Richard's desire to deflect his energies from love (for which his deformity renders him unsuitable) to intrigue and murder, but rather a more sympathetic message for which the resolution to 'prove a villain' acts as a 'screen.' The 'something much more serious'[12] that Freud describes behind the screen is, essentially, a variation on the theme of the family romance. His Richard declares

> Nature has done me a grievous wrong in denying me that beauty of form which wins human love ... I have a right to be an exception, to overstep those bounds by which others let themselves be circumscribed. I may do wrong myself, since wrong has been done to me – and now [says Freud] we feel that we ourselves could be like Richard, nay, that we are already a little like him. Richard is an enormously magnified representation of something we can all discover in ourselves. We all think we have reason to reproach nature and our destiny for congenital and infantile disadvantages; we all demand reparation for early wounds to our narcissism, our self-love ... Why were we born in a middle-class dwelling instead of a royal palace?[13]

For Freud, then, Shakespeare's Richard III represents not so much a particular aberrant personality warped by the accident of congenital deformation, as (or, but rather) the general psychological fact of deformation at birth and by birth, the congenital deformation that results 'in ourselves,' in 'all' of us, by the fact that we are born to certain parents, and in certain circumstances, incurring, inevitably, certain narcissistic wounds. Thus for Freud the character of Shakespeare's Richard marks the fact of deformation in the register of the psychological, just as we shall see the same character mark the inevitability of deformation in the registers of the political and the historiographical.

Moreover, in Freud's narrative the political is also explicitly present, though it is signified by a lacuna, a lapse in the progress of his exposition:

> For reasons which will be easily understood, I cannot communicate very much about these ... case-histories. Nor do I propose to go into the obvious analogy between deformities of character resulting from protracted sickliness in

childhood and the behavior of whole nations whose past history has been full of suffering. Instead, however, I will take the opportunity of pointing to that figure...[14]

and so on to Shakespeare and Richard III. What is the 'obvious analogy' he resists? It seems reasonable to associate the 'deformities of character resulting from protracted sickliness in childhood,' and, indeed, the 'behavior of whole nations whose past history has been full of suffering' with some specific rather than merely general referent. And if we consider the year in which this essay was first published, in *Imago* 1915–1916, we may be reminded of the circumstances of Germany in the First World War, and, most directly, of the personal circumstances of Kaiser Wilhelm. For Wilhelm II of Prussia was born with a withered arm, a congenital defect that made him the target of gibes from his childhood playmates, including his cousin, who would become Czar Nicholas of Russia. As a recent historical study describes him, Wilhelm II

> was a complicated man of painful insecurity – his left arm was withered and useless – who sought in pomp and bluster, in vulgar displays of virility, to mask his handicap and to assert what he devoutly believed in: his divine right to rule. But he craved confirmation of that right and yearned to be loved and idolized. Beyond the flawed character was a man of intelligence and vision.[15]

Wilhelm II, then, is also considered – or considered to have considered himself – an 'exception' to normal rules. Freud takes exception to mentioning him – or even, perhaps, to consciously identifying him – and instead displaces his analysis onto the safely 'literary' character of Shakespeare's Richard. And Richard's opening soliloquy, descanting on deformity, provides a revealing narrative of the ways in which the line between the 'psychological' and the 'historical' is blurred.

'Unlick'd,' 'unfinished,' 'indigested' – 'not shaped' for sportive tricks, 'scarce half made up.' The natal circumstances and intrapsychic discourse of Shakespeare's Richard, who ironically resolves, despite his initial disclaimers, to 'court an amorous looking-glass' (I. i. 15, I. ii. 255, I. ii. 262), uncannily anticipate the language of Jacques Lacan's description of the 'mirror stage.' Lacan writes of

> the view I have formulated as the fact of a real specific prematurity of birth in man...This development is experienced as a temporal dialect that decisively projects the formation of the individual into history. The *mirror stage* is a drama whose internal thrust is precipitated from insufficiency to anticipation – and which manufactures for the subject, caught up in the lure of spatial identification, *the succession of phantasies that extends from a fragmented body-image to a*

form of its totality that I shall call orthopaedic – and, lastly, to the assumption of
the armour of an alienating identity, which will mark with its rigid stricture the
subject's entire mental development.[16]

Characteristically, Richard turns his chaotic physical condition into a rhetorical benefit, suggesting that he can 'change shapes with Proteus for advantages' (*3 Henry VI*, III. ii. 192); be his own parent and his own author, lick
himself into shape – whatever shape the occasion requires. Queen Elizabeth
tells him that he cannot win her daughter 'Unless thou couldst put on some
other shape' (*Richard III*, IV. iv. 286). But the shape in which we encounter
him is already a deformed one – the natural deformity of historical record.

Peter Saccio gives a highly useful account of the evolution of Richard the
monster in his study of Shakespeare's English kings:

> This lurid king, hunchbacked, clad in blood-spattered black velvet, forever
> gnawing his nether lip or grasping for his dagger, has an enduring place in
> English mythology. He owes something to the facts about the historical Richard
> III. He owes far more to rumor and to the political bias, credulity and especially
> the literary talent of Tudor writers...
>
> As myth, the Tudor Richard is indestructible...As history, however, the
> Tudor Richard is unacceptable. Some of the legend is incredible, some is
> known to be false, and much is uncertain or unproved. The physical deformity,
> for example, is quite unlikely. No contemporary portrait or document attests
> to it and the fact that he permitted himself to be stripped to the waist for
> anointing at his own coronation suggests that his torso could bear public
> inspection.[17]

In fact, when we come to examine the portrait evidence, we find that it is
of considerable interest for evaluating Richard's alleged deformity. A portrait
now in the Society of Antiquaries of London, painted about 1505, shows a
Richard with straight shoulders. But a second portrait, possibly of earlier
date, in the Royal Collection, seems to emblematize the whole controversy,
for in it, X-ray examination reveals an original straight shoulder line, which
was subsequently painted over to present the raised right shoulder silhouette
so often copied by later portraitists.[18]

Richard is not only deformed, his deformity is itself a deformation. His
twisted and misshapen body encodes the whole strategy of history as a necessary deforming and *un*forming – with the object of *re*forming – the past.
Shakespeare exemplifies this strategy with precision in a remarkable moment
in *Much Ado About Nothing*, when the vigilant and well-intentioned Watch
overhears a comment by Borachio. 'Seest thou not what a deformed thief
this fashion is?' 'I know that Deformed,' remarks the Second Watch wisely
to himself, ''a has been a vile thief this seven year; 'a goes up and down like
a gentleman. I remember his name' (III. iii. 125–7). Like Falstaff's eleven

buckram men grown out of two, this personified concretion takes on an uncanny life of its own in the scene. When Borachio and Conrade are confronted with their perfidy, Deformed is identified as a co-conspirator: 'And
one Deformed is one of them; I know him, 'a wears a lock' (ll. 169–70),
and agaîn, 'You'll be made bring Deformed forth, I warrant you' (ll. 172–3).
This is precisely what happens to the reinvented historical figure of Richard
III.

Created by a similar process of ideological and polemical distortion,
Richard's deformity is a figment of rhetoric, a figure of abuse, a catachresis
masquerading as a metaphor. In a viciously circular manifestation of neo-
Platonic determinism, Richard is made villainous in appearance to match
the desired villainy of his reputation, and then is given a personality warped
and bent to compensate for his physical shape.

For Shakespeare's play, in fact, encodes what we might call a suppositious
presupposition. Richard's deformity is not claimed, but rather presupposed,
given as fact in service of the question, 'was his villainy the result of his
deformity?' – a question not unlike 'have you stopped beating your wife?'
Jonathan Culler has shown that the presuppositions that govern literary
discourse are mistakenly designed as givens, as 'moments of authority and
points of origin,' when in fact they are only 'retrospectively designated as
origins and ... therefore, can be shown to derive from the series for which
they are constituted as origin.' As with literary conventions, so also with
historical presuppositions that constitute the ground of a discursive continuum – here the 'History' of Richard III. To adapt Culler's argument
about speech acts, 'None of these [claims of historical veracity] is a point of
origin or moment of authority. They are simply the constituents of a discursive space from which one tries to derive conventions.'[19]

Richard's deformity, itself transmitted not genetically but generically
through both historiography and dramaturgy, becomes the psychological and
dramatic focus of the play's dynamic. Shakespeare has written history backward, taking Hall's and More's objective correlative (he looked the way he was;
he should have looked this way because he was in fact this way; he should have
been this way, so he must have looked this way) and then presupposed it.
Richard's own claim that he can 'change shapes with Proteus for advantages' is
a metahistorical comment on his Lamarckian evolution as villainous prototype,
every misshaped part an over-determined text to be interpreted and moralized,
descanting on his own deformity. Shakespeare's play brings 'Deformed forth' as
an embodiment of the historical process that it both charts and epitomizes.

History is indeed shown by the play to be a story that is deformed from
the outset, by its very nature. The figure of Hastings, for instance, seems
predestined to bring out particularly uncanny modes of deformation through
the ghostly doublings of the Scrivener and the Pursuivant. The Pursuivant
(an official empowered to serve warrants) who accosts Lord Hastings in

Richard III, Act III, scene 2 is also named Hastings, and appears by that name not only in the Quarto text but also in Hall's *Union of the Two Illustre Families of Lancaster and York*. The absence of his name from the Folio has caused some editorial speculation, and the Arden editor's long discussion of this absent name emphasizes the strangeness of the figure:

> The entire episode as it appears in F seems pointless: it merely repeats what has already been said by Hastings, adds a superfluous character, and would probably be cut by an economy-minded producer. The fact that it was not cut in Q suggests that someone felt strongly enough about it to retain it, and that the identity of the pursuivant served to make an ironical point.[20]

According to both Hall and Shakespeare, Hastings receives a number of warnings of the fate that is to befall him. His horse stumbles, Stanley dreams that the boar will rase their helms and sends a cautionary word to Hastings, and still Hastings remains adamantly blind to his danger.

At this point, in a remarkable scene reported by Hall and dramatized by Shakespeare, Hastings encounters the Pursuivant who bears his own name. He greets him warmly, reminiscing about the last time they met, when Hastings was fearful for his life. Now, ironically feeling more secure, he rejoices to note that his former enemies, the Queen's allies, have been put to death, and he himself is 'in better state than ere I was' (III. ii. 104). Hall moralizes with some satisfaction on this latest ironic twist: 'O lorde God, the blyndnesse of our mortal nature, when he most feared, he was in moste surety, and when he reconed him selfe most surest, he lost his lyfe, and that within two houres after.'[21] Shakespeare makes the same point more subtly and forcefully by prefacing this encounter with Richard's decision to 'chop off his head' if Hastings will not agree to their 'complots' (III. i. 192–3) and then following it with a knowing aside from Buckingham to the audience. The encounter with the Pursuivant (literally, a 'follower') named Hastings is an example of the uncanny in one of its most direct forms, recognizable and strange at once. The action itself is doubled, as Hastings meets 'Hastings' coming and going, and does not understand what he sees. Hastings's own name functions in a subdued allegorical way throughout this scene, which could be emblematized as *festina lente*, making Hastings slowly.[22]

Another example of doubling and displacement within a historical event is provided by the odd little scene with the Scrivener (III. vi.). Borrowed by the playwright from his chronicle sources, this scene becomes in its dramatic embodiment a model of history as a kind of ghost writing, since it encodes and 'engross[es]' the fashioning of a rival text. The Scrivener complains that he has spent eleven hours copying the indictment of Hastings 'in a set hand,' or legal script. The first draft, or 'precedent' (l. 7), 'was full as long a-doing, / And yet within these five hours Hastings liv'd / Untainted, unexamin'd, free, at liberty' (ll. 7–9). The Scrivener laments the duplicity of the times – 'Who is so gross / That cannot see this palpable device' (ll. 10–11) 'engross'd' by his own set hand (l. 2) – and yet who dares to say he sees it?

This packed little scene demonstrates at once the play's preoccupation with writing and the preemptive – indeed pre*scriptive* – nature of its political design. The Scrivener's indignation is both moral and professional, for his task of scriptwriting had begun before the incident that was to occasion it, and ended too late to authorize – although it will retrospectively 'legitimitize' – the death of Hastings. Since the previous scene has already presented the spectacle of Hastings's decapitated head, displayed by Lovell and Ratcliffe to the London populace and an apparently grief-stricken Richard, the existence, belatedly revealed, of a meticulously crafted indictment undercuts the idea of historical accident or spontaneous action. History is not only deformed but also pre-formed. Hall recounts the story with particular attention to the length of time the drawing of the indictment would take:

> Nowe was thys proclamacion made within two houres after he was beheaded, and it was so curiously endytcd and so fayre writen in Parchement in a fayre hande, and therewith of it selfe so long a processe, that every chyld might perceyve that it was prepared and studyed before (and as some men thought, by Catesby) for all the tyme betwene hys death and the proclamacion proclaimyng, coulde skant have suffyced unto the bare wrytyng alone, albeit that it had bene in paper and scribeled furthe in haste at adventure.[23]

Like the disparity between the 'truth' of Shakespeare's play and the historical figure it encodes, the 'palpable device' of the long-prepared indictment and the apparent hasting of Hastings's demise opens the question of authority. Which comes first, the event or the ghost writer?

So far is Richard from being merely the passive psychological victim of his deformity, he early on becomes deformity's theorist and manipulator, not only 'descanting' upon it, but projecting and displacing its characteristics onto others. The death of Clarence is a good example of how this works in the play. Clarence is imprisoned at Edward's order, but at the instigation of Richard. The two murderers who go to the Tower to carry out the execution bear Richard's warrant for entry. And Edward is nonplussed when, at the worst possible time from a political standpoint, Clarence's death is announced. 'Is Clarence dead?' he asks, 'The order was reversed.' 'But he, poor man, by your first order died,' says Richard. 'And that a winged Mercury did bear; / Some tardy cripple bare the countermand, / That came too lag to see him buried' (II. i. 87–91).

The phrase 'tardy cripple' spoken by the crippled Richard is doubly ironic. He himself is represented in this account not by the cripple, but by 'winged Mercury,' fleet of foot, who bears the message of execution – here, in fact, made possible by Richard's forged warrant. The 'tardy cripple,' coming 'too lag' to save Clarence, is Richard's displacement of deformity onto the foiled intentions of his well-formed brother the King.

An even more striking instance of this crippling or deforming of the world outside Richard occurs in the scene at Baynard's Castle (III. vii.) in which Richard enters aloft between two bishops, 'divinely bent to meditation' (l. 62), and Buckingham stages a public entreaty to persuade him to accept the throne. Buckingham describes Richard as the rightful heir, with 'due of birth' and 'lineal glory' (ll. 120–1), able to prevent the resigning of the crown 'to the corruption of a blemish'd stock' (l. 122). But his description of the present state of governance is oddly pertinent (and impertinent) to the man he is apparently addressing:

> The noble isle doth want her proper limbs;
> Her face defac'd with scars of infamy,
> Her royal stock graft with ignoble plants,
> And almost should'red in the swallowing gulf
> Of dark forgetfulness and deep oblivion.
>
> (ll. 125–9)

Here the cripple is England, wanting 'proper limbs' (compare Richard's own ironic description of 'me that halts and am misshapen thus' as 'a marv'llous proper man' in the eyes of the Lady Anne [I. ii. 250–4]). 'Defac'd' and especially 'should'red' make the transferred anatomical references unmistakable.

In the final scene of *3 Henry VI* an ambitious and disgruntled Richard had murmured aside, 'yet I am not look'd on in the world. / This shoulder was ordain'd so thick to heave, / And heave it shall some weight, or break my back' (V. vii. 22–4). In the scene of the wooing of Anne, Richard protests that Queen Margaret's slanderous tongue 'laid their guilt upon my guiltless shoulders' (*Richard III*, I. ii. 98), again mischievously calling attention to his own physical deformity; later he is twitted by young York to the same effect ('Because that I am little like an ape / He thinks that you should bear me on your shoulders' [III. i. 130–1]). Richard's deformed shoulder is what 'shoulders' the noble isle of England into near oblivion, but in Buckingham's anatomy of the deformed state the 'proper man' is the well derived Richard, who will restore the kingdom to its wonted shape. In both of these cases a condition of deformity is transferred, to the hypothetical messenger or the diseased polity.

Deformity as a self-augmenting textual effect, contaminating the telling of Richard's story as well as Richard's story itself, has been associated with his literary presence almost from the first. More's account of the notorious sermon of Dr Shaa is a good example. Dr Shaa had been persuaded to preach a sermon in which he would impute the bastardy of Edward's sons and point out Richard's physical resemblance to his father the Duke of York. He was to have intoned these sentiments, comparing Richard's visage and behavior to those of the admired Duke, at the point when Richard himself appeared in the congregation. Richard, however, was late, and the key passage already past when he did turn up. Seeing him enter, Dr Shaa, in a flurry of discomfiture, began to repeat his point for point comparison, but 'out of al order, and out of al frame,'[24] to the consternation of the audience. The 'shamefull sermon' having backfired, Shaa fled to his house and was forced to 'kepe him out of sight lyke an owl,' and soon 'withered away' of shame.

In this little story Dr Shaa sees himself as a writer of predictive history, predicating the future on a repetition of the past (the second Richard an image of the first). But his narrative, out of all order and out of all frame, like Richard's own misshapen body, becomes in More's retelling the perversion and distortion of its intended form and design. Moreover, Dr Shaa himself is contaminated by the rhetorical force of the prevailing mythology about Richard. In the course of More's account Shaa himself becomes deformed, or 'withered,' as if by the disseminated agency of his ignoble association with Richard, whose own arm is 'like a with'red shrub' (*3 Henry VI*, III. ii. 156), 'like a blasted sapling, with'red up' (*Richard III*, III. iv. 69). The figure of Richard keeps escaping its own boundaries, to appear uncannily replicative in the authors of his twisted history.

Other putative sources for Shakespeare's play have suffered the same suggestive narrative contamination. Francis Seager's complaint, *Richard Plantagenet, Duke of Gloucester*, one of the tragedies published in the 1563 *Mirror for Magistrates*, is described by a prose commentator in the volume as appropriate to its subject. The roughness of the meter was suitable, since 'kyng Rychard never kept measure in any of his doings ... it were agaynst the *decorum* of his personage, to use eyther good Meter or order.'[25] The 'decorum of his personage' seems also to have affected the Arden editor, Antony Hammond, who describes this same poem as 'a dull, lame piece of verse.'[26]

Such observations reflect the powerful ghostly presence of the lame and halting Richard. E. M. W. Tillyard, writing of the first tetralogy, remarks upon 'the *special shape* in which the age of Elizabeth saw its own immediate past and its present political problems,' and again of 'the *shape* in which the War of the Roses appeared to Shakespeare's contemporaries.'[27]

That 'special shape' is Richard's. Images of 'the beauty of virtue and the deformity of vice' were commonplace in Tudor writings (this particular phrase comes from the second preface to Grafton's *Chronicle at Large* [1569], probably written by Thomas Norton, the author of *Gorboduc*); but when the subject turned explicitly to Richard, the correspondence of physical, moral, and poetic or stylistic deformity seems particularly overdetermined.

Bacon's essay 'Of Deformity,' reads like a description of Richard III, though it may have been provoked more directly by Robert Cecil:

Deformed persons are commonly even with nature; for as nature hath done ill by them, so do they by nature; being for the most part, as the Scripture saith, 'Void of natural affection,' and so they have their revenge of nature. Certain there is a consent between the body and the mind, and where nature erreth in the one, she ventureth in the other ... Whosoever has anything fixed in his person that doth induce contempt, hath also a perpetual spur in himself, to rescue and deliver himself from scorn; therefore all deformed persons are extreme bold ... Also it stireth in them industry... to watch and observe the weakness of others that they may have somewhat to repay. Again, in their superiors it quencheth jealousy and it layeth their competitors and emulators asleep; as never believing they should be in possibility of advancement, till they see them in possession. So that, upon the matter, in a great wit deformity is an advantage to rising... they will, if they be of spirit, seek to free themselves from scorn, which must be either by virtue or malice.[28]

Samuel Johnson cites these sentiments with approbation in his notes on *3 Henry VI*, making explicit their relevance to Richard ('Bacon remarks that the deformed are commonly daring, and it is almost proverbially observed that they are ill-natured. The truth is, that the deformed, like all other men, are displeased with inferiority, and endeavour to gain ground by good or bad means, as they are virtuous or corrupt').[29] And, indeed, this too may be an instance of overdetermined contamination. Dr Johnson's stress on 'deformities' reflects his own self-consciousness of deformation. Suffering from scrofula as an infant, Johnson was marked throughout life by 'scars on the lower part of the face and on the neck'[30] which he sought to conceal in his portraits by presenting the better side of his face to the painter's view. Until the age of six he bore on his arm an open, running sore, or 'issue,' cut and left open with the idea of draining infection. This, and the partial blindness also induced by tuberculosis in infancy, produced in him a 'situation so appalling,' writes Walter Jackson Bate, that 'we are naturally tempted to speculate on the psychological results.'[31]

But Johnson's most striking observations about deformity in Shakespeare occur in another connection. 'We fix our eyes upon his graces, and turn them from his deformities, and endure in him what we should in another loathe or despise.' The subject of these comments, astonishingly, is not Richard III, but Shakespeare himself – and the 'deformities' are those of literary and dramatic creation. 'I have seen,' he continues, 'in the book of some modern critic, a collection of anomalies, which shew that he has corrupted language by every model of depravation, but which his admirer had accumulated as a monument of honour.'[32] 'Anomalies,' 'corrupted language,' 'model of depravation' – all this sounds very like Richard III as he is received by a reluctantly admiring audience. Not only does Richard theorize his own deformity, he generates and theorizes deformity as a form of power.

II

In a response to a recent collection of essays on *'Race,' Writing, and Difference*, Houston A. Baker, Jr discusses Shakespeare's Caliban as an example of what he calls 'the deformation of mastery,' the way in which a representative of the indigenous population finds a voice within the colonialist discourse of the master, Prospero.[33] Caliban, the 'hooting deformed of Shakespeare's *The Tempest*,' provides for Baker an opportunity to describe 'a drama of deformation' as it is articulated by the indigenous Other that advertises itself through a phaneric mask of display. Caliban's metacurses, his deployment of language against language, are a result of his conscription by Western culture, his 'willingness to barter his signs for the white magician's language.'[34] His physical deformity and his curses are alike indices of this double bind. What Baker proposes – and he is here troping the present-day Afro-American scholar's discourse on Caliban's – is a '"vernacular" invasion and transcendence of fields of colonizing discourse in order to destroy white male hegemony.'[35] Unable to go back to a pre-lapsarian or pre-Prosperian innocence (another impossible and hypothetical origin only fantasized in retrospect by the play) Caliban and his twentieth-century heirs must find a solution to the double bind in a 'triple play' of what Baker calls 'supraliteracy,' the deployment of the vernacular, 'hooting' phaneric deformities that are the sign of the slipped noose, of the freed, independent, and victorious subject.

What Baker is here calling for, in an elegant phaneric display of his own, is essentially a rhetoric and a politics of deformation. His word 'hoot,' which he takes from an ethological description of gorilla display, nowhere appears in *The Tempest*, but it suggests the 'mimic hootings' of Wordsworth's Boy of Winander, and even the phaneric 'hoos' of Stevens' Chieftain Iffucan of Azcan.

The 'deformed slave' who is Caliban has lately been taken as the site of deformation for a number of contemporary debates. Thus we might consider Caliban not only as a figure for the colonized subject, but also as a figure for mixed genre, as Paul Howe has suggested,[36] or (on the model of Frankenstein's monster) as a figure for woman. And this kind of deformation, too, has potential relevance for Richard III. Because in the course of Shakespeare's play Richard himself develops what is in effect a rhetoric of deformation, calling attention to the novelties of his physical shape and the ways in which that shape liberates him from the constraints of conventional courtly deportment. 'Cheated of feature by dissembling nature,' Richard himself feels free to cheat and dissemble; 'deformed, unfinished,' he freely descants on his own deformity.

'Man,' writes Nietzsche in his essay 'The Use and Abuse of History,' 'braces himself against the great and ever greater pressure of what is past: it pushes him down or bends him sideways, it encumbers his steps as a dark invisible burden which he would like to disown.'[37] So Richard 'Crook-back' (*3 Henry VI*, I. iv. 75; II. ii. 96; V. v. 30) is bent not only by specific historical distortions but by the intrinsic distortion of history, which Richard bears, like an ape, on his shoulders. Again, as *Titus Andronicus* particularizes in its decapitations and cutting off of hands the dismembering of historiographical writing, so *Richard III* anatomizes the dangers of re-membering, of history as an artifact of memory.

Writing of what he describes as 'monumental history,' Nietzsche argues that

> as long as the soul of historiography lies in the great stimuli that a man of power derives from it, as long as the past has to be described as worthy of imitation, as imitable and possible for a second time, it of course incurs the danger of becoming *somewhat distorted*...there have been ages, indeed, which were quite incapable of distinguishing between a monumentalized past and a mythical fiction...Monumental history deceives by analogies: with seductive similarities it inspires to fanaticism; and when we go on to think of this kind of history in the hands of gifted egoists and visionary scoundrels, then we see empires destroyed, princes murdered, wars and revolutions launched and the number of historical 'effects in themselves,' that is to say, effects without sufficient cause, again augmented.[38]

'Gifted egoists and visionary scoundrels'; 'wars and revolutions launched'; 'princes murdered'; the past 'somewhat distorted' in the direction of mythical fiction – Nietzsche is uncannily describing not only monumental history but also Richard III – and *Richard III*. Moreover, Richard himself in his opening soliloquy articulates the process of monumental history:

> Now are our brows bound with victorious wreaths,
> Our bruised arms hung up for monuments,
> Our stern alarums chang'd to merry meetings,
> Our dreadful marches to delightful measures.
> (I. i. 5–8)

This is the description of something completed and assimilated, something finished – against which Richard remains defiantly incomplete and imperfect: 'curtail'd of this fair proportion, / Cheated of feature by dissembling nature, / Deform'd, unfinish'd, sent before my time / Into this breathing world scarce half made up' (ll. 18–21). Yet Nietzsche, too, writes of the consciousness of history as something that reminds man of 'what his existence fundamentally is – an imperfect tense that can never become a perfect one.'[39] So the imperfect and unperfected Richard stands over against 'the phrase "it was".'[40]

It is in the multiple narratives of birth that Richard comes most clearly to stand as an embodiment of the paradoxical temporality of history. On the one hand, he is premature: 'Deform'd, unfinish'd, sent before [his] time.' Yet on the other, he is born too late, 'held for two years in his mother's womb, emerging with teeth,' overdeveloped and overarmed. Both Robert N. Watson and Janet Adelman[41] have identified, in psychoanalytic terms, another birth scene, a fantasized one in which the 'unlick'd bear-whelp' carves his own way out of the womb, making a birth canal where none exists:

> Seeking a way, and straying from the way,
> Not knowing how to find the open air,
> But toiling desperately to find it out –
> Torment myself to catch the English crown;
> And from that torment I will free myself,
> Or hew my way out with a bloody axe.
> (*3 Henry VI*, III. ii. 176–81)

Figuratively, this may be seen as a process of violently willful biological birth; politically, it presents itself as a birth of historical process. Premature, Protean, fully and functionally toothed, Richard here hews out an historical path, the way to the crown (and to the chronicles). The violence of his act is inseparable and indistinguishable from that act itself. His use of history is simultaneously and necessarily its abuse.

There is another retelling of the birth story in *Richard III*, this one by the Lady Anne:

> If ever he have child, abortive be it,
> Prodigious, and untimely brought to light,
> Whose ugly and unnatural aspect
> May fright the hopeful mother at the view,
> And that be heir to his unhappiness!
> (I. ii. 21–5)

This passage, too, can be conceived as a description of autogenesis. The fantasy child who is to be the only offspring of Richard and Anne is Richard himself.[42] A different construction, or reconstruction, of Anne's speech, however, might read this predictive curse as the birth of history. History – the historical subject and the synthetic Shakespearean history play – is the prodigious and untimely result of the union of chronicle and drama. Anne's imagined scene of the mother's dismay (she does not, of course, envisage *herself* as the 'hopeful mother' of his child) strongly recalls King Henry VI's account of the birth of Richard: 'Thy mother felt more than a mother's pain, / And yet brought forth less than a mother's hope' (*3 Henry VI*, V. vi. 49–50).

As I have argued elsewhere,[43] recent critical displacements of the once-fashionable notion of 'providential history' by a politically self-conscious, ideologically determined reshaping of historical 'fact' have foregrounded the degree of belatedness intrinsic to and implicit in Elizabethan history plays. The 'now' of these plays is always preeminently the 'now' of the time of their literary genesis – the time is manifestly out of joint, and the retrospective reconstruction of history ('to tell my story,' to pursue Hamlet's own chronicling of the process) is the only means of shaping time at either the protagonist's or the dramatist's command. 'May not an ass know when the cart draws the horse?' asks Lear's Fool (*King Lear*, I. iv. 223), but the cart, or tumbril, of historical events inevitably draws the hero's charger in its wake. Thus the repudiation of the fiction of historical accuracy or 'objectivity,' the self-delusive and far from benign assumption that the past can be recaptured without contamination from the present, has become a crucial starting point of both the Foucauldian and the deconstructive projects. For history is always in the process of deconstructing itself – of becoming, as it always was, 'his-story,' the story that the teller imposes upon the reconstructed events of the past.

This is not new news to the chroniclers of chroniclers. Sidney's famous description of the historian in his *Apologie for Poetrie* characterizes him as 'loaden with old mouse-eaten records, authorizing himself (for the most part) upon other histories, whose greatest authorities, are built upon the notable foundation of hearsay, having much ado to accord differing writers, and to pick truth out of partiality.'[44] The historian is constrained by his burden of facts; 'Many times he must tell events, whereof he can yield no cause; or if he do, it must be poetical'[45] – must, that is, make the move from 'fact' to fiction, 'for that a feigned example, hath as much force to teach, as a true example.' One of the best known passages in the *Apologie* addresses the question of theatrical fictions, mimesis, and allegoresis.

> What child is there, that coming to a play, and seeing Thebes written in great letters upon an old door, doth believe that it is Thebes? If then a man can arrive, at that child's age, to know that the poet's persons and doings, are but pictures what should be, and not stories what have been, they will never give the lie, to things not affirmatively, but allegorically, and figuratively written. And therefore, as in history, looking for truth, they go away full fraught with falsehood; so in poesy, looking for fiction, they shall use the narration, but as an imaginative groundplot of a profitable invention.[46]

This quotation, often cited, is frequently truncated by the omission of the last sentence. Its sense seems to be that poesy – which here includes drama – is less culpable of distortion than history, because it does not pretend to objectivity. Or, to put the position somewhat differently, its distortion is the product of design. A very similar position is adumbrated in 'The Use and Abuse of History,' in Nietzsche's argument that the only possible 'objectivity' in the framing of history comes in the work of the dramatist, who alone writes history *as* an expression of the 'artistic drive' rather than as a putatively authoritative and objective record of *what was*. For drama, in Nietzsche's terms, offers

> an artistically true painting but not an historically true one. To think of history objectively in this fashion is the silent work of the dramatist; that is to say, to think of all things in relation to all others and to weave the isolated event into the whole: always with the presupposition that if a unity of plan does not already reside in things it must be implanted into them. Thus man spins his web over the past and subdues it, thus he gives expression to his artistic drive – but not to his drive towards truth or justice. Objectivity and justice have nothing to do with one another.[47]

By contrast to drama all other modes of historical writing are fundamentally unsatisfactory, constructive in some ways but destructive in others. Since they are written by historical subjects in effect created by the very history they seek to document, there can be no objective or authoritative vantage point for their observations. And this point is oddly but firmly insisted upon by both Sidney and Nietzsche. Thus Sidney claims that 'the best of the historian is subject to the poet; for whatsoever action, or faction, whatsoever counsel, policy, or war stratagem, the historian is bound to recite, that may the poet (if he list) with his imitation make his own.'[48] And Nietzsche writes that the human subject must situate himself or herself *'against history'*;[49] 'if you want biographies, do not desire those who bear the legend "Herr So-and-So and his age," but those upon whose title-page there would stand "a fighter against his age".'[50]

The title page of *biographies*; 'the *history* of great men.'[51] It is often asked about Shakespeare's *Richard III*, as about other pivotal works in the Shakespeare canon (e.g. *Julius Caesar*): is it a tragedy or is it a history? Is it, as both Quarto and Folio title pages call it, 'the tragedy of Richard III,' or, as the Folio classifies it, generically to be listed under the histories? Nietzsche has here uncannily provided an answer to the question of *why* this is a question: the birth of history can only be presented as the birth of tragedy.

'The Use and Abuse of History' (1874) is indeed in some sense a coda or extrapolation of Nietzsche's great study of the rise and fall of the tragic vision in ancient Greece, *The Birth of Tragedy* (1871). In that work, as Hayden White has noted, Nietzsche 'lamented the decline and fall of ancient tragedy, and named the modern historical consciousness as its antitype.'[52] 'The Use and Abuse of History' continues this exploration of what has gone wrong, of what has been lost with the loss of the classical tragic vision.

But Nietzsche's remarks are not confined to the Greeks alone. There is another dramatist who haunts Nietzsche's text, and that dramatist, perhaps unsurprisingly, is Shakespeare. Twice he takes as his starting point what someone else has said about Shakespeare's intersection with the modern historical world. Quoting Franz Grillparzer, Nietzsche critiques the contemporary German's sensibility, developed, so he says, 'from his experience in the theater. "We feel in abstractions," [Grillparzer] says, "we hardly know any longer how feeling really expresses itself with our contemporaries; we show them performing actions such as they no longer perform nowadays. Shakespeare has ruined all of us moderns." '[53] Shortly thereafter, Nietzsche quotes Goethe:

> Goethe once said of Shakespeare: 'No one despised outward costume more than he; he knew very well the inner human costume, and here all are alike. They say he hit off the Romans admirably; but I don't find it so, they are all nothing but flesh-and-blood Englishmen, but they are certainly human beings, human from head to foot, and the Roman toga sits on them perfectly well.'

Nietzsche takes this opportunity to condemn present-day literati and officials, who could not be portrayed as Romans

> because they are not human beings but only flesh-and-blood compendia and as it were abstractions made concrete...creations of historical culture, wholly structure, image, form without demonstrable content and, unhappily, *ill-designed form* and, what is more, *uniform*. And so let my proposition be understood and pondered: *history can be borne only by strong personalities, weak ones are utterly extinguished by it*...He who no longer dares to trust himself but involuntarily asks of history 'How ought I to feel about this?' finds that his timidity gradually turns him into an actor and that he is playing a role, usually indeed many roles and therefore playing them badly and superficially.[54]

'*Ill-designed form* and, what is more, *uniform*.' For Nietzsche the modern politician's failure lies precisely in his conformity to unthinking standards of political correctness, what Nietzsche scornfully calls 'objective' standards, as if any strong personality, in his view, could be 'objective' or subscribe to an 'objective' reading of history. 'Ill-design' for Nietzsche is thus the obverse of what it is for *Richard III*. In Shakespeare's play Richard's physical appearance, his ill-design, perversely glories in its difference from the usual, the uniform, the fully formed.

The famous scene in which he woos and wins the Lady Anne ('and will she yet abase her eyes on me...On me, that halts and am misshapen thus?/My dukedom to a beggarly denier,/I do mistake my person all this while!/Upon my life she finds (although I cannot)/Myself to be a marv'llous proper man./I'll be at charges for a looking glass ...' [I. ii. 246–55]) displays a Richard whose narcissistic posturing translates ill-design ('misshapen thus') into 'proper' or handsome appearance – and thus to *proprietary* and *appropriative* behavior, made possible by his flouting of the conventional *proprieties*.

Shakespeare appears a third time in this relatively short essay, when Nietzsche is offering a critique of the 'philosophy of the unconscious' of Eduard von Hartmann. Von Hartmann's description of the 'manhood of man' is ironically disparaged by a citation from Jaques's celebrated speech in *As You Like It* on the seven ages of man – a citation that not surprisingly encodes the word 'history'.[55]

> Last scene of all,
> That ends this strange, eventful history,
> Is second childishness, and mere oblivion,
> Sans teeth, sans eyes, sans taste, sans every thing.
> (II. vii. 163–6)

The Richard who comes into the world already provided with teeth is an apt counter-image to this toothless historical deterioration. Yet, as these citations make clear, the power of drama as a historical force can be enfeebling as well as enabling, reducing men to actors in the very act of raising history to drama. 'Overproud European,' writes Nietzsche in an apostrophe that neatly deconstructs Pico's *De dignitate hominis*,

> you are raving! Your knowledge does not perfect nature, it only destroys your own nature. Compare for once the heights of your capacity for knowledge with the depths of your capacity for action. It is true you climb upon the sunbeams of knowledge up to Heaven, but you also climb down to chaos. Your manner of moving, that of climbing upon knowledge, is your fatality; the ground sinks away from you into the unknown; there is no longer any support for your life, only spider's threads which every new grasp of knowledge tears apart. – But enough of this seriousness, since it is also possible to view the matter more cheerfully.
>
> The madly thoughtless shattering and dismantling of all foundations, their dissolution into a continual evolving that flows ceaselessly away, the tireless unspinning and historicizing of all there has ever been by modern man, the great cross-spider at the node of the cosmic web – all this may concern and dismay moralists, artists, the pious, even statesmen; *we* shall for once let it cheer us by looking at it in the glittering magic mirror of a *philosophical parodist* in whose head the age has come to an ironical awareness of itself.[56]

Self-irony, proclaimed by a philosophical parodist eying history (and the construction of the human subject) in a glittering magic mirror. It is a stunning evocation of Richard III. 'Shine out, fair sun, till I have bought a glass, / That I may see my shadow as I pass' (*Richard III*, I. ii. 262–3). Over and over again, Shakespeare's Richard Crook-back is compared to a spider, spinning plots. Queen Margaret refers to him as a 'bottled spider, / Whose deadly web ensnareth thee about' (I. iii. 241–2), and the hapless Queen Elizabeth recalls her warning when it is too late: 'O, thou didst prophesy the time would come / That I should wish for thee to help me curse / That bottled spider, that foul bunch-back'd toad!' (IV. iii. 80–1). The Lady Anne likewise classes him with 'spiders, toads, / Or any creeping venom'd thing that lives' (I. ii. 19–20) – even as she succumbs to his designs. Indeed Richard's father, the Duke of York, his predecessor in vengeful soliloquy, had claimed for himself the same identification: 'My brain, more busy than the laboring spider, / Weaves tedious snares to trap mine enemies' (*2 Henry VI*, III. i. 339–40).

Is the present afflicted or instructed by the power of tragedy to 'weave the isolated event into the whole?' Can the 'tireless unspinning and historicizing of all there has ever been by modern man, the great cross-spider at the node of the cosmic web' – occupied with weaving 'spider's threads which every new grasp of knowledge tears apart'[57] – be seen as that which cripples as well as empowers the observer who would profit from historical models, historical example, historical textualizations? This is perhaps the question Shakespeare forces us to ask of our own ambivalent fascination with 'that bottled spider / Whose deadly web ensnareth [us] about': Richard III – and *Richard III* – as the dramatization of the power of deformity inherent in both tragedy and history.

Notes

1 See *The Riverside Shakespeare*, ed. G. Blakemore Evans (Boston: Houghton Mifflin, 1974). All citations from the plays are to this edition unless noted in the text.

2 Charles Ross, *Richard III* (Berkeley, CA: University of California Press, 1981).

3 Ibid., p. li.

4 Ibid., p. 229.

5 Ibid., p. li.

6 René Girard, 'Hamlet's dull revenge', *Stanford Literary Review*, 1 (Fall 1984): 159.

7 *Narrative and Dramatic Sources of Shakespeare*, ed. Geoffrey Bullough (London: Routledge and Kegan Paul, 1975), vol. 3, p. 223.

8 *The Yale Edition of the Complete Works of Sir Thomas More*, vol. 2, *The History of King Richard III*, ed. Richard Sylvester (New Haven, CT: Yale University Press, 1963), p. 7. Sir Horace Walpole, one of the earliest defenders of Richard's reputation, characterized More as 'an historian who is capable of employing truth only as cement in a fabric of fiction' (Walpole, *Historic Doubts on the Life and Reign of Richard III* (London: J. Dodsley, 1768 [1965 edn]), p. 116 and recent scholars have explicitly identified the kind of 'fiction' More is writing as *drama*. Thus

A. R. Myers asserts that 'his history is much more like a drama, unfolded in magnificent prose, for which fidelity to historical fact is scarcely relevant' (Myers, 'The character of Richard III', originally published in *History Today*, 4 (1954), reprinted in *English Society and Government in the Fifteenth Century*, ed. C. M. D. Crowder (Edinburgh and London, 1967), p. 119; cited in Ross, *Richard III*; and Alison Hanham argues that the *History* is really a 'satirical drama' meant to display More's own cleverness rather than his command of fact (Hanham, *Richard III and his Early Historians* [Oxford: Clarendon Press 1975], pp. 152–90).

9   I am indebted to Richard Strier for this observation.

10   Sigmund Freud, 'Some character-types met with in psychoanalytic work', in *Character and Culture*, ed. Philip Rieff (New York: Collier Books, 1961), p. 159.

11   Ibid., p. 160.

12   Ibid., p. 161.

13   Ibid.

14   Ibid., p. 160.

15   Fritz Stern, *Gold and Iron* (New York: Vintage Books, 1979), p. 437.

16   Jacques Lacan, 'The mirror stage as formative of the function of the I', in *Écrits*, trans. Alan Sheridan (New York: W.W. Norton, 1977), p. 4.

17   Peter Saccio, *Shakespeare's English Kings* (New York: Oxford University Press, rpt 1978), pp. 158–9. In a recent study of biography and fiction in Tudor–Stuart history writing (*Biographical Truth: The Representation of Historical Persons in Tudor–Stuart Writing* [New Haven, CT: Yale University Press, 1984]), Judith H. Anderson notes that historians regularly impeach Shakespeare's play for its lack of fidelity to historical fact, and points out accurately that the play would lose its power if it did not convince the audience that it was 'somehow real history' (p. 111) – 'Despite ourselves, we believe it' (p. 123). Yet Anderson's view of Richard's deformity is a relatively conventional one. Citing Freud, and reasserting the humanistic commonplace that suffering creates art, she describes Richard as 'the misshapen product of his nature and time and also, as we watch him in the play, the product of his own making' (p. 117). Whether self-fashioned or twisted by his own deformity, Richard is seen as compensating for a disability, rather than seizing that disability as the occasion for a theoretical exploration of the nature of deformation.

18   Pamela Tudor-Craig, *Richard III* (London: National Portrait Gallery, 1973); cited in Ross, *Richard III*, pp. 80, 92–3.

19   Jonathan Culler, 'Presupposition and intertextuality', in *The Pursuit of Signs* (Ithaca, NY: Cornell University Press, 1981), p. 177.

20   *King Richard III*, ed. Antony Hammond, The Arden Shakespeare (London: Methuen, 1981), p. 338.

21   Edward Hall, *The Union of the Two Noble ... Families of Lancaster and York* (1548), cited in *King Richard III*, ed. Hammond, p. 353.

22   See Sigmund Freud, 'The uncanny' (1919), in *Studies in Parapsychology*, ed. Philip Rieff (New York: Macmillan, 1963), pp. 19–60, especially pp. 38–42 on 'the double' and the repetition-compulsion.

23   Hall, cited in *King Richard III*, ed. Hammond, p. 354.

24 More, *Richard III*, p. 68.

25 *Narrative and Dramatic Sources*, ed. Bullough, p. 232.

26 *King Richard III*, ed. Hammond, p. 87.

27 E. M. W. Tillyard, *Shakespeare's History Plays* (New York: Collier Books, 1962), p. 72 (emphasis added).

28 Francis Bacon, *Essays Civil and Moral* (London: Ward, Lock, 1910), pp. 69–70.

29 *Johnson on Shakespeare*, ed. Arthur Sherbo (New Haven, CT: Yale University Press, 1968), vol. 7, p. 605.

30 Walter Jackson Bate, *Samuel Johnson* (New York: Harcourt Brace Jovanovich, 1979), p. 7. See Bate's sensitive treatment of these physical deformities and Johnson's apparent repression of their origins, esp. p. 9. My thanks to Joseph Bartolomeo for reminding me of the relevance of Johnson's own physical disabilities.

31 Bate, *Samuel Johnson*, p. 7.

32 Samuel Johnson, 'Preface to Shakespeare,' in *Johnson on Shakespeare*, ed. Sherbo, vol. 7, p. 91.

33 Houston A. Baker, Jr, 'Caliban's triple play', in *'Race,' Writing, and Difference*, ed. Henry Louis Gates, Jr (Chicago: University of Chicago Press, 1986), p. 390.

34 Ibid., p. 392.

35 Ibid., p. 382.

36 Paul Howe, personal communication, January 1987.

37 Friedrich Nietzsche, 'The use and abuse of history', in *Untimely Meditations*, trans. R. J. Hollingdale (Cambridge: Cambridge University Press, 1983), p. 61. Hollingdale translates this famous essay as 'On the Uses and Disadvantages of History for Life'. I use his translation, as being the most accurate modern version, but take the liberty of retaining the title by which the piece is best known to English readers – and, I think, most suggestively rendered for argumentation.

38 Ibid., pp. 70–1. (emphasis added).

39 Ibid., p. 61.

40 Ibid., p. 70.

41 Robert N. Watson, *Shakespeare and the Hazards of Ambition* (Cambridge, MA: Harvard University Press, 1984), p. 20. Janet Adelman, 'Born of woman, fantasies of maternal power in *Macbeth*', in *Cannibals, Witches, and Divorce: Estranging the Renaissance*, ed. Marjorie Garber (Baltimore, MD: The Johns Hopkins University Press, 1986), pp. 91–3.

42 See Watson, *Hazards of Ambition*, p. 26.

43 Marjorie Garber, 'What's past is prologue: temporality and prophecy in Shakespeare's history plays', in *Renaissance Literary Genres: Essays on Theory, History and Interpretation*, ed. Barbara Lewalski, Harvard English Studies 14 (Cambridge, MA: Harvard University Press, 1986), pp. 301–31.

44 'An apology for poetry', in *Sir Philip Sidney: Selected Poetry and Prose*, ed. David Kalstone (New York: Signet Classic, 1970), p. 227.

45 Ibid., p. 233.

46 Ibid., p. 249.

47   Nietzsche, 'Use and abuse of history', p. 91.
48   Sidney, 'An apology', p. 234.
49   Nietzsche, 'Use and abuse of history', p. 106.
50   Ibid., p. 95.
51   Ibid.
52   Hayden White, *Metahistory: The Historical Imagination in Nineteenth-century Europe* (Baltimore, MD: The Johns Hopkins University Press, 1973), p. 356.
53   Nietzsche, 'Use and abuse of history', p. 81.
54   Ibid., pp. 85–6 (emphasis added).
55   Ibid., p. 115.
56   Ibid., p. 108.
57   Ibid.

The Instability of History in the *Henry IV* Sequence

Paola Pugliatti

Pugliatti's analysis of both Henry IV *plays focuses on moments of explicit engagement with different and sometimes opposing concepts of time, causality and historical record. Pugliatti does see integral connections between the two parts, but it is a relationship of increasing recapitulation and distortion of themes, rather than of their development, fulfilment or conclusion. By connecting time with space and, in particular, with the contested spaces of tavern/court and rebels/king, she is able to develop a sophisticated and allusive relationship between parts 1 and 2.*

Paola Pugliatti, 'Time, Space and the Instability of History in the *Henry IV* Sequence', in *Shakespeare the Historian* (Basingstoke: Macmillan, 1996), pp. 102–31.

The General Frame: Rumour, or the Falsifications of Historiography

The issue of the 'structural problem' of the *Henry IV* plays seems still to attract the attention of critics. In a recent article, Paul Yachnin has taken up the subject once again, remarking that those critics who have argued for the unity of the two plays have normally not developed 'the idea of sequence into an interpretive approach'.[1] Starting from what are considered discrepancies in the sequence (Hal's two reformations being the main one), Yachnin adopts an interpretative model which, far from viewing change as an element producing discontinuity, '*includes* change as the central condition of the production of meaning'[2] and in the second play shows a revisionist attitude which, he holds, works as a critique and even as an undoing of the first.

Yachnin's model is interesting in the first place because it rejects the assumption, which has been fundamental to virtually all discussions of the 'structural problem', that we should 'render Shakespeare's meaning full, stable, and permanent'; and in the second place because it pertinently discusses the 'structural problem' in close connection with the kind of historical vision that the sequence presents. In particular, Yachnin argues that the two plays 'develop Shakespeare's critique of Renaissance historiography, and enact the revisionist, open-ended nature of historical change', 'persistently altering the basic shape of history, and so depriving history of basic shape altogether'.[3]

However, although I agree with Yachnin's general claims, I prefer to consider the second play as a development of certain equivocal elements which are present in the first rather than, like Yachnin, as an outright contradiction of its meanings; I will therefore discuss 'change' and 'open-endedness' from a different set of premises. In particular, I see destabilisation in the progressive corruption of the value system which the first play presents. Apparently neatly defined and delimited and mutually contrasted, the three axiologies which determine the conflicts of the sequence – rule, misrule and rebellion – are in reality blurred right from the start, and they get more and more disfigured as the action progresses: basically, the space of rule is corrupted by being occupied by an illegitimate king;[4] the popular nature of the sphere of misrule is contaminated and deflected from 'low' style by the presence in it, and belonging to it, of the heir apparent (in the sphere of misrule, we may say, the disruption of the *norm* is accompanied by a corruption of the *form*); while the sphere of rebellion tends to present itself as a space of legitimation, for it supports the restoration of someone who is presented as the legitimate heir of Richard II. These discrepancies vitiate the plays' alleged system of values and therefore compromise the possibility of clear moral and political discriminations.

More generally, the sequence puts forward the idea that instability of meaning is a problem which also affects historiography: there are, as we shall see, more or less explicit suggestions that transmission may corrupt historical truth and that knowledge of past events is in any case problematic; but even more problematic is the business of foreseeing and planning future developments for, principally in the sphere of rule, the course of (historical) events does not develop according to either projects or expectations. Time corrupts, infects, contaminates and disfigures, and future developments often bring the frustration of expectations. Thus, both historical knowledge and political project are presented as uncertain predicaments, and historical time tends to be reduced – again, mainly in the sphere of rule – to the mere consciousness of the present.

The whole structure of meaning is developed progressively and cumulatively, although this is brought about in the two plays by means of different strategies. As regards the 'structural problem', then, my idea is that the second play strengthens and clarifies certain premises of the first; that what have been considered discrepancies cease to be problematic if we acknowledge the fact that the framework of the sequence is one of instability rather than one of coherence or consistency; and that this framework is precisely the means by which the sequence questions the pattern of coherence which is at the basis of all providential views of history. Nevertheless, while it is undoubtedly true that Part Two integrates Part One, I would not go so far as to affirm that Part One would be incomplete without Part Two.[5] Simply, as Harold Jenkins argued, *Henry IV* 'is both one play and two', and if 'The two parts are complementary, they are also independent and even incompatible.'[6]

My presentation of the framework described will start from a reading of the *incipit* of the two plays where I consider many of the premises of future developments to be laid. As a start, I will go back to Yachnin's article and pick up a few of the points he makes, which, I believe, call for some comment.

Yachnin quotes, as one of the moments in the sequence in which 'the meaning of actions and words is changed and destabilized by subsequent actions and words',[7] Henry's speech which opens the first play. However, he reads the speech as expressing in the first part the king's intention to go on a crusade and as disclaiming this same intention in the second. In particular, he interprets Henry's meaning in ll. 28–30 ('But this our purpose is now twelve month old, / And bootless 'tis to tell you we will go; / Therefor we meet not now') as 'his statement . . . that a crusade is out of question at this time'. Yachnin's reading of the speech as 'Henry's actorly performance of zeal', then, triggers a series of metatheatrical comments about 'the actorly nature', in the play, 'of characters' actions and words' as intended 'to crystallize their own meanings in the face of the fluidity of meaning'; 'actorly', then, is equated with 'non-stable' and 'changeable', as opposed to a not altogether clear *authentic*, meaning.[8] These assumptions, I believe, and in particular the unclear relationship obtaining between the notions evoked (revisionist attitude, actorly performance, instability, authentic meaning), obscure Yachnin's arguments; besides, I believe that Henry's opening speech in the first play may be read in a light which might better support Yachnin's main claims about the representation of history as unpredictable and open-ended, albeit on the basis of a different set of arguments.

Let us bear in mind, in the first place, that the speech is the statement which opens the sequence and that, therefore, it is through that speech that the spectators – and the readers – are introduced into the world of the play; and in the second place that the occasion is official and ceremonial and that it involves onstage witnesses of a certain importance who are listening to a public statement from the king. The speech has, therefore, a decisive function in establishing the text's historiographical perspective.

Whether Henry is here putting up an 'actorly performance' or not (an attitude which, besides, does not seem to be suggested by the text, either explicitly or implicitly) is, I believe, hardly important. What is crucial, instead, is his recognition – and both the onstage and offstage audience's recognition – of the inanity of his own purposes and of the unreliability of (historical) predictions. (Henry had expressed the same purpose to go on a crusade, in an almost prophetic tone, when, so to speak, we last saw him, in the lines with which he closes *Richard II.*)

It seems clear to me that in the first part of his speech Henry is expressing his purpose with perfect assurance ('As far as to the sepulchre of Christ / ...Forthwith a power of English shall we levy', ll. 19–22) and that in the last part he is simply reminding the nobles – and the audience – that the project is long rife and that its execution is beyond doubt. At the same time, he stresses his conviction with a negation of the necessity of the reminder ('But this our purpose now is twelve month old, / And bootless 'tis to tell you we will go', ll. 28–9); the sentence which follows ('Therefor we meet not now', l. 30) means precisely that the decision has been taken, and that the present meeting is not meant to establish *whether* to go or not. Instead, the king's purpose *now* is simply to hear what suggestions the Council has made 'in forwarding this dear expedience' (l. 33). Besides, Henry does not seem to depend on the Council's opinion; on the contrary, he is merely expecting them to 'decree' what support or marginal advice they can supply *in forwarding* the enterprise.

It is, in all evidence, Westmoreland's speech which introduces a new and unexpected element which disrupts the fulfilment of Henry's purpose. This, moreover, is characteristically unexpected for, as Westmoreland explains, it was determined by a sudden interruption of the Council's meeting with the irruption of the post from Wales. None of the 'heavy news' (l. 37) that the post has brought to the Council has as yet been disclosed to Henry, who is informed of them at the same time as the audience and is *therefore* forced to abandon his 'twelve month old' project: the decision to abandon the expedition is therefore dictated by an external destabilising factor which gives an unexpected turn to what the king appeared to envisage as the predictable chain of (historical) events. The spectacle of the king's failure is displayed before our eyes.

But the sequence stages an even more explicit and crucial instance of destabilisation. It is again an opening, again the audience's first contact with a dramatic world: *Enter Rumour, painted full of tongues.*

Directly addressing the audience, Rumour opens his speech imposing attention:

> Open your ears; for which of you will stop
> The vent of hearing when loud Rumour speaks?
> (*2 Henry IV, Induction*, ll. 1–2)

Rumour proceeds to communicate – albeit somewhat indirectly – the news of Henry's victory at Shrewsbury and of Hal's killing of Hotspur, but he then goes on to say that he has been spreading news to the contrary. It might seem reasonable to suppose that the *Induction* was intended as a device to sum up the main events of Part One, or at least as a reminder of the outcome of the battle of Shrewsbury. However, it deserves attention for it is unique in the whole corpus of histories (why, in the first place, did Shakespeare not feel that a similar link was needed to connect the events of the *Henry VI* plays?), with perhaps the sole exception of Gloucester's soliloquy which opens *Richard III* (this, however, focuses much more on future events than on past ones).

Yet, by the time we get into the first scene of the play we feel that Rumour's speech was by no means necessary as a means of setting out past events. The play might in fact easily have started around line 30 with Travers arriving and informing Northumberland of the disaster at Shrewsbury. No clumsiness in the exposition would have followed, for no information already possessed by the characters would have been transmitted. But quite apart from that, the *Induction* triggers a rather peculiar scene in which the audience's attention is strongly directed towards the workings of the mechanism of news-spreading. This involves three onstage 'messengers' (Lord Bardolph, Travers and Morton), two offstage 'gentlemen' who in turn communicated the news, good to Bardolph and bad to Travers; it makes it impossible the first two messengers (Lord Bardolph and Travers) to be eyewitnesses – which is rather unusual – and the questions from Northumberland to Bardolph, 'How is this deriv'd? / Saw you the field? Came you from Shrewsbury?' (ll. 23–4), which sound slightly odd, since it is conventionally agreed that messengers are considered to be reliable. Obviously, the mechanism of the *Induction* was not meant to create suspense in the audience, for it is precisely from the *Induction* that the spectators know what the truth is (but, do they really *know*?); nor does Northumberland's grief at his son's death deserve the emotional enhancement which may come from the strain of absorbing subsequently contrary truths (we, again, *know* from Rumour that the sickness which he alleged as an impediment to his taking part in the battle was *crafty*).

In other words, the device is not technically necessary; on the contrary, its inclusion renders necessary an overelaboration of the first scene which is not easy to justify in terms of dramatic logic. But, apart from its uniqueness, this particular *Induction* may seem rather surprising as an introduction to a historical play because it is eminently and overtly destabilising.[9] What

Rumour in the final analysis seems to communicate to the audience is a reflection on the instability of meaning in historiography: past events, when they are reported, are subjected to distortions; 'rumour' stands, therefore, for one of the possible factors which contribute to the falsifications of historiography, of its 'continual slanders' (l. 6), others being 'surmises, jealousies, conjectures' (l. 16). The implication is clear: what has already been told about this story – in the first play of the sequence – may have suffered from falsification, and may therefore stand in need of revision.

A different reading of the *Induction* is possible, one which once again focuses on instability, change and uncertainty but which treats these as an unavoidable part of the pursuit of historical awareness and thus as inherent in historiographical practice. By spreading false news, Rumour is in fact suggesting that witnesses need to be evaluated on the basis of their proximity to the events ('Saw you the field? Came you from Shrewsbury?'), and of their reliability ('A gentleman well bred, and of good name', l. 26; 'A gentleman almost forspent with speed', l. 37; 'some hilding fellow that had stol'n / The horse he rode on', ll. 57–8); in short, he is prompting research. Naturally, research may lead us to change and revise our account of events, and change and revision are, as Yachnin says, the central conditions of the production of meaning in the *Henry IV* plays.

In the following pages, I aim to show that the moral and political system of values is not only presented right from the start as unstable, but also gets progressively more and more distorted and corrupt. This is achieved by means of different but concurring strategies in the two plays: in Part One it is time – both as a topic of discourse and as an element in the plot's development – which is used to compare and contrast the three axiologies mentioned above; while in Part Two the corruption of those same axiologies is brought out mainly through space manipulation and in particular through the trespassing implicit in the action of border-crossing.

As I have suggested, the various spaces of the plays – roughly, what is commonly identified with the double plot plus the rebels' space (to which is assigned an independent semantic space in both plays) – adumbrate notions which are obviously not simply spatial, since they evoke the easily identifiable and highly charged political and moral models of *rule*, *misrule* and *rebellion*. My aim is to show that the sorts of political and moral evaluations that the plays apparently encourage are undermined by the way in which the various spatial configurations are organised and interconnected in time and by the way in which they are made to interfere with each other.[10] In particular, following certain suggestions by Lotman regarding the organisation of space, I am interested in developing the notion of *border*, holding that peculiar meanings may be connected – in a given text and in a given culture – with the ideas of keeping within or transgressing certain boundaries.[11]

In Part One, each of the three semantic spheres is presented as managing and, up to a point, controlling its own space and time; the separation between them is responsible for the comparatively neat differentiation of the political and moral issues which each of the spaces stands for: rule, rebellion and misrule each dominate certain relevant space–time loci which are mutually contrasted by means of sequential juxtapositions and of the contrasts produced by certain of their characteristics: night / day, north-west / south, inside / outside, moving / still, etc., are some of the ways in which the various axiological differences are made relevant and by which the various settings and their inhabitants are made to make sense. But the overall structure of meaning is constructed sequentially and is developed in time. While, in fact, the first play mainly establishes those axiologies and meanings and gives them a comparatively clear set of distinctive prerogatives, in the second we see their progressive disfigurement and finally their utter corruption: trespassings and interferences, in fact, are comparatively ineffectual in the first play, where they figure merely as hints and suggestions of what may in the end happen and as partial and temporary distortion of the prerogatives of each of the spaces; while in the second they are responsible for the blurring and final collapse of the issues for which each of the spaces stands. Besides, although the *dénouement* of the sequence is the triumph of the space of *rule*, the way this comes about involves an interesting exchange of prerogatives, for it is achieved by means of a double betrayal: the betrayal by John of Lancaster of the forces of rebellion and the betrayal by Hal of the forces of misrule.

This general frame is established in different ways in the two plays: while in the first it relies principally on time (the impression of simultaneity is the means by which the various spheres are both contrasted and interrelated), in the second it is constructed mainly by playing on the different spaces and on the various events which involve crossings of their boundaries, with violations which become more and more frequent and more and more fatal.

1 *Henry IV*: Time's Masters and Time's Fools

That time, in a number of aspects, is an extremely important component of *1 Henry IV* is evident throughout the text.[12] Indeed, nowhere else does Shakespeare emphasise the time component so punctiliously or underline its importance for almost all the characters in so many different circumstances. Scarcely a scene goes by without our attention being drawn to time or without some discussion of the meaning of time: thus, there are occasions where basic information about the time of day (or of night) is given, occasions where some future time is envisaged and looked forward to, occasions where it is stated that the time has come for some enterprise to be set in motion; finally there are occasions where alien times (and spaces) thrust themselves before us through the arrival of posts and through the delivery of letters. Allusions to and specifications of time tightly connect the sequences developing in the various spaces activated by the action; they help to create contrasts between diverging thoughts occurring at the same time to different characters while connecting and / or contrasting axiologies and attitudes by creating an impression of temporal contiguity or coexistence. Indeed, the play exploits this basic historical (and theatrical) component almost obsessively, although it suggests that there is profound difference between the various views of time (and therefore utter instability in any definition of historical time), a difference which is determined by the characters that inhabit the various times and by the way they manage and master – or are not able to master – time; this until the battle of Shrewsbury forces all to meet in one and the same time and space – a space which is alien to all and which is entrusted with the task of dispersing, albeit temporarily, Henry's rival axiologies.

Henry's time is indeed unquiet. The time which he mentions in the second line of the play, which he has planned to devote to the 'frighted peace' and to the crusade is, as we have seen, turned into a time of war by the news which arrives from Wales and Scotland. But it is in the second scene of the play that the temporal component is made thematically relevant. The very first words we hear from Falstaff at the opening of the scene concern time ('Now, Hal, what time of day is it, lad?', I. ii. 1), and they are used in Hal's reply and in the subsequent five speech turns in a way that completely deautomatises the casual character of Falstaff's question. Hal does not answer it but replies elaborating on its absurdity and thus uses his speech to introduce Falstaff to the audience:

> *Prince*: ... What a devil hast thou to do with the time of the day? Unless hours
> were cups of sack, and minutes capons, and clocks the tongues of
> bawds, and dials the signs of leaping-houses, and the blessed sun
> himself a fair hot wench in flame-coloured taffeta, I see no reason
> why thou shouldst be so superfluous to demand the time of the day.
> (I. ii. 6–12)

Falstaff then further elaborates on Hal's cue in two subsequent speeches, establishing the first significant opposition of the play regarding time, namely, the night / day opposition:

> *Falstaff*: ... we that take purses go by the moon and the seven stars, and not by
> Phoebus, he 'that wand'ring knight so fair' ... Marry then sweet wag,
> when thou art king let not us that are squires of the night's body be
> called thieves of the day's beauty: let us be Diana's foresters, gentlemen
> of the shade, minions of the moon; and let men say we be men of good

> government, being governed as the sea is, by our noble and chaste
> mistress the moon, under whose countenance we steal.
>
> (I. ii. 13–15, 23–9)[13]

Even Falstaff's space is inhabited by some kind of temporal prospect: there we find both short-term forward projections ('tomorrow morning, by four o'clock', ll. 120–1, 'tonight', l. 125, 'tomorrow night', ll. 126, 187, 'tomorrow', ll. 156–7), which envisage in advance supper-time and the time appointed for the highway robbery, and a long-term one (the often repeated 'when thou art king', ll. 16, 58, 60, 141–2), in which Falstaff foresees a better legitimation of his revels once Hal has assumed the role of king and maybe even an extension of his own kind of time to the space of rule. But the scene is sealed by Hal's mention of a different kind of time, which makes us perceive the groundlessness of Falstaff's expectations. In the closing line of his soliloquy, in which he reveals his project to forsake his present friends (one of the few projects in the sequence which are not destined to be frustrated), it is not by chance that Hal chooses time – Falstaff's transgressive time – as the present offence to be 'redeemed'.

Following what appears to be a neat expositional pattern, the third scene presents the face of rebellion, and with it yet another view of time. Hotspur's time is forward-projected and characterised by impatience. Once the plot is sketched and the rebellious enterprise is agreed between him, Northumberland and Worcester, Hotspur produces an explicit statement of his attitude towards time: 'O, let the hours be short / Till fields, and blows, and groans applaud our sport!' (I. iii. 295–6), which pertinently concludes the encounter.

All three spaces have by now been presented, and all three have been associated with the different projects which are going to fill out the play's plot. In the space of rule, the initial project is thwarted by the intrusion of external circumstances; in that of misrule, time appears short-winded, and the project of betrayal formulated by Hal (who is the spurious element in that space) also makes it short-lived; while in that of rebellion it appears characterised by impetuosity and presumptuousness. The idea that the conflict between the three main spaces is going to be a conflict between different conceptions of time is thus suggested right from the start. Quite surprisingly, however, the king's time is presented as the least stable and the most powerless. Henry's inability to formulate a project of his own, unaffected by external pressures, condemns the time of state politics and the locus of political power to the instability of unplanned action.

But it is in Act II (with a coda in Act III, scene 1) that we encounter the most interesting treatment of time and a clearer juxtaposition of, and confrontation between, the two destabilising axiologies of the play, those of misrule and rebellion.

In the sequence of scenes which I am going to discuss, time is on the one hand *used* as a dramaturgical tool to produce contrasts by suggesting simultaneity and on the other *evoked* as a topic for reflection. In the first scene, which is set in Rochester, time is repeatedly mentioned and specified as a relevant element of the plot. The first line, spoken by one of the two Carriers ('An it be not four by the day I'll be hanged'), signals the man's impatience to leave for London, to which he and his companion have to transport goods and passengers; Gadshill enters asking 'what's o'clock?' (l. 31) and is answered by the First Carrier 'I think it be two o'clock' (l. 32); when he further asks the Carrier 'what time do you mean to come to London?' (ll. 40–1), he is answered 'Time enough to go to bed with a candle, I warrant thee' (ll. 42–3). Obviously, 'two o'clock' has a different meaning for the Carriers and for Gadshill: the former are concerned to leave as soon as possible in order to deliver their goods, to get their passengers to their destinations in due time and not to spend too many hours of the day travelling; while for Gadshill, who is 'one of the squires of the night's body', two o'clock is the right time for purse-cutting. Scene 2, with the highway robbery and the trick played on Falstaff by Hal and Poins, who rob the robbers of their booty, presumably takes place a little later, the same night. By the end of the scene, Hal's night of revels seems to be concluded after Falstaff, Gadshill and Bardolph have fled. Leaving the prince and Poins on the highway, we are abruptly introduced to the presence of Hotspur, *solus*, Hamlet-like, reading a letter (the first of many epistolary intrusions from a different space and time in the space of rebellion). One of his possible allies in the dangerous enterprise of revolt has forsaken him. Nevertheless, in the dialogue which he starts with the absent and unknown (to us) sender of the letter, Hotspur shows a courageous heart: he will proceed relentlessly in his project.

In the first moments of this scene, the evident discrepancies – linguistic, stylistic and situational – with the preceding one prevent us from appreciating Hotspur's mood and from siding with the seriousness of his undertaking. However, by the end of the Hotspur scene, emotion and sympathy have been raised, mainly thanks to the dialogue which follows the appearance of Lady Percy (the encounter is an antecedent of that between Brutus and Portia in *Julius Caesar*, II. i. 233–309); so that when, with equal abruptness, the Eastcheap scene is revealed, we feel that the pressure of estrangement is also working in the opposite direction: for a few moments, in fact, laughter is blocked and we are compelled to absorb the irreconcilable diversity of the two worlds.

The technical need to interpose a scene which takes place in a different space between two scenes showing the space of Hal's revels does not by itself fully account for the interpolation of the incongruous fragment. More compelling seems to be the need to contrast Hal's wild night with the

serious and pathetic thoughts and activities which *in the meantime* are keeping his rival awake. In this case, it is not clear whose interests are served by
the perception of the discrepancy. Certainly, however, the audience's tendency to side with the prince is blurred, and we are compelled to discern
and discriminate; even to choose between the time and space of comedy and
those of tragedy, between the laughter that accompanies Falstaff's cowardice
and Hal's idleness and the pathos that attends on Hotspur's desperate
courage; and finally, we are made to consider that events and motivations
are neither neutral nor transparent and that our shifts in sympathy from
the prince to his rival have been meticulously planned, directed and moni-
tored.

Hotspur's monologue (a dramatic privilege which he shares with Hal and
which gives him a chance to make the audience appreciate his point of view)
closes with yet another mention of time ('I will set forward tonight', l. 35)
which, again, presents rebellion's time as wilful and rash. In his dialogue
with Lady Percy, then, Hotspur repeats his intention to leave 'within these
two hours' (ll. 36–7), and we leave him making preparations for the journey.

At this point, the text makes a temporal leap of more or less 24 hours,
and once again presents two scenes which seem to be taking place simultaneously, probably the following night.[14]

In Act II, scene 4, the first tavern scene of the sequence, time is again a
conspicuous topic, while we have an explicit comparison between Hal's and
Hotspur's time. The first 100 lines of the scene are occupied by Hal's
ungenerous jest towards Francis. This, which is suggested by Francis's busy
although inconsequential running here and there and answering calls with
'anon, anon', reveals yet another attitude towards time which is peculiar to
this character. It has been argued that Francis lacks both memory – he
cannot answer the simple question about his age – and forward vision and
that 'he is the man who is never capable of questioning his immediate
predicament...lacking what Augustine called *distensio animi*, memory and
project'.[15] In his 'dialogue' with Francis, Hal is precisely exposing the man's
lack of future perspective: to his question 'when', which requests the specifi-
cation of a time in the future, Francis in fact replies again with 'Anon, anon'
(ll. 61–3).[16] The prince's reply is jestingly didactic in its superfluous listing
of possible future times, while the redundancy of the drawer's name is
perhaps meant to prompt a further 'anon' from him ('Anon, Francis? No,
Francis, but tomorrow, Francis; or, Francis, a-Thursday; or indeed, Francis,
when thou wilt', ll. 64–6); but the drawer further confirms his perception of
the present time as merely 'anon' when, to Hal's direct question 'What's
o'clock, Francis?', he again replies 'Anon, anon, sir.'[17]

Hal's final comment on Francis's 'fewer words than a parrot' and on his
inconsequential running here and there triggers the thought of 'the Hotspur
of the north':

Prince: That ever this fellow should have fewer words than a parrot, and yet
            the son of a woman! His industry is up-stairs and down-stairs, his
            eloquence the parcel of a reckoning. I am not yet of Percy's mind, the
            Hotspur of the north, he that kills me some six or seven dozen of Scots
            at a breakfast, washes his hands and says to his wife, 'Fie upon this
            quiet life, I want work'. 'O my sweet Harry', says she, 'How many hast
            thou killed today?' 'Give my roan horse a drench', says he, and answers,
            'Some fourteen', an hour after; 'a trifle, a trifle'.

                                                              (II. iv. 96–106)

The shift from Francis to Percy has always been considered a sudden and
almost inexplicable change of subject; this has led commentators to explain it
as prompted by Hal's declaration, in line 90, about his being 'of all humours',
and therefore as a contrast with Hotspur's gloomy bent on war. The interpolation of the comment on Francis between l. 90 and the mention of Hotspur starting on l. 99, however, remains unexplained unless Francis, too, is
included as one of the elements in the comparison;[18] and it seems to me that
the incongruity vanishes if we acknowledge time as the element which triggers the associative link which brings Percy into Hal's mind. The 'Hotspur of
the north' (and the mention of Hotspur's space of action is not irrelevant) is
evoked by Hal in a parodic mood in which his rival's headstrong way of living
his time is equated to Francis's amnesic (namely, not historically-oriented),
non-projectual and inconsequential sheer present (see, 'at a breakfast', l. 101,
and 'an hour after', l. 106).[19]

Twice more time is specified in the scene, and on both occasions in connection with an interference from a different space. When the hostess announces that 'a nobleman of the court' (l. 283), 'an old man' (l. 289) is at the
door and asks to speak to Hal, Falstaff's comment is 'What doth gravity out
of his bed at midnight?' (l. 290; the gentleman's appearance seems to him
improper, for he comes from a space whose time is the day). Together with
the call to duty from the king, who sends word to the prince that he 'must to
the court in the morning' (ll. 330–1), the messenger brings the 'villainous
news' (l. 329) of the rebellion of those who, in Falstaff's words, are 'That
same mad fellow of *the north*' and 'he of *Wales*' (ll. 331–2, my emphasis). This
first attack on the space of misrule, brought jointly by the king and the rebels,
is followed a little later by the attack of justice: 'The sheriff and all the watch'
(l. 483), accompanied by the Carrier whose passengers have been robbed the
night before, are at the door. In the brief exchange between Hal and the
Sheriff at the end of the latter's visit, clock time is again specified:

Sheriff: Good night, my noble lord.
Prince: I think it is good morrow, is it not?
Sheriff: Indeed, my lord, I think it be two o'clock.

                                                              (II. iv. 516–18)

The two invasions from an alien space have spoiled the night's fun. In an impatient projectual mood which he manifests for the first time, before Falstaff 'fast asleep behind the arras' (ll. 521–2), Hal seals the sequence and the night with words which dispel the lazy atmosphere of the tavern. The space which contains misrule has been invaded by the pressure of its rival axiologies and, besides, the coming of day disbands the night's revels:

> I'll to the court in the morning. We must all to the wars, and thy place shall be honourable. I'll procure this fat rogue a charge of foot, and I know his death will be a march of twelve score. The money shall be paid back again with advantage. Be with me betimes in the morning; and so, good morrow, Peto.
> (II. iv. 536–42)

Between Hal's night in Eastcheap and his interview with the king the following morning, we are introduced to the heart of rebellion. The scene in Bangor, like the one in Warkworth, takes place during the night, and its location – immediately after the Eastchèap night and before Hal's encounter with the king the following morning – means that we perceive it as taking place simultaneously with the tavern events in Act II, scene 4.[20]

Unlike Hal's, Hotspur's night is packed with events, of which the most important is the agreement between him, Mortimer and Glendower about the 'indentures tripartite' to be drawn and 'sealed interchangeably' (III. i. 76–7). Space in this scene is mainly the map of the country, a model territory and a figure of dominion by which the rebels are measuring their influence and building up their expectations of future sway. South-east, west and north, reduced to contractual items, are the terrains on which the rebels are constructing their potential power. Time, intensely projectual, is again charged with the haste to achieve the desired results which we by now recognise as Hotspur's main characteristic, and which is repeatedly signalled in the scene.[21] The night is spent drawing the deed of partition and in the encounter with the ladies; Hotspur says to Lady Percy that he will soon leave ('And the indentures be drawn I'll away within these two hours', ll. 254–5), and the scene is concluded with yet another hint of his haste as compared to the attitude of 'slow' Mortimer:

> *Glendower*:   Come, come, Lord Mortimer, you are as slow
> As hot Lord Percy is on fire to go:
> (III. i. 257–8)

The following two scenes have closings which present the remaining two spaces of the play, which are both equally projected towards the meeting with the enemy. In Act III, scene 2, once the news that the rebels' forces have gathered in Shrewsbury reaches Henry, the king's time, too, becomes forward-bent. (Henry's time, however, remains inhabited and determined by the moves of others):

> *King*: ...
>> On Wednesday next, Harry, you shall set forward,
>> On Thursday we ourselves will march.
>>
>> ...
>>
>> Our business valued, some twelve days hence
>> Our general forces at Bridgnorth shall meet.
>> Our hands are full of business, let's away,
>> Advantage feeds him fat while men delay.
>>
>> (III. ii. 173–80)

The effects of the invasion of justice and war into the space of misrule start to be felt in the following scene. Falstaff complains that he has been robbed of a ring in the tavern and the Hostess replies by accusing him of not paying his debts. Hal, who joins them, does not appear to have changed attitude after his interview with his father; rather, he seems to be profiting from his recovered friendship with the king ('I am good friends with my father and may do anything', III. iii. 180–1); and rather than reform his friends in view of the war, he seems to be willing to bring the tavern's space of misrule into the final conflict:[22]

> *Prince*: ...
>> Go, Peto, to horse, to horse, for thou and I
>> Have thirty miles to ride yet ere dinner-time.
>> Jack, meet me tomorrow in the Temple hall
>> At two o'clock in the afternoon:
>> There shalt thou know thy charge, and there receive
>> Money and order for their furniture.
>>
>> (III. iii. 196–201)

In the last two lines of this speech, however, Hal's impatience to meet Hotspur and the impression that he is inflamed by patriotism are somewhat quelled by the formal tone suggested by the sudden use of verse for his speech and by the rhyme which appears in the closing lines ('The land is burning, Percy stands on high, / And either we or they must lower lie', ll. 202–3).

In Acts IV and V, it is messages to and from the rebels and 'rebel letters' that are responsible for the border-crossings of time and space. Letters are delivered to Hotspur before the battle, but he 'cannot read them now' (V. ii. 80).[23] Why does he not? What might their function be, given that we are never going to be allowed to know their contents? Again, border-crossing seems to be the point. By now, signals of discomfiture have gathered over the rebels' heads, and the spectators may imagine that the unread letters

contain more defections on the part of prospective allies. For letters to the
rebels, as we know by now, contain betrayal since a letter cannot but convey
absence: 'it is only letters that arrive at the battlefield: death is their destin-
ation.'[24] Here, again, time and space play an important role. For, by definition, letters come from a different time and a different space. Those letters,
then, apart from conveying absence, reveal that the betrayal of the rebellion
has already been planned and executed and that the death sentence on the
rebels was in fact pronounced in a time in which the rebellion still nourished expectations of solidarity and help: those that even now were still
thought to be co-conspirators, have at a certain moment in the past forsaken
the rebellion. It is here, maybe, that Hotspur realises for the first time that
he – as one of his last sentences will reveal – is being made 'time's fool'. The
letters remain sealed: we, like Hotspur, know that death has already been
decreed and is now trying to force the boundaries of rebellion, that death,
coming from afar and from the past, is the message of the unsealed letters.
By refusing to read them, Hotspur is making a last desperate attempt to
keep away the death sentence they carry.

When he meets Hotspur on the battlefield, Hal speaks in spatial terms of
the impossibility of them both living on the same historical scene:

> Two stars keep not their motion in one sphere,
> Nor can one England brook a double reign
> Of Harry Percy and the Prince of Wales.
>   (V. iv. 64–6)

while Hotspur acknowledges the coming of his own death in terms of time:

> But thoughts, the slaves of life, and life, time's fool,
> And time, that takes survey of all the world,
> Must have a stop.
>   (V. iv. 80–2)

However, neither rebellion nor misrule is actually vanquished. York and
Wales are the spaces where the first is still 'busily in arms' (V. v. 38), and the
king's prospective closing leads us to meet the circumstance of 'such another
day' (l. 42); besides, we also perceive from Hal's complicit aside to Falstaff in
Act V, scene 4 ('if a lie may do thee grace / I'll gild it with the happiest terms
I have', ll. 156–7) that misrule has by no means been dispersed.

The spaces – as well as styles and persons – that we encounter in Part One
are comparatively independent from each other and remain in the end con-
flictual. Although there have been a number of border-crossings (war and
justice have violated the space of misrule and rebellion has openly insinuated
itself into both the opposing spaces), the boundaries of each sphere have not

been fatally affected by those attacks and by the end of the play they seem to have been reconstituted – except for the uncertainty of Hal's position. The lasting violation of spaces will be a decisive feature of the next play.

2 *Henry IV*: Border-crossing, Sickness and Corruption

Rather than considering the second play as a revision and even an *undoing* of the meanings of the first (as Yachnin does), I prefer to describe it as enacting a process of corruption whose seeds are already present – albeit hardly stressed – in Part One.[25] Various forms of sickness now attack the core of the three spaces and, in the end, the axiologies which militate against the king are defeated by a process of pollution which changes their very nature; but even the natural body of the king is attacked by corruption, and illness decrees the end at least of that power which is associated with the illegitimate Henry IV.

In *2 Henry IV* there are repeated and open allusions to sickness, bodily decay, old age and the prospect of death; at the same time, the violations of what in Part One are comparatively independent and 'healthy' spaces become more and more frequent and aggressive. Border-crossing thus becomes the agent of malady: almost literally, a foreign body is insinuated into a healthy organism where it produces disease and corruption. Repeatedly, inversions and exchanges of attributes are given explicit verbal expression, and these represent an attack on the axiological integrity of the various spaces, whose nature is finally perverted.[26]

In his first appearance in Act I, scene 2, Falstaff questions his Page about the doctor's examination of his urine; 'He said', the Page answers, 'the water itself was a good healthy water; but, for the party that owed it, he might have moe diseases than he knew for' (ll. 2–4): Falstaff's, then, is a hidden disease, impossible to detect physically. In the same scene, we witness Sir John's first encounter with justice. After attempting to avoid the encounter by pretending to be deaf, he tries to exorcise the presence of the Lord Chief Justice and to undermine his sphere of action by alluding to an illness which supposedly affects him and to his age:

> I am glad to see your lordship abroad. I heard say your lordship was sick. I hope your lordship goes abroad by advice; your lordship, though not clean past your youth, have yet some smack of age in you, some relish of the saltness of time; and I most humbly beseech your lordship to have a reverend care of your health.
> (I. ii. 93–9)

The Chief Justice does not seem to be affected by Falstaff's allusions to his health. It is Falstaff, instead, who appears troubled by the thought of illness. First, he mentions the king's sickness ('I hear, his majesty is returned with some discomfort from Wales', ll. 102–3; 'And I hear, moreover, his Highness is fallen into this same whoreson apoplexy', ll. 106–7), which he describes at length, simply annoying the officer: 'This apoplexy, as I take it, is a kind of lethargy, and't please your lordship, a kind of sleeping in the blood, a whoreson tingling' (ll. 110–12). The attempted attack on the king is rejected by the Chief Justice: 'What tell you me of it? Be it as it is' (l. 113), but Falstaff repeats the assault with a more precise diagnosis of causes: 'It hath it original from much grief, from study, and perturbation of the brain; I have read the cause of its effects in Galen, it is a kind of deafness' (ll. 114–16). But 'deafness' is Falstaff's malady, as the Lord Chief Justice promptly retorts. The exchange that follows reveals that it is Sir John who has been infected by the disease he has mentioned and defined:

> *Chief Justice*: I think you are fallen into the disease, for you hear not what I say to you.
> *Falstaff*: Very well, my lord, very well. Rather, and't please you, it is the disease of not listening, the malady of not marking, that I am troubled withal.
> *Chief Justice*: To punish you by the heels would amend the attention of your ears, and I care not if I do become your physician.
> (I. ii. 117–24)

The last attack on the integrity of the space of misrule is launched by the king: 'The king has severed you and Prince Harry' (ll. 202–3), says the Lord Chief Justice, and although Falstaff and Hal will meet again later on in the play, we know that the process of separation is already under way.

After the exit of the Lord Chief Justice, Falstaff enquires of the Page about his cash in hand; and, again, he comments on the emptiness of his pockets in terms of sickness: 'I can get no remedy against this consumption of the purse; borrowing only lingers and lingers it out, but the disease is incurable' (ll. 237–9). Then, passing from metaphor to the literal meaning, he curses his gout:

> A pox of this gout! or a gout of this pox! for the one or the other plays the rogue with my great toe. 'Tis no matter if I do halt; I have the wars for my colour, and my pension shall seem the more reasonable. A good wit will make use of anything; I will turn diseases to commodity. (I. ii. 244–50)[27]

Act II is, as in Part One, almost entirely devoted to the space of misrule and develops the idea of the corruption and dissolution of the Eastcheap world. When we next see Falstaff (in Act II, scene 1) he is being sued by the Hostess, who is trying to have him arrested on account of his debts and the breach of a marriage promise. Again the Lord Chief Justice crosses the border of Falstaff's space. Those wrongs, he says, must be redressed promptly: the one 'with sterling money, and the other with current repentance' (ll. 119–20). But, while the Justice is trying to patch up the quarrel, a further disturbance breaks in. This time it is war, news of which is brought by Gower from the king and the Prince of Wales, together with a letter giving details of the present situation. From line 135 to line 162, the scene presents the interesting configuration of a divided space. While the Chief Justice is absorbed in the reading of the letter, Falstaff tries to recover what is left of his space and succeeds in softening the Hostess's heart and in having her withdraw her action. By the end of the exchange, the Hostess promises to give him supper and to invite Doll Tearsheet to cheer him up. But after the Hostess and his other friends are gone, Sir John loses control of the situation. Once the space he dominates has dissolved, he is left alone with the Chief Justice and Gower and obliged to share the space of their present preoccupations and the subject of their conversation, which he tries to do to no effect. His repeated questions – 'What's the news, my lord?' (l. 164), 'I hope, my lord, all's well. What is the news, my lord?' (l. 167), 'Comes the King back from Wales, my noble lord?' (l. 172) – are left unanswered by the Chief Justice, who thus, by breaking a basic conversational rule, manifests his utter contempt for Sir John. For the first time in the whole sequence, the audience, too, may tend to abandon Falstaff in his pathetic attempt to gain credibility in the sphere of state politics. His invitation of Gower to dinner and Gower's refusal do not raise laughter, for Falstaff's endeavour to captivate Gower's sympathy appears disturbingly grotesque and out of place; and there is more than a chance that we may share the Chief Justice's scorn and agree with his final verdict on the fat knight: 'thou art a great fool' (ll. 189–90).

In the following scene, the space we are in is even more equivocal and more distorted. The first part of the conversation between Hal and Poins was the starting point of Auerbach's essay on 'The weary prince'.[28] However far one may be from sharing Auerbach's interpretation of the scene as the epitome of Shakespeare's tendency to attribute dignity only to 'high' characters (the most surprising of Auerbach's examples of this is Shylock), one cannot but agree with the importance that he attributes to the Prince's sadness. The blending of styles – which Auerbach reads, through the intrusion of the 'humble' element represented by Poins and 'small beer', as a shame to Hal's greatness – is certainly relevant in this scene; for no other reason than simply because it is here that Hal remarks – and makes the audience realise – that there is a (stylistic) difference and discrepancy between him and his 'friends'. Indeed no such discrepancy is noticeable in the tavern scenes, where Hal seems to be perfectly at home in the 'low'-style discourse. In the scene with Poins, the discordance of styles is being openly enunciated and presented, as it were, as one of the problems that arise at this stage in the dissolution of the space of misrule and in Hal's gradual assumption to the space of power. The mixture of styles and persons is now for the first time seen as a disease in the body both of the story's development and of the text's decorum.

The reason the Prince gives for his sadness is his father's illness. But Hal's weariness may well derive from a more complicated mixture of feelings. He knows that in the world's eyes his father's sickness is not an adequate reason for his sadness ('it is not meet that I should be sad now my father is sick', ll. 38–9), but perceives that the real reason behind his sadness is unspeakable: the mortal disease affecting the very heart of the space of rule is also infecting the space of misrule, and will in the end decree its dissolution. Besides, Hal's weariness, and the very fact that he speaks of his sadness, are also a hint to the audience: a melancholy separation is near, and in a short time the spectators will have to cope with the prince's betrayal of his former friends and the dissolution of the comic plot. While, on the one hand, by revealing his sadness, Hal is trying to increase the audience's sympathy through its appreciation of his divided mind, on the other, by showing contempt for his 'low' friend Poins, he is preparing the audience for his final desertion of Falstaff.

The next time we see Hal at the Boar's Head (Act II, scene 4) is also the last.[29] The prince is wearing a drawer's costume – at this stage the disguise is necessary for him to meet his former friends on the same (stylistic) level. By the end of the scene, time in the tavern undergoes an acceleration which is wholly extraneous to the rhythm of laziness that we tend to associate with the space of misrule; the prince's last verbal jest is left incomplete ('You, gentlewoman, –', l. 346), for war knocks at the door in the person of Peto. Hal's farewell to Falstaff's world is couched in a formal style which once more signals the (stylistic) gap:

> By heaven, Poins, I feel me much to blame,
> So idly to prophane the precious time,
> When tempest of commotion, like the south
> Borne with black vapour, doth begin to melt
> And drop upon our bare unarmed heads.
> (II. iv. 358–62)[30]

and his farewell to Falstaff is cold and distant ('Falstaff, good night', l. 363).

A further (Bardolph's) knocking at the door summons Sir John to court, away from Doll and the prospect of yet another night of revels. After a last boast of self-praise ('You see, my good wenches, how men of merit are sought after', ll. 371–2), Falstaff pronounces a warm farewell to the women

('Farewell, good wenches: if I be not sent away post, I will see you again ere I go', ll. 374–5). And while not a single word has accompanied Hal's exit, Falstaff's departure is followed by tears of deep nostalgia.

The comic plot is soon to find other participants, in a space which is even more affected by war and almost obsessively corrupted by the thought of old age and death.

In his home in Gloucestershire, old Justice Shallow has gathered a company of ragged men for conscription. While waiting for Falstaff's arrival together with Justice Silence, he strikes the keynote which is going to colour the whole encounter: nostalgia for the mad days of his youth at Clement's Inn and the thought of his old acquaintance:

> *Shallow:* . . . Jesu, Jesu, the mad days I have spent! And to see how many of my old acquaintance are dead!
> *Silence:* We shall all follow, cousin.
> *Shallow:* Certain, 'tis certain, very sure, very sure. Death, as the psalmist says, is certain to all, all shall die.
>
> (III. ii. 32–7)

Shallow's inane comments on death go on for a while. He asks Silence about an old common friend:

> *Shallow:* Death is certain. Is old Double of your town living yet?
> *Silence:* Dead sir.
> *Shallow:* Jesu, Jesu, dead! A drew a good bow, and dead! A shot a fine shoot. John a Gaunt loved him well, and betted much money on his head. Dead!
>
> (III. ii. 40–5)

After Falstaff has examined and 'pricked' the men, Shallow resumes the topic, and asks Sir John about Jane Nightwork (obviously, a prostitute). Falstaff himself seems to be affected by the thought of old age: the woman is living, he says, but she is 'Old, old, Master Shallow' (l. 201). His answer gives the JP an opportunity to produce more silly and entirely tautological comments, this time on old age: 'Nay, she must be old, she cannot choose but be old, certain she's old' (ll. 202–3).

But corruption also makes its appearance in other forms in this scene: Bardolph and Falstaff accept money from Mouldy and Bullcalf to free them from conscription; besides, according to Falstaff, Shallow's account of his 'mad days' at Clement's Inn is sheer corruption of the truth (again, an instance of distortion of past events), 'every third word a lie' (l. 301). Here, again, the thought of old age affects Falstaff, who produces a melancholy comment in a reflective mood, an entirely new note in his humour: 'Lord, how subject we old men are to this vice of lying!' (ll. 297–8).

But the sphere of rule, too, is affected by an incurable disease which endangers the life of its very heart, the King. We see Henry for the first time in Act III, scene 1, but his illness has already been hinted at on several occasions. From his first speech, moreover, we know that sleep has abandoned him.[31] But sickness is not simply attacking the King's natural body: in the shape of rebellion, it is attacking the body politic and the country itself. To Warwick and Surrey, Henry speaks of the danger coming from the north as of a malady which has attacked the body of his kingdom:

> *King*:   Then you perceive the body of our kingdom
> How foul it is, what rank diseases grow,
> And with what danger, near the heart of it.
> (III. i. 38–40)

Warwick takes over the metaphoric suggestion and further elaborates it:

> *Warwick*:   It is but as a body yet distemper'd,
> Which to his former strength may be restor'd
> With good advice and little medicine.
> (III. i. 41–3)

Other hints at sickness appear in the same scene. To Henry's preoccupations about the large number of soldiers in the rebels' army, Warwick answers by recalling that rumour may corrupt the truth ('Rumour doth double, like the voice and echo, / The numbers of the feared', ll. 97–8); then he explains Henry's present state of mind with his illness:

> Your Majesty hath been this fortnight ill,
> And these unseason'd hours perforce must add
> Unto your sickness.
> (III. i. 104–6)

The next and last time we see the King (Act IV, scene 4), he is again projecting a crusade, this time in a sort of delirium.[32] If the present ordeal meets with success, Henry says, 'We will our youth lead on to higher fields, / And draw no swords but what are sanctified' (ll. 3–4). But the news that the rebels have suffered a defeat hardly cheers him, and the thought of illness returns implacably: 'And wherefore should these good news make me sick?' (l. 102). The end, we know, is near:

> I should rejoyce now at these happy news,
> And now my sight fails, and my brain is giddy.
> O me! come near me, now I am much ill.
> (IV. iv. 109–111)

But, before he dies, Henry is still to experience a final violation of his space in what is perhaps the most serious of the trespasses perpetrated by the heir apparent. The theft of the crown, by which Hal performs his premature appropriation of the space of rule, accelerates the King's death: 'This part of his conjoins with my disease, / And helps to end me' (IV. v. 63–4).

But sickness has attacked the rebels' camp as well: when acting as messenger from John of Lancaster, Westmoreland remarks on the paradox of seeing the Archbishop in arms. He comments on the absurdity of York's transformation in terms of linguistic translation, and remarks that his presence produces a corruption of the nature of rebellion (IV. i. 32–52). Quite pertinently, the Archbishop answers by claiming that his transformation into a warrior was dictated by the sickness of the whole realm and the necessity to cure it. His speech, a long medical metaphor (ll. 53–87), employs in thirteen lines no less than eleven expressions related to sickness ('disease'd', 'burning fever', 'bleed', 'disease', 'infected', 'physician', 'diet', 'rank minds', 'sick', 'purge the obstruction', 'veins of life'). The encounter between the rebels and the emissaries of the King ends with John of Lancaster's arrival (the most fatal of all the border-crossings happening in the rebels' space) and with the rebels being sent to death. Quite pertinently, while they are drinking with Lancaster to what they still believe is their reestablished friendship, Mowbray feels 'on the sudden something ill' (IV. ii. 80). The fatal disease, this time, has come from the King's sphere; rebellion is defeated in much the same way as misrule is going to be defeated. But misrule lingers on longer, and we are still to encounter what is left of Falstaff's world in Act V.

Again, the last scenes of the play give us the impression that the various fragments take place simultaneously. While Falstaff and Bardolph visit Shallow in Gloucestershire (Act V, scene 1), the news of the King's death is given to the Lord Chief Justice (Act V, scene 2), and we first see the prince as Henry V who reconciles himself with the judge and promises to 'frustrate prophecies' (l. 127); and while Pistol brings Falstaff news of the king's death (Act V, scene 3), Quickly and Tearsheet (we are driven to think, as an effect of Henry's reconciliation with justice) are brought to jail (Act V, scene 4). The last scene of the play seals the triumph of power and the unification of rule with justice by means of another betrayal. If it is true that Hal has mocked 'the expectation of the world' (V. ii. 126), he has certainly not frustrated the spectator's forecasts. Time is finally redeemed, although by means of a cruel dramatic sin: the annihilation of the universe of comedy.[33]

There remains to discuss the moment where we encounter what is perhaps the most lengthy and elaborate, but also the most ambiguous meditation on (historical) time and change in the whole canon.

The passage, it seems to me, enunciates two distinct views of historical time and change, which reveal two opposed historiographical conceptions: on the one hand, we have Henry's conception, the weak choiceless view of a world dominated by chance – or maybe by an inscrutable providence; on the other hand, we have Warwick's empirical view, which shows greater confidence in the possibility of formulating historical predictions. Warwick's somewhat facile forecast ('My Lord Northumberland will soon be cool'd', l. 44), obviously intended to soothe the king's anxiety, triggers Henry's meditation on our impotence in predicting what is in store for us:

> *King*:   O God, that one might read the book of fate,
> And see the *revolution* of the times
> Make mountains level, and the continent,
> Weary of solid firmness, melt itself
> Into the sea, and other times to see
> The beachy girdle of the ocean
> Too wide for Neptune's hips; how *chance's mocks*
> And *changes* fill the cup of *alteration*
> With divers liquors!
>
> (III. i. 45–53, my emphasis)

Henry's speech is remarkably confused – as is his state of mind – for it oscillates between the idea of inspired prophecy (the conjunction of the expressions 'read the book of fate' and 'see the revolution of the times' evokes the prophecies produced by astrologers) and that of mere chance. The shape of events is written in the 'book of fate', and to read in that book the changes that time will bring is not given to us. To signify change, Henry chooses the alterations which take place in nature: mountains being made level and the ground being invaded by the waters; but he insists on a weak explanation of change – one which does not apply to the kind of mutational phenomena he has described – indicating 'chance's mocks', the unforeseeable tricks produced by mere chance, as the various causes ('divers liquors') which actually bring about changes ('fill the cup of alteration').[34] What is interesting in Henry's speech is his insistence on the idea of *change* and the hidden thought which it reveals. Although the images of his speech are taken from the natural world, and although the starting point of his meditation seems to be the change in attitude on the part of the Percies, it is evident that the kind of change he is envisaging if he should be defeated by the rebels is one which will take the form of the transference of power to a different person. Not improperly, in fact, the word he uses is *revolution*. The word's meaning is ambiguous: Henry might here simply be suggesting a 'process of change' in a linear causative chain of events,[35] but he might also be using *revolution* in its astronomical (and etymological) sense, where it connotes a revolving, a cyclic movement in a course which ends where it started (in this way he might be connecting the idea of prophecy to astrology and at the same time alluding to the possible repetition of his act of usurpation). To a modern

reader, however, the word conveys the political connotations which are connected with the kind of change which is produced by the overthrow of an
established government, a connotation by no means improbable in the passage quoted, since it has been shown that by the end of the sixteenth century
the word was already on the way to acquiring its modern meaning.[36] That
this last meaning is at least coexistent with the old ones is further shown by
the fact that immediately following these lines Henry evokes the revolution
he himself produced by overthrowing Richard,[37] although he evokes the
event by recalling the change in attitude of the Percies:

> ... It is but eight years since,
> This Percy was the man nearest my soul;
> Who like a brother toil'd in my affairs,
> And laid his love and life under my foot;
> Yea, for my sake, even to the eyes of Richard
> Gave him defiance.
>   (III. i. 60–5)

But the course of Henry's meditation on time and (historical) change is at
this point complicated by yet another different theme: that of political
prophecy and of Richard's ability – which contrasts with his own impotence
– to produce a foretelling of future events:

> But which of you was by –
> [*To Warwick*] You, cousin Nevil, as I may remember –
> When Richard, with his eye brimful of tears,
> Then check'd and rated by Northumberland,
> Did speak these words, now prov'd a prophecy?
> 'Northumberland, thou ladder by the which
> My cousin Bolingbroke ascends the throne'
>   ...
> 'The time will come, that foul sin, gathering head,
> Shall break into corruption' – so went on,
> Foretelling this same time's condition,
> And the division of our amity.
>   (III. i. 65–79)

Warwick's speech in answer to Henry's tends to steer the king's weak and
confused acknowledgement of his impotence towards the idea of political
prediction, by suggesting that careful observation of human behaviour is all
that is needed to make the foretelling of future events possible. Warwick at
the same time explains how Richard was able to foresee what was to happen
eight years later and suggests that the present situation, too, if examined in
the light of past events, will allow predictions to be made:

> *Warwick*: There is a history in all men's lives
> Figuring the nature of the times deceas'd;
> The which observ'd, a man may prophesy,
> With a near aim, of the main chance of things
> As yet not come to life, who in their seeds
> And weak beginnings lie intreasured.
> Such things become the hatch and brood of time;
> And by the necessary form of this
> King Richard might create a perfect guess
> That great Northumberland, then false to him,
> Would of that seed grow to a greater falseness,
> Which should not find a ground to root upon
> Unless on you.
>
> (III. i. 80–92)

In other words, if we observe the events in the life of a person, we can detect a pattern, or, as it were, a sort of personal behavioural norm in accordance with which each of us tends to act; and, by observing this pattern, we can predict 'with a near aim' what this person's future actions will be ('the main chance of things as yet to come').[38] Thus, predictions may be made by observing the 'seeds' and 'weak beginnings', the basic tendencies of human behaviour. In other words, Warwick is suggesting that a reading of the future presupposes the capacity to read the past.[39]

Warwick's speech, I believe, should be read as a more general and complex statement than is suggested by Yachnin's reading of it as 'a pragmatic analysis of personality types'.[40] Indeed, the passage illustrates a historiographical procedure which places inference at the basis of historical research: although Warwick is exposing the procedure in the direction of prediction which goes from cause to effect, his speech may imply the contrary direction – the eminently historiographical one which proceeds from effects to their causes.

Indeed, it seems not improper to connect Warwick's idea of reading the 'seeds' and 'weak beginnings' to the circumstantial and conjectural model (particularising versus generalising) described by Carlo Ginzburg as the basic paradigm of historiography.[41] In his essay, Ginzburg envisages the possibility of formulating *retrospective prophecies* starting from the close, microscopic, analysis of details, a procedure which he sees as common to all the historical sciences. His claim is that scraps and marginal data, the fingerprints, as it were, of past events, allow the historian to grasp and discern a reality which would otherwise be unattainable, and that minimal details and circumstances have often been the key elements in the understanding of more general phenomena.

What Warwick is talking about is essentially the same procedure, although he is concerned with applying it in the direction of historical prediction. Indeed, the two perspectives share a method of close reading and of sign interpretation that allows both diagnosis and prognosis, and both are founded on intuition and on inferential procedures.[42]

It is easy to see how closely the conjectural paradigm applies to the (historical) dramatist. Unable to produce generalisations owing to the constraints of the genre, the dramatist cannot but produce a particular experience, whose decoding cannot but be indirect and conjectural.

But Warwick's idea of change taking place in time and his stress on the observer's activity also epitomises the spectator's experience, which is obviously the mirror image of the dramatist's. The 'weak beginnings' of the conflict, which we saw 'intreasured' in the first play and which Henry was not able to read – let alone dominate – have grown to produce the second play's 'necessary form'. Through the ten acts of the sequence, the audience has been driven to forecast 'with a near aim' the present state of affairs. This, however, is not the end of the story. To remind us at the same time that historical 'closings' are always open-ended and that the closing of a history play is never a conclusion, the play enacts two different endings: John of Lancaster's forecast of a campaign to conquer France as historical prediction and the Epilogue's promise that 'our humble author will continue the story, with Sir John in it' (*Epilogue*, 27–8) as dramaturgical projection.

Notes

1 P. Yachnin, 'History, theatricality and the "structural problem" in the *Henry IV* plays', *Philological Quarterly*, 70 (1991), pp. 163–79, p. 164. Recently, the 'structural problem' has been discussed also by S. Hawkins, 'Structural pattern in Shakespeare's histories', *Studies in Philology*, 88 (1991), pp. 16–45.

2 Yachnin, 'History', p. 164.

3 Ibid., pp. 164, 163, 173.

4 I wish to point out that in the second play legality occupies a sphere of its own, that of the Lord Chief Justice, who never shares the same scenic space with Bolingbroke.

5 In the wake of Dover Wilson (ed.), *1 Henry IV* (Cambridge: Cambridge University Press, 1946) and E. M. W. Tillyard, *Shakespeare's History Plays* (London: Chatto and Windus, 1944), Sherman Hawkins has restated this claim, speaking of 'a premeditated second part' ('*Henry IV*: the structural problem revisited', *Shakespeare Quaterly*, 33 [1982], pp. 278–301, p. 281). In his later essay ('Structural pattern') Hawkins is less explicit on this point.

6 H. Jenkins, *The Structural Problem in Shakespeare's 'Henry IV'* (London: Methuen, 1956), p. 26.

7 Yachnin, 'History', p. 168.

8 Ibid., pp. 168–9.

9 G. Melchiori discusses the importance of the exceptional prescription of costume ('painted full of tongues') in the 1600 Q stage direction (the prescription is absent

in F) and suggests that the actor playing Rumour might reappear immediately after as Lord Bardolph, 'the bringer of false news, the personification of Rumor in the world of history': G. Melchiori, 'The primacy of philology', in *Shakespeare Today*, ed. K. Elam (Florence: La casa Usher, 1984), pp. 39–50, 44.

10 This claim, like many others in [*Shakespeare the Historian*], is certainly of the kind that would be challenged by Richard Levin as an 'ironic' reading. Levin's article on 'Performance-critics vs close readers in the study of English Renaissance drama', *Modern Language Review*, 81 (1986), pp. 545–59, has raised in radical (although ironic) terms the serious question of the spectator's perception as different from the reader's. His conclusion against the extremities of both performance-critics and ironic readers, however, leaves the issue unsolved. Granted, as Anthony Dawson argues, that performances cannot deliver, and audiences cannot 'absorb, the same kind of meaning that reading can produce' ('The impasse over the stage', *English Literary Renaissance*, 21 [1991], 309–27, p. 317), one fails to see why criticism should not construct readers' (ironic) meanings and why a performance should not use those – and other – hidden, implied, indirect or even possible meanings and convey them with its own communicative tools. On this topic, see H. Berger, *Imaginary Audition* (Berkeley, CA: University of California Press, 1989).

11 The way in which time and space are represented in literary texts has produced a number of differently focused theories. From a dramaturgical perspective, Elam is interested in the construction and reception of time as it is transmitted through the organisation of the play's syntagmatics in connection with action development. A dramatic text, he holds, is discontinuous and incomplete; the audience, therefore, needs to actualise the logical connectives suggested by the text's organisation in order to fill in the gaps and complete its furnishing: K. Elam, *The Semiotics of Theatre and Drama* (London: Methuen, 1980), chapter 4. Such implicit connections are, I believe, particularly relevant to historical drama for they constitute the most efficacious substitute for the category of causation. Bakhtin considers the representation of time and space in literary texts (what he calls the *chronotope*) as the way in which literature takes hold of historical reality and masters it. Space and time are, in texts, fused into an inseparable whole: time, Bakhtin says, is in literary texts a fourth dimension of space (Mikhail Bakhtin, 'Discourse in the novel' in *The Dialogic Imagination*, ed. H. Holquist [Austin: University of Texas Press, 1981]). Lotman attributes an exceptional importance to the way in which space is represented in texts, holding that through a particular space configuration we tend to simulate notions which are not of a spatial nature, but are ways of representing cultural, social, religious and moral models. Lotman shows how such antitheses as high / low, open / closed, right / left, inside / outside, and so on, are used to represent hierarchies, moral evaluations or value judgments and so on. Ju. M. Lotman, *The Structure of the Artistic Text* (Ann Arbor: University of Michigan Press, 1977), pp. 217–31; see also 'The notion of boundary', in *Universe of the Mind: A Semiotic Theory of Culture* (London: Tauris, 1990), pp. 131–42.

12 See M. Hunt, 'Time and timelessness in *1 Henry IV*', *Explorations in Renaissance Culture*, 10 (1984), pp. 56–66.

13 The editor of the Arden edition, A. R. Humphreys explains 'squires…beauty' as 'Since we serve the night's excitements, do not complain that we are inactive by

day'; he also signals a possible pun 'night–knight': '"Squires of the body" were a nobleman's attendants.' But perhaps the most interesting passage of Falstaff's speech is the possible topical allusion to Elizabeth–Diana, 'our noble and chaste mistress, the moon'; Falstaff alludes to some form of royal protection in the play's situation ('under whose countenance we steal') and to its legitimation in the future when Hal will be king. Kastan comments on these lines, saying that 'for Falstaff this is not a submission to authority but an authorization of transgression'. David Scott Kastan, '"The king has many marching in his coat": or, what did you do during the war, daddy?', in *Shakespeare Left and Right*, ed. I. Kamps (London: Routledge, 1991), pp. 241–58, p. 248.

14 In Act II, scene 3 Hotspur is leaving Warkworth for Bangor and tells his wife: 'Whither I go, thither shall you go too: / Today will I set forth, tomorrow you' (ll. 116–17). In Act III, scene 1 Hotspur has joined Mortimer and Glendower in Bangor, and Lady Percy is with them. As regards Hal, we leave him on the highway in Act II, scene 2, presumably towards the break of day, given the intense activity during the night which started at two o'clock in the inn-yard at Rochester; and find him again in Act II, scene 4 at the 'Boar's Head' in Eastcheap, again at night (see, 'this present twelve o'clock at midnight', ll. 92–3); it seems reasonable to suppose that this is the night immediately following the robbery, given Hal's impatience to follow up the joke played on Falstaff.

15 G. Martella, '*Henry IV*: the form of history', unpublished, p. 8. To a certain extent, Francis shares these characteristics with Henry's impotence of prediction and project. The same idea of the unconsciousness of the present is expressed in *Macbeth*: 'Thy letters have transported me beyond / This *ignorant* present' (I. v. 56–7, my emphasis).

16 E. P. Thompson argued that 'in general, the populace has little predictive notion of time': 'Eighteenth-century English society: class struggle without class?', *Social History*, 3 (1978), pp. 133–65, p. 158.

17 That with his question Hal is simply testing Francis's awareness of time is shown by the fact that the question comes immediately after his own 'this present twelve o'clock at midnight' (ll. 92–3).

18 Certain editors also suggest that the connection may lie in 'Francis's busy-ness, or his limitation of ideas' (Humphreys); or that 'Perhaps, too, this thought of Hotspur is prompted by Francis's feverish activity'. D. Bevington, *Henry IV Part 1* (Oxford: Oxford University Press, 1987).

19 Bevington suggests that 'Like Francis, Hal is being pulled simultaneously in two directions, and has not devised as yet a better response than Francis's own "Anon, anon, sir!"' (ibid., p. 60); interpretations of the passage are in M. Rose, *Shakespearean Design* (Cambridge, MA: The Belknap Press of Harvard University Press, 1972), pp. 50ff; Sheldon P. Zitner, 'Anon, anon: or, a mirror for a magistrate', *Shakespeare Quarterly*, 19 (1968), pp. 63–70; Tillyard, *Shakespeare's History Plays*, p. 275.

20 In Act III, scene 2 the dialogue between Henry and Hal is interrupted by Sir Walter Blunt, who communicates to the king 'That Douglas and the English rebels met / The eleventh of this month at Shrewsbury' (ll. 165–6). This piece of news locates the Bangor scene earlier than the preceding night (a few days are

needed for the journey, and Henry answers Blunt that 'this advertisement is five days old', l. 172). The possible anachronism, however, does not cancel the impression of simultaneity between the two preceding scenes.

21 No other reason than a need to stress Hotspur's impetuousness can be given for his imprecation 'A plague upon it! I have forgot the map' (III. i. 4–5) while the map is before him; and the same can be said of his quarrel with Glendower and his complaint that 'He held me last night at least nine hours / In reckoning up the several devils' names' (ll. 150–1). These two lines, however, run counter to the hypothesis that Hotspur's previous night was the night in Warkworth, although, again, the spectator's perception of its simultaneity with the highway robbery is not likely to be affected by this punctualisation. That Hotspur's time is precipitous is stressed even in Lady Percy's description of his way of speaking in Part Two (II. iii. 24–5).

22 Falstaff seems to pick up the feeling when he seals the scene by asking the Hostess for breakfast and adding: 'O, I could wish this tavern were my drum' (III. iii. 204–5).

23 Goldberg develops the idea that rebellion is strictly allied with writing while there is an 'ideological and logocentric suppression of any connection between power and writing': 'Rebel letters: postal effects from *Richard II* to *Henry IV*', *Renaissance Drama*, new series, 19 (1988), pp. 3–28, p. 13. It should be remarked, however, that in the second play of the sequence letter-writing and the reception of written messages are mainly connected with the king and his entourage.

24 Ibid., p. 12.

25 The idea of revision largely depends on the importance that we attribute to Hal's 'reformation' in the battle. If we don't expect absolute coherence from Hal's behaviour and see his final conversion as a sequence of comparatively irregular false starts, we tend to attribute much less importance to Shrewsbury as the expected moment of his reformation. There is even a danger that we may mistake for patriotic involvement his aggressiveness and 'unruly disposition' if we conclude that Shrewsbury constitutes his reformation. Is Hal not simply harnessing to his father's service the riotous habits which he normally puts to quite different use in the tavern and on the highway? Jenkins remarks that 'The only man at court who believes in the Prince's reformation, the Earl of Warwick, believes that it will happen, not that it has happened already' (Jenkins, *Structural Problem*, p. 25).

26 Among these inversions, see Mortimer's statement that success will follow thanks to the fact that 'the Bishop / Turns insurrection to religion' (I. i. 200–1); we encounter another verbal and conceptual inversion in Act I, scene 2:

> *Chief Justice*: God send the prince a better companion!
> *Falstaff*: God send the companion a better prince!
> (I. ii. 199–200)

When planning with Poins to dress as servants, Hal describes the disguise as an exchange of attributes: 'From a god to a bull? A heavy descension! It was Jove's case. From a prince to a prentice? A low transformation, that shall be mine…' (II. ii. 166–8). Later on, Westmoreland remarks on the transformation of the

Archbishop of York into a man of war and a rebel. Using a linguistic metaphor, he asks York: 'Wherefore do you so ill translate yourself' (IV. i. 47) from a discourse of peace into the 'tongue of war' (l. 49), 'Turning your books to graves, your ink to blood,/Your pens to lances, and your tongue divine/To a loud trumpet and a point of war?' (ll. 50–2).

27 In this speech, Falstaff makes use of two inversions: the one between pox and gout and the turning of disease into a commodity. This last reminds us of Pistol's speech in *Henry V* (V. i. 84–93).

28 'Der Müde Prinz', in *Mimesis* (Bern: Francke, 1946); English translation, *Mimesis* (Princeton, NJ: Princeton University Press, 1953), pp. 312–33.

29 In the dialogue which opens Falstaff's encounter with the Hostess and Doll, venereal diseases are one of the topics of conversation.

30 Peto, in his role of war messenger, is allowed a verse speech (ll. 352–7). Earlier I remarked on a similar formal closing with the switch to verse in Part One, at the end of Act III, scene 3.

31 Henry develops the conventional kingly theme of sleep which abandons the great on account of their cares and responsibilities while it visits the untroubled subject. In the preceding scene, Falstaff put forward a similar claim to greatness: 'the undeserver may sleep, when the man of action is called on' (II. iv. 372–3).

32 In Act IV, scene 3 John of Lancaster informed us that the king is 'sore sick' (l. 75); to Lancaster, in turn, has been attributed by Falstaff 'a kind of male green-sickness' (l. 91) on account of his sober habits ('thin drink', l. 89); 'green sickness', Humphreys explains, is 'anaemia incident to unmarried girls'.

33 L. Falzon Santucci says that 'the task that faces Shakespeare at this point... is that of guiding *2H4*, and the audience, as swiftly and credibly as possible out of the world of comedy into that of serious historical drama; the closure must authenticate seriousness and not the irresponsible Falstaff world' ('Theatrical transactions', *Strumenti Critici*, 15 [1991], pp. 317–33, p. 327).

34 Commentators remark that the imagery in ll. 46–51 is analogous to that of Sonnet 64, 5–8, and also recall a passage of Ovid's *Metamorphoses* (xv. 262 ff) in Golding's translation (1567).

35 Melchiori's reading in the footnote to this passage in G. Melchiori, *The Second Part of King Henry IV* (Cambridge: Cambridge University Press, 1989).

36 The modern meaning is reported in the *OED* as first occurring after the 1688 revolution. As I have shown elsewhere (P. Pugliatti, 'Shakespeare's names for rebellion', in *Early Modern English: Trends, Forms and Texts*, ed. C. Nocera Avila, N. Pantaleo and D. Pezzini [Fasano: Schena, 1992], pp. 81–93), it seems that the transition from a conservative meaning, deriving from astrology and indicating a revolving movement leading back to the starting point, to the modern one indicating a sudden breach with the past, was achieved through an intermediary phase where the word started to mean a 'change in condition'. In its five occurrences in Shakespeare's canon (*Hamlet*, V. i. 88, *Antony and Cleopatra*, I. ii. 125, *Love's Labour's Lost*, IV. ii. 68, Sonnet 59, 12 and the one I am discussing here), the word seems to me to be well on its way to the modern meaning. It is quite possible, therefore, that the semantic change in English is to be attributed to Shakespeare. Christopher Hill has shown that the word acquired its modern

political implications long before the 1688 revolution: 'The word revolution', in *A Nation of Change and Novelty* (London: Routledge, 1990), pp. 82–101.

37   Three and a half lines which appear in Qb (in Qa the entire scene is omitted) and do not appear in F are interposed between the end of the passage quoted and the beginning of the evocation of Richard:

> O, if this were seen,
> The happiest youth, viewing his progress through,
> What perils past, what crosses to ensue,
> Would shut the book and sit him down and die.
> (III. i. 53–6)

Whatever the reasons for the omission of these lines in F, it should be noticed that the first half of l. 53 ('With divers liquors!') is completed by the otherwise inexplicably short l. 57 ('Tis not ten years gone'); and that the meaning of the added (or subtracted) lines contradicts Henry's wish to foresee future events. The lines, in fact, express the idea that even if it were possible to read the future we would become passive and sit still, waiting for death.

38   The word *chance* here does not have the same meaning as in Henry's speech; Warwick simply means 'the way in which things will fall out' rather than a capricious and therefore unforeseeable turn of events.

39   This idea appears, once again in connection with prediction or prophecy, in *Macbeth*. The expression is used by Banquo when he questions the witches about his future: 'If you can look into the seeds of time, / And say which grain will grow, and which will not...' (*Macbeth*, I. iii. 58–9).

40   Yachnin, 'History', p. 173.

41   C. Ginzburg, 'Spie. Radici di un paradigma indiziaro', in *Crisi della vagione*, ed. A. Gargani (Turin: Einaudi, 1979).

42   Ginzburg mentions the word *intuition* only in the last page of his essay. His claim is that the human sciences, confronted by the dilemma of choosing a weak scientific status and reaching remarkable results or choosing a strong one and reaching less remarkable results, should choose the first, opting for the 'elastic rigour' of conjectural paradigms.

3

Language

Shakespeare's plays are, first, words on the page. D. H. Lawrence's poem 'When I Read Shakespeare' opens: 'When I read Shakespeare I am struck with wonder / that such trivial people should muse and thunder / in such lovely language'. The different approaches to this 'lovely language', through the varied lenses of historical linguistics, studies of imagery, and post-structuralism, have produced extremely varied criticism over the past century, and some of the key movements in this critical history are described in this chapter.

There have been many studies of early modern English and Shakespeare's plays. Margreta de Grazia's overview 'Shakespeare and the Craft of Language' in de Grazia and Wells (2001) provides an introduction to rhetoric, punning and historical linguistics. Joseph (1947), Hulme (1962), Blake (1983), Salmon and Burness (1987) and Hussey (1992) all offer more detailed studies or collections of essays on Shakespeare's language. The historical context of Shakespeare's language is discussed by Barber (1997) and Hope (1999), and Cercignani (1981) writes about Elizabethan pronunciation. Houston (1988) and Wright (1988) discuss Shakespeare's metre and syntax; Ness (1941) catalogues Shakespeare's use of rhyme. Lanham (1969/1991) is the standard work on rhetorical terms. There are interesting approaches to Shakespeare's language from the point of view of actors speaking the verse in Barton (1984), Berry (1993) and Rodenburg (2002). Crystal and Crystal (2002) take a readably lexicographical approach to *Shakespeare's Words*.

Literary studies of Shakespeare's language have made a major contribution to criticism over the past century. L. C. Knights's argument that 'the only profitable approach to Shakespeare is a consideration of his plays as dramatic poems' (Knights, 1946: 6), Wilson Knight's attempt 'to see each play as an expanded metaphor' (Knight, 1930: 16), and C. S. Lewis's injunction 'to surrender oneself to the poetry and the situation' (Lewis, 1964: 208) are all instances of a critical reaction against the stress on character promoted by A. C. Bradley (1904) and his Romantic antecedents. In her study *Shakespeare's Imagery and What it Tells Us* (1935), however, Caroline Spurgeon is less concerned with individual characters than with the overall linguistic mood of a play. She offers 'suggestions as to the light thrown by the imagery (1) on Shakespeare's personality, temperament and thought, (2) on the themes and characters of the plays' (Spurgeon, 1935: ix). The book groups image clusters together by theme and also identifies dominant strains of imagery in specific plays. In the early history plays up to *Richard II*, the running metaphor is 'that of growth as seen in a garden and orchard, with the deterioration, decay and destruction brought about by ignorance and carelessness on the part of the gardener' (1935: 216); Spurgeon sees this as a precursor to the more complex image clusters of the tragedies. She also traces the imagery of butchery, of animals, of ships and the sea, and the king as sun. Turning to *King John*, Spurgeon sees this play as unusual among the histories for the intensity of its metaphorical patterning. The 'dominating symbol' 'is the body and bodily action' (1935: 245). Kenneth Muir's *Image and Symbol in Shakespeare's Histories* (1967) develops these analyses, demonstrating that the sequence of history plays shows 'a gradual progression in the use of imagery. In the three parts of *Henry VI* the usual form of image is the simile; in the later Histories it is the metaphor' (1967: 122).

Wolfgang Clemen, in his *The Development of Shakespeare's Imagery* (1951/1977), focuses on the tragedies, and argues that Shakespeare's early history plays demonstrate a 'lack of organic relation of the imagery to the play, the characters, and the situation as well as to its decorative rather than expressive purpose'. 'Characterization by individual speech is barred' (Clemen, 1977: 40), as Shakespeare prefers the sententious and proverbial rhetorical style. *Richard III* develops this style towards 'individual characterization', and, by *Richard II*, Shakespeare is exhibiting 'a greater variety of expression and a more subtle modulation' (1977: 52–3), where imagery serves the character of the poet-king. Frank Kermode's *Shakespeare's Language* (2000) also argues that there is a significant shift in Shakespeare's deployment of language for individual characterization, and, like Clemen, he dates this to around the time of *Hamlet*. Thus he also gives comparatively little attention to the histories of the 1590s, except to the extent that they anticipate the works to come. *Henry VI* shows the rhetorical style of Shakespeare's early work, in which the drama uses language in the manner of a 'non-dramatic poem, or possibly an oration' (Kermode, 2000: 29), although Kermode does caution that 'in Shakespeare's time ornament was generally thought of as more integral to meaning than we are likely to think it' (2000: 40). Kermode gives a careful analysis of Richard II's soliloquy in Act V, scene 5 as 'very much in the middle' of Shakespeare's career: showing signs 'of high intelligence at work, signs of a language formidably changing to meet greater challenges' (2000: 45). In *The Shakespearean Metaphor* (1978), Ralph Berry discusses the development of metaphorical language through the 'camp' aestheticism of Richard III's rhetoric (1978: 11), to the incarnate metaphor of illegitimacy in *King John*, the Bastard, and the obfuscation of political rhetoric in *Henry V*.

Brian Vickers's analysis of *The Artistry of Shakespeare's Prose* (1968) discusses its particular use in *Henry IV* in his chapter 'The World of Falstaff'. In the exchanges between prince and knight, Vickers analyses 'the way in which Shakespeare has extended the application of familiar prose devices – such as equivocation, repartee, deflating imagery, and symmetrical syntax – until they have become the real expression of the personalities involved', mixing 'comic and serious overtones' (Vickers, 1968: 99). The only history to be given extensive treatment in M. M. Mahood's *Shakespeare's Wordplay* (1957) is *Richard II*:

> Richard is a poet, but not, of course, for the reason that as a character in a poetic drama he speaks verse which is magnificent in its imagery and cadence. If the whole play were in prose, he would still be a poet by virtue of his faith in words; his loss of this faith and his consequent self-discovery that for all the wordy flattery of others he is not agueproof, constitute Richard's tragedy. Bolingbroke, on the other hand, knows words have no inherent potency of meaning, but by strength of character and force of arms he is able to make them mean what he wants them to mean. (Mahood, 1957: 73–4)

James Calderwood develops this idea in his *Metadrama in Shakespeare's Henriad*, arguing that 'the main metadramatic plot centers in the "fall of speech"' (1979: 5): 'Instead of regarding language as a means towards political ends, I would find Shakespeare solving problems of language by means of politics. Political affairs, in other words, become metaphors for art' (Calderwood, 1979: 4). Thus 'the shift of power in England from Richard to Bolingbroke marks a movement from, among other things, verbal realism to skepticism' (1979: 30); 'the *Henry IV* plays center in a fallen language whose once time-honoured truths have been called into cynical doubt by a world governed at the top by the lying king at Westminster and at the bottom by the lying knight at Eastcheap' (1979: 169–70); 'just as Harry, lacking Divine Right sovereignty, earns his title to kingship through an ordeal by combat at Agincourt, so rhetoric, lacking the automatic sovereignty of poetry, earns its keep in action, substituting for inherent validity an achieved validity' (1979: 179). Joseph Porter's *The Drama of Speech Acts: Shakespeare's Lancastrian Tetralogy* (1979) develops similar themes.

R. A. Foakes's 'Suggestions for a New Approach to Shakespeare's Imagery' (1952) tackles a lack of methodological sophistication in the work on

Shakespeare's imagery. He argues that there has been little assessment of the difference between 'poetic' and 'dramatic' imagery (Foakes, 1952: 81–2), and that a definition of imagery derived from drama is needed:

> While it is possible for a poem to be a metaphor, to exist only in an image or images, this cannot properly be said of a Shakespearian play. The poetic image in a play is set in a context not of words alone, but of words, dramatic situation, interplay of character, stage-effect, and it is also placed in a time sequence. (Foakes, 1952: 85–6)

Thus, a

> discussion of dramatic imagery then would include reference to the subject-matter and object-matter of poetic imagery, to visual and auditory effects, iterative words, historical and geographical placing, and to both the general and particular uses of these things. Dramatic imagery would be examined primarily in relation to context, to dramatic context, and to the time-sequence of a play; the general or overall patterns of word and image would be examined in relation to other effects as well as for their own value. (1952: 90)

Also on methodological questions is Robert Weimann's essay 'Shakespeare and the Study of Metaphor' (1974) which reminds us that 'The essence of metaphor is to connect' (Weimann, 1974: 150) and that the study of metaphor cannot therefore be separated from these points of reference. Weimann suggests that the formalist study of Shakespeare's language has 'not considered the theatrical functions of dramatic speech and the way it is correlated to non-verbal means of expression. To read the figures in the carpet is to see them in their two-dimensional extension, not as part of a process in time, and on the stage' (1974: 158–9). Weimann argues for the interrelation of metaphor in 'the total meaning of Shakespeare's poetry in the theater' (1974: 167).

Bawdy innuendo in puns can be excavated with reference to Eric Partridge's *Shakespeare's Bawdy*, an essay and an extensive glossary first published in 1947 with revised editions in 1958 and 2001. For Terry Eagleton (1986) Shakespeare's puns are a radical challenge to the ostensible conservatism of the drama:

> Even those who know very little about Shakespeare might be vaguely aware that his plays value social order and stability, and that they are written with extraordinary eloquence, one metaphor breeding another in an apparently unstaunchable flow of what modern theorists might call 'textual productivity'. The problem is that these two aspects of Shakespeare are in potential conflict with one another. For a stability of signs – each word securely in its place, each signifier (mark or sound) corresponding to its signified, (or meaning) – is an

integral part of any social order: settled meanings, shared definitions and regularities of grammar both reflect, and help to constitute, a well-ordered political state. Yet it is all this which Shakespeare's flamboyant punning, troping and riddling threaten to put into question. His belief in social stability is jeopardized by the very language in which it is articulated. It would seem, then, that the very act of writing implies for Shakespeare an epistemology (or theory of knowledge) at odds with his political ideology. This is a deeply embarrassing dilemma, and it is not surprising that much of Shakespeare's drama is devoted to figuring out strategies for resolving it. (Eagleton, 1986: 1)

Eagleton considers *Richard II* and *1 Henry IV* in this light. Elsewhere, connecting linguistic approaches to politicized and theoretical methodologies has produced some exciting work. In *Shakespeare from the Margins* (1996) Patricia Parker returns to Shakespeare's wordplay with a more theoretically informed attention to punning, metaphor and the subterranean connections within and between plays which can be revealed by close, historically aware reading. She is particularly concerned with the status of homophone puns in an era before standardized orthographic and printing conventions. One of her *Literary Fat Ladies* (1987) is Falstaff. Her discussions offer densely argued and stimulating re-evaluation of the practice of close reading, not as an activity which divorces literature from its culture but which can imbricate it more closely in social and cultural linguistics. In *Poetic Will: Shakespeare and the Play of Language* (1997), David Willbern discusses *Henry IV* with a combination of psychoanalytic framework and close textual analysis, engaging with historicist criticism and its limitations. Essays taking a similarly theoretical approach are collected by Atkins and Bergeron in *Shakespeare and Deconstruction* (1988). There are specific articles on Shakespeare's language and the history plays by MacDonald (1984), Skura (1997), and Steinsaltz (2002) on the use of French.

References and Further Reading

Atkins, G. Douglas and Bergeron, David M. (1988) *Shakespeare and Deconstruction*. New York: Lang.

Barber, Charles Laurence (1997) *Early Modern English*. Edinburgh: Edinburgh University Press.

Barton, John (1984) *Playing Shakespeare*. London: Methuen.

Berry, Cicely (1993) *The Actor and the Text*, rev. edn. London: Virgin.

Berry, Ralph (1978) *The Shakespearean Metaphor: Studies in Language and Form*. London: Macmillan.

Blake, N. F. (1983) *Shakespeare's Language: An Introduction*. London: Macmillan.

Bradley, A. C. (1904) *Shakespearean Tragedy: Lectures on Hamlet, Othello, King Lear, Macbeth*. London: Macmillan.

Calderwood, James L. (1979) *Metadrama in Shakespeare's Henriad: Richard II to Henry V.* Berkeley, CA: University of California Press.

Cercignani, Fausto (1981) *Shakespeare's Works and Elizabethan Pronunciation*. Oxford: Clarendon Press.

Clemen, Wolfgang (1951) *The Development of Shakespeare's Imagery*. London: Methuen, 2nd edn, 1977.

Crystal, David and Crystal, Ben (2002) *Shakespeare's Words: A Glossary and Language Companion*. London: Penguin.

de Grazia, Margreta and Wells, Stanley W. (eds) (2001) *The Cambridge Companion to Shakespeare*. Cambridge: Cambridge University Press.

Eagleton, Terry (1986) *William Shakespeare: Rereading Literature*. Oxford: Blackwell.

Edwards, Philip, et al. (eds) (1980) *Shakespeare's Styles: Essays in Honour of Kenneth Muir*. Cambridge: Cambridge University Press.

Foakes, R. A. (1952) 'Suggestions for a new approach to Shakespeare's imagery', *Shakespeare Survey*, 5: 81–92.

Gross, Kenneth (2001) *Shakespeare's Noise*. Chicago: University of Chicago Press.

Hope, Jonathan (1999) 'Shakespeare's "Natiue English"', in A *Companion to Shakespeare*, ed. David Scott Kastan, pp. 239–55. Oxford: Blackwell.

Houston, John Porter (1988) *Shakespearean Sentences: A Study in Style and Syntax*. Baton Rouge: Louisiana State University Press.

Hulme, Hilda M. (1962) *Explorations in Shakespeare's Language: Some Problems of Lexical Meaning in the Dramatic Text*. London: Longman.

Hussey, S. S. (1992) *The Literary Language of Shakespeare*, 2nd edn. London: Longman.

Joseph, Miriam (1947) *Shakespeare's Use of the Arts of Language*. New York: Columbia University Press.

Kermode, Frank (2000) *Shakespeare's Language*. London: Allen Lane,

Knight, George Wilson (1930) *The Wheel of Fire: Essays in Interpretation of Shakespeare's Sombre Tragedies*. London: Oxford University Press.

Knights, L. C. (1946) *Explorations: Essays in Criticism, Mainly on the Literature of the Seventeenth Century*. London: Chatto and Windus.

Lanham, Richard A. (1969) *A Handlist of Rhetorical Terms: A Guide for Students of English Literature*. Berkeley, CA: University of California Press, 2nd edn, 1991.

Lewis, C. S. (1964) 'Hamlet: the prince or the poem', in *Studies in Shakespeare: British Academy Lectures*, ed. Peter Alexander, pp. 201–18. London: The British Academy.

MacDonald, Ronald R. (1984) 'Uneasy lies: language and history in Shakespeare's Lancastrian tetralogy', *Shakespeare Quarterly*, 35: 22–39.

Mahood, M. M. (1957) *Shakespeare's Wordplay*. London: Methuen.

Muir, Kenneth Arthur (1967) *Image and Symbol in Shakespeare's Histories*. Manchester: Manchester University Press.

Ness, Frederic W. (1941) *The Use of Rhyme in Shakespeare's Plays*. New Haven, CT: Yale University Press.

Parker, Patricia (1987) *Literary Fat Ladies: Rhetoric, Gender, Property*. London: Methuen.

——(1996) *Shakespeare from the Margins: Language, Culture, Context*. Chicago: University of Chicago Press.

Partridge, Eric (1947) *Shakespeare's Bawdy: A Literary and Psychological Essay, and a Comprehensive Glossary.* London: Routledge.

Porter, Joseph (1979) *The Drama of Speech Acts: Shakespeare's Lancastrian Tetralogy.* Berkeley, CA: University of California Press.

Rodenburg, Patsy (2002) *Speaking Shakespeare.* London: Methuen.

Salmon, Vivian and Burness, Edwina (1987) *A Reader in the Language of Shakespearean Drama.* Amsterdam: John Benjamins.

Spurgeon, C. F. E. (1935) *Shakespeare's Imagery and What it Tells Us.* Cambridge: Cambridge University Press.

Skura, Meredith (1997) 'Marlowe's Edward II: penetrating language in Shakespeare's Richard II', *Shakespeare Survey*, 50: 41–55.

Steinsaltz, David (2002) 'The politics of French language in Shakespeare's history plays', *Studies in English Literature, 1500–1900*, 42: 317–34.

Vickers, Brian (1968) *The Artistry of Shakespeare's Prose.* London: Methuen.

Weimann, Robert (1974) 'Shakespeare and the study of metaphor', *New Literary History*, 6: 149–67.

Willbern, David (1997) *Poetic Will: Shakespeare and the Play of Language.* Philadelphia, PA: University of Pennsylvania Press.

Wright, George T. (1988) *Shakespeare's Metrical Art.* Berkeley, CA: University of California Press.

Psychoanalysing the Shakespeare Text

Harry Berger

Berger's methodologically explorative article proposes different ways of approaching the tetralogy through an exemplary analysis of the first scenes. Taking in psychoanalysis, questions of theatricality and a close attention to language, the argument suggests that patriarchal reproduction – the matter of genealogy – and mimetic reproduction – the matter of historiography – are intertwined and contradictory. 'Psychoanalysing the text' emerges as a rigorous and informed close textual reading.

Harry Berger, 'Psychoanalyzing the Shakespeare Text: The First Three Scenes of the "Henriad"', in *Making Trifles of Terrors: Redistributing Complicities in Shakespeare* (Stanford, CA: Stanford University Press, 1997), pp. 148–67.

Patriarchal ideology is shown in the *Henriad* to create deep tensions that are not dispelled, and are often exacerbated, by its mechanisms of repression and displacement. This is partly because the problems inherent in the cultural constructions of 'natural' or jural fatherhood are carried into the wider sphere of national and dynastic politics in two uneasily related forms of symbolic fatherhood: the Christian principle of divine paternity and the aristocratic principle of what might be called heraldic genealogy. The name of the Father, God, is used to authorize the distribution of patriarchal power onto two axes of 'descent': the 'vertical' axis of substitution called hierarchy, and the 'horizontal' axis of succession, heraldic genealogy. In both axes, the formal 'cause' or criterion is *mimesis*, but whereas in the first, descent is organized in terms of declining resemblance to the Father, in the second, the Father ideally achieves genealogical immortality by reproducing its image in progenial replicas.[1] My emphasis in this essay will be on a certain disorder in the mimetic principle itself, a contradiction that, as Plato saw, causes the structure of genealogical mimesis to be contaminated by that of hierarchical mimesis.

The ideal of genealogical mimesis is appealed to early in *Richard II* by the Duchess of Gloucester, who reminds Gaunt that his father's seven sons 'Were as seven vials of his sacred blood,/Or seven fair branches springing from one root' (I. ii. 12–13), and that his murdered brother, her late husband, 'was the model of thy father's life' (l. 28).[2] Similarly, in Act II, scene 1, York appeals to it when he urges Richard to live up to the standards set by his father, reminding him that 'His face thou hast, for even so look'd he' (l. 176). A little later, he gives the principle its classic statement:

> Is not Gaunt dead? and doth not Herford live?
> Was not Gaunt just? and is not Harry true?
> Did not the one deserve to have an heir?
> Is not his heir a well-deserving son?
> Take Herford's rights away, and take from time
> His charters, and his customary rights;
> Let not to-morrow then ensue to-day:
> Be not thyself. For how art thou a king
> But by fair sequence and succession?
>
> (II. i. 191–9)

Although these appear to be blandly constative articulations of the mimetic principle, they are being uttered in the face of its violation, and York's rhetoric is already charged with a sense of its fragility – a sense of the generational malaise that he will betray later in the play, and that may be imagined to motivate the blandness and the appeal of heraldic genealogy.

Consider, for example, the third and fourth lines: their chiasmic bonding does not quite efface the tension between the claims stated in the two separate rhetorical questions. Gaunt 'deserves' an heir not only because he was just but also because he is dead. His son 'deserves' to be an heir not only because he is true (we could read this mimetically as 'true to his father,' 'in his image') but also because he is alive. The heir represents his father's death, the loss of authority, power, life – 'no less than all' – and he can plead his right to this appropriation by appealing to the plague of custom and curiosity of nations.

Edmund's pungent if pathetic braveries – the clichés of knavery and folk cynicism – take on a different kind of life when transplanted to the soil of primogeniture and legitimate inheritance. For they clearly apply:

> This seems a fair deserving, and must draw me
> That which my father loses; no less than all:
> The younger rises when the old doth fall.
>
> (*King Lear*, III. iii. 25–7)

York tries to secure the rhetorical icon of the transmission he is defending by the chiasmus 'one – deserve – heir – heir – deserving – son': 'the one' reappears at the end, but not quite, in *son*; mimesis implies and demands a difference which it tries to overcome by a mirroring that recuperates the lost identity, but the inversion that expresses the difference at the heart of the process also expresses opposition between the two orders of 'the one' and 'son.'

The threat of external violation that York addresses in his protest to Richard thus reflects a problem lurking within the mimetic process itself, and may partially account for the ineffectuality of the protest. Such persuasions meet stiff competition in paternal criticism of sons, as exemplified by Gaunt early in *Richard II* and much later by Gaunt's son in *2 Henry IV*:

> O, had thy grandsire with a prophet's eye
> Seen how his son's son should destroy his sons,
> From forth thy reach he would have laid thy shame...
>
> (*Richard II*, II. i. 104–6)
>
> ...See, sons, what things you are...
>
> (*2 Henry IV*, IV. v. 64)

The negative and positive sides of paternal ideology are expressed in the following two statements by Bolingbroke, the first to York, who has just disclosed his son's treason, and the second to Harry:

> O loyal father of a treacherous son!
> Thou sheer, immaculate and silver fountain,
> From whence this stream, through muddy passages,
> Hath held his current, and defil'd himself,
> Thy overflow of good converts to bad...
>
> (*Richard II*, V. iii. 58–62)
>
> And now my death
> Changes the mood, for what in me was purchas'd
> Falls upon thee in a more fairer sort;
> So thou the garland wear'st successively.
>
> (*2 Henry IV*, IV. v. 198–201)

But the negativity and positivity of these utterances are complicated and indeed challenged as soon as they are contextualized.

Psychoanalytic criticism has tended to approach the problems these statements adumbrate by resituating them within the network of explanations made available by the institutionalized lore of psychoanalysis. I propose as an alternative taking a scion from that root and grafting it onto a different explanatory network, whose stock is the mimetic process. As I mentioned earlier, there is a disorder, a structural flaw, in the very notion of mimesis, and it is magnified by confusion in the paternal deployment of the genealogical principle. The father's desire of immortality may produce a desire to clone and control an endless series of identical replacements. This, incidentally, implicates a latent ideal of male parthenogenesis that may be expressed in the fear, scapegoating, and repression of the feminine. But this desire is crossed by the desire to overgo one's replacements, to be the unrepeatable archetypical eponymous progenitor whose all-giving cannot be matched. What the father then wants to reproduce are not replicas but images, imitations. It is of the nature of an imitation to be defective, to fall short of what it represents so that it can represent itself *as* the representation of an exemplar. A perfect imitation, as Derrida notes, 'is no longer an imitation'; the tiny difference between imitated and imitation makes all the difference; imitation 'is not what it is...unless it is in some way at fault or rather in default.'[3] The paternal project entails the reduction of the son's difference, his otherness, to assure both the genealogical continuity of the paternal archetype and its hierarchic superiority to the weaker vessels that transmit its image. This is a project of symbolic filicide, and it is nourished by the desire of immortality, that is, by the fear of death that, projected onto the potential replacement, makes of a 'true inheritor' a true competitor. In the space or gap of otherness that the act of paternity creates, and that symbolic filicide cannot efface, indeed can only render more alien, arises the answering project of symbolic parricide.

The centrality of this theme to the *Henriad* has often been recognized and discussed, but with two limitations that I shall try to confront in this essay. First, the burden of critical discussion has been placed on Henry IV as father; virtually no attention has been paid to him as son, and this will be the subject of the following interpretation. Second, I know of no serious attempts to correlate psychoanalytic criticism with the two other major lines of interpretation addressed to the *Henriad*: political and metatheatrical criticism. While I do not have space to consider these in any detail, I shall illustrate and formulate a methodological hypothesis for connecting metatheatrical issues to the intratextual representation of political and generational conflict. For reasons that will become clearer as we proceed, a metatheatrical approach to the dramatic and theatrical dimensions of the 'story' of the *Henriad* presupposes a standpoint outside the normative limits of what has been called 'stage-centered' reading. It calls for a project that is doggedly textual in orientation, and is thus *anti*theatrical: it will generate readings that don't readily lend themselves to performance and that will necessarily draw fire from stage-centered critics. But that, in a perverse way, is my point – that is, that the antitheatricality of the readings I shall give reflects an antitheatricality in the Shakespeare text. By calling that text antitheatrical I mean that it throws into question all the dramatic structures – narrative, episode, scene, character, and body – that theatrical performance privileges and the author of Shakespeare's plays clearly loves. I include among these structures the political and historical scenarios as embodiments of the patriarchal ideology with its two axes of hierarchy and orderly succession. I shall read the critique of drama and theater politically as a critique of that ideology, but what I am chiefly interested in is its relation not to the politics of the state but to that of father / son conflicts. I therefore view psychoanalytic, political, and dramatico-theatrical interpretation as closely intertwined striations of a single activity.

Mimesis is the common representational principle informing the organization of genealogical and hierarchic relationships, and of relationships among the text, the dramatic narrative, and theatrical performance. Thus I assume the text to be performing a critique of mimesis – and of its own mimetic status – in the very act of producing a mimesis. In exploring the critique I shall not bother with its possible relevance for allegories of the playwright's literary or psychological development. I prefer to seek within the dramatic community and its generational conflicts for the motives that lead to the production and critique of mimetic structures. What regulative and representational functions do these structures fulfill in relation to the father / son conflicts depicted in the *Henriad*? And since 'in the *Henriad*' here means in the language of the play as it offers itself directly to readers rather than to actors, what functions do those structures fulfill in relation to the text?

I consider these two questions to be the same question, and I shall respond to it by exploring, in the interpretations that follow, a particular hypothesis: that Shakespeare's mimetic structures – theater, drama, and the narrative sequences they represent – are related to the text as manifest to latent contents; that they are explicitly and conspicuously presented as displaced, condensed, and dramatized visualizations of latent textual meanings they thereby repress. This hypothesis will now be tested by excavating from the text of the first act of *Richard II* the shadowy evidence of the first major father / son conflict in the *Henriad*.

In the opening scenes of *Richard II*, the inflation of speech is no more conspicuous than the silences it constitutes as hidden behind it. Participants within the drama share with audiences and readerships an uneasy awareness that the ceremonially dramatic but otherwise noncommittal language pushes much into the background, that ritual speech is being used to hide, mystify, or justify other motives than those expressed, and that no one knows exactly what those motives may be – perhaps, in some cases, those whose motives they are least of all. Since the characters seem for the most part to be maneuvering in the dark, it may be risky to venture into one of the more charged and salient pockets of silence, the one that encloses what goes on between John of Gaunt and his son. That pocket is peripheral to the more central one enclosing what goes on between Richard and Bolingbroke, but since both pockets are mediated, or set off, or circumscribed, by the more accessible relationship between Richard and Gaunt, I shall observe due caution and begin there. The Gaunt / Bolingbroke relation remains a mystery throughout the *Henriad*. Bolingbroke's obsession with his relation to Richard crops up frequently in the *Henry IV* plays, and his revisionary retrospects afford at least limited access to what went on (or goes on) in *Richard II*. The relation between Gaunt and Richard is resolved with considerable stridency by the time Act II, scene 1 of the first play is over.

The general tenor of Richard's attitude toward Gaunt may be caught by trying to listen to the former's opening words with Gaunt's ears:

> Old John of Gaunt, time-honored Lancaster,
> Hast thou according to thy oath and band
> Brought hither Henry Herford thy bold son,
> Here to make good the boist'rous late appeal,
> Which then our leisure would not let us hear,
> Against the Duke of Norfolk, Thomas Mowbray?
> *Gaunt*:   I have, my liege.
>
> (I. i. 1–7)

The chiasmic patterning of name – title – title – name in the first and last lines works to Gaunt's detriment, since the last line lacks modifiers, which Richard so pointedly uses in the first. The blunt and familiar opening, 'Old John of Gaunt,' edges the elegant variation that follows it with faint sarcasm. Richard pushes on the tonal difference between personal and ritual address, converts apposition into opposition, makes the second epithet sound like a euphemistic or mystified equivalent of the first. Then, turning from father to son, his alliterative coupling of *bold* with *boist'rous* reduces the ambivalent first term to its negative connotation: under the pressure of the meanings of *boisterous* (rough, coarse, clamorous, unskillful), *bold* shifts from 'fearless' or 'confident' to 'presumptuous' or 'forward.' At the same time the combination of *son* and *boist'rous* tends to diminish Bolingbroke – to *boy* him – and to stress Gaunt's responsibility for his son's good behavior.

In the lines that follow the opening exchange, Richard continues to press on Gaunt's role as surety:

> *Richard*:   Tell me, moreover, hast thou sounded him,
>   If he appeal the Duke on ancient malice,
>   Or worthily as a good subject should
>   On some known ground of treachery in him?
> *Gaunt*:   As near as I could sift him on that argument,
>   On some apparent danger seen in him,
>   Aim'd at your highness, no inveterate malice.
>
>   (I. i. 8–14)

Although Richard's questions are clearly ceremonial, and therefore rhetorical, he puts them to aggressive use not merely in picking away at Gaunt's responsibility for the good faith of the appeal but also in trying to elicit a response that will reveal the extent of the knowledge, and perhaps complicity, Gaunt shares with his son. The response is evasive: not '*known* ground of treachery,' but '*apparent* danger seen.' The measured, heavily stopped blank verse of Gaunt's vague reply expresses the care he takes to dissociate himself from any appearance of complicity or knowledge. We hear much in later scenes about his view of Richard and England, but never a word about his relation to Bolingbroke's appeal – or, for that matter, about his relation to Bolingbroke. This is the subject that the following textual excavation aims to elucidate.

Bolingbroke prefaces his accusation of Mowbray with words in which, as the Arden editor observes, he 'takes care to explain ... the purity of his motives':

> In the devotion of a subject's love,
> Tend'ring the precious safety of my prince,
> And free from other misbegotten hate,
> Come I appellant to this princely presence.
>
>   (I. i. 31–4)

While 'other misbegotten hate' answers to Richard's 'ancient malice' and thus apparently has Mowbray as its object, the vagueness of both phrases gives them a wider sweep, for in the background of the appeal lies the murder of Gloucester, which is the climactic and most heavily stressed of the three articles in Bolingbroke's accusations: 'misbegotten hate' may refer to the family feud and the motive for revenge.

In the rhetorical climax of his accusation, Bolingbroke asserts that Gloucester's blood,

>   like sacrificing Abel's, cries
> Even from the tongueless caverns of the earth
> To me for justice and rough chastisement;
> And by the glorious worth of my descent,
> This arm shall do it, or this life be spent.
>
>   (I. i. 104–8)

His generational logic is less shaky than it seems, for why should Gloucester's blood be like the archetypal murdered *brother's*, and why should it cry to *him* to be God's surrogate in this affair, unless he is replacing the father whose consenting silence amounts to symbolic fratricide, and whose 'unwilling tongue' (I. iii. 245) diminishes 'the glorious worth' of Bolingbroke's descent from Edward III? It is to these lines that Richard / Cain responds: 'How high a pitch his resolution soars!' (I. i. 109). A few lines later, assuring Mowbray of his impartiality, he redefines the lineal scheme to his own advantage:

> Were he my brother, nay, my kingdom's heir,
> As he is but my father's brother's son,
> Now by my scepter's awe I make a vow,
> Such neighbor nearness to our sacred blood
> Should nothing privilege him...
>   (I. i. 116–20)

As Kittredge observes, the second line is a 'slighting antithesis to "my kingdom's heir."' Although the derogation of Gaunt is here only a move in the game of lineal checkers, the opening words of the play had already begun to establish Richard's disdain for his uncle, and this impression is situationally reinforced shortly after when Gaunt participates in the tactic Richard employs to frustrate Bolingbroke's justice. In jingling rhymes whose flippancy sharpens the calculated tone of affront, Richard makes Gaunt share the onus of his arbitrary interruption of the ritual: 'Good uncle, let this end where it begun; / We'll calm the Duke of Norfolk, you your son' (ll. 158–9). Gaunt complies with a disingenuous aphorism that avails itself of Richard's opening, 'Old John of Gaunt,' to activate the weakling's plea, senility: 'To be a make-peace shall become my age. / Throw down, my son, the Duke of Norfolk's gage' (ll. 160–1).

Bolingbroke directs his bitter refusal to Richard and continues insulting Mowbray, but if in reading his words we pretend once again to be listening with Gaunt's ears we may feel that his son's sentiments are not entirely displaced to those two targets:

> O God defend my soul from such deep sin!
> Shall I seem crest-fallen in my father's sight?
> Or with pale beggar-fear impeach my height
> Before this outdar'd dastard? Ere my tongue
> Shall wound my honor with such feeble wrong,
> Or sound so base a parle, my teeth shall tear
> The slavish motive of recanting fear,
> And spit it bleeding in his high disgrace,
> Where shame doth harbor, even in Mowbray's face.
>   (I. i. 187–95)

The second line contains the only verbal acknowledgment of his father's presence Bolingbroke makes in this scene. It is ceremonially correct: he salutes the immediate source of 'the glorious worth of my descent' and states his unwillingness to dishonor the source by displaying cowardice before his father's eyes. Nevertheless, this line gives the whole speech the capacity to strike daggers into any ears pretending to be Gaunt's.

Since Gaunt commanded the display, the ritual force of the rhetorical question changes to 'Shall I let my father have the satisfaction of watching me perform the base act he and Richard urged on me?' The question that follows may then be heard as intensifying the speaker's sense of outrage: 'Is this what you ask me to do, lower my crest by impeaching my height with a display of fear?' The parallelism of the prepositional clauses that end each question places Gaunt and Mowbray in the same position. This adds interest to *outdar'd*: it does not characterize Mowbray's behavior, and as a ritual insult it does not have to, but it can be applied with some justice to Gaunt who, unwilling to avenge or speak up for his brother himself, seconded the king's attempt to frustrate Bolingbroke's appeal 'for justice and rough chastisement.' His son's refusal to be infected with this shameful fear-bred silence challenges Gaunt's self-imposed tonguelessness: the amputated tongue symbolizes the father's 'feeble wrong' ('Ere my father / Shall wound my honor'), and the hyperbolic violence directed at this ritual surrogate is at once masked and enabled by the careful emphasis of the final clause, 'even in Mowbray's face.' This displacement effectively makes the speech self-referential, for Bolingbroke is spitting his challenge to Gaunt in Mowbray's face.

Our evidence for decoding the meant or unmeant messages one character receives from another's words comes from the meant or unmeant meaning transmitted through his own words. Gaunt's words to the Duchess, which follow almost immediately after Bolingbroke's speech, register an uneasiness that suggests he is belatedly directing toward her the kind of lame excuse he might wish to make toward his son; yet at the same time, they register more aggressive feelings:

> Alas, the part I had in Woodstock's blood
> Doth more solicit me than your exclaims
> To stir against the butchers of his life;
> But since correction lieth in those hands
> Which made the fault that we cannot correct,
> Put we our quarrel to the will of heaven,
> Who, when they see the hours ripe on earth,
> Will rain hot vengeance on offenders' heads.
>
> (I. ii. 1–8)

Gaunt is very careful here with his plural forms and shifters, and although we immediately identify 'the butchers,' 'those hands,' and 'offenders,' 'they' in line

7 is less obvious – what divine, angelic, or human avengers pluralize 'the will of heaven'? When will they judge the time to be ripe? And into what saving community of 'we' does the first person of lines 1–2 vanish? If the apocalyptic excuse is meant to suggest a more legitimately sanctioned revenge than his son's effort, and one from which Gaunt will be spared, what could that possibly be? The vagueness of 'offenders,' lacking the article that would link it more closely to particular 'butchers' and 'hands,' implies something no less encompassing and remote than the Psalmist's wish for fire and brimstone, or the Last Judgment; it measures the sense of justified helplessness Gaunt encodes in the 'we' of line 5, hence according to the logic of his argument those who wrongly attempt correction will join the offenders at the general doom. In Act I, scene 1 he had heard his son say that he would make his challenge to Mowbray 'good on earth, / Or my divine soul answer it to heaven' (ll. 37–8), and buried in Gaunt's words to the Duchess is a protest against that arrogance.

The Duchess, however, does not let Gaunt slip off into the Elizabethan world picture or even into the sunset of his declining years: 'Finds brotherhood in thee no sharper spur? / Hath love in thy old blood no living fire?' (I. ii. 9–10). She accuses him of something very like the 'pale beggar-fear' and 'feeble wrong' spat out by Bolingbroke:

> thou dost consent
> In some large measure to thy father's death
> In that thou seest thy wretched brother die,
> Who was the model of thy father's life.
> Call it not patience, Gaunt, it is despair;
> In suff'ring thus thy brother to be slaught'red,
> Thou showest the naked pathway to thy life,
> Teaching stern murder how to butcher thee.
> That which in mean men we intitle patience
> Is pale cold cowardice in noble breasts.
> What shall I say? to safeguard thine own life,
> The best way is to venge my Gloucester's death.
>
> (I. ii. 25–36)

In these words Gaunt could well hear Bolingbroke's allusion to symbolic fratricide repeated as a direct accusation, intensified by conversion to symbolic parricide.

He defends himself with an aggressive restatement of the Tudor ideology:

> God's is the quarrel – for God's substitute,
> His deputy anointed in His sight,
> Hath caus'd his death; the which if wrongfully,
> Let heaven revenge, for I may never lift
> An angry arm against His minister.
>
> (I. ii. 37–41)

These words both acknowledge his feeble wrong and register the need to justify it more fully by rejecting the Duchess's appeal to the vendetta ethic. The concluding lines use the Tudor theory to rationalize his own 'patience,' but they also imply a criticism of Bolingbroke's impatient arm. To Dover Wilson they seemed to 'condemn in advance the usurpation of his son... after his death,'[4] but I think the observed connection to Bolingbroke is strengthened by being shifted from the prospective mode of dramatic irony to the retrospective mode of structural irony.

When Gaunt suggests that the Duchess should direct her complaint to 'God, the widow's champion and defence,' her reply is definitive, and Gaunt makes no answer to it:

> Why then, I will. Farewell, old Gaunt.
> Thou goest to Coventry, there to behold
> Our cousin Herford and fell Mowbray fight.
> O, sit my husband's wrongs on Herford's spear,
> That it may enter butcher Mowbray's breast!
> Or if misfortune miss the first career,
> Be Mowbray's sins so heavy in his bosom
> That they may break his foaming courser's back
> And throw the rider headlong in the lists,
> A caitive recreant to my cousin Herford!
> Farewell, old Gaunt; thy sometimes brother's wife
> With her companion, grief, must end her life.
> *Gaunt*:   Sister, farewell; I must to Coventry,
> As much good stay with thee as go with me!
> (I. ii. 44–57)

The Duchess refuses to call Bolingbroke Gaunt's son. In the first of her three references to him he is '*Our* cousin' – she shares him equally with Gaunt in a general classificatory relation – and by the third, at line 53, her possession has become singular. This shift destabilizes the modifier in the next line: we may read it either as 'thy brother's sometimes wife' or as 'the wife of thy sometimes brother,' cut off from Gaunt not only by his death but also by the recreancy that would leave 'sacrificing Abel' unavenged – that is, 'you are no longer of "our faith," and our extended kin group is now represented by our cousin, not by you; he has assumed your lapsed responsibility.' But since the Duchess has already described that lapse as a wrong done to her husband, the implication is even stronger. 'O, sit my husband's wrongs on Herford's spear': to replace Gaunt and to redress his wrong is to challenge him to combat. Once again, the 'recreant' Mowbray is a ritual scapegoat, and the violent imagery of trial by combat provides a hyperbolic image, a melodramatic outlet, for the displaced expression of sentiments that might be less easy to entertain toward Gaunt.

The argument I have excavated from the tongueless caverns of the Duchess's language is that Bolingbroke has replaced – indeed, displaced – his father as the true son of Edward III and brother of Gloucester, and that some defensive and even resentful recognition of the argument is embedded in Gaunt's language. When I read 'Hath love in thy old blood no living fire?' I recall and refocus Gaunt's 'to be a make-peace shall become my age,' seeing it now tinged by rueful and bitter if resigned acknowledgement of the trimmer's role he has assumed in others' eyes, tinged also by a more aggressive complement: 'to be a troublemaker becomes his youth.'

The Duchess names Gaunt four times in this scene: she calls him 'Gaunt' twice in her opening speech when she still hopes to persuade him to action, but switches to 'Old Gaunt' after he has referred her to God the widow's champion and she turns instead to Herford for succor. I think the contexts in which the Duchess, Richard, and Gaunt himself refer to his age – whether in epithets, descriptions, or puns – almost always skewer the reference on the sharp sword of the father–son interaction: when his authority over Bolingbroke is invoked or being called into question (I. i. 1, 160, 162–3); when – as here – Bolingbroke's challenge is contrastively related to his own ideologically toned evasions; and when, after being party to his son's banishment, he complains to Richard that it will hasten his death (I. iii. 216–32).

Under the pressure of these contexts and their language, 'old' and 'gaunt' become Gaunt's defensive weapons in the struggle between father and son that marks the passage of patriarchal authority from predecessor to successor, aged to young, old to new – it would be better to say the passage of phallic power, since my excavation leads me to conclude that the play's language characterizes Gaunt not only as pleading impotence and not only as accused of it but also as symbolically 'castrated' by Bolingbroke's challenge. And this is the conclusion I want to carry as a hypothesis into the third scene of Act I: Bolingbroke's presence and behavior are a standing rebuke to Gaunt; he feels accused and challenged, replaced and excelled, by his son; Bolingbroke's innuendoes in Act I, scene 1, reinforced by the Duchess's charges in Act I, scene 2, point toward a father who has been 'deposed,' or self-deposed, having allowed his son to 'usurp' his place and function in the generational order. Thus to see and be seen by his son ('in my father's sight') may not cause him unmitigated joy, and this occasions another speculation – that is, will it cause him unmitigated grief to be relieved of that presence?

'As much good stay with thee as go with me': the limp sentiment with which Gaunt takes his leave hardly suggests that he is any more eager to rush off to Coventry than he is to linger on and hear the Duchess talk about it. The contrast to Bolingbroke is driven home in the opening lines of Act I, scene 3:

> *Marshal*: My Lord Aumerle, is Harry Herford arm'd?
> *Aumerle*: Yea, at all points, and longs to enter in.

Bolingbroke does not immediately appear, however; Mowbray enters and speaks first. Ritual purists complain that the appellant should have preceded the defendant into the lists.[5] But the reversed order makes possible an interesting variation in Richard's two requests to the Marshal to administer the oath of justice. For Mowbray, he uses these words: 'swear him in the justice of his cause.' For Bolingbroke, however, the formula is significantly altered, and I think the significance is underlined by its contrast to the earlier request: 'Depose him in the justice of his cause.' Reading the word that names the central action of the play I succumb to the charm of several temptations. First, of course, the pun invites a proleptic interpretation – as if Richard already sees Bolingbroke crowned and pronounces a curse ('Let him be deposed') that nevertheless reflects awareness of his own unjust regime. This implies a second alternative – 'Depose *me* in the justice of his cause' – from which I slide helplessly into the pleasure of imagining either or both statements as expressions of Gaunt's dilemma: 'if my son is "deposed" by Mowbray, his cause will be proved unjust, ergo I shall be justified, but if his cause is just, I am "deposed."'

A similar temptation is dropped in my path by Richard's leave-taking of Bolingbroke:

> We will descend and fold him in our arms.
> Cousin of Herford, as thy cause is right,
> So be thy fortune in this royal fight!
> Farewell, my blood; which if to-day thou shed,
> Lament we may, but not revenge thee dead.
>   (I. iii. 54–8)

In the first line I see not only a foreshadowing of the deposition scene but a condensed visualization of Richard's latent project as it unfolds through the play, here displaced to the physical circumstance of a ceremonial gesture. The rhythm accentuates the *will* to descend; the second phrase is a kinesic hyperbole that mimes the desire coupling Richard to Bolingbroke in their dance toward deposition and regicide, and toward the subsequent regime, when the embrace gradually becomes a stranglehold. This line chimes with 'depose' and with the odd reference to 'royal fight' as an element of the proleptic rhetoric threading glints of the latent project through the first and third scenes of the play.

The second couplet adds another element: Richard's message is that if Bolingbroke loses he will unjustly have shed the 'high blood' his royal kinsman shares, but his language also lets the alternate message, 'if you kill me,' flicker briefly before us. In the final line, the alert excavator might discern another displacement. While the statement is sardonic in Richard's mouth – as if he might be expected to avenge his kinsman and has to explain that he won't – it crisply epitomizes the attitude Gaunt expressed in Act I, scene 2: 'Lament' = 'Alas, the part I had in Woodstock's blood'; 'but not revenge' = 'I may never lift / An angry arm,' since Mowbray will have proved to be heaven's minister.

In the balanced duplicity of these lines Richard flaunts his mastery of the rhetorical tease. He (con)descends to favor Bolingbroke with a hug and a word of tepid encouragement (by the judicial logic of trial by combat, 'as' in line 55 must mean 'if,' not 'since'), then devotes the last line and a half to harping on his possible defeat. Rhymes, end-stopping, and echoing caesuras add bite to his wicked tongue – the finality, certainty, and witty detachment of aphoristic or recited speech. This is political, not merely poetic, mastery. Even as he folds the successor-to-be in his arms, he sends the usurper-to-be off with a dry-eyed mock. Bolingbroke parries the mock in answering couplets that are more forceful but less balanced and assured:

> O, let no noble eye profane a tear
> For me, if I be gor'd with Mowbray's spear!
> As confident as is the falcon's flight
> Against a bird, do I with Mowbray fight.
>
> (I. iii. 59–62)

This begins well with 'profane a tear': the lament would be profaned not only by his unworthiness but also because it would indubitably be feigned. Yet the expansive energy of his heroic clichés flags suddenly at the end of each enjambment. The falcon comes down on its prey more confidently than the figure does on 'a bird.' The trajectory of Bolingbroke's career, its brief upward surge and long anticlimax, is epitomized in this rhythm. His real contest is not the physical encounter with Mowbray but the verbal encounter with Richard and, behind that, the silent encounter with Gaunt. The putative referent of the words – the anticipated fight with Mowbray – is actually the signifier of the present power struggle that goes on, and will continue to go on, within the 'fair designs' of the rhetorical lists.

After two unrhymed lines of farewell to Richard and Aumerle, and a summary couplet broadcasting his self-assurance, Bolingbroke winds up for the climax of his speech – his farewell to Gaunt – with an odd simile: 'Lo, as at English feasts, so I regreet / The daintiest last, to make the end most sweet' (ll. 67–8). The figure implies that these 'ceremonious' farewells and salutes are things to be savored, things to be consumed. The farewell salute to Gaunt will be the tastiest morsel. Bolingbroke's emphasis is on rhetorical pleasure and performance rather than on the illocutionary force of the sentiment; he will confect a filial dessert of sweetly end-stopped pieties. Yet once again, the language wries out of his control and serves up a more disconcerting message:

> O thou, the earthly author of my blood,
> Whose youthful spirit in me regenerate
> Doth with a twofold vigor lift me up
> To reach at victory above my head,
> Add proof unto mine armor with thy prayers,
> And with thy blessings steel my lance's point,
> That it may enter Mowbray's waxen coat,
> And furbish new the name of John a Gaunt,
> Even in the lusty havior of his son.
>
> (I. iii. 69–77)

The frame or crust of this trifle is a request for blessing; the filler is a respectful *aemulatio*. But from under the mock modesty of the fourth line something interesting begins to bubble forth. 'To reach... above my head' can hardly refer to victory over Mowbray; whatever the speaker intends, the words are steeled (or stolen) by another sky-aspiring proleptic allusion: they point toward Richard. Then, with 'furbish,' they become more abrasive as their lance passes almost too easily from Mowbray's waxen coat to Gaunt's rusty name. Ure makes a good case for preferring the Quarto's *furbish* to the Folio's *furnish*: 'Besides its more general meaning of "clean up", *furbish* means "scour the rust from armor"... so Gaunt's name (honor, repute) is also his armor, and the metaphor continues the references to arms and armor in the preceding lines.'[6] But it also joins with *new* to scratch away at the film of self-apology Gaunt has coated his name with – '*Old* John of *Gaunt*.' It is the *former* spirit of Gaunt's youth that Bolingbroke invokes to help the falcon soar to the height of his heavenly author's quarrel; a spirit that died and now revives only in the 'lusty havior' of the son whose angry arm will 'scour the rust' from his earthly author's (and his family's) once untarnished honor.

Bolingbroke's English confection thus concludes as a challenge to Gaunt to support his cause: the son's victory will clear his father's name. The name-clearing problem places Gaunt in a classic double bind, since he also seems to want a clear name in the court's eyes and those of God's anointed deputy. This problem comes into focus after the interruption when Richard reminds him that his 'tongue a party-verdict gave' to his son's banishment (I. iii. 234). Gaunt's rueful reaction to the verdict and to his share in it is troubled by his strident protest of nonresponsibility. But I think it is also troubled by the deceptively truistic distinction with which he justifies himself:

> You urg'd me as a judge, but I had rather
> You would have bid me argue like a father.
> O, had it been a stranger, not my child,
> To smooth his fault I should have been more mild.
> A partial slander sought I to avoid,
> And in the sentence my own life destroy'd.
> Alas, I look'd when some of you should say
> I was too strict to make mine own away;
> But you gave leave to my unwilling tongue
> Against my will to do myself this wrong.
>   (I. iii. 237–46)

The first couplet says that if he had been arguing as a father he would have been more mild. The second couplet says that if he had been arguing as a non-father he would have been more mild. The first couplet implies that he argued as a non-father in order to avoid the charge of prejudice. The second couplet implies that being less mild in order to avoid the charge of prejudice is acting like a father. But consider also the following variation: 'Because it was no stranger but my child, / I could not smooth his fault or be more mild.' This more directly conveys the message that the partiality of the loving father is not toward any child but toward a guilty child. Gaunt acknowledges his son's fault, confesses to a father's impulse to overlook it (only a 'child,' after all), and goes on to lament the strictness of the loyal and obedient subject forced to suppress the impulse in the interest of justice. In this parable, the primary focus of self-presentation is on the trials of the Good Father. Gaunt is smoothing faults all around – Richard's, his own – and the smoothness penetrates the syrupy rhymes and rhythms of his speech.

What the speech actually suppresses is the fear and guilt of the Bad Father, who pleads the avoidance of partiality to cover other motives for being less mild to a son than to a stranger. He blames others for letting himself destroy his life and for not telling him 'I was too strict to make mine own away.' The elliptical strain of this phrase betrays the pressure of his not mentioning what he is doing to his 'child': insofar as 'make ... away' is apposite to 'my own life destroy'd' it means 'do away with,' but insofar as it refers to Bolingbroke's exile it means 'send away.' In the blurring together of these senses, 'mine own' opens up to include not only his upright self-sacrifice but also the sacrifice of his son that enables him to avoid a partial slander. 'Mine own' justifies both sacrifices because it suggests that his son, like his life, is his possession, to dispose with as he judges right. This judgment, he explains, is the source of his grief. Yet further reflection will show that it is also the effect of his guilt, which it reinforces.

Since Gaunt's conversation with the Duchess established his interest in making himself and others believe that it is wrong to oppose the king, we can imagine him seeing Bolingbroke's de facto challenge to Richard through the medium of Mowbray as a fault in which he could easily be implicated as an accomplice to a plot fomented by the Gloucester faction. This changes the import of 'partial slander' from 'accusation of leniency' to 'accusation of complicity': it would have been easier for him to smooth the fault of a stranger whose questionable motives did not glance at him. What could make his party-verdict doubly painful is his sense that he has sacrificed his son to clear himself. His behavior constitutes a betrayal of Bolingbroke and his cause; worse than that, it expresses a desire to betray his son. He looked in vain for others to temper this ignoble impulse. The unstable syntax of the final couplet betrays the effect of their failure. Construed as a redundant negative construction, it says that both he and his tongue were unwilling to do himself the injury of voting for his son's exile, or to inflict on his son the injury he ignobly desired to inflict. But construed as an antithetical con- struction – '[my unwilling tongue] / Against [my will to do myself this wrong]' – it says that he had a will, a desire, to do this wrong, that he was unwilling to actualize the desire in speech, but that Richard's urging pre- vailed upon him.

The conclusion of this strenuous excavation of Gaunt's lines is that they betray his fear of being contaminated by Bolingbroke's action; his reluctant agreement to the sentence of exile in response to that fear; the desire to defeat the son who challenges him; the guilt occasioned in him by that desire and by an agreement that sacrifices his son's interest to his own; and the attempt to assuage that guilt by blaming his party-verdict on others, an attempt that could only increase the corrosive power of self-despite. What destroys his life, then, what makes him gaunt for the grave, is not merely grief at being separated from his son, perhaps forever, but guilt at having willed to do his son that wrong. On Bolingbroke's side, the father / son conflict is concealed, enabled, exacerbated, by a double displacement: from Gaunt to Richard to Mowbray; from father to king to peer. Mowbray serves as the medium in which are condensed Bolingbroke's darker purpose – to accuse the king – and his darkest purpose – to rebuke his father.

The centrality of this conflict in the *Henriad* is obvious and has often been noted, but never with reference to Gaunt and Bolingbroke. As I stated at the beginning of the essay, my purpose in excavating their relationship has been to situate an interpretation in the most antitheatrical reaches of the text in order to position myself 'outside' the politico-historical and dramatico-theat- rical narrative privileged by stage-centered criticism. This positioning (or positing) allows me to interpret the emergence of that narrative in functional terms as a defensive transformation of latencies in the text, and to explore the dialectic by which Shakespeare represents the meaning of theatrical drama in those terms. I conclude with a brief reading of a passage that will open up onto a summary overview of the process I have been discussing.

Early in the play Richard commands the appearance of Bolingbroke and Mowbray in characteristically tortured syntax:

> Then call them to our presence; face to face,
> And frowning brow to brow, ourselves will hear
> The accuser and the accused freely speak.
>
> (I. i. 15–17)

'Face to face, / And frowning brow to brow': leading off thus with a pair of unbound modifier phrases frees them up for serial redefinition. In a first fleeting mirage they seem to describe Richard confronting the other two as *his* antagonists and / or appellants. This gives way to a second when the strangely pluralized royal plural suggests that he confronts and / or accuses himself. Finally, the opposed selves are bound to their proper ritual representatives in line 17, and their proper ritualized representation in lines 18–19, an event celebrated with the play's first rhymed couplet: 'High-stomach'd are they both and full of ire, / In rage, deaf as the sea, hasty as fire.'

The shift in these five lines from enjambed internally stopped blank verse to end-stressed rhymed verse reinforces the shift from uncertain syntax and rapidly changing impressions to the too predictable formulas of chivalric rhetoric, which in this case produces an oxymoronic relation between what is said and how it is said: the analogies of nature are clichés of art; the reported unruliness of the combatants is overruled by the measured rhythm of the report, by its discountable literary hyperboles. And there is a sense in which their rage will be as artificial and literary as the language, a sense in which the 'report' is actually a self-fulfilling stage direction that prescribes the emotions and behavior appropriate to culturally prefabricated roles embedded in a certain institutional narrative. The rage will also be artificial because it will be ritually displaced and misdirected.

The shifts described above combine to mark the most fundamental process that structures this drama: the passage and transformation of conflict from the tongueless caverns of some 'hidden imposthume' to the safety of the sanctioned artifice and 'fair designs' of ritualized combat and behavior. In the *Henriad* the equivalents of Hamlet's phrase are, like his, carefully vague, as if keeping their distance from the miasma they fear to touch: 'buried fear,' 'some other grief,' 'inward wars.' The passage from this latent content to the manifest fictions of ritual embodiment is perfectly described by Lafew in *All's Well That Ends Well*: 'we make trifles of terrors, ensconcing ourselves into seeming knowledge when we should submit ourselves to an unknown fear' (II. iii. 3–6). A sconce is a fortress, and in *Richard II* the conspicuous trifles, the stiff and stilted formulas, of ritual are the palisades that impose quarantine against the miasma:

> I'll answer thee in any fair degree
> Or chivalrous design of knightly trial...
>
> (I. i. 80–1)

> On pain of death, no person be so bold
> Or daring-hardy as to touch the lists,
> Except the marshall and such officers
> Appointed to direct these fair designs.
>
> (I. iii. 42–5)

The textual confusions buried in Richard's call to the combatants resonate with obscure, labile, and dangerous power struggles – rooted in fear, guilt, aggressivity, self-contempt, and Janus-faced desire – that defy closure and shun exposure; his final couplet visualizes the dramatic form in which they can find legitimate heroic expression and narrative resolution.

Trial by combat displaces, condenses, dramatizes, and thereby at once represses and represents such 'inward wars' as those that divide a father from his son and from himself. Shakespeare's achievement lies in making the 'fair designs' represent and be touched by the miasma they eschew. The prescribed rhetoric of ritual speech and action is shown to be inadequate to deal with or represent whatever 'other grief' is buried in the language of the dramatic community. It is precisely its inadequacy, its parodic and artificial character, that lets the ritual function as a mode of concealment enabling the hidden struggles to continue. To borrow René Girard's terms,[7] if trial by combat is a caricature of *differentiation*, Shakespeare presents it as such by encouraging us to search his text for the undifferentiating forces that produce the caricature as its instrument. Cutting across the differentiating boundaries of the nominal combatants and subjects of dispute, the text throws anamorphic shadows that bathe the empty glitter of ceremonial speech in a rich chiaroscuro.

Girard's distinction was formulated for the analysis not of a particular ritual but for all ritual, including what he refers to as the 'surface play,' and I have argued elsewhere that the surface play is the one privileged by theatrical performance.[8] My concluding incautious generalizations are that the preceding comments on trial by combat apply to Shakespeare's representation of the 'fair designs' of theatrical performance on its audience; apply to dramatic fiction, whether staged or not; apply to any transformational interaction between the excavated meanings of the text and the speech assigned to names we conventionally reify and imagine as persons. They apply wherever language is distributed among the embodied subjects who speak it. The *meta*morphosis of text into bodies produces conspicuous *ana*morphosis that has the same function and effects as those of the 'fair designs' of trial by combat. Socially or culturally produced structures of embodiment – of presences, subjects, characters, roles, individuals – are quarantines against the 'discourse of the Other' that smokes the edges of clear visualization and ambiguates simple location. The plastic design behind that mode of production is to *pre-vent* 'bad humors' by providing identities and stories the actors can live with, narratives that enable them to discharge those humors while preserving unawareness and self-esteem. The embodiment of presence is thus the building of Lafew's sconce.

Shakespeare's text, then, is not the representation of drama per se but rather the representation of its construction *out of* the text's discourse of the Other and *against* that discourse – the representation and, in the positive sense, the critique of the self-concealing motivational conditions of embodiment. Insofar as theatrical performance is the ritual reinforcement of the drive to embodiment, is its actualization in living bodies, it intensifies the defensive flight of drama from text, imposing itself on the contours of drama like a template that masks off its underlying textuality. Shakespeare's metatheatrical critique of theater is, as we know, contained within his metadramatic critique of drama. These are enabling, not inhibiting, critiques: they support his production of dramatic fictions and theatrical performances in a transgressive manner, that is, by clearly signaling their limits, laying bare the motives behind their production, adumbrating a textual dimension at once implicit in them and beyond them. To represent performed drama *as* a flight from text is to enrich it with the transcendent fringe of meanings, the signifying nothing conspicuously concealed by the sound and fury of the words, conspicuously frustrated by the splendors of embodiment. The fury, splendor, and frustration can be experienced together only in performance; we have to feel the presence and pressure of the theatrical template, submit to its fair designs, in order to measure both *its* power and the shadowy counterforce of the power it represses. The politics of that repression cannot be borne home to us in any other way. But the fury, splendor, frustration, and politics can only be understood and evaluated by the excavation that psychoanalyzes the text.

Notes

1 Property interests may not account for all aspects of the appeal of primogeniture. Both the hierarchic and the genealogical principles of mimesis surely contribute something. The father wishes to replicate *himself*, not *himselves*. There is support for the primacy of the firstborn as *image* in both Testaments.

2 All quotations are from *King Richard II*, ed. Peter Ure, The Arden Shakespeare, 5th edn (1961; repr. London: Methuen, 1966).

3 Jacques Derrida, 'Plato's pharmacy', in *Dissemination*, trans. Barbara Johnson (Chicago: University of Chicago Press, 1981), p. 139.

4 *The Life and Death of King Richard the Second*, ed. Matthew W. Black, A New Variorum Edition of Shakespeare, vol. 27 (Philadelphia: Lippincott, 1955), p. 44.

5 Ibid., pp. 50–1. Another complaint is that Mowbray should have been summoned by a herald, not by 'the appellant's trumpet' (I. iii. 4). It is as if a second trial, a shadow trial, is being conducted, with the appellant usurping the function of the 'officers / Appointed to direct these fair designs' (ll. 44–5), but doing so to peculiar effect, since Mowbray and whomever he represents (Richard? Gaunt?) thereby usurp Bolingbroke's role as appellant and are placed in a position to accuse him. And this, in short, is the story of Henry Bolingbroke in the *Henriad*.

6 *King Richard II*, ed. Ure, p. 26.

7 René Girard, 'To entrap the wisest: a reading of *The Merchant of Venice*', in *Literature and Society*, ed. Edward W. Said (Baltimore, MD: The Johns Hopkins University Press, 1980), pp. 100–19.

8 See chapter 6 [of *Making Trifles of Terrors*].

Value and Metaphor in the Lancastrian Tetralogy

Sandra K. Fischer

Through a close and historically informed analysis of the language of economics in the Henry IV *plays, Sandra Fischer gives a new perspective on their sense of historical and political process. She argues for the significance of image clusters based around debt and repayment in a wider context of national economic prosperity as an index of strong leadership. The idea of contract theory is developed in the context of relations between play and audience and monarch and subject.*

Sandra K. Fischer, '"He means to pay": Value and Metaphor in the Lancastrian Tetralogy', *Shakespeare Quarterly*, 40: 2 (1989), pp. 149–64.

Samuel Johnson reproved Shakespeare for using too many quibbles, an excess that, according to Johnson, led him away from his thematic point and marred his effectiveness as a dramatist.[1] Shakespeare's reiterated metaphor clusters, however, which could be perceived as verbal quibbles, lend unity to his plays; and his characters' habits of troping reveal their attitudes toward the spoken word.[2] The metaphorical cast of a character's mind – the analogies he uses to perceive, order, and explain his vision of reality – in turn shows how effectively that character vies for perceptual authority, how potent is his view of experience. When a character's own metaphors become a shared language, he has both posited and assigned the values of his world; he has, in effect, created meaning through his interpretation.

Especially in the history plays, Shakespeare's characters struggle with the public tongue as they attempt to control history, master their roles, and assert their identities within history's chaotic process. Falstaff most notably and joyfully exploits language, stretching its lexical and moral possibilities not only for money or advancement but also to betoken his personal value in a society that prefers to judge him in terms of physique or virtuous action. Though the most comic in his linguistic playfulness, Falstaff is not the sole quibbler here; he is simply a contender in the serious rivalry in troping that the Lancastrian tetralogy dramatizes. The winner is able to fashion and effect his own reality; his metaphors become ways to reshape and justify his actions and to establish his personal value during the liminal social period portrayed.[3] In these plays, the authority of words begins to replace the valor of deeds; significance resides in interpretation more than in action. As James L. Calderwood observes of the tetralogy, 'metaphor is not merely a verbal device with which to align symbolic counters...but rather an authentic reflection of the world's true shape and nature,'[4] a reflection formed by an interaction between the speaker and the resemblance that he perceives.

Metaphor so used is aptly described by Puttenham as 'a figure of transporte' that effects 'a kinde of wresting of a single word from his owne right signification, to another not so naturall, but yet of some affinitie or conueniencie with it...'[5] In the Lancastrian tetralogy, the players strive for such a language, one that can accurately interpret their new and turbulent social relations. Specifically, as they experience the rise of the new economics as an historical reality, they begin to test the metaphorical suitability of the lexicon of economics for assigning human values and describing personal relations. As the characters habitually appropriate economic language, they do more than simply unify the metaphorical experience of the drama for the audience. They reveal a startling link between word and value, discovering in language a flexible and variable medium of exchange that creates their world and their identities anew. To adopt a mercantile attitude toward the word is to abandon feudalism and to accept a different economic construct of reality. The vocabulary of economics offers a surprisingly accurate 'conueniencie' for describing and justifying both political strategy and personal action during this period of historic transition.

To examine 'transporting' figures may reveal the heart of both character and dramatic theme. Terence Hawkes argues that Shakespearean drama, despite its ostensible subject, is inevitably about language itself, celebrating the flexibility and ambiguity of the spoken word and simultaneously cementing a perceived social reality. Ted Cohen suggests, further, that shared metaphors may also serve a social purpose in helping to establish a sense of community and camaraderie in both *dramatis personae* and audience. Acting as a lens through which relationships and events are filtered, metaphors define social values and *modi vivendi*. Michael D. Bristol emphasizes the cohesive plebeian experience of theatrical performance and the subversive nature of its language, finding in Renaissance drama an idiom of alternatives. Plays offer an experience as 'liminoid' as was the life of popular culture, which 'operated in the light of values that were neither feudal nor bourgeois.'[6]

Certainly seminal metaphors become authoritative when employed by the rulers manqué of that society. Because the word of the king has the symbolic power to establish value (as it does on currency), the metaphorical perceptions of Richard, Henry, and Hal reveal not only individual character but also social policy and direction.[7] Richard in effect banishes communication from his realm, replacing the exchange transaction of speaking and listening with a conception of rhetoric as flourish or embellishment, the word for its own sake, divorced from content, empty of value. As Ronald R. Macdonald notes, 'Richard does not use the language of sacred kingship: he allows it to use him'; or, as Joseph A. Porter says, 'for Richard language is a medium for constructing expressions rather than for expressing.'[8] Both Henry and Hal, in contrast, contrive a different way of kingly speaking, each inventing a new kind of metaphorical language that better approximates the social realities they encounter.[9]

In this series of history plays, the *dramatis personae* must master language and its 'transporting' metaphors, for, as Joan Webber argues, political success relies on the 'creative use of language,' on an effective manipulation of rhetoric as a form of control.[10] The power offered to those who understand the link between language and value is perhaps nowhere as succinctly illustrated as in such an historical context, where the play itself both tests and judges a changing concept of value as manifested in metaphorical flexibility and expertise. The most recent studies of the Henriad have in fact altered our notions of historical theme: the plays are not so much about the innate qualities of monarchy as they are about the kingly perception of the world and self-presentation to one's subjects. Macdonald best summarizes this contemporary hermeneutic:

> To speak effectively in the new world created by the usurpation requires the exploitation of all the figurative resources of language, of irony, of understatement, of wary hyperbole and deft paronomasia. The days are gone when simple grandiloquence...will do...The changes of history demand changes of language, and to survive in the world of the two parts of *Henry IV* is to learn to speak in ways that are adequate to the occasion. Much of Hal's 'education' in the course of the plays, if that is what it is, may be described as his attempt to master new languages...to speak like a king; or to speak like himself...It is a rigorous process of learning the languages of others and inventing a language of your own...It is those who do not grow in language, who do not submit themselves

to its shifting substance and stubborn materiality, who are defeated by history...[11]

The Henriad portrays a political conflict that is in essence based on the proper use of language and the use of a proper language, or as Calderwood says, based 'not merely in who will possess the word in England but in what conception of language will prevail.'[12]

The metaphorical center of the Lancastrian cycle lies in a cluster of tropes that spill from the mouths of all the major characters, revealing larger concerns of political alliance, concerns with the individual in history. It is a pattern that equates human relations with economic transactions, and at its base is an experimentation with new ways of finding identity and defining human value in the context of a quickly developing social-exchange mentality.[13] Hal must learn the language of this new, mercantile world of exchange in order to avoid repeating the fiscal mistakes of Richard and to reaffirm himself as his father's son and heir with a comparable set of economic ethics: a steely sense of opportunism, an ability to self-legitimize newly minted or stolen value, a recognition of the ambiguous nature of keeping one's word, and a sense of both *when* and *how* to pay a debt (in whatever currency). As H. R. Coursen explains, the movement of the tetralogy is toward 'economic determinism,' an environment in which characters 'must compete with each other ruthlessly in a world drained of intrinsic value' and where, after alternative values are tested, 'the "ethic" is "what works."'[14]

To extend natural economy to the sphere of human economics is to show that individual value must be asserted and retained; stealing (whether by means of usurpation or low-life roguery) must be justified; contracts must be made and debts paid; and breaches of one's ethical debt to God must be redeemed – all of which actions apply to Henry as well as to Hal and link father and son in a tight alliance, no matter how disparate their characters may sometimes seem. In addition to fixing an identity between father and son, king and heir, these nodes of metaphor also establish a set of structural foils that make the behaviors of both the more readily understood by contrast.[15]

In the speech of both Henry and Hal, four structural patterns of economy and economic metaphor emerge: the testing of language as a currency that lends value to its manipulator; the comparing of the historical ripening of time to a contract maturing; the marking of a backdrop of macroeconomic transition and the debasement of traditional values; and the asserting of the contractual basis of all human endeavor and relation. Indeed, in the same way that *King Lear* and *The Merchant of Venice* can be described as plays that are 'about' bonds, the Lancastrian tetralogy can aptly be said to be 'about' economic contracts and their metaphorical applications in the process of history. As Alan C. Dessen observes, 'Both parts of *Henry IV* display prominently the breaking of vows and the non-payment of debts';[16] more importantly, they also investigate the very metaphor of indebtedness.

I

Shakespeare surely found the tracings of his econo-contractual pattern in Holinshed, his major source; but he would have found it as well in the very nature of his political subject: as David Scott Kastan notes, political history is 'the matter of the fallen world.'[17] The Gardener of *Richard II*, 'old Adam's likeness, set to dress this garden' (III. iv. 73), inhabits not an Eden but a fallen version of Paradise, where constant labor and diligence are required to maintain an artificial rather than a natural order. Gaunt's accusations of Richard underscore this image of the perversion of natural hierarchy into a mercenary contractualism:

> this dear dear land...
> Is now leas'd out...
> Like to a tenement or pelting farm.
> England...
> ...is now bound in with shame,
> With inky blots and rotten parchment bonds.
> (II. i. 57–64)

Such emphasis upon the materiality and contractuality of the post-lapsarian world was, of course, a Renaissance commonplace, deriving from the *Summa* of Aquinas and passed down through various glosses and reinterpretations. For example, Johannes Nider in *De contractibus mercatorum* (1468) bases his entire discussion on the implications of the Fall. The concept of individual ownership of property, for instance, and the necessity of artificial machinery for exchange and contracts exist, writes Nider, because of our loss of innocence: 'that precept of the law of nature, of holding all things in common, was revoked by the Fall.'[18] Richard's 'fallen world' kingdom must thus participate in contractual economy (it is his misunderstanding and abuse of the system that in part allow for Bolingbroke's usurpation).

Moreover, Shakespeare also saw the dramatic power of comparing post-lapsarian economy to the basic socioeconomic changes that had begun in the fourteenth and fifteenth centuries (the period under scrutiny in the history plays) and that were becoming conventional in his own time.[19] Precisely because contracts were attaining a frightening prominence, writers like Nider and others, who felt the need to justify and codify their rules of operation, had begun to debate the nature and status of contractual relations. The story of contracts under the Common Law begins in the thirteenth century with instruments called 'covenants'; by the fourteenth century a seal was mandatory for the document to have legal weight, and, as we see reflected in Shakespeare's economic metaphors, 'debt was...the central contractual action in medieval law.'[20] Although these contracts are defined in the legal glosses as (rather specifically) necessitating mutual consent and exchange of property, Shakespeare seized upon the larger implications of behavior defined by writ and bargain. In a society where 'contract ...assumed an entirely new role,'[21] the king's conception, and expression, of his own social function required a mastery of the language and ethics of contract and trade.

Seeing an historical connection between language and social value has its parallel in Renaissance views about the functions of history and historical fictions. If, in addition to illustrating God's providential plan for England and vindicating the Tudor myth, Shakespeare's history plays attempt to offer a thinly veiled symbolic forum for the analysis of current social phenomena (as many critics believe), a direct clash between the ethics of feudalism and mercantilism such as we witness in the Lancastrian tetralogy lends itself perfectly to applications of the 'new man' morality in Elizabethan society. The connection between coinage, value, and political success was also known in Renaissance study of the past, for the debasement of the coinage was almost universally held (during the Renaissance) to have been the immediate cause of the fall of the Roman Empire and thus a greatly feared contemporary threat to economic and social stability.[22]

A focus on economy and contract is, then, historically appropriate. It is also encouraged by Holinshed's use of econo-contractual metaphor in the *Chronicles'* reading of historical event. One hallmark of the *Chronicles'* relation of the history of this period is an insistent legalistic tone: from the pledges offered initially to procure Hereford's release from arrest, to the justification for Henry V's sally into France, to the final judgments passed on each of the three rulers, the chronicler stresses the reciprocal and contractual nature of human interaction. Shakespeare, as is commonly noted, appropriates verbatim several of Holinshed's phrases, including the 'farm[ing]' of the realm, the 'blanke charters' used for unequal taxation, the 'instrument' (also called a 'schedule or bill of renouncement') that Henry requires Richard to read and approve when transferring the kingship, the 'indenture' of the Westminster conspirators, 'sealed with their seales and signed with their hands,' that York discovers hidden in his son's bosom, and the 'tripartite indenture' of the Percy rebellion.[23]

Judging by the substance of the chronicle and the language used to explain and justify individual behavior, Holinshed seems to recognize above all that his personages are engaged in what Hawkes calls 'a crucial turning-point in British social and political history,'[24] one in which a changing social structure affects the language men use in dealing with one another and in which a profit-motivated money economy in part defines their interactions. Hereford's initial complaint against Mowbray is essentially economic: Mowbray retained money given him to pay the king's soldiers. To this accusation Hereford adds the personal complaint of 'false suggestions and malicious counsell' (p. 494), which extends the conception of economy to the abuse of language in a consistent word–coin analogy: speaking falsely becomes a form of counterfeiting and thus a distortion or misrepresentation of reputation, a measure of human social value. Appropriately, part of the punishment or remedy for this economic abuse of contractual word must be econolinguistic, enforcing congruency between word and truth, word and value: Mowbray must be made to pay as he had been charged.[25] Not only did Richard abuse kingship by 'farm[ing]' the realm[26] and unfairly taxing the citizens with blank charters and 'a new and strange subsidie... the leuieng of [which] monie' caused '[g]reat grudging and manie a bitter cursse' (p. 428), but he was also charged with the violation of his own contractual word of obligation: acting 'without law or custome, contrarie to his oth taken at his coronation' (p. 502).[27]

When the nobles, churchmen, and government officials can bear no further economic abuse (fines, tallages, taxes), they rally to Bolingbroke's cause, violating their own contract of allegiance to their king. Henry returns not only contractually, to claim his birthright,[28] but also economically, 'to cause the paiment of taxes and tallages to be laid downe, & to bring the king to good gouernment' (p. 498). Henry's power in this endeavor, moreover, is cemented by an economic ruse of his own: 'those that came not [to Henry's side], were spoiled of all they had, so as they were neuer able to recouer themselues againe, for their goods being then taken awaie, were neuer restored. And thus what for loue, and what for feare of losse, they came flocking vnto him from euerie part' (p. 498). When Henry confronts the king, he speaks contractually and economically, eventually claiming the crown as his legal right through the support of his blood, his kinsmen,[29] and God, and as redress for the wrongs done to him and to his kingdom 'for default of good gouernance and due iustice' (p. 505). According to the legal historian Bracton, Richard forfeits his right when he violates law and oath: 'there is not *rex* where will rules rather than *lex*.'[30] The concept of economic obligation to the commonweal underlies charges leveled against him by Henry and by Holinshed. Henry urges the populace to indict Richard on the grounds that 'he was an vnprofitable prince to the commonwealth' (p. 502), and Holinshed judges him finally: 'He was prodigall' (p. 508).

Although in Holinshed's account Henry seems to understand royal economic obligation better than does Richard, he similarly suffers because of economic and contractual abuses. His border wars become monetary concerns, and even the dead cannot be claimed for burial 'without great summes of monie giuen for libertie to conueie them awaie' (p. 520). The Percys unite against their former ally because they 'began now to enuie his wealth' (p. 521), and treason becomes a matter of contractual word: many 'did not onelie promise to the Persies aid and succour by words, but also by their writings and seales confirmed the same. Howbeit, when the matter came to triall, the most part of the confederates abandoned them, and at the daie of the conflict left them alone' (p. 522).[31] A new kind of moral relationship is being tested here and failing: the contract represented by spoken words no longer signifies. As Feste judges in another context, 'words are very rascals since bonds disgrac'd them' (*Twelfth Night*, III. i. 21); words become rescindable, alterable in interpretation, and devoid of the integrity of intrinsic value, reflecting the vacuum of standards ushered in by Richard.

The Percys' list of complaints against Henry includes, as a fatal reenactment of Richard's cycle, 'leuieng of taxes and tallages, *contrarie to his promise*' (p. 523, emphasis mine). Henry's onerous wars are additionally disastrous for the commonwealth because they pervert natural, Edenic economy, keeping men from 'their woonted trades and occupations.' Holinshed's final judgment of Henry deems his economic abuses so hateful that – 'what with such taxes, tallages, subsidies, and exactions as he was constreined to charge the people with' (p. 541) – he could not have redeemed himself even with a much longer reign. Henry seems to have understood the social change but to have been unable to adjust to it completely. His kingdom spanned two moral economies. He understood and used opportunistic contractualism and the mercantilist ethic yet still at base put too much faith in the old symbols of value: a man's word, the king's body, and stalwart, unwavering individual human mettle.

Hal begins his reign more auspiciously, in relation to both legal contracts and economic matters. When, in the second year of his reign, he proposes (as had his father) to seize the church lands for 'the honor of the king, and defense of the realme ... [and] for reliefe onelie of the poore, impotent, and needie persons' (p. 545), his religious advisors support his invasion of France both contractually and economically: 'for the recouerie of his ancient right and true inheritance ... they had granted to his highnesse such a summe of monie, as neuer by no spirituall persons was to any prince before those daies giuen or aduanced' (p. 546). Keeping his word and caring economically for his people, Henry V receives nothing but praise from Holinshed. He restores the right spirit of economy (that is, commonweal) to his realm but also learns to use the modern legalistic language of contracts to justify his actions. The *Chronicles'* final judgment on his character is substantially economic: 'For bountifulnesse and liberalitie, no man more free, gentle, and franke, in bestowing rewards to all persons, according to their deserts: for his saieng was, that he neuer desired monie to keepe, but to giue and spend' (p. 583). Hal studies and uses the new economics, yet he is careful to bow to the still-operative medieval theories governing the right use of riches: i.e., as Aquinas had prescribed, he was munificent and liberal. A guise of value is restored when the king rewards his people according to both their need and their merit.[32] The 'affinitie or conueniencie' of the language of money and contracts, when applied to kingship and individual action, is apparent in the source in both its language and its judgments. Shakespeare's appropriation and expansion of these metaphorical tendencies for his Lancastrian cycle considerably enrich our experience not only of each king but also of the emerging patterns of historical process.

II

It is in *Richard II* that the tropic and structural contexts are established for the econo-contractual metaphors that will dominate *1 Henry IV*. Recent criticism of *Richard II* often focuses on its language, on Richard's use of the word as empty gesture, devoid of power because abstracted from its representative reality and thus its intrinsic value. To Richard, language is nothing more than ceremonious self-indulgence, and part of his failure is his depriving language of its communicative, relational capacity. Richard's attitude toward the word is linked to a changing economic context in two ways: first, his feudal utterance reflects, in its anachronicity, how the facts of political economy have altered; and, second, Richard, like Henry, applies the principles of economy equally to his kingdom and to his speech – Richard is a squanderer, Henry a careful weigher of expense.[33] Richard is everywhere cited for his abuses: his prodigality on frivolous personal expenses, his onerous taxes to support the war effort, his confusing of ceremony and practicality (e.g., in buying new uniforms rather than weapons for the soldiers), his violation of patrimony, and his dependence upon the extrinsic royal title rather than on intrinsic regal character and action. By contrast, Henry justifies his return in careful contractual terms: he presents himself as Lancaster rather than Hereford, claiming with this new identity a new set of rights and obligations; he insists upon the written and acknowledged bill of resignation.[34] Bolingbroke also reestablishes the power of the word with Richard's execution, finding, to his seeming surprise, that language breeds deed: the word of the ruler once again passes current.

In the opening scenes of *1 Henry IV*, the context of contract and exchange links the apparently disparate worlds of government and tavern. It is King Henry himself who implies the first economic metaphors of this play: his description of the civil broils suggests that they are an expense of time and a waste of lives; the king is worried about not having fulfilled his promise to redeem his guilt in Richard's death; victory in war is determined by counting up human and material gains and losses; prisoners are considered 'prizes' and 'spoils.' Moreover, his initial complaints against the prince are economic, as Hal is accused of 'riot' (i.e., extravagance) and of debasing his reputation as heir. Hal is linked to Hotspur in an exchange metaphor (which will bear interest later), and Percy's violation of his contract with the king is stated in economic terms: he 'keeps' his prisoners 'to his own use.' The king demands that Hotspur 'answer' the complaints[35] and thus establishes a pattern of paying, justifying, and redeeming one's economic actions by linguistic act or verbal value in an extension of the lesson of Richard's murder.

Act I, scene 2, then, is not such a world away from the metaphoric context of the court and the battlefield as it might seem. In Act I, scene 2 Hal counts himself among the unpunished thieves, just as Henry has admitted that he needs to redeem Richard's murder; and Falstaff reveals to us the importance of linguistic mastery and the exchange of words in establishing individual value. His company is tolerated and his social value determined primarily by his linguistic dexterity. Additionally, we begin to understand as Hal and Sir John converse that even intangible values can, in this transitional society, be bought – intangibles like reputation and a 'commodity of good names' (I. ii. 83). The prince and Falstaff eventually jest about varieties of contracts and the ambiguities involved in keeping one's word, uncovering an economic crux that will apply equally to the king, his heir, and the Percys. In Poins's joking attack, Falstaff has, by contract, sold his soul to the devil for a cup of Madeira and a capon's leg on Good Friday; however, as Hal and Poins explain, if the knight keeps his word and pays his debt to the devil, he is damned for breaking the contract of life owed to God in return for the implicit promise of redemption (ll. 114–21). Though expressed in jest, this dilemma of conflicting contracts suggests that men are saved not by merit but by deals, expediency, and crafty manipulation of contractual debt (we will see more of this later on the battlefield). Knowing which debts to keep and when and how to pay are vital assets for the prince; he learns these conventions equally from the behavior of Falstaff and that of his father.

In *2 Henry IV* Warwick explains the prince and his method to both the king and the audience: 'The Prince but studies his companions / Like a strange tongue, wherein, to gain the language...' (IV. iv. 68–9). Understanding the potency of words as variable payment for debt and as a commodity lending value to the speaker is vital for success in this economically volatile society. By showing us a variety of attitudes toward linguistic value, Shakespeare illuminates Hal by means of foils, a principle that Hal himself recognizes and affirms in his first soliloquy (*1 Henry IV*, I. ii. 195–217) and which, in mercantile strategy, is referred to as 'glozing' or 'setting a glosse on wares.'[36] Hotspur proves himself inflexible in the face of values other than traditional honor and *virtù*: three separate times he violently objects to and refuses to receive as current a linguistic coinage other than his own. The first time he rejects the 'holiday and lady terms' (I. iii. 46) of the king's emissary; later he reacts to Henry's language of courteous persuasion (I. iii. 250–6); and finally he mocks and disdains the Welsh tongue of Glendower as an unfit currency (III. i. 117–18). As Dessen notes, Hotspur maintains a 'self-induced deafness,' while Hal has the thespian facility to play parts and learn words other than his own.[37] Even with this confident assurance of the value of a true and valorous Englishman's tongue, Hotspur finds that his misunderstanding of the value of language sets up his defeat: the false message that Worcester takes to the Percys about the king's offer constitutes a kind of counterfeiting or false coinage that Hotspur, rigid in his understanding of linguistic value, is unable to discern.

Hal, in contrast, understands the slippery nature of language and allows himself to experience its values firsthand in, for example, Falstaff's account of the Gadshill robbery. The prince is explicit about the motivation of the trick perpetrated on Francis the tapster in the same scene; he explains that, having learned their language, he may now 'command all the good lads in East-cheap,' the mercantile sector of London (II. iv. 14–15). Further, he parries with Falstaff in a series of puns and equivocations in mutual recognition and admiration of the characters' inverse values. Hal has intrinsic 'mettle,' as he himself often asserts. Because his face, when he becomes king, will be stamped on the coinage as a symbol of value, now its features themselves are a form of credit or IOU – that is, an implied contract for payment. Falstaff's intrinsic 'mettle' is his wit, and this he must coin into an exchange value of multisignifying words. Both reveal their knowledge of this value relationship in the telling exchange in which, after the 'true Prince' has proposed a feeble pun, the 'Prince of Puns' chastises him:

> *Falstaff*: How now, how now, mad wag? What, in thy quips and thy quid-dities? What a plague have I to do with a buff jerkin?
> *Prince*: Why, what a pox have I to do with my hostess of the tavern?
> *Falstaff*: Well, thou hast call'd her to a reckoning many a time and oft.
> *Prince*: Did I ever call for thee to pay thy part?
> *Falstaff*: No, I'll give thee thy due, thou hast paid all there.
> *Prince*: Yea, and elsewhere, so far as my coin would stretch, and where it would not, I have us'd my credit.
> *Falstaff*: Yea, and so us'd it that, were it not here apparent that thou art heir apparent –
>
> (I. ii. 44–58)

and with that masterly paronomasia drives home the point of their relative values at the same time as he wins the verbal parrying with the most brilliant and thus most valuable rhetorical figure.

Metaphors of contractual economy can underscore alliances as well as foils. Henry and Hal reveal their affinity not only because, as David Boyd notices,[38] they are drawn to the same figures of speech, but also because both understand the growth of historical process in terms of a maturing contract. The Lancasters are eventually successful because of an *economic* attitude toward power and the unfolding of history.[39]

Hal displays a sophisticated understanding of mercantile strategies when he describes his plan to maximize demand through scarcity – what economists would term 'increasing his marginal utility.' (Elsewhere Shakespeare and his contemporaries refer to this process as 'engrossing the market.')[40] In his Act I, scene 2 soliloquy, the prince describes how he will augment his ultimate value by counterfeiting lack of value. When he is most 'wanted,' he says, he will emerge like the sun from the mists covering his glory and be *better* than his word by paying a debt for which he has not been bound – the debt he never promised – a kingly act that exceeds the Common Law obligations. Hal's 'redemption of time,' then, goes beyond his merely using it wisely for self-instruction; it also recognizes the Lancastrian contract. Hal must not assert himself as the true ruler until the time is ripe, until the contract is mature. Interestingly, his father gained the crown by use of the same mercantile principle, as he eventually explains to his heir: though he did not counterfeit lack of worth, he hid his value so that when he did appear his virtue had not been sullied by acquaintance and he could out-shine *his* foil, Richard (*1 Henry IV*, III. ii. 44–57). According to Dessen, 'Everyone else in the play readily finds reasons not to pay their debts or keep their vows. But, in striking contrast, Prince Hal pays all his debts, even those he never promised, and keeps his vow to his father (by saving the king's life, killing Hotspur, and distinguishing himself at Shrewsbury) ...Hal fulfills his promises and debts: to the Sheriff, to the King, to England.'[41]

Henry fails to realize fully until the last that Hal is as astute as he as an econo-political theorist. Just as Henry uses and then abandons his 'agents,' the Percys, who have bought the throne for him (I. iii. 165), so Hal employs Hotspur as an unwitting 'factor' whose economic successes – as Hotspur engrosses up glorious deeds – Hal will exact in a strict accounting on the battlefield and claim as his own (III. ii. 144–52).[42] Momentarily heartened by his son's economic justifications of his political actions, the king looks forward to battle as an economic transaction, a 'business' full of 'advantage' (III. ii. 163, 177, 180), where Hal shall have 'charge and sovereign trust' (III. ii. 161). Both expect the accounts to be settled in the fray, Henry having now finally appreciated Hal's delayed payment. As Hotspur notes in a haughtily ironic tone, 'The King is kind, and well we know the King/ Knows at what time to promise, when to pay' (IV. iii. 52–3); in an equally strong moment, Hal seizes the proper instant in battle to identify himself, name his worth, and assert his value and his knowledge of contracts: 'It is the Prince of Wales that threatens thee,/Who never promiseth but he means to pay' (V. iv. 42–3).

The best payment (or the most desirable redemption) stems from an affirmation of contractual economic understanding. The Percys, though expecting a reward for their assistance to Bolingbroke in helping him seize the crown, lose redemption through a series of weak and ineffectual contracts culminating in the 'indentures tripartite' that are ultimately disastrously broken (III. i. 1–2, 79–85). Henry washes the blood from his hands symbolically by dying in the Jerusalem chamber, but his real redemption is enacted by Hal when Hal breaks with Falstaff in *2 Henry IV*, fulfilling the early promise of 'I do, I will' (*1 Henry IV*, II. iv. 481). This redemption, however, begins on the battlefield in *1 Henry IV*, where the prince 'redeem[s]' his reputation by making 'tender' (that is, value) of his father's life (V. iv. 48–9). Recognizing his obligation as heir and affirming his father's place and worth as king, Hal asserts both individual and Lancastrian identity within the contractual flow of history.[43] Hal has learned that power inheres in a new economic ideology and language of exchange.

Hal's enduring hereditary value is made even more striking by being set against a backdrop of economic transition and debasement of traditional values. Metaphors of counterfeiting permeate the play, from the tavern in Act I to the battlefield in Act V. These metaphors reflect Henry's numismatic manipulations, which caused great confusion regarding steadfast stores of value. Stow, who links the monetary event with the future of the crown, reports of Henry in his *London Chronicle*, 'Y^e xj. yere of his reygne [1410] began ye alaye of goulde: & ye kyngs sons betyn in ye Chepe.'[44] Throughout the plays, however, Hal is characterized, especially by the economically astute Falstaff, as a 'true piece of gold' (II. iv. 492). Hal loses nothing by counterfeiting (that is, by playing roles) because he *is* value; he embodies value. His intrinsic worth is punningly underscored by comparing the prince with slang words for such coins as 'royal' (I. ii. 141). Hal may play at being a rogue; he may steal in jest and then repay the money; he may dismiss a court messenger by toying with his status and worth (II. iv. 287, 291); but he risks nothing by this symbolic counterfeiting because, as Falstaff philosophizes, 'Never call a true piece of gold a counterfeit. Thou art essentially made, without seeming so' (II. iv. 491–3).

Inheriting nobility and right rule from his father, Hal fares better than others in this time of inflation and debasement, a confusion in values caused by a confusion in true and proper government. Thus we learn that Robin the hostler died when the price of oats rose (II. i. 10–13), just as Richard was deposed partly because of economic disasters. The civil war itself reflects economic debasement and uncertainty: it causes, as Hotspur says, 'bloody noses and crack'd crowns' (that is, in one meaning, coins of a debased issue or faulty minting), and he complains that we must 'pass them current too' (II. iii. 93–4) – that is, accept them as valuable.[45] Strife is so prevalent that soldiers, like new coins, are stamped each season as a new assertion of might and value (IV. i. 4–5); and land, which traditionally lent prestige and nobility to its owner, '[y]ou may buy... now as cheap as stinking mack'rel' (II. iv. 359–60). Negation of the traditional status and power base afforded by land ownership reveals a vacuum of values for which alternative modes and more appropriate economic metaphors must be found.

Hal's understanding of the violable nature of contracts, of when and how to fulfill an obligation, stands him in good stead. War may be viewed metaphorically as a contractual economic venture, where soldiers are commodities, the king is counterfeited, and 'payment' is death. Treason too is a contract, with rigid stipulations of reward if the hazard succeeds. But Hal's primary contracts are elevated ones: to king and to God. He is able to instruct Falstaff in the latter contract before battle – 'thou owest God a death' (with a paronomasia on 'debt') – and Falstaff in turn continues to teach the prince about crafty contractual manipulation: ''Tis not due yet, I would be loath to pay him before his day' (V. i. 126–8).[46] Indeed, by counterfeiting death, Falstaff is able to forestall payment, which may be why Hal so lightly gilds the demeanor of his friend at the end of *1 Henry IV*. He will wait until the end of Part 2 to fulfill his word to Falstaff, a fitting reward for this contractual education. Again, proper timing is crucial. According to Porter, as Richard denies the existence of time until it destroys him, so Hal understands that he exists in time and will of necessity grow and change.[47] Similarly, Henry invests in the Lancastrian future by 'ventur[ing]' Hal on the field of battle (V. i. 101), and his interest or return is the shining forth of his son's true mettle.

III

2 Henry IV will show the full accrual of the king's contractual investment. At his father's death, Hal becomes surety for the Lancastrian line, accepting completely the terms of the contract of kingship: 'You won it, wore it, kept it, gave it me' (IV. v. 221). As Hal next fulfills his promise to Falstaff by banishing him, the aging knight turns to tallying up *his* debts – 'Master Shallow, I owe you a thousand pound... Sir, I will be as good as my word' (V. v. 73, 85) – realizing that the time of the contract has matured as he is growing old, and that he too will now be called to account. In this action of promised banishment, Hal, as D. J. Palmer suggests, restores some measure of Edenic perfection to his kingdom. Falstaff, the old man, has become an image of 'the unregenerate Adam in the self.'[48] When Hal keeps his promise by sloughing him off, the word itself has been reinvested with value.

Shakespeare employs as well the economics of theatrical self-consciousness to make us complicit in the bargain. At the end of *2 Henry IV*, the 'Epilogue' takes the stage to inform us of *our* contractual obligations: by paying our ticket price, we have contracted for pleasure, but, as we have witnessed with Falstaff, Henry, and Hotspur, our expectations must not exceed our invest- ment. If we are dissatisfied, we must, he says, 'Bate me some, and I will pay you some, and (as most debtors do) promise you infinitely' (ll. 14–16). He refers metaphorically to a common Renaissance economic practice: to pull debtors further into their clutches, usurers often pretended to forgive part of the debt, renewing the rest at an even higher rate of interest, compounded. Manner and message, vehicle and tenor of econo-contractual metaphor are thus merged in this final allusion to 'usurer's kindness.'[49]

Similarly, the lengthy wooing of Katherine in *Henry V* fulfills our expect- ation of Hal's comfortable and successful mastery of the language of contract- ing. Their union is arranged by both word and article; it is based on 'downright oaths' (V. ii. 144) and looks forward to interest on the venture, a son and heir 'compound[ed]' (l. 207).[50] Henry V restores intrinsic value to the kingship, being 'a fellow of plain and uncoin'd constancy' (ll. 153–4), at the same time as he establishes relationship in his kingdom by the more realistic and modern method of contract, employing its lexicon with all whom he encounters (as in, for example, his contract with Williams). In the final mar- riage contract, he merges public and private welfare in an attempt to ensure a prosperous economic future and a confident moral underpinning to his reign.

Through his 'quibbles' Shakespeare chronicles the historical process of linguistic / lexical valorization in the tetralogy. We have observed his investi- gation of the economics of contractual obligation in his dramatic language, and we have experienced the prevalence of contract theory ourselves as an audience community and as implicit beneficiaries of England's promised prosperity. The 'affinitie or conueniencie' of econo-contractual metaphor as 'a figure of transporte' is effectively illustrated throughout the cycle: life is a contract from God; kingship is an hereditary and political contract; treason is a doomed venture; and intrinsic values still supersede transitory exchange values in the contractual flow of history.

Acknowledgement

This paper was presented in shorter form at the 1982 annual meeting of the Modern Language Association, held in Los Angeles.

Notes

1   Samuel Johnson, 'A Preface to Shakespeare' (1765) in *Johnson on Shakespeare*, The Yale Edition of the Works of Samuel Johnson, 15 vols. (New Haven, CT: Yale University Press, 1958–85), vol. VII, ed. Arthur Sherbo, p. 74.

2   See Kenneth Muir, 'The uncomic pun', *Cambridge Journal*, 3 (1950), pp. 472–85, esp. p. 472; and Hilda Hulme, *Yours That Read Him: An Introduction to Shakespeare's Language* (London: Ginn, 1972), p. 40. In his seminal article, 'Symphonic imagery in *Richard II*', *Proceedings of the Modern Language Association*, 62 (1947), pp. 339–65, Richard D. Altick analyzes metaphor clusters in *Richard II* with a focus on earth, land, and ground as the most prominent recurring figures.

3   D. J. Palmer, interpreting this historical process in light of St Paul's advice to the Ephesians about 'redeeming the time,' suggests that Hal's reformation is a *de facto* '"recreation" of his identity in men's eyes.' To 'redeem' is in essence to be 'judged anew.' See 'Casting off the old man: history and St Paul in *Henry IV*', *Critical Quarterly*, 12 (1970), pp. 267–83, esp. pp. 268, 273.

4   James L. Calderwood, *Shakespearean Metadrama* (Minneapolis, MN: University of Minnesota Press, 1971), p. 178.

5   George Puttenham, *The Arte of English Poesie* (London: 1589), sig. V4ᵛ.

6   Terence Hawkes, *Shakespeare's Talking Animals: Language and Drama in Society* (London: Edward Arnold, 1973), pp. 37–52, 73; Ted Cohen, 'Metaphor and the cultivation of intimacy', in *On Metaphor*, ed. Sheldon Sacks (Chicago: University of Chicago Press, 1979), pp. 6–8; and Michael D. Bristol, *Carnival and Theater: Plebeian Culture and the Structure of Authority in Renaissance England* (London: Methuen, 1985), pp. 1–53, esp. pp. 37–8, 48.

7   As suggested by Marc Shell, *The Economy of Literature* (Baltimore, MD: The Johns Hopkins University Press, 1978), pp. 3–8; and Ernst H. Kantorowicz, *The King's Two Bodies: A Study in Medieval Political Theology* (Princeton, NJ: Princeton University Press, 1957), pp. 3–23.

8   Ronald R. Macdonald, 'Uneasy lies: language and history in Shakespeare's Lancastrian tetralogy', *Shakespeare Quarterly*, 35 (1984), pp. 22–39, esp. p. 26; Joseph A. Porter, *The Drama of Speech Acts: Shakespeare's Lancastrian Tetralogy* (Berkeley, CA: University of California Press, 1979), p. 37. See also Calderwood, who maintains in *Shakespearean Metadrama* that Richard's words are as bankrupt as his morality, that he uses 'a heavily ornamented, richly stylized language suited to poetic recitation,' and that he asks his subjects to play 'roles in which true words are denied' (pp. 154–63). In his subsequent development of this theme specifically in the Lancastrian tetralogy, however, Calderwood modifies this judgment. In *Metadrama in Shakespeare's Henriad: Richard II to Henry V* (Berkeley, CA: University of California Press, 1979), he suggests that Richard believes initially in the (false) equation between signifier and signified; his tragedy is the realization that metaphors are not true, that God no longer sanctions kingship as the king no longer embodies value (pp. 11–17). His study differs from mine primarily in its relation of the historical process and attitudes toward language to the self-conscious playwright and in his limited mention of the language of contracts and its implications.

9   Hawkes, *Shakespeare's Talking Animals*, pp. 79, 85.

10 Joan Webber, 'The renewal of the King's symbolic role', *Texas Studies in Literature and Language*, 4 (1963), pp. 530–38, esp. pp. 530–1.

11 Macdonald, 'Uneasy lies', pp. 33–4.

12 Calderwood, *Shakespearean Metadrama*, p. 172. On its most basic level, a critical focus on dramatic language is not a new method. Ever since Caroline Spurgeon

conveniently categorized Shakespeare's images, a popular exercise for organizing the metaphorical experience of the plays has been to search for image clusters and to realize their cumulative thematic function. Ralph Berry has recently extended and refined the cluster approach by locating in Shakespeare's dramatic method linked 'metaphor as a controlling structure.' A vital component of this formal function of metaphor clusters is cumulative impact: 'The essence of the matter is repetition and recall: a word retained in a new context receives new meanings, and retroactively affects the old.' See Caroline Spurgeon, *Shakespeare's Imagery and What it Tells Us* (New York: Macmillan, 1936); note a recent reorganization of Spurgeon's categories in Louis Charles Stagg, *The Figurative Language of the Tragedies of Shakespeare's Chief 16th-century Contemporaries, An Index* (New York: Garland, 1984); Ralph Berry, *The Shakespearean Metaphor: Studies in Language and Form* (Totowa, NJ: Rowman and Littlefield, 1978), pp. 1 and 6 (Berry includes in his methodological introduction what could be termed an anti-Levin clause, which can also be applied to my critical intent here: 'I argue, simply, for a sustained act of perception from a single angle, for the description that allows me best to account for the drama' [p. 1]; see also Altick, 'Symphonic imagery'). Kenneth Muir, in 'The uncomic pun', delineates a fourfold dramatic function of clusters of metaphor that he terms 'serious puns': they 'illogically' underscore the logical progression of the play, they act as links between seemingly unrelated linguistic figures, they work to reveal complex multiplicities on an unconscious level, and they operate by allusion to make us aware of the larger experiential reality as well as its component parts (p. 483). Following the logic of metaphorical clustering, Paul Jorgensen suggests that 'honor' and 'time' are the most prominent recurring figures in *Henry IV* and explains the problematic behavior of the prince by redefining his promised redemption of time as using it well, spending it wisely. Both J. Dover Wilson and Herschel Baker have stressed, in relation to this idea of 'using time,' the allusive prodigal son pattern of Hal's behavior, noting that his reformation is all the more stirring for his having been tempted for a time by waste and riot. See Paul A. Jorgensen, '"Redeeming time" in Shakespeare's *Henry IV*' in *Shakespeare: Henry IV Parts I and II*, ed. G. K. Hunter (London: Macmillan, 1970), pp. 231–42, esp. p. 235; J. Dover Wilson, 'Riot and the prodigal prince', in ibid., pp. 92–101, esp. pp. 96–7; and Herschel Baker, 'Introduction' to *Henry IV, Parts 1 and 2* in *The Riverside Shakespeare*, ed. G. Blakemore Evans et al. (Boston: Houghton Mifflin, 1974), pp. 842–6, esp. p. 843. Subsequent line numbers for quotations from Shakespeare's plays refer to this edition.

13 See my *Econolingua: A Glossary of Coins and Economic Language in Renaissance Drama* (Newark: University of Delaware Press, 1985), esp. pp. 16–23.

14 H. R. Coursen, *The Leasing Out of England: Shakespeare's Second Henriad* (Washington, DC: University Press of America, 1982), pp. 3–4. See also Palmer, 'Casting off the old man', p. 272.

15 Robert Hapgood organizes the language of the tetralogy by finding in each play a consistent thematic mode of speech: for him, the focus of *Richard II* is 'denunciation,' of *1 Henry IV* 'retrospection,' of *2 Henry IV* 'true and . . . false report,' and of *Henry V* 'dispute.' Porter, in part devising his own figures for the linguistic patterns of the *Henriad*, names three 'summary metaphors': an historical movement

from 'the demise of the universal authoritative language of Latin and the concurrent rise of the vernaculars,' the Tower of Babel as 'the proliferation of tongues,' and the fall of man as the loss of pure linguistic signification (*The Drama of Speech Acts*, pp. 3–4). As helpful and provocative as these patterns are, a more consistent and unified approach relating theme and metaphor would recognize the extent to which microeconomics defines the goals, reasoning, relationships, and utterances of all the characters in the process of the entire tetralogy. R. J. Dorius in part recognizes this center when he examines the figures of natural economy – like 'carelessness, excess, waste, and disease' – and their sources in an Aristotelian mean in an attempt to discern the larger thematic shape of the *Henriad*. For him, shared metaphors offer a convenient system of comparison. See Robert Hapgood, 'Shakespeare's thematic modes of speech: *Richard II* to *Henry V*', *Shakespeare Survey*, 20 (1967), pp. 41–9, esp. pp. 41–5; R. J. Dorius, 'A little more than a little', *Shakespeare Quarterly*, 11 (1960), pp. 13–26, esp. p. 13; and, for example, David Boyd, 'The player prince: Hal in *Henry IV Part 1*', *Sydney Studies in English*, 6 (1980–81), pp. 3–16, esp. p. 3.

16   Alan C. Dessen, *Shakespeare and the Late Moral Plays* (Lincoln: University of Nebraska Press, 1986), p. 80; see also Jan Lawson Hinley, 'Bond priorities in *The Merchant of Venice*', *Studies in English Literature*, 20 (1980), pp. 217–39.

17   David Scott Kastan, *Shakespeare and the Shapes of Time* (Hanover, NH: University Press of New England, 1982), p. 51.

18   Johannes Nider, *On the Contracts of Merchants*, ed. Ronald B. Shuman, trans. Charles H. Reeves (Norman: University of Oklahoma Press, 1966), p. 68.

19   It is standard critical opinion that Shakespeare employed the history play in part as contemporary commentary. See, for example, 'Introduction' in *Twentieth-century Interpretations of Richard II*, ed. Paul M. Cubeta (Englewood Cliffs, NJ: Prentice-Hall, 1971), pp. 2–3; Lily B. Campbell, *Shakespeare's 'Histories': Mirrors of Elizabethan Policy* (San Marino, CA: Huntington Library, 1947), pp. 3–7; M. M. Reese, *The Cease of Majesty: A Study of Shakespeare's History Plays* (London: Edward Arnold, 1961), pp. vii and 162; and Calderwood, *Metadrama in Shakespeare's Henriad*, pp. 1–2.

20   S. J. Stoljar, *A History of Contract at Common Law* (Canberra: Australian National University Press, 1975), pp. 5–7. See also Bracton, *De legibus et consuetudinibus angliae*, ed. George E. Woodbine, trans. Samuel E. Thorne, 4 vols (Cambridge, MA: Belknap Press, 1968), vol. II, p. 119.

21   Stoljar, *History of Contract*, p. 33.

22   See, for example, Irving Ribner, *The English History Play in the Age of Shakespeare* (1957; rev. edn, New York: Barnes and Noble, 1965), pp. 2–29; and Sir Robert Cotton, 'A Speech Touching the Alteration of Coyn' (given before Parliament in 1626 and printed in 1651) in *Select Tracts and Documents Illustrative of English Monetary History 1626–1730*, ed. William A. Shaw (1896; rpt London: George Harding, 1935), p. 24.

23   Raphael Holinshed, *The Third Volume of Chronicles* (London: 1587), pp. 496–521. The name 'Holinshed' is used throughout this essay to refer to all material contained in the *Chronicles* even though Holinshed himself was often quoting earlier chroniclers. Subsequent quotations are from this volume, and page references will be cited parenthetically in the text.

24 Hawkes, *Shakespeare's Talking Animals*, p. 76.
25 Covenant 'commands the defendant's *keeping* of an agreement: *ut teneat conven-tionem*' (Stoljar, *History of Contract*, p. 5). Interestingly, slander allows tort damages to be awarded to the plaintiff because of economic losses suffered through the impugning of reputation.
26 On the distinction between the obligations of king and landlord, see Donna B. Hamilton, 'The state of law in *Richard II*', *Shakespeare Quarterly*, 34 (1983), pp. 5–17.
27 Richard seems most to violate the second and portions of the third part of his oath: 'that he will forbid rapacity to his subjects of all degrees' and 'that he will cause all judgments to be given with equity and mercy' (Bracton, *De legibus*, vol. II, p. 304).
28 Henry had proprietary right, and he returns for his possessory right. Bracton notes the necessity of the first for legal action: 'immediately after the death of his ancestor the *proprietas* descends to the nearer heir, whether he is a minor or of full age, a male or a female, a madman or a fool, as an idiot, one who is deaf and dumb, present or absent, ignorant of the matter or apprised of it ... [P]ossession and the possessory right ought always to follow the *proprietas*' (ibid., p. 24).
29 Stoljar (*History of Contract*, p. 8) notes the widespread use of 'compurgators or oath-helpers' in early cases of breach of covenant: these people, usually twelve in number, would vouch for the veracity of the litigant's claim and could sway the case for him even if all of them were committing perjury.
30 Bracton, *De legibus*, vol. II, p. 33.
31 According to Bracton, one bound in debt by writing is *irrevocably* bound, whether or not the conditions of exchange have actually been performed. The promise stands simply 'because he has written that he owes it' (Stoljar, *History of Contract*, p. 10).
32 Fischer, *Econolingua*, p. 125.
33 Hawkes, *Shakespeare's Talking Animals*, p. 93; and Leonard F. Dean, 'From *Richard II* to *Henry V*: a closer view', in *Twentieth-century Interpretations*, ed. Cubeta, p. 61.
34 Even though the king may not be legally judged by anyone except God, 'one may say that the king has committed an *injuria*, and thus charge him with amending it ... [I]f he is without bridle, that is without law, they [the earls and barons] ought to put the bridle on him' (Bracton, *De legibus*, vol. II, p. 110; see also p. 305).
35 It was the king who initiated the actions and principles that would later become the Common Law; remedies for debt and breach of contract were awarded only in the royal courts (Stoljar, *History of Contract*, p. 3).
36 See 'The Epistle Dedicatorie' to John Wheeler, *A Treatise of Commerce* (Middelburg: 1601), sig. A4ʳ; and William Perkins, 'A Treatise of the Vocations', in *The Workes of William Perkins*, 3 vols. (London: 1612), vol. I, sig. Ttt6ʳ.
37 Dessen, *Shakespeare and the Late Moral Plays*, p. 69.
38 Boyd, 'The player prince', p. 9.
39 See Elliott Krieger, who observes that 'setting something aside implies a faith in the future, just as redeeming implies a knowledge of the past ... To exert this

control over history, people need a way of quantifying the abstract relations they as participants hold to past and future' (*A Marxist Study of Shakespeare's Comedies* [London: Macmillan, 1979], p. 138).

40   Fischer, *Econolingua*, p. 72. For examples of this use of the word 'engross,' see *Volpone*, I. i. 82; *A Mad World, My Masters*, I. i. 159; *All's Well That Ends Well*, III. ii. 65; *Romeo and Juliet*, V. iii. 115; *The Merry Wives of Windsor*, II. ii. 196; and *The Bond-Man*, I. iii. 195–6.

41   Dessen, *Shakespeare and the Late Moral Plays*, pp. 81–2.

42   Shakespeare may be underscoring his metaphor here with the legal action, developing during his time, called *assumpsit*. This was a cause of action arising from deceit in an exchange or 'breach of an express warranty of quality' (Stoljar, *History of Contract*, p. 31). Hotspur can only act for the prince, not replace him.

43   As Kastan notes, the genre of history play affords not so much a form as an 'ethical category': an examination and testing of personal action and value (*Shakespeare and the Shapes of Time*, p. 171). Jonathan Dollimore supports this function of Jacobean drama, which 'interrogates ideology... seizing on and exposing its contradictions and inconsistencies and offering alternative ways of understanding social and political process' (*Radical Tragedy: Religion, Ideology and Power in the Drama of Shakespeare and his Contemporaries* [Chicago: University of Chicago Press, 1984], pp. 3–8, esp. p. 8). See also Pierre Macherey and Etienne Balibar, 'Literature as an ideological form: some Marxist propositions', *Oxford Literary Review*, 3 (1978), pp. 4–12, esp. p. 10; and my 'Drama in a mercantilist world', *Mid-Hudson Language Studies*, 6 (1983), pp. 29–39, esp. pp. 30–1.

44   John Stow, *Two London Chronicles* in *A Camden Miscellany*, 94 vols (London: Camden Society, 1910), 3rd series, vol. XVIII, p. 1.

45   Fischer, *Econolingua*, pp. 61, 65, 99.

46   The concept of life as a contract from God is a widespread Renaissance metaphor. It was disseminated in such sermons as 'Of Almes deedes, and mercifulnesse toward the poore and needy', in *Certaine Sermons or Homilies appointed to be read in* CHVRCHES (London: John Bill, 1623), as well as in plays, as in *Cymbeline*, V. iv. 151–71.

47   Porter, *The Drama of Speech Acts*, p. 79.

48   Palmer, 'Casting off the old man', p. 268.

49   Fischer, *Econolingua*, pp. 45, 134.

50   On a similar use of this metaphorical application, see Janet P. Alwang, 'Contractual Wyatt', in *Abstracts of the Papers Presented at the Eighth Annual Mid-Hudson MLA Conference* (1982), p. 2: 'Beneath the aristocratic courtly love metaphor lies embedded the metaphor of the bargain-maker who insists on a fair return on any expenditure of devotion. The metaphor is subtle but substantial, created out of bourgeois trading terms.' See also Thomas M. Greene, 'Pitiful thrivers: failed husbandry in the sonnets', *Shakespeare and the Question of Theory*, ed. Patricia Parker and Geoffrey Hartman (New York: Methuen, 1985), pp. 230–44.

4

Gender and Sexuality

In her groundbreaking study, *Shakespeare and the Nature of Women* (1975), Juliet Dusinberre proposes that 'the drama from 1590 to 1625 is feminist in sympathy' (Dusinberre, 1975: 5). Chapters on the significance of boy-players, on chastity and virtue and on female authority develop the thesis that the stage reflected changing attitudes to women in contemporary society, and that 'Shakespeare's feminism consists of more than a handful of high-born emancipated heroines: it lies rather in his scepticism about the nature of women' (1975: 305): '[Shakespeare] did not divide human nature into the masculine and the feminine, but observed in the individual woman or man an infinite variety of union between opposing impulses. To talk about Shakespeare's women is to talk about his men, because he refused to separate their worlds physically, intellectually, or spiritually' (1975: 308).

Having established the specificity of her subject, Dusinberre seems here to conclude by erasing it. But this was only the beginning of a burgeoning critical field. Philip Kolin takes *Shakespeare and the Nature of Women* as the starting-point for his bibliography *Shakespeare and Feminist Criticism* (1991), and countless critics cite it in approbation or disagreement. Looking back over the two decades of revisionist literary scholarship since the first edition of her study, Dusinberre cites the book's place in a wider feminist politics, a 'battle about ownership' (Dusinberre, 1996: xii), connecting the debate about Shakespeare with modern gendered struggles for a critical and social position from which to speak. She admits that 'if I were rewriting the book I would have to address the theoretical problems surrounding the relation of history to the play as fiction' (1996: xxi), that 'I wouldn't now use the language of authorial intention' (1996: xxii), and that the need to discuss the plays in performance is now firmly established. This list of additional factors and changing methodologies, as well as Dusinberre's double focus on the historical context of Shakespeare's plays and current feminist debates, make her review of the state of recent feminist scholarship on Shakespeare a good introduction to the lively and wide-ranging field of gender criticism.

Following Dusinberre, Marilyn French's *Shakespeare's Division of Experience* (1981) proposed that the antagonistic 'gender principle' was of fundamental importance to Shakespeare's drama, arguing for a movement from 'profound suspicion of "feminine"' qualities in his early work towards some 'fear' of the 'masculine principle' and an idealization of the feminine (French, 1981: 17). French describes *1 Henry VI* as a war 'waged by the masculine principle against the feminine' (1981: 49), and reads in *Richard III* 'misogyny... raised in this play into a general attitude towards life' (1981: 69). In her *Comic Women, Tragic Men: A Study of Gender and Genre in Shakespeare* (1982), Linda Bamber makes it clear that her approach 'locates the feminism in the critic – not in the author or even the work'. Her argument on the history plays, excerpted in Holderness (1992), is that 'the feminine develops from an almost undifferentiated participant in the masculine adventure into an emblem of what is left out in the masculine-historical mode. Initially similar to the masculine Self, the feminine changes into something essentially different' (Holderness, 1992: 64).

Jean Howard and Phyllis Rackin's *Engendering a Nation: A Feminist Account of Shakespeare's English Histories* (1997) notes that gender analysis has tended to avoid history as a genre in which 'female characters can threaten or validate the men's historical projects but they can never take the center of history's stage or become the subjects of the narratives of patriarchal succession' (1997: 44). Their chapter on *King John* is reprinted below. As Howard and Rackin point out, sustained engagement with issues of gender and sexuality in relation to the history plays has been relatively scant. Essays by Jackson (1988) and Gutierrez (1990) on *Henry VI*, and by McMillin (1984) and Holderness (1991) on *Richard II* are outweighed by the burden of articles on the comedies and tragedies. Standard collections of feminist approaches, including Dympna Callaghan's *A Feminist Companion to Shakespeare* (2000), Kate Chedgzoy's collection of important essays representing a range of approaches to *Shakespeare, Feminism and Gender* (2001), and Barker and Kamps's *Shakespeare and Gender: A History* (1995), tend to focus on genres other than history, although these volumes offer useful methodological showcases. Barker and Kamps's historicist approach to questions of gender may seem to have gained total dominance. Writing in 1987, however, Lynda Boose defended more psychoanalytical approaches to gender criticism against this historicist orthodoxy, arguing that new historicism tended to marginalize issues of gender, and that the stress on male actors often seemed to imply that 'there are no more women in Shakespeare's plays' (Boose, 1987: 730). For a vehemently argued account challenging the premise of feminist or gender-based approaches, see Brian Vickers's

Appropriating Shakespeare (1993), and, in particular, his chapter 'Feminist Stereotypes: Misogyny, Patriarchy, Bombast'.

Gender criticism has also focused on masculinity and on male identity. Coppélia Kahn's *Man's Estate: Masculine Identity in Shakespeare* (1981) argues that Shakespeare's 'male characters are engaged in a continuous struggle, first to form a masculine identity, then to be secure and productive in it' (Kahn, 1981: 1). Father–son bonds in the history plays are considered by Kahn, and by Peter Erickson in his *Patriarchal Structures in Shakespeare's Drama* (1985). Erickson is less concerned with individual masculine identity, and instead engages with the social structure – sometimes benevolent, sometimes tyrannical – of patriarchal power in the plays. He argues that *Henry V* proposes 'male bonding between brothers as an alternative to the problematic tension of father–son relations' (1985: 64) and draws interesting connections to *Hamlet*.

In his *Shakespeare and Masculinity* (2000), Bruce R. Smith derives from feminist criticism an understanding of gender as historical and social construction, and applies this to concepts of masculinity. The politics Robert B. Pierce focuses on are familial. His *Shakespeare's History Plays: The Family and the State* (1971) uses conduct books to establish Elizabethan expectations of family bonds and obligations, particularly focusing on the relationship between fathers and sons, and the analogy between the family and the state. Thus, 'the family is significant in the structure of *1 Henry VI*. Its system of values provides a standard to measure the disorder and moral nihilism that are infecting England and even beginning to corrupt the domestic lives of the rulers' (Pierce, 1971: 51); and the imagery of the prodigal son makes Hal 'both a son reconciled with his father and a soul reconciled with the principle of order and virtue in the universe' (1971: 219). Also on issues of masculinity are articles by Moulton (1996) and Bach (1999–2001). Robin Headlam Wells's *Shakespeare on Masculinity* (2000) discusses Shakespeare's plays as responses to and interventions in contemporary debates about militant Protestant heroic masculinity. He argues that, through his career, Shakespeare develops a more sceptical relation to this version of masculinity, and studies Prospero as the ultimate embodiment of this shift. The 'concatenation of aggression, male bonding, and homoerotic desire' in the history plays is developed in Bruce Smith's careful and thorough *Homosexual Desire in Shakespeare's England* (1991: 59). Smith reads legal, medical and literary texts to establish the relationship between the homosocial and the homosexual. Shakespeare's works are discussed in a nexus of references, including poems by Donne, Spenser and Barnfield, and plays by Marlowe and Marston.

References and Further Reading

Adelman, Janet (1992) *Suffocating Mothers: Fantasies of Maternal Origin in Shakespeare's Plays, Hamlet to The Tempest.* New York: Routledge.

Alexander, Catherine M. S. and Wells, Stanley W. (eds) (2001) *Shakespeare and Sexuality.* Cambridge: Cambridge University Press.

Bach, Rebecca Ann (1999–2001) 'Tennis balls: Henry V and testicular masculinity; or, according to the *OED*, Shakespeare doesn't have any balls', *Renaissance Drama*, 30: 3–23.

Bamber, Linda (1982) *Comic Women, Tragic Men: A Study of Gender and Genre in Shakespeare.* Stanford, CA: Stanford University Press.

Barker, Deborah and Kamps, Ivo (eds) (1995) *Shakespeare and Gender: A History.* London: Verso.

Boose, Lynda (1987) 'The family in Shakespeare studies; or – studies in the family of Shakespeareans; or – the politics of politics', *Renaissance Quarterly*, 40: 707–42.

Callaghan, Dympna (1999) *Shakespeare without Women: Representing Gender and Race on the Renaissance Stage.* London: Routledge.

——(ed.) (2000) *A Feminist Companion to Shakespeare.* Oxford: Blackwell.

Chedgzoy, Kate (ed.) (2001) *Shakespeare, Feminism and Gender.* Basingstoke: Palgrave.

Drakakis, John (ed.) (1985) *Alternative Shakespeares.* London: Methuen.

Dusinberre, Juliet (1975) *Shakespeare and the Nature of Women.* London: Macmillan, 2nd edn, 1996.

Erickson, Peter (1985) *Patriarchal Structures in Shakespeare's Drama.* Berkeley, CA: University of California Press.

French, Marilyn (1981) *Shakespeare's Division of Experience.* New York: Summit Books.

Garber, Marjorie B. (1992) *Vested Interests: Cross Dressing and Cultural Anxiety.* New York: Routledge.

Goldberg, Jonathan (1992) *Sodometries: Renaissance Texts, Modern Sexualities.* Stanford, CA: Stanford University Press.

Greenblatt, Stephen J. (1988) *Shakespearean Negotiations: The Circulation of Social Energy in Renaissance England.* Berkeley, CA: University of California Press.

Gutierrez, Nancy A. (1990) 'Gender and value in *1 Henry VI*: the role of Joan de Pucelle', *Theatre Journal*, 42: 183–93.

Holderness, Graham (1991) '"A woman's war": feminist readings of *Richard II*', in *Shakespeare Left and Right*, ed. Ivo Kamps. London: Routledge.

——(ed.) (1992) *Shakespeare's History Plays: Richard II to Henry V.* Basingstoke: Macmillan.

Howard, Jean (1988) 'Cross-dressing, the theater and gender struggle in early modern England', *Shakespeare Quarterly*, 39: 418–40.

—— and Rackin, Phyllis (1997) *Engendering a Nation: A Feminist Account of Shakespeare's English Histories.* London: Routledge.

Jackson, Gabriele Bernhard (1988) 'Topical ideology: witches, Amazons and Shakespeare's Joan of Arc', *English Literary Renaissance*, 18: 40–65.

Jardine, Lisa (1983) *Still Harping on Daughters: Women and Drama in the Age of Shakespeare.* Brighton: Harvester, 2nd edn, 1989.

Kahn, Coppélia (1981) *Man's Estate: Masculine Identity in Shakespeare*. Berkeley, CA: University of California Press.

Kolin, Philip C. (1991) *Shakespeare and Feminist Criticism: An Annotated Bibliography and Commentary*. New York: Garland.

Lenz, Carolyn Ruth Swift, Neely, Carol Thomas and Greene, Gayle (eds) (1980) *The Woman's Part: Feminist Criticism of Shakespeare*. Urbana: University of Illinois Press.

Levine, Laura (1994) *Men in Women's Clothing: Anti-theatricality and Effeminization, 1579–1642*. Cambridge: Cambridge University Press.

McMillin, Scott (1984) 'Shakespeare's *Richard II*: eyes of sorrow, eyes of desire', *Shakespeare Quarterly*, 35 (1984), pp. 40–52.

Moulton, Ian (1996) '"A monster great deformed": the unruly masculinity of Richard III', *Shakespeare Quarterly*, 47: 251–68.

Pierce, Robert B. (1971) *Shakespeare's History Plays: The Family and the State*. Columbus: Ohio State University Press.

Smith, Bruce R. (1991) *Homosexual Desire in Shakespeare's England: A Cultural Poetics*. Chicago: University of Chicago Press.

—— (2000) *Shakespeare and Masculinity*. Oxford: Oxford University Press.

Traub, Valerie (1992) *Desire and Anxiety: Circulations of Sexuality in Shakespearean Drama*. London: Routledge.

Vickers, Brian (1993) *Appropriating Shakespeare: Contemporary Critical Quarrels*. New Haven, CT: Yale University Press.

Wayne, Valerie (ed.) (1991) *The Matter of Difference: Materialist Feminist Criticism of Shakespeare*. London: Harvester Wheatsheaf.

Wells, Robin Headlam (2000) *Shakespeare on Masculinity*. Cambridge: Cambridge University Press.

Elizabeth

Leah S. Marcus

Leah Marcus's promulgation of a particular historicized consciousness she calls 'local reading' produces this densely allusive and engaging investigation of Elizabeth's refracted image in the Henry VI *plays. Marcus argues that ambivalence towards Elizabeth's rule is relayed through the portraits of female dominance, particularly in the anti-type of Joan la Pucelle in* 1 Henry VI. *Through a close attention to historical specifics, Marcus is able to reanimate a provocative topical parallel.*

Leah S. Marcus, 'Elizabeth', in *Puzzling Shakespeare: Local Reading and its Discontents* (Berkeley, CA: University of California Press, 1988), pp. 51–83.

Shakespeare is very English – too English.
Victor Hugo

In 'To the great Variety of Readers' Heminge and Condell guaranteed customer satisfaction: 'Reade him, therefore; and againe, and againe: And if then you doe not like him, surely you are in some manifest danger, not to vnderstand him. And so we leaue you to other of his Friends, whom if you need, can bee your guides: if you neede them not, you can leade your selues, and others. And such Readers we wish him' (A3r). It is a stimulus to recuperative interpretation, individual and collective: readers are bound to 'like him,' either on their own or with the guidance of those who are already his 'Friends.' Even as applied to the Bard, however, the promise is too optimistic. Readers and editors have indeed needed to 'like' Shakespeare, but in order to do so they have sometimes felt obliged to sacrifice another idea equally associated with the First Folio's editors – the idea that the plays are pure Shakespeare. What could not be 'liked' was cast off so that the universal called Shakespeare could remain intact.

The *Henry VI* plays were among the first to fall to the salvage operations of the Disintegrators. Beginning with Edmund Malone in the 1780s, numerous editors argued that only the trilogy's best scenes are 'Shakespeare'; the rest were fragments of older plays or contributions by other dramatists – Marlowe, Nashe, Peele, or Greene. Part 1 of the trilogy has been particularly vulnerable to the strategy: unlike Parts 2 and 3, *1 Henry VI* does not exist in any early printed version, and its apparent date is hard to reconcile with its apparent place in the cycle.[1] Even more than Parts 2 and 3, *1 Henry VI* is steeped in topical materials, using events from the French wars of 1422–50 to evoke numerous details of England's ongoing campaigns in France during 1591 and 1592. The play was enormously popular. It is one of the few attributed to Shakespeare for which we have a record of audience response. Thomas Nashe commented sometime before August 1592:

> How would it haue ioyed braue *Talbot* (the terror of the French) to thinke that after he had lyne two hundred yeares in his Tombe, hee should triumphe againe on the Stage, and haue his bones newe embalmed with the teares of ten thousand spectators at least (at seuerall times), who, in the Tragedian that represents his person, imagine they behold him fresh bleeding.[2]

That Talbot had been a 'terror' to the French was part of the play's appeal at a time of extreme Francophobia and 'war fever.' But the blatant patriotism that helped endear *1 Henry VI* to its 1592 audiences has repelled more recent readers. Those who have insisted most strongly on its 'newsreel' topicality have also been its most avid Disintegrators, finding it little but 'crowding, clamour and confusion,' a 'thing of threads and patches' – a piece of crude wartime propaganda which could not be 'true' Shakespeare because it was too insistently local to be 'liked.'[3]

We will never know precisely how much of *1 Henry VI* is 'true' Shakespeare. It is interesting, however, that when the play was reinstated in the canon during the 1930s and 1940s, there was one element that continued to carry the taint of inauthenticity. Readers and critics began to develop sophisticated arguments for the integrity and artistry of the trilogy as a whole, but held out for composite authorship in the portrayal of Joan La Pucelle, who appeared an impossible pastiche of laudable and despicable traits; the scurrilous, 'shameful' spectacle of her trial was particularly singled out as spurious.[4] The exposure of the sublime Maid of Orleans as a witch and strumpet was a low gesture that had to be separated from Shakespeare, lest both idealized figures fall together.

Local reading of *1 Henry VI* needs to focus on the disquieting figure of Joan. She is a key to the other topical issues engaged by the play, the unstable center of a whole set of strong contemporary resonances which we have been oddly reluctant to pick up. A third highly idealized (and deidealized) figure has to be brought into the discussion – Queen Elizabeth herself. She bore ultimate responsibility for the French campaigns of 1591–2, but her lukewarmness in pursuing them caused massive frustration among her subjects. In some ways during those war years, at least to those among her subjects who fretted under her extreme caution, Queen Elizabeth was altogether too comparable in terms of her effect on English militarism to a stage figure like Shakespeare's Joan La Pucelle.

We are accustomed to thinking of the Virgin Queen in terms of a set of clearly female identities. As celebrated in the 1580s and 1590s, she was the divine Astraea returned or, in place of the Holy Virgin banished from Protestant spirituality, a secularized Virgin Mother to the nation. She was a Queen of Shepherds, a new Deborah, a Cynthia or Diana, the unreachable object of male desire and worship. But alongside such womanly identifications, which she certainly did nothing to discourage, the queen possessed a set of symbolic male identities which are much less familiar to us, in part because they surface most frequently in her speeches and public pronouncements, in part, I suspect, because her rhetoric confounds our own preconceived notions about gender. Her subjects had similar difficulties. They were far better acquainted than we are with her complex balancing of male and female attributes, but not necessarily comfortable with her strategies. In *1 Henry VI*, Joan La Pucelle functions in many ways as a distorted image of Queen Elizabeth I. She, like Elizabeth, is a woman who 'acts like a man.' She collects about her a markedly similar set of idealized symbolic identities. Yet she belongs to the enemy camp. The figure of Joan brings into the open a set of suppressed cultural anxieties about the Virgin Queen, her identity, and her capacity to provide continuing stability for the nation. Elizabeth was loved by her subjects, but also feared and sometimes hated. She was, in the wry formulation of one of her own officials, 'More than a man, and (in troth) sometyme less than a woman.'[5]

The Queen's Two Bodies

To recognize the power and pervasiveness of the queen's disruption of ordinary gender categories, we need to plunge – for a few brief pages – into the morass of historical data, the records of sexual anomaly. As a virgin queen who steadfastly clung to her singleness, Elizabeth was unprecedented in England. Her virginity exempted her from most of the recognized categories of female experience, allowing her to preserve her independence while simultaneously tapping into the emotional power behind the images of wife and mother through fictionalized versions of herself. But the identity which lay behind all the others and lent them much of their authority was her identity as ruler. Elizabeth envisioned this primary public identity in clearly male terms. Like the earlier Tudors, she relied heavily on the juridical concept of the king's two bodies and referred to it explicitly in speeches: the monarch is at once a frail earthly being, subject to death and disease, and an immortal being, the incarnation of a sacred principle of kingship which exists along with the merely mortal body from the monarch's first anointing as king. The Boy King Edward VI's advisers had insisted that the transcendental powers of his office resided in him despite the childish weakness of his person; so Queen Elizabeth frequently appealed to her composite nature as queen: her 'body natural' was the body of a frail woman; her 'body politic' was the body of a king, carrying the strength and masculine spirit of the best of her male forebears.[6]

Even when she did not invoke the doctrine directly, as she did as early as 1558, she used it to structure an interplay between male and female royal identities. In her famous Armada speech before the troops massed at Tilbury in 1588, for example, she offered herself as a model of kingly courage:

> I have the body of a weak and feeble woman, but I have the heart and stomach of a king, and of a king of England too; and I think foul scorn that Parma or Spain, or any Prince of Europe, should dare to invade the borders of my realm; to which, rather than any dishonour should grow by me, I myself will take up arms, I myself will be your general, judge, and rewarder of every one of your virtues in the field.

Spanish invasion would be a 'dishonor' linked to her womanly weakness, a violation of intact territorial borders that would 'grow' through the Virgin Queen in particular because it would bring with it a shame like that of sexual violation. To avert the peril, Elizabeth temporarily sloughed off the marks of her vulnerable female identity and portrayed herself as a king prepared to 'take up arms' and lead the troops into battle. Her costume at Tilbury gave visual embodiment to her verbal appeal. She carried a truncheon as she rode between the ranks and wore, according to some accounts, a 'silver cuirass' – appropriate covering for the 'heart and stomach of a king.'[7]

Her strategies were successful – perhaps too successful. After the initial dispersal of the Armada, the Spanish forces never returned to renew the invasion as everyone expected them to. The queen's martial self-presentation at Tilbury was a glorious moment of patriotic triumph, but also (as we will note later on) a spectacle that aroused distinct uneasiness among Englishmen. Poets and balladeers rose gamely to the occasion, however, celebrating her Amazonian bearing and attire, praising her 'tough manliness,' her '*mascula vis*,' and her resemblance to her father, Henry VIII, 'Whose valour wanne this *Island* great renowne.' As a young woman, Elizabeth had liked to place herself directly in front of the giant Holbein portrait of Henry VIII at Whitehall, challenging those present to measure her own bearing and authority against the majestic 'splendour' of her father. At Tilbury, she claimed for herself her father's military éclat.[8]

The appearance at Tilbury was the only recorded occasion on which Elizabeth went to the extreme of adopting male attire. She and the earl of Leicester, who helped orchestrate her visit to the troops, appear to have felt that the extraordinary threat posed by the presence of the Spanish Armada off the coast demanded an extraordinary display in response.[9] But the basic rhetorical strategy Elizabeth employed on that occasion was by no means atypical. Her manly garb was not a mere warlike accoutrement, but a revelation of essence for a queen who claimed to be 'man and woman both.' In dealing with internal affairs, Elizabeth placed special emphasis on her composite nature when she needed to enforce her will upon groups of recalcitrant men. As early as 1563, for example, when she began to encounter parliamentary opposition, she argued, 'The weight and greatness of this matter might cause in me, being a woman wanting both wit and memory, some fear to speak and bashfulness besides, a thing appropriate to my sex. But yet, the princely seat and kingly throne wherein God (though unworthy) hath constituted me, maketh these two causes to seem little in mine eyes, though grievous perhaps to your ears.'[10] Or to take a more elaborate example from 1566, in response to a petition that she do the proper womanly thing – marry and declare a successor:

> As for my own part, I care not for death; for all men are mortal. And though I be a woman, yet I have as good a courage, answerable to my place, as ever my father had. I am your anointed Queen. I will never be by violence constrained to do

anything. I thank God I am endued with such qualities that if I were turned out
of the realm in my petticoat, I were able to live in any place in Christendom.

Your petition is to deal in the limitation of the succession. At this present it is
not convenient . . . But as soon as there may be a convenient time, and that it
may be done with least peril unto you – although never without great danger
unto me – I will deal therein for your safety, and offer it unto you as your Prince
and head, without request; for it is monstrous that the feet should direct the
head.[11]

These passages adapt the theory of the king's two bodies to a rhetorical
formula which Elizabeth I was to use successfully throughout her reign. She
concedes to male discomfort at being commanded by a woman through her
open acknowledgment of her weakness. But that disarming confession of
the visible truth disables her audience's resistance to the invisible truth that
follows. As monarch she exceeds them all; her participation in the undying
principle of kingship outranks their masculinity. Small chance that she
would be turned out of the nation in her petticoat! That belated reference
to her femininity in the 1566 speech, appearing after the appeal to her
father's authority and her continuation of his 'place,' takes on almost the
quality of self-inflicted sacrilege. Her self-demeaning corners the market on
that potential strategy and renders it unavailable to her subjects. In the
meantime, she has forced her audience to accept a slight reworking of the
language of sexual hierarchy. John Knox's *The First Blast of the Trumpet
against the monstrous regiment of Women* (1558) had argued vehemently that
allowing a woman to govern was as ungainly and incongruous as requiring
the 'head' to 'folowe the feet.'[12] Elizabeth's speech corrects the analogy: she
is a woman, but also the 'Prince and head.' The truly 'monstrous regiment'
would be for her male subjects, her 'feet,' to direct her.

We could argue that such appeals to kingship do not amount to the construction of a second, male identity. But Elizabeth I used a number of other
strategies which reinforced the sense of her 'body politic' as male. For one
thing, she took great care with the vocabulary used to describe her position
on the throne. She had no objection to the term *queen* and used it herself
throughout her reign. But more habitually, she referred to herself as *prince*.
The word's most basic sixteenth-century meaning was ruler, especially male
ruler; it was also applied to the eldest son of a reigning monarch. The equivalent female term was *princess*. But although Queen Elizabeth was frequently
called 'princess' in the early years of her reign and used the word of herself,
with the passing of time that feminine epithet tended to disappear in favor of
the more masculine *prince*. *Princess* was quite often, in the queen's own later
usage, a term of disparagement applied to discredited female monarchs like
Mary Queen of Scots. In her policy statements weighing the fate of the
deposed Scottish 'princess' Mary, Elizabeth calls herself 'prince.'

We can trace the gradual masculinization of Queen Elizabeth's epithets quite clearly in the formulaic openings to her proclamations. Mary Tudor's proclamations had, as often as not, begun 'The Queen our sovereign Lady,' with explicit reference to her sex. That formula is also quite common at the very beginning of Elizabeth's reign, but tends gradually to be replaced by more sexually ambiguous formulas: first 'The Queen's majesty,' then more elaborate formulas like 'the Queen's most excellent majesty in her princely nature considering' or 'Monarch and prince sovereign' substituting for the earlier 'sovereign lady.' In the early years proclamations frequently referred to her as 'princess,' in the later years, almost never. The formula 'The Queen our sovereign Lady' lingered on in contexts for which an evocation of her feminine nature was particularly appropriate: during a plague, when the measures she took assumed the aura of maternal concern for her stricken people, or in famine, in connection with feeding the hungry.[13] But otherwise she was almost always a 'prince.' In parliamentary speeches or court audiences, it was quite common for the queen to be addressed as 'princess'; in her response, she would deftly underline her own authority (and chide the presumption of her interlocutor) by referring to herself as 'prince.' Subtly, perhaps not always consciously, she constructed a vocabulary of rule which was predominantly male-identified. Gradually, perhaps not consciously, her subjects yielded to the symbolic truths she sought to convey through her precision with vocabulary and modeled their language upon her own.

At the very end of her life, as her 'mortal body' became older and frailer, she insisted more strongly upon the male component of her regal identity and began to refer to herself with increasing frequency as 'king'; for 'King,' Tudor jurists argued, 'is a Name of Continuance.'[14] In her famous Golden speech of 1601, for example, which was printed and disseminated throughout England, Elizabeth protested, in a variation of the rhetorical formula which had served her well for forty years,

> I know the title of a King is a glorious title; but assure yourself that the shining glory of princely authority hath not so dazzled the eyes of our understanding, but that we well know and remember that we also are to yield an account of our actions before the great Judge. To be a King and wear a crown is a thing more glorious to them that see it, than it is pleasant to them that bear it. For myself, I was never so much enticed with the glorious name of a King or royal authority of a Queen, as delighted that God hath made me His instrument to maintain His truth and glory... Shall I ascribe anything to myself and my sexly weakness? I were not worthy to live then; and, of all, most unworthy of the mercies I have had from God, who hath given me a heart that yet never feared any foreign or home enemy.

In a message to Parliament that same year, the speaker noted, 'She said her kingly prerogative (for so she termed it) was tender.'[15] 'For so she termed it':

the queen's contemporaries were aware of something distinctly anomalous in her adoption of male epithets for her 'body politic.' But they also grasped what she was trying to convey, commenting that in her 'Stately and Majestick comportment' she carried 'more of her Father than Mother,' and that she had 'too stately a stomach to suffer a commander'; she was 'king and queen both.'[16]

It was not only officialdom who encountered the idea of the queen's composite identity. Her proclamations were usually both printed and read with fanfare in towns and villages throughout the kingdom; her most important speeches were printed and others circulated widely in manuscript versions through alehouses and other gathering places. She herself appeared frequently in public in London and the counties. Nearly everyone living in southeast and central England would have seen her in person at one time or another and she may have used elements of her usual formulas in extemporaneous speeches on many such occasions.[17] In sermons and public entertainments, she was associated with male heroes along with the more familiar female ones. As she was a Belphoebe or Astraea, so she was often portrayed as a St George or a David, Moses or Solomon, an Alexander, an Aeneas who (symbolically) had sacrificed the Dido of her own femininity out of duty to the future of the nation. Then too, for the most educated segment of the public, the notion of the monarch as androgynous may have had a certain familiarity; this quality was not uncommonly claimed as an attribute even by male rulers like François Premier, who had himself painted with the head of a virago emerging from his breast.[18]

On at least one occasion, a subject's sudden apprehension of the queen's composite nature appears to have saved her life. The Catholic conspirator Dr William Parry revealed in 1583 that he had approached the queen intending to assassinate her as she walked alone in the Privy Garden. Just as he raised his dagger to stab her, he stopped himself, wonderfully 'appalled and perplexed,' for he saw 'in her the very likeness and image of King Henry the Seventh.' What he saw was the sacred image of kingship, of 'Continuance.' The royal composite did not always arouse such awe, however. Among ordinary people, there was rife covert speculation as to what the queen's precise gender was. A carter at Windsor complained once in her hearing that at last 'he knew the Queen was a woman,' since she had repeatedly countermanded his orders. The remark is brief but revealing: like others among her subjects, he had been doubtful whether she was female or not.[19]

As king and queen both, how could Elizabeth accommodate a husband? The politically expedient courtships which she entertained, sometimes in apparent indifference to the anxiety of her subjects, allowed her to create a particularly complex interplay of sexual identities. When actual marriage was not at issue, she won male allegiance by giving rein to her flirtatious, feminine side, as she did in the symbolic, half-playful courtships of admirers like Sir Christopher Hatton and Sir Walter Ralegh. But genuine courtship was a more complicated matter. During the years of her reign when she at least appeared to entertain the possibility of marriage, she frequently used her chosen epithet 'prince' to cool potential suitors: the subtle masculine identification of her language repulsed the potential lover even as she seemed in other ways to encourage him. The duke of Anjou (earlier Alençon) was a prime victim of the tactic: through her teasing, bewildering shifts in sexual attitude and identity, she kept her 'frog' dangling for years.[20]

One of Elizabeth's usual ploys when Parliament or her advisers pleaded with her to marry was to insist that she was already married to her kingdom. On one such occasion early in her reign she held up the hand bearing her coronation ring, seeming to portray herself symbolically as the nation's wife. She continued to use the same analogy in later years, as in an exchange recorded by Sir John Harington:

> The Queene did once aske my wife in merrie sorte, 'how she kepte my goode wyll and love, which I did alwayes mayntaine to be trulie goode towardes her and my childrene?' My Mall, in wise and discreete manner, tolde her Highnesse, 'she had confidence in her husbandes understandinge and courage, well founded on her own stedfastness not to offend or thwart, but to cherishe and obey; hereby did she persuade her husbande of her own affectione, and in so doinge did commande his' – 'Go to, go to, mistresse, saithe the Queene, you are wisely bente I finde: after such sorte do I keepe the good wyll of all my husbandes, my good people.'[21]

Toward the end of her reign, however, Elizabeth more and more frequently placed herself in the role of husband. In 1596, for example, she claimed, 'Betweene Princes and their Subiects there is a most straight tye of affections. As chaste women ought not to cast their eye upon any other than their husbands, so neither ought subiects to cast their eyes upon any other Prince, than him whom *God* hath given them. I would not have my sheepe branded with another mans marke; I would not they should follow the whistle of a strange Shepheard.' This language was not some sudden, isolated reversal of expected gender roles; by the 1590s it was familiar.[22]

One of Queen Elizabeth's most clearly womanly self-portrayals was as virgin mother to her people. She used this role throughout her reign, but particularly when the matter of the succession reared its ugly head: how, she would protest, could her people demand that she marry and produce an heir when she was already mother to them all? In an interesting recent paper, Carole Levin has shown how versions of the unsolved problem of the succession would surface to plague her at moments of political vulnerability. There were persistent rumors that the Boy King Edward VI was still alive and ready to claim his throne and a series of impostors claimed to be the long-lost king. There were also persistent rumors that Elizabeth had given birth to illegitimate children: in 1587, for example, a young man claimed to be Arthur Dudley, her unacknowledged son by the earl of Leicester. The longing for a male succession got expressed in other ways as well: one particularly impudent rebel protested 'that the land had been happy if Her Majesty had been cut off twenty years since, so that some noble prince might have reigned in her stead' – that prince, of course, being male.[23]

The longing for a male successor to Elizabeth was intense, even among the queen's most adoring subjects. One of the ways she tried to assuage that longing was by depicting herself, on a subliminal, symbolic level, as a son, her own son. Her favored term *prince* conveys this to some degree: even though it was a generic term for monarch, its more specific use was for a male heir apparent. Her perpetual status as young virgin or 'virgin Prince' even as she passed far beyond the childbearing years may have fostered the idea of her sonship, since in the sixteenth century women were commonly regarded, like boys, as immature men.[24] Costume emphasized the connection: young Tudor boys wore skirts just like their mother and sisters, with only a sword at their sides to suggest their sexual differentiation. So long as Elizabeth I's identity continued to allow the symbolic potential of growth into manhood, however irrational that hope given the fact of her womanhood, she was able to alleviate at least some of the longing for an heir.

Occasionally, she seemed to deploy her public language in ways that fostered the fantasy. When Mary Queen of Scots gave birth to a prince, Prince James, the English still hoped for the like from Elizabeth. The issue became particularly delicate when James was hailed by the Scots as 'Prince of Scotland, England, France and Ireland.' Queen Elizabeth issued a proclamation denying reports on the Scottish succession, rumors that Prince James was to 'be delivered into her majesty's hands, to be nourished in England as she should think good' and that Elizabeth meant to control the Scottish succession 'after the decease of the young prince or King without bairns.' In this context, the word *prince* is used to mean male heir to the throne. But the language that follows seems subtly to suggest that the English have no need of such a prince and such rumors. Elizabeth herself is their prince: she 'is (and by God's grace intendeth during her life to be) a prince of honor and a maintainer of truth.'[25] Like the emblematic phoenix, a device closely associated with the queen, she embodied – or tried to embody – her own succession.

Non-Western cultures offer frequent analogues to the dazzling multiform figure of Elizabeth: a woman, either a young virgin or an aging woman past menopause, who is set apart from the usual female functions and allowed access to otherwise exclusively male activities, who is perceived as androgynous and given hieratic status. In Protestant sixteenth-century England, however, there was no established institutional niche for such a figure to occupy. If it partook of the sacred, it nevertheless lacked the defined cultural status that would have allowed it to be separated from the merely deviant.[26] By emphasizing the maleness of her 'body politic,' Elizabeth was able to alleviate some of the anxiety her subjects felt about the 'monstrous regiment of Women.' In effect, she was denying that there was a woman on the throne, or at least that she as ruler was no more than a 'mere' woman. But the very strategies by which she preserved received cultural assumptions in one way violated them in another.

In Renaissance England, the image of a ruler who dressed like a woman but acted with the force and leadership of a man was an image associated with riot and festival disorder. As part of the holiday overthrow of normal hierarchy, a 'disorderly woman,' often a man in female disguise, could be placed on top: a Maid Marion or a Robin Hood disguised as an old hag, or 'Lady Skimmington,' the central figure in one of the English versions of the *charivari*, who was impersonated by men dressed as women and led a raucous procession which commonly boiled over into riot.[27] The opposite form of cross-dressing aroused the same fears. During the 1580s, women who followed the mode for wearing doublets, jerkins, and hats 'as men haue' were furiously castigated by moralists for violating the Book of Deuteronomy's injunctions against cross-dressing and creating a dangerous confusion of 'kinds': 'If they could as wel chaunge their sex, & put on the kinde of man, as they can weare apparel assigned onely to man, I think they would as verely become men indeed as now they degenerat from godly sober women, in wearing this wanton lewd kinde of attire, proper onely to men.'[28] Queen Elizabeth's self-portrayal as both man and woman, a 'woman who acted like a man,' perpetuated a complex of attributes associated with danger and 'misrule.'

The queen had ways of stifling this set of potential associations. One of the most important was that she almost never allowed her composite identity to be depicted visually. Except at Tilbury in 1588, she did not violate sexual boundaries through her actual attire. Nor, it would seem, did she allow the composite to be suggested in portraiture, except through subtle and esoteric iconography. Pictures of Elizabeth as an Amazon are all of foreign origin, or date from after her death. There is, for example, a Dutch engraving from the 1590s that depicts Elizabeth in the threatening posture of Amazonian combat which she had assumed at Tilbury. With sword raised in bellicose threat against an invading Catholic fleet, she both incarnates and protects Protestant Europe. But such images did not proliferate within England. In the 'official' Armada portraits, Elizabeth appears as a female monarch, an intact virgin whose boundaries and powers remain inviolate as a result of the dispersal of the fleet.[29] Visualizations of her *mascula vis* like that offered in the Dutch engraving were perhaps too disquieting for domestic consumption, too disruptive of the delicate balancing of male and female identities which she had imposed through language.

James Aske's *Elizabetha Triumphans* (1588), one of the most elaborate of the Armada poems, shows inklings of such disquietude. The poem sets out to record the 'wonders passing strange' accomplished by Elizabeth, wonders which surpass those of her 'Sire' Henry VIII, exceed everything, in fact, but the miracles of God. All of her 'strange' feats are triumphs over international Catholicism. By the rising of her 'Sunne,' the wolfish pope has been made to slink away and all 'Popish reliques' are 'burnt.' She has routed the French out of Scotland, defeated Mary Queen of Scots and the many conspirators who supported Mary's claim to the English throne. She has also dispelled the 'devillish arte' of popish magicians, seminary priests, and Irish rebels, and – finally and climactically – triumphed over the pope and his minions through the defeat of the Spanish Armada. Aske's poem includes bits of paraphrase of Elizabeth's speech at Tilbury. He also attempts an epic description of the strangest of her 'wonders,' her appearances before the troops. She came before them a 'Queen most like herselfe' when she was most like a male warrior:

> Not like to those who coutch on stately doune,
>   But like to Mars, the God of fearefull Warre,
>   And heaving oft to skies her warlike hands,
>   Did make herselfe Bellona-like renowned.

Despite the murkiness of his attempts at epic elevation, Aske's poem is fairly specific about Elizabeth's attire and demeanor. On the first day of her visit, she 'marched King-like' to survey the ranks as they knelt in submission before her sacred majesty. On the second day, inspired by the 'warlike show' of her troops marching in display and mock combat before her, she adopted their prowess for herself:

> Most bravely mounted on a stately steede
>   With trunchion in her hand (not used thereto)
>   And with her none, except her Liutenant,
>   Accompanied with the Lord Chamberlaine,
>   Come marching towards this her marching fight.
>   In nought unlike the Amazonian Queene,
>   Who beating downe amaine the bloodie Greekes,
>   Thereby to grapple with Achillis Stout,
>   Even at the time when Troy was sore besieged.[30]

According to Aske, Elizabeth's donning of male battle gear was an act of courage inspired by the valor of her men. And yet, once equipped, she marches out against them as though they are the enemy – she is likened to the Amazon queen (Penthesilea) who battles her way through the Greek ranks in order to fight Achilles. Once activated, her androgynous power is a threatening, implacable force that annihilates anything in its way.

Aske's account was almost certainly based on eyewitness information. Probably he was there himself. Along with the thousands of soldiers, there were numerous civilian onlookers at Tilbury. But it is unlikely that he or anyone else there saw the queen mowing down Englishmen. The menacing overtones of his description register suppressed anxiety over the uncanny image of the queen in warlike male attire. After her appearance, according to Aske, the soldiers talked of nothing but how she had showed herself before them. The dominant reaction was fervent acclaim suggestive of a 'marvellous concord, in a mutual love, betwixt a queen and her subjects.' One Spanish agent who visited Tilbury reported, 'All that day, wandering from place to place, I never heard any word spoken of her, but in praising her for her stately person, and princely behaviour.'[31] On the great day itself, discomfort at the 'strange wonder' of the queen's violation of sex roles was apparently not articulated, at least not in public. But there were signs of anxiety later on of the kind that had been expressed earlier by John Knox. He had speculated that if ancient Greeks who had argued against the rule of women were brought back to life in the Renaissance to see

> A woman sitting in iudgement, or riding frome parliament in the middest of men, hauing the royall crowne vpon her head, the sworde and sceptre borne before her, in signe that the administration of iustice was in her power: I am assuredlie persuaded, I say, that suche a sight shulde so astonishe them, that they shuld iudge the hole worlde to be transformed into Amazones, and that such a metamorphosis and change was made of all the men of that countrie, as poetes do feyn was made of the companyons of Vlisses, or at least, that albeit the outwarde form of men remained, yet shuld they iudge that their hartes were changed frome the wisdome, vnderstanding, and courage of men, to the foolishe fondnes and cowardise of women.[32]

At Tilbury, the soldiers were indeed, for a time, living under the regimen of an Amazon. Where could the blurring of sexual identities be expected to stop: if the queen, a woman, was also a man, did that mean, according to the fears of contemporary moralists about the effects of cross-dressing, that men were turned into women? In a dedicatory preface to Julius Caesar (one of Elizabeth's Masters of Requests), as Aske is discussing proper requital for benefits received, he suddenly and illogically expresses a concern 'least, I should make myselfe suspected to be of both sex.' This seemingly gratuitous remark relates to nothing in the immediate context but reverberates insistently with the subject matter of his poem, which he describes in quasi-maternal terms as the 'first fruit that my barren wit yeelded.' Other popular materials from the immediate post-Armada years display an upsurge of similar fascination with, and horror of, the Amazonian confusion of gender. Long Meg of Westminster provided a living London example: she dressed in male clothing, fought men and bested them (particularly if they were French or Spanish), and was overtly likened to the queen.[33] Aske's anxiety was a common cultural phenomenon after Tilbury. He is able to praise the sexual multivalence of his 'King-like' queen, but shows signs of fearing a like sexual indeterminacy for himself.

In Shakespeare's *1 Henry VI*, the warrior Joan of Arc has a similar uncanny, befuddling effect on English warriors and their accustomed roles. The play was staged less than four years after England's victory over the Armada, and after Elizabeth's glorious, troubling appearance at Tilbury. On that memorable occasion, she had vowed to lead a life corresponding to her mode of dress: 'I myself will take up arms; I myself will be your general, judge, and rewarder of every one of your virtues in the field.' Joan of Arc in *1 Henry VI* performs the military roles Elizabeth had promised to play in the event of Spanish invasion. Joan, however, acts the victorious soldier through nefarious supernatural means. The figure of Joan airs a wide range of anxious fantasies which had eddied about the English queen in the years leading up to the Armada victory and in the Armada year itself, fantasies which could be allowed to surface only after the worst of the Catholic threat had receded.

Astraea's Daughter

In Shakespeare's play, the dominant man–woman is demonized. Almost from her first appearance at the court of the Dauphin, Joan of Arc is associated with a mystique of virginity and power like that which surrounded Elizabeth. She is a 'holy Maid' who can work 'wondrous feats,' who has sacrificed the usual womanly roles in order to serve the nation and 'free my Countrey from Calamitie' (TLN 283).[34] Her public rhetoric often sounds like a tinny echo of Elizabeth's habitual tactics with Parliament. Joan promises the French courtiers, 'I exceed my Sex. / Resolue on this, thou shalt be fortunate, / If thou receiue me for thy Warlike Mate' (TLN 291–3). She claims to enjoy an infallible election and divine support which has some of the quality of Elizabeth's sacred 'Continuance.' And the heroic language with which her adoring 'subjects' honor her is also markedly like that which surrounded the English queen. What Elizabeth did to her recalcitrant subjects through rhetoric, Joan manages through combat. When she fights with the Dauphin Charles and 'ouercomes' him, he hails her, 'Stay, stay thy hands, thou art an

Amazon, / And fighteth with the Sword of *Debora*' (TLN 307–8). Her prowess overturns normal hierarchy – 'head' and 'feet' change places. Charles vows to be her servant, kneeling to the 'Amazon' warrior as the Tilbury troops had knelt before Elizabeth, or as her parliamentary opponents had more than once yielded to the 'male' authority of her 'body politic.'

After the victory at Orleans, Charles hails La Pucelle as 'Diuinest Creature, *Astrea's* Daughter' (TLN 644) and vows to honor her through processions, images, and 'high Festiuals': 'No longer on Saint *Dennis* will we cry, / But *Ioane de Puzel* shall be France's Saint' (TLN 669–70). In a markedly similar way, the English hailed the English Astraea – most recently in the 1591 London pageant *Decensus Astraeae*. They celebrated Elizabeth's Accession Day as a public holiday; to commemorate the victory over the Armada, they were ordered to begin celebrating a new 'saint's day' as well, St Elizabeth's Day (November 19). All the popish rites with which the French surround their venerated martial maid eerily resemble the quasi-religious ritual that surrounded England's Virgin Queen, particularly in the 1580s and after, when the cult of Elizabeth became most prominent and elaborated.

At the same time, the spectacle of the 'woman on top' in *1 Henry VI* evokes some of the same anxieties about female dominance, at least from those characters who are not immediately dependent on Joan's military prowess:

> Burgundy: ... But what's that *Puzell* whom they tearme so pure?
> Talbot: A Maid, they say.
> Bedford: A Maid? And be so martiall?
> Burgundy: Pray God she proue not masculine ere long:
> If vnderneath the Standard of the French
> She carry Armour, as she hath begun.
>
> (TLN 698–703)

The interchange can, of course, be understood as a series of bawdy puns like so many of the English remarks about the '*Puzell*.'[35] But it can also be taken literally. Contemporary moralists expressed precisely the same fear about actual women who wore elements of male attire. If Joan persists in her violation of accepted sex roles, she may eventually turn male, perhaps through the same magic that allows her to triumph over men, or perhaps through some obscure physiological mechanism, like those catalogued by Stephen Greenblatt, by which a deviant male sexuality could be stimulated in an apparent female.[36] Joan's crossing of the gender boundaries marking men off from women threatens a whole set of cultural polarities by which the categories were kept distinct. The English forces in *1 Henry VI* are markedly less tolerant of cross-dressing for military purposes than the English had been at Tilbury. Joan provokes English skepticism and anxiety of a kind which could not be voiced openly in 1588 about Queen Elizabeth and the anomalous identities she claimed.

Yet even when Joan is unmasked as a sorceress, she continues to throw off echoes of Elizabeth. Almost incredibly, the two Frenchmen she confesses to have taken as lovers are the duke of Alençon and the duke of Anjou (Reignier) – precisely the names of the two French noblemen Elizabeth had come closest to marrying in the decades before: first the duke of Anjou, then his brother the duke of Alençon, later also called Anjou.

These highly charged details are not to be found in Shakespeare's sources.[37] There are too many of them and they form too insistent a pattern to be attributable to mere chance. Rather, we are dealing here with a deliberate strategy. But what the playwright sought to accomplish through such an insistent topical overlay is another and more complicated matter. It is possible, of course, that some or all of the potentially explosive details were omitted from at least some performances. We have the play only in the 1623 folio version. The early quartos of Parts 2 and 3 of *Henry VI* omit many of the classical references which exist in the folio texts, perhaps in order to simplify the plays for performance; the same excisions could have been made for performances of Part I.[38] Yet even without the most explicit echoes, the similarities between French *Puzell* and English 'Virgin Prince' are insistent enough to have registered on some level with 1591–2 audiences. Those were years in which war fever and the passion for topical decoding were both so intense that, as one dramatist complained, he had only to mention 'bread' to be taken as referring to 'Bredan in the low countries.'[39] The image of Joan could not have been impervious to similar, probably covert, speculation.

The echoes have also registered on some level with more recent editors and critics, even though they have not been acknowledged. The unease generated by the play's impossible, insistent topicality gets expressed as something else – as vague irritation at the ungainliness of Shakespeare's language, for example, or at the incoherence of Joan's character. Despite his usual attention to historical detail, G. B. Harrison remarked of the phrase 'Astrea's Daughter,' 'The excessive use of classical names in this passage is typical of Shakespeare's early work.'[40] It is interesting that he singled out the particular passage he did to make the complaint. For the Disintegrators, similarly, the blatant but inadmissible echoing of attributes between the English Astraea and the French 'Astrea's Daughter' has almost invariably registered as textual contamination. The scenes in which men fight heroically or engage in political maneuvering (as in the Temple Garden) are most likely to be 'Shakespeare'; those containing the disturbing echoes of the language surrounding Elizabeth are 'certainly not Shakespeare.'[41] The play's topicality – even though unacknowledged – has been read as bad aesthetics, unsettling textual turbulence.

As local reading of *1 Henry VI* forces us to recognize, 'Shakespeare' in this play is inextricable from something that looks suspiciously like political sacrilege. It is not the moderate image of the Bard of the chronicle plays that we have traditionally been offered, but it is just as much Shakespeare as other things we have felt more comfortable calling by that name. That is not to say that the issue of intentionality in the play is at all clear-cut. Even as the dramatist plants the specific details which could generate subversive thoughts about the queen, he makes them part of a structure so unstable that it refuses to settle into a single set of political implications. The play's topical overlay sets in motion a broad, indefinite set of speculations about the extent to which the parallels between the two celebrated virgins can be said to hold. There is not one topical interpretation of the play, but a burgeoning, proliferating array of possible interpretations, any one or more of which might have been seized on by members of a contemporary audience. The play sets off chains of local associations, but without the subtle shaping and end-capping which we might expect to control them given the sensitivity of its subject matter. Instead, its very unsettledness is its protection. What it does is create such an open field for speculation that audience response is scattered as a prism scatters colors. What might have been taken even at this early date as the Author's Intent is unreadable because it can be read in too many different ways.

In one area of the play, according to the testimony of Thomas Nashe, audience response in 1591–2 was quite uniform: everyone (or nearly everyone) thrilled over the deeds of 'braue Talbot' and sorrowed over his death. To the extent that they admired English Talbot, early audiences probably hated French Joan, who humiliates him in combat and mocks his 'Stinking and fly-blowne' corpse. But Joan's odd resemblance to Elizabeth undercuts the appeals to patriotism, or at least sets them apart from attributes and images associated with the English queen. Let us survey, in rather scatter-shot fashion, some of the areas of possible signification in which this rift can be observed.

Most obviously, perhaps, the play's vision of an outwardly immaculate virgin 'ruler' who turns out to be a slut underneath brings common gossip about Elizabeth to pungent dramatic life. Rumors about the sexual appetites of her 'mortal body' had plagued the queen throughout her reign, but became particularly rife in the 1580s and early 1590s. One Henry Hawkins claimed in 1581 that Elizabeth had had five illegitimate children by Dudley – all of them delivered while the queen was on one of her summer progresses, for 'she never goethe in progress but to be delievered.' In 1587, as we have noted, a young Englishman who was arrested in Spain on charges of espionage claimed to be the queen's illegitimate child by Dudley: he provided interrogators with an elaborate story about how he had been kept in England incognito and finally escaped to the Continent. In 1590, one

Dionisia Deryck declared that Elizabeth 'hath already had as many children as I, and that two of them were yet alive, one a man child and the other a maiden child, and the others were burned.' Leicester, their father, had 'wrapped them up in the embers in the chimney which was in the chamber where they were born.' According to another similar account from the same year, Leicester 'had four children by the Queen's Majesty, whereof three were daughters and alive, and the fourth a son that was burnt.'[42] These rumors were likeliest in places and times of extreme disaffection, but could be encountered almost anywhere. The queen's openly flirtatious, sometimes scandalous behavior with Leicester and other favorites did nothing to dispel them. Before 1588, such 'slanderous words against Her Majesty' were often punished with imprisonment or worse; after the Armada threat had passed, perpetrators were likely to get off more lightly, perhaps by being sentenced to the pillory, where they would wear their seditious words on a paper attached to their foreheads for all passers-by to read.[43]

Joan of Arc's naming of her lovers is both a displacement and a display of rumors like those which dogged the English queen. If Elizabeth, according to persistent and seemingly independent accounts, had had secret liaisons with her favorites and made a practice of burning her unwanted offspring, the French *Puzell* confesses to very similar liaisons; she and the unborn child she claims to be carrying are both burned together. It is not entirely clear, however, that the image of the virgin-whore perishes along with Joan of Arc. The play can be viewed as 'pillorying' scandals about Queen Elizabeth – airing them for public inspection and repudiation through the figure of Joan of Arc, who admits her scarlet past as she stands under guard in a situation rather like that of an Elizabethan doing penance for slander. But like the pillory, the play gives public visibility to the very scandals it brands as shameful. *Henry VI Part 1* can easily be viewed as *reinforcing* the illicit English passion for 'slanderous words against Her Majesty,' again through a process of displacement and display. Its endless bawdy punning about the fallen female appetites that can lurk beneath a public self-presentation of sacred, untouchable virginity would, for contemporary audiences, have been hard to dissociate from rumors about Elizabeth.

And what are we to make of Joan's specific choice of lovers? By the 1590s, the prospect of a French marriage was dead and the queen herself was past childbearing. Nevertheless, the spectacle of a 'Pucelle' or 'Puzzell' who confesses that she has taken Alençon and Anjou as lovers conjures up grim earlier fears about the queen's seeming appetite for Frenchmen. If she married Anjou, many of her Protestant subjects were convinced she would inevitably revert to Catholicism, since, as John Stubbs put it in *The Discoverie of a Gaping Gulf whereinto England is Like to be Swallowed* (1579), 'If woman, that weaker vessel, be strong enough to drawe man through the aduantage whiche the deuill hath within our bosome, (I meane our naturall corruption and proonesse to Idolatry) how much more forcibly shall the stronger vessell pull weake woman considering that with the inequalitie of strength there is ioyned, as great or more readinesse to Idolatrye and super-stition.' The public spectacle of Elizabeth and Anjou together, as their miniatures appear together in her prayer book, enclosing between them the queen's own devotions, aroused strong anxieties among the English about the future of Protestantism. Moreover, as Stubbs argued, since the wife is subject to the husband, Elizabeth through her marriage would in effect cede England to France. In Stubbs's horrific imaginings, marriage to Anjou would engulf Elizabeth – and the nation with her – in French duplicity and disease. England would become a playground for dread agents of the Cath-olic League like Catherine de' Medici, who had engineered the St Bar-tholomew's Day Massacre and surrounded herself with 'familiar spirits' who obeyed her every wish against the Protestants.[44]

This complex of fears involving Catholic superstition, female danger, and demonism was not Stubbs's isolated vision. Although he was sentenced to lose the hand with which he had written his seditious book, there were many who shared his feelings. The queen's attempt to suppress *The Discoverie of a Gaping Gulf* merely increased public agitation. According to Ambas-sador Mendoza, Elizabeth's proclamation calling in extant copies, 'instead of mitigating the public indignation against the French, has irritated it and fanned the flame.' William Camden recorded the silent 'commiseration,' the 'apprehensions of strange doubts' and 'secret inward repining' with which spectators witnessed Stubbs's punishment.[45]

After the Armada, the secret repinings began to be vented more openly – as though with a collective sigh of relief that finally the marriage issue was defunct. In 1591, for example, Edmund Spenser had published his *Mother Hubbard's Tale*. That work was so transparently an allegory of court intrigues surrounding the French match that it was immediately suppressed, to re-appear in print only in 1611. Shakespeare's play was not, so far as we know, suppressed on stage, but unlike the other two parts of *Henry VI*, it was never published in a quarto edition – perhaps because it too, although far more fragmented and piecemeal than Spenser's political allegory, could give rise to similar associations.[46]

A common tactic during the crisis over Anjou had been to associate the French match with a return of the Wars of the Roses. Elizabeth's proclam-ation against Stubbs complained that whereas previously her subjects had conjured up images of the English civil wars in order to convince her to marry, 'to avoid all such or greater civil wars and bloodsheds as betwixt the houses of York and Lancaster,' they now used the same historical argument to *dissuade* her, thereby claiming 'contrary' effects of 'one self Cause.'[47] In *1 Henry VI*, which chronicles the opening skirmishes in the bloodshed 'betwixt' York and Lancaster, many of the chauvinistic beliefs which had fueled opposition to the queen's match with Anjou circulate around 'Astrea's Daughter.' Despite the play's pre-Reformation setting, its Englishmen are sturdy, manly 'Protestants' who mock at French Catholic credulity and cowardice. They keep their own Cardinal Winchester (the 'Scarlet Hypocrite') at arm's length on account of his association with Rome and popish corruptions. From the first, they brand Joan of Arc as a witch. In fighting the French, they fend off the specter of what England itself could become if it were absorbed back into popery, and by destroying Joan, they banish the dread vision of a debased French Catholic Elizabeth, a queen become travesty of her Protestant self. Or at least, they evacuate it temporarily. No sooner is Joan condemned to the flames than another overbearing Frenchwoman, Margaret of Anjou, emerges to reign over England.

Shakespeare's treatment of Joan could have given rise to many other associations with French and 'Popish' queens and claimants – with Elizabeth's half-sister Mary Tudor, for example, who had scourged English Protestants, or with Mary Queen of Scots, who had briefly been queen of France, who had plotted endlessly against Elizabeth and Protestantism until her execution in 1587, and who was much more openly (and justifiably) reviled as a whore than Elizabeth. But the play's reverberations between Joan and Elizabeth are by far the most insistent and most troublesome. By a perverse magnetism, the figure of Joan picks up not only contemporary fantasies about Elizabeth in her 'mortal body' as a woman but also more covert and extraordinary fantasies about Elizabeth's self-presentation in her 'immortal body' as a man. Reading John Stubbs's tract, we can sense that after the terrible fright caused by the French marriage negotiations of the 1560s and 1570s, the idea of Elizabeth as male in her 'body politic' came to have a certain attractiveness. Stubbs calls her the 'Eue' but also the 'Adam' of the national Eden, 'our Adam & soueraigne Lord or lordly Lady of this Land,' as though to remind the queen in that way that her composite identity as ruler was incompatible with marriage.[48] And yet, as we have already noticed, the queen's *mascula vis* could give rise to its own set of anxieties, particularly after Tilbury, 1588.

Throughout the *Henry VI* cycle, female dominance is associated with bloody rites of violence and 'misrule.' But there is a particular concentration of such motifs in Part 1, which is presided over, as Renaissance riots frequently were, by a cross-dressed woman. In Part 1 carnivalesque inversions proliferate like Hydra heads, almost always at the expense of the English. There is, for example, the episode of the 'Master Gunner of Orleance, and his Boy.' Taught to spy out the enemy as they file through the secret gate, the boy is able to strike down two English heroes, one of them the great Salisbury, who had overcome in 'thirteene Battailes.'[49] Similarly, after the first English victory of the play, Alençon compares the victorious English to '*Samsons* and *Goliasses*' (TLN 230). What he intends is a reference to military might: in

Edward III's time, England had bred Olivers and Rowlands; now she has given birth to a new race of heroes. But the names he chooses are both associated with the motif of destruction through inversion: Samson was defeated by Delilah, a woman; Goliath, by David, a young boy. Throughout the play, Talbot is a particular target for just such reversals. He is verbally humiliated in the episode with the countess of Auvergne, who is incredulous that such a 'Child' and weak 'shrimpe' can be the mighty warrior. His dealings with the young Henry VI have some of the same quality of topsy-turvydom: the hero must defer to the sovereign authority of a child. But the play's most flamboyant inversion is the figure of Joan triumphant. She is lethal to English manhood – on stage, she drives English troops like 'Doues' and puppies before her without so much as a fight (TLN 618). Whenever she encounters Talbot, she bests or equals him. Even after her powers have been proved fallible by the English recovery of Orleans and Rouen, Joan maintains that Frenchmen will triumph so long as they keep her 'on top':

> Let frantike *Talbot* triumph for a while,
> And like a Peacock sweepe along his tayle,
> Wee'le pull his Plumes, and take away his Trayne,
> If Dolphin and the rest will be but rul'd.
> (TLN 1590–3)

And she does turn the tables once more. Talbot and his son die valiantly in battle against overwhelming odds, and Joan mockingly shatters the high-flown titles with which the English bear witness to his glory. Talbot the 'Earle of Shrewsbury,' and 'Great Earle of *Washford, Waterford*, and *Valence, /* Lord *Talbot* of *Goodrig* and *Vrchinfield, /* Lord *Strange* of *Blackmere*, Lord *Verdun* of *Alton*,' and so on (TLN 2295–9), lies 'fly-blowne' at her feet.

These reversals follow the pattern articulated by John Knox: when women turn Amazons and rule, men become like women, or at least lose the ability to show themselves in traditional cultural terms as men. Eventually, of course, some of the topsy-turvydom is righted. Joan's reign of 'misrule' ends when she is captured and executed. But she leaves behind her a disquieting set of associations with another woman in authority. In *1 Henry VI*, the ability to tolerate female rule is exclusively (and risibly) French. The play offers two competing visions of a society with the 'woman on top.' Initially, Joan appears France's savior. The Dauphin and his nobles submit to her gladly because they are caught up in her mythos of holy virginity and believe she will bring them victory. It is a partially secularized version of the traditional festival message *Deposuit potentes et exaltavit humiles*, and reverberates with the kind of self-sacrificing veneration which the English queen was also able to inspire. But the overturn of sexual hierarchy in the service of more exalted patriotic goals is something for which the English in the play express nothing but scorn. They perceive it as the effect of French superstition and credulity, and label Joan's 'monstrous regiment' over men as dangerous and deviant from the start. It is as though, in *1 Henry VI*, despising female dominance is a necessary part of being male, English, and 'Protestant.' How are we to read this pattern, given the strong topical associations between Joan and Elizabeth? The easiest response would be to take the figure of Joan as blatant and unambiguous travesty, a debased caricature of Elizabeth that is finally empty and demonic because it lacks an essential element of the queen's self-presentation, the sacred 'immortal body' of kingship. Such an interpretation would smooth over some of the play's most potentially subversive edges, but would also close off interesting areas of possible signification which emerge when *1 Henry VI* is located in terms of the national situation in 1591–2. It is time we turned briefly to the play's other and less volatile area of topicality, its evocation of materials relating to England's French campaigns during the early 1590s.

After the Armada, the English were quite unaware that they had just passed over an important national watershed. Both before and after the brief period of euphoria following the news that the Spanish fleet had been destroyed, there was widespread restiveness and disappointment that no more had been accomplished. Part of this was let-down of the type that could be expected after such a stunning triumph, but part of it was frustration that the English had been (and were continuing to be) denied the chance to come face to face with the enemy and defeat them decisively in battle. Francis Walsingham himself had written gloomily from Tilbury, 'Our half-doings doth breed dishonour and leaveth the disease uncured.' After Tilbury, the 'half-doings' had maddeningly continued.[50] In the three and a half years between the Armada and *1 Henry VI*, England had remained at war, but relatively little had happened. English troops had fought against elements of the Catholic League on the Continent, but with little to show for their efforts but yet more frustration. Moreover, some of the English commanders who had made the most brilliant showing at Tilbury were gone. The earl of Leicester, who had marched alongside the queen, had died only six weeks later; the earl of Shrewsbury, who together with his son, Lord Talbot, had made the most impressive display of troops at the camp, had died in 1590.[51]

The situation of England at the beginning of *1 Henry VI* – a time of depression and confusion after a major military triumph – closely parallels the situation of England in the early nineties. *Henry VI Part 1* begins shortly after Henry V's glorious victory at Agincourt, but the young warrior-king is dead and his French conquest is dissolving away; England in 1591–2 had experienced a similarly miraculous victory followed by a similar series of reversals and disappointments in France. Shakespeare massively rearranges fifteenth-century history in order to bring out the parallels between the two times of waning heroism. Even some of the names of heroes are the same, such as

Talbot, created earl of Shrewsbury in one of the play's seemingly extraneous scenes, and his son, Lord Talbot. The obstacles that stand in the way of clear-cut victory are, in each case, the same: a 'want of Men and Money,' a desire to gain the fruits of success without the passionate force and unanimity required to bring it about. The messenger's critique of affairs in fifteenth-century France at the beginning of *1 Henry VI* precisely parallels English objections to the conduct of the French wars of the 1590s.

> Amongst the Souldiers this is muttered,
> That here you maintaine seuerall Factions:
> And whil'st a Field should be dispatcht and fought,
> You are disputing of your Generals.
> One would haue lingring Warres, with little cost;
> Another would flye swift, but wanteth Wings:
> A third thinkes, without expence at all,
> By guilefull faire words, Peace may be obtayn'd.
> Awake, awake, English Nobilitie,
> Let not slouth dimme your Honors, new begot.
>
> (TLN 80–9)

After the assassination of Henry III of France in 1589–90, it seemed possible that France could be brought into the Protestant fold. Reformed Englishmen yearned for a commitment of money and men large enough to tilt the balance in favor of the Protestant king Henry IV and French Huguenots in their war against the Catholic Guise. Elizabeth did send some money and ammunition and promised troops, but because of severe factional feuding among the chief ministers and her own dislike for massive embroilment on the Continent, England offered French Protestants only feeble support – more 'half-doing' of the kind that 'bred dishonour.' From the point of view of militant English Protestants, there was, once again, a burning need for the 'English Nobilitie' to 'Awake, awake.'

Parallels between the French campaigns in Shakespeare's play and the earl of Essex's expedition to Rouen in 1591–2 have frequently been remarked. The expedition was intensely popular in England and volunteers flocked to join the effort. Those at home paid avid attention to the smallest scrap of information from the Continent. And Shakespeare's play gave them 'information.' Joan's signal of fire from a high tower, the English officers' surveys of fortifications and decisions about the placement of artillery, Talbot's challenge to '*Alanson*, and the rest' in Rouen, 'Will ye, like Souldiors, come and fight it out?' (TLN 1501–2), and his visit to the countess of Auvergne, even the ribald jokes about the Dauphin and his 'shriving' of Joan – all of these episodes resemble events of the Essex campaign, which were hot news in 1591–2. The parallels are not precise – and would not have had to be – in order to create a feeling of intense contemporaneity. When English audiences watched *1 Henry VI*, what they saw was a bustling, bloody palimpsest of past and present militarism.[52]

But let us not overemphasize Essex, as topical readings of Shakespeare generally do. In terms of its depiction of valor under impossible circumstances, *1 Henry VI* is even closer to a slightly earlier campaign, the French rescue mission undertaken by Baron Peregrine Bertie Willoughby and four thousand men in 1589–90. Queen Elizabeth had first authorized the expedition, then countermanded it at the last minute, too late to prevent the troops from sailing. Willoughby's men aided Henry IV's forces in the successful capture of Vendôme, 'wading through the river and ditches and climbing over the walls in most valiant manner,' and in the capture of Le Mans and Alençon. According to Willoughby himself, the Alençon garrison said 'that they would not have surrendered if they had not been more afraid of the English behind them than of the French at the breach.' Henry IV of France also praised the valor of the English troops. More than once, their presence appears to have made the difference between Huguenot victory and defeat.[53]

Elizabeth wrote Willoughby of her pride that his troops had given the lie to 'such as have conceived an opinion either of our weakness or of the decay and want of courage or other defects of our English nation.' Nevertheless, despite the continuing success of Willoughby's zealous Protestant warriors, Elizabeth failed to send them adequate money and supplies. As time wore on, they continued to fight bravely, but suffered increasingly from sickness and want of food and clothing. One of Willoughby's men was his cousin John Stubbs – the same John Stubbs who had sacrificed his right hand in 1579 to the cause of preventing Elizabeth's French match. He wrote back from France (left-handed) that it was 'an honour to [have] been in this journey,' but he included a pathetic description of the hardships suffered by the men. Stubbs and most of the rest of Willoughby's soldiers never made it back from France, despite all their 'forward endeavours and valour,' but perished of hunger and neglect. When Henry IV officially dismissed Willoughby's men (because he could not afford to pay them himself), some eighty of them stayed on to fight in the French king's army. Others straggled back to England at the beginning of 1590.[54] It is a tale very like the story of Talbot and other doughty Englishmen in *1 Henry VI*, a tale of English Protestant heroism against impossible odds and defeat as a result of a maddening and seemingly unnecessary 'want of Men and Money.' Essex's expedition, of course, renewed hopes, but it was quickly bogged down in factionalism and conflicting orders. In 1591–2, when 'ten thousand spectators at least (at seuerall times)' beheld Talbot's 'triumphe' on the stage and shed tears over his 'bleeding,' they were bewailing as well the cause of French Protantism and the doomed heroism of many of the Englishmen who had fought for it. They were shedding, perhaps, tears of rage and frustration, as well as tears of sorrow.

The villain in the affair, or at least the government official easiest to cast in the role of villain, was Queen Elizabeth herself. She had, of course, good reasons for her reluctance to enter into prolonged wars on the Continent. Money was in very short supply; she may have perceived earlier than some others that Henry IV simply could not defeat the Catholics in France. By 1593, he had himself converted with the famous comment that Paris was well worth a mass. We are dealing here, however, with public passions, not measured, judicious assessments. During the brief period when victory in France seemed to be tantalizingly within England's grasp, Elizabeth's delay and endless vacillation brought ultra-Protestants to rage and despair. If what they saw in *1 Henry VI* was a palimpsest of fifteenth-century and contemporary martial adventures in France, then the part played by Queen Elizabeth herself in the present could easily enough be related to Joan's obstruction of proto-Protestant heroism in the past. We could put the matter in terms of our own language of psychodynamics. From the perspective of militant English Protestantism, the figure of Joan is a projection of hatred and pent-up resentments which it was impossible to vent directly in full vehemence against the English monarch.

Many of the xenophobic plays of 1588–91 restaged and reworked the Armada events. John Lyly's *Midas* (1589 or 1590) refers to the Armada defeat and satirizes Philip of Spain. In Robert Wilson's *The Three Lords and Three Ladies of London* (printed 1590), Londoners bravely face a 'mighty host' of Spaniards and engineer a victory over the Armada that is 'London's achievement alone.' Wilson's *The Cobbler's Prophecy* also commemorates the Armada, focusing on treason at home.[55] Shakespeare's *1 Henry VI* follows the pattern of many of the post-Armada plays, identifying, as many of the others do, a foreign scapegoat for divisions at home, reenacting the events of the Great Year with an obsessive intensity. But Shakespeare's play is unusually explicit in its probing of the queen's part in the memorable events.

We are obviously entering a highly speculative area here, but let us press further. It is not only that Joan La Pucelle frustrates English heroism. She does so while at the same time being, in covert ways, dependent on it. Almost immediately after the death of Talbot, Joan is revealed as the witch he had all along argued her to be. With 'charming Spelles and Periapts' she summons her 'Familiar Spirits' as usual, but they refuse to do her bidding and slink away in silence (TLN 2427–39). Without them, Joan loses her ability to 'rule' over men. It is as though her black magic loses its force once it no longer has Talbot's heroism to feed on. The link is reminiscent of the 'strange wonders' of Elizabeth at Tilbury – inspired, according to contemporaries, by the martial valor of her troops, but simultaneously taking away from that valor by depriving them of the opportunity to fight. It is characteristic of the dynamics of witchcraft belief that what is attributed to divine influence in times of success can easily be reinterpreted as demonic in the case of failure. So long as Joan succeeds she and others on her side attribute her incredible victories to divine intervention. But in failure, she is associated instead with heretical traffic with demons. If we read this pattern back into the English situation at Tilbury and after, we uncover a set of covert associations between the uncanny image of Elizabeth in her *mascula vis* and ideas about witchcraft.

The witch was a particularly virulent subspecies of the Renaissance 'disorderly woman.' Witches were sexually ambiguous creatures who, according to widespread contemporary belief, often used their occult powers to prey upon male strength and sexual potency. So close was the cultural association between witchcraft and other forms of sexual reversal that individual instances of female domination were often considered evidence of witchcraft or demonic possession.[56] Queen Elizabeth faced the peculiar challenge of keeping the 'white magic' of her sacred power as ruler separate from these strong cultural associations. Disaffected subjects attempted to use witchcraft against her – at various times during the 1580s and 1590s, officials found doll-sized replicas of the queen stuck through with pins and portraits which had been stabbed or otherwise defaced. But she was also suspected of witchcraft herself during the same years, usually by England's enemies. Scottish Catholics accused her of having been 'cosenede by the devile' in the sentencing and execution of Mary Queen of Scots, and Mary herself had made similar insinuations. In fact, Elizabeth did keep up an interesting friendship with the astrologer and 'cunning man' John Dee, but the precise nature of their relationship is unclear.[57]

After the Armada, especially on the Continent, there was occasional covert speculation that such a seemingly miraculous victory could only have been accomplished through witchcraft. Not only had the Spanish fleet been harried from the English coast after only brief naval skirmishes, but it had been almost completely destroyed by gales and mysterious naval disasters on the way home. The Armada portrait depicts just such storms in the vignette to the queen's upper right; in *1 Henry VI*, Joan's first appearance against the English is marked by a similarly portentous 'tumult,' thunder, and lightning (TLN 569–70). Particularly in the aftermath of the Armada victory, the English, like their adversaries, may have had secret questions about the power behind the queen's androgynous 'wonders' at Tilbury. In Shakespeare's play, the figure of the witch brings such anxieties into the open. The furthest limit of our speculations about Joan of Arc and Elizabeth is to suggest that Joan's demonism in the play evokes contemporary fears about Elizabeth's 'strange' and unfathomable powers – in particular, a fear that the queen's anomalous self-display as a male warrior had in some mysterious fashion drained away the efficacy of the English forces. It is yet another version of Knox's formula by which the Amazon, by taking on male attributes, reduces men to women.

Witchcraft beliefs provide a language and explanatory system contemporaries would have been likely to invoke to account for the puzzling series of post-Armada failures and the feelings of military impotence that went along with them. We in the late twentieth century might invoke a different explanatory system. In addition to the more concrete reasons for failure, we can speculate, for example, that the queen's violation of sexual boundaries may have had a real (if temporary) psychological impact upon her male subjects' sense of sexual identity and military acumen. The mighty Talbot describes his state of mind after his first encounter with Joan triumphant as a temporary loss of identity:

> I know not where I am, nor what I doe:
> A Witch by feare, not force, like *Hannibal,*
> Driues back our troupes, and conquers as she lists.
> (TLN 615–18)

If we substitute the divine for the demonic, we have a reasonable approximation of James Aske's reaction in *Elizabetha Triumphans* to the dazzling sight of the queen marching at Tilbury. She is a mysterious force that amazes and scatters her own men as though they are the enemy.

There are, of course, other aspects of the queen's complex self-presentation which could easily be read out of the play: the matter of Joan's pastoralism, for example, which can easily enough be associated with the pastoral imagery surrounding 'Eliza Queene of Shepheardes,' or the matter of Joan's bastardy (Elizabeth had also been declared illegitimate by a father), or the play's handling of ideas about succession. Once the mind starts working on the parallels between Astraea and her 'Daughter,' there is no end to the tangled speculations which the play can set in motion. What needs to be emphasized, however, is their half-formed, equivocal nature. It is easy to interpret *1 Henry VI* as a blatant call to arms in the aftermath of the Armada: 'Awake, awake, English Nobilitie, / Let not slouth dimme your Honors, new begot.' But the play's many echoes of the language surrounding Elizabeth do not add up to a similarly uniform statement unless we lean hard on one possible line of interpretation while simultaneously suppressing others.

And yet, although they do not yield an interpretation, the echoes do seem to arrange themselves according to a repeated pattern – the pattern already referred to of airing through displacement. Various possibilities for meaning collect about the figure of 'Astrea's Daughter' like a vast heap of cultural fragments. What must remain unspoken is spoken of somebody else who is either an alter ego of the queen or her debased image, but neither definitively, so that it is hard to judge whether the play would have registered with contemporaries as subversion or as containment of subversion.[...]

Notes

1   For examples of Disintegrationism, see John Dover Wilson's edition of *The First Part of King Henry VI* (1952; reprinted Cambridge: Cambridge University Press, 1968), pp. vii–lv; his 'Malone and the upstart crow', *Shakespeare Survey*, 4 (1951), pp. 56–68; and the useful overview in *Evidence for Authorship: Essays on Problems of Attribution*, ed. David V. Erdman and Ephim G. Fogel (Ithaca: Cornell University Press, 1966), pp. 438–50. The problems of authorship, dating, and sequence have been discussed by almost every editor of the play. See in particular *The Heritage Shakespeare: The Histories*, ed. Peter Alexander (New York: Heritage Press, 1958), pp. 574–87; Alexander's *Shakespeare's Henry VI and Richard III* (Cambridge: Cambridge University Press, 1929); and Madeleine Doran, *Henry VI, Parts II and III: Their Relation to the 'Contention' and the 'True Tragedy'*, University of Iowa Studies, Humanistic Studies vol. IV, no. 4 (Iowa City: University of Iowa, 1928). The consensus now is that the early quarto editions are not sources for Shakespeare's *Henry VI* plays, but either pirated editions of Parts 2 and 3 based on stage performance or (as seems even more likely) actual performance versions. See Steven Urkowitz's parallel argument for the *Richard III* quarto as acting text in 'Reconsidering the relationship of quarto and folio texts of *Richard III*', *English Literary Renaissance*, 16 (1986), pp. 442–66. The best explanation I have encountered of how the *Henry VI* plays could have been composed in chronological order with Part I coming first, yet receive contemporary notice when they did, is Hanspeter Born, 'The date of *2, 3 Henry VI*', *Shakespeare Quarterly*, 25 (1974), pp. 323–34.
2   *The Works of Thomas Nashe*, ed. Ronald B. McKerrow, vol. I (London: A. H. Bullen, 1904), p. 212. It is now generally agreed that Nashe's comment is a reference to Shakespeare's play. Since my discussion will be complex enough already, I am not dealing with variant reactions to the play – those of devout Catholics, for example, who might have been sympathetic toward French ritualism, or the reactions of women in the audience as differentiated from men. To a large degree, they probably shared the response recorded by Nashe – those were years during which the appeal to national unity overrode many other factors. Nevertheless, I should make clear in advance that my discussion will be geared toward what was perceived by Nashe as the universal response.
3   See the introduction to John Dover Wilson's edition, cited in note 1 above; S. C. Sen Gupta, *Shakespeare's Historical Plays* (London: Oxford University Press, 1964), p. 69 (Gupta is citing A. W. Ward's characterization of *1 Henry VI*); Thomas Marc Parrott, *Shakespearean Comedy* (1949; repr. New York: Russell and Russell, 1962), p. 207; W. Schrickx, 'Nashe, Greene and Shakespeare in 1592', *Revue des langues vivantes*, 22 (1956), pp. 55–64; and Leo Kirschbaum's spirited polemic against the Disintegrators, 'The authorship of *1 Henry VI*', *Proceedings of the Modern Language Association*, 67 (1952), pp. 809–22.
4   See Gupta, *Historical Plays*, p. 63; Parrott, *Shakespearean Comedy*, pp. 209–10; Hardin Craig, *An Interpretation of Shakespeare* (1948; repr. New York: Citadel Press, 1949), pp. 47–56; and E. M. W. Tillyard's discussion of critics' attitudes toward Joan of Arc in *Shakespeare's History Plays* (New York: Barnes and Noble,

1944), pp. 162–8. In a related maneuver, George Bernard Shaw argued that Shakespeare wanted to make Joan a 'beautiful and romantic figure' but was forced by his company to cater to contemporary taste, producing as a result a play that was 'poor and base in its moral tone': *Saint Joan: A Chronicle Play in Six Scenes and an Epilogue* (New York: Brentano's, 1924), xxxvi.4.6.

5 From Sir Robert Cecil's 1603 letter to Sir John Harington, printed in *Nugae Antiquae: Being a Miscellaneous Collection of Original Papers...by Sir John Harington and by Others*, ed. Thomas Park (London: J. Wright, 1804), vol. I, p. 345.

6 See Ernst Kantorowicz, *The King's Two Bodies: A Study in Mediaeval Political Theology* (Princeton, NJ: Princeton University Press, 1957), pp. 7–14; and Marie Axton, *The Queen's Two Bodies: Drama and the Elizabethan Succession* (London: Royal Historical Society, 1977), p. 38.

7 See Winfried Schleiner's important article, '*Divina Virago*: Queen Elizabeth as an Amazon', *Studies in Philology*, 75 (1978), pp. 163–80. For other references to the queen's androgynous image and related strategies, see Jonathan Goldberg, *Endlesse Worke: Spenser and the Structures of Discourse* (Baltimore, MD: The Johns Hopkins University Press, 1981), pp. 150–3; Louis Adrian Montrose, '"Shaping fantasies": figurations of gender and power in Elizabethan culture', *Representations*, I (1983), pp. 61–94; and Leonard Tennenhouse, *Power on Display: The Politics of Shakespeare's Genres* (New York: Methuen, 1986). For Elizabeth's explicit use of the doctrine of the king's two bodies, see her speech before the Lords cited in Axton, *Queen's Two Bodies*, p. 38. The fullest account of Tilbury by a biographer of Elizabeth is in Alison Plowden, *Elizabeth Regina: The Age of Triumph 1588–1603* (New York: Times Books, 1980), pp. 10–12. Contemporary accounts of Tilbury vary considerably and there is no way of being certain which is the most accurate version. Like Elizabeth's coronation, the episode remains shadowy despite its prominence: it was too anomalous to fit readily into contemporary descriptive categories. The queen's speech was apparently not printed until 1651, but that version is regarded by historians as reasonably reliable. As she spoke, her chaplain took down her words and they were read later to the troops who were too far away to hear her. The manuscript circulated widely. See Paul Johnson, *Elizabeth I: A Biography* (New York: Holt, Rinehart and Winston, 1974), p. 320 (I have cited the speech from Johnson's text); and J. E. Neale's discussion of the text of the speech in 'The sayings of Queen Elizabeth', *History*, n.s. 10 (1925–6), pp. 212–33. We will never know precisely what the queen said at Tilbury, but there is corroboration of key elements of her speech as we have it from unexpected places. See notes 30 and 31 below.

8 Schleiner, '*Divina Virago*', p. 173; Johnson, *Elizabeth I*, p. 79.

9 As Plowden points out (*Elizabeth Regina*, pp. 10–11) Leicester suggested Elizabeth's visit to his camp at Tilbury, east of London, at least in part as a way of diverting her from going down to the coast to meet the enemy in person. Her martial appearance at the camp was a symbolic display, not a genuine military encounter. However, there remained the possibility of such an encounter later on, since the Spaniards were expected to return.

10 Quoted in J. E. Neale, *Elizabeth I and her Parliaments, 1559–1581* (London: Jonathan Cape, 1953), pp. 107–8. I am also indebted to Allison Heisch's study,

'Queen Elizabeth I: parliamentary rhetoric and the exercise of power', *Signs*, I (1975), pp. 31–55, which gives excerpts from many of Elizabeth's speeches in the queen's manuscript versions.

11   Neale, *1559–1581*, pp. 149–50. At least some of her contemporaries noted the skill with which she used the strategy. See Neale, *Elizabeth I and her Parliaments, 1584–1601* (London: Jonathan Cape, 1957), pp. 248–9.

12   John Knox, *The First Blast of the Trumpet against the monstrous regiment of Women (1558)*, ed. Edward Arber (London: English Scholar's Library, 1878), p. 23. Knox's marginal note attributes the analogy to one of the homilies of Chrysostom, but it was so familiar that Elizabeth was not necessarily alluding directly either to Knox or to Chrysostom. As is well known, Knox somewhat amended his views out of deference to the Protestant queen, but the move came belatedly and grudgingly.

13   See Paul L. Hughes and James F. Larkin (eds), *Tudor Royal Proclamations*, vols 2 and 3 (New Haven, CT: Yale University Press, 1969). For illustrations of the masculinization of epithets, see, for example, vol. 2, pp. 100, 103, 144, 210, 258, 273; vol. 3, pp. 119, 121, 125, 185, 193, 198, 236, 242, 245, 256; for proclamations issued during a plague, vol. 2, pp. 236, 317, 321, 345, 420, 430, and for the later, more masculine plague-time proclamations, vol. 3, p. 121; for feeding the hungry, vol. 3, pp. 193–4. Another place where she kept the feminine forms was in contexts which also mentioned her father, but even that vestige dropped out in time. See vol. 2, pp. 364, 435, and vol. 3, p. 97. For examples of the use of *princess* to imply demeaned status, see Neale, *1584–1601*, p. 127; George P. Rice, Jr (ed.), *The Public Speaking of Queen Elizabeth* (1951; repr. New York: AMS Press, 1966), pp. 89–91; and G. B. Harrison (ed.), *The Letters of Queen Elizabeth* (1935; repr. New York: Funk and Wagnalls, 1968), pp. 180 and 219.

14   Cited from Edmund Plowden in Kantorowicz, *King's Two Bodies*, pp. 23, 407.

15   Neale, *1584–1601*, pp. 385, 388–92, 432.

16   See Johnson, *Elizabeth I*, p. 111; and Sir Robert Naunton, *Fragmenta Regalia*, ed. Edward Arber (1870; repr. New York: AMS Press, 1966), p. 15.

17   Johnson, *Elizabeth I*, pp. 323–4; Neale, *1584–1601*, p. 392; see also Louis Montrose, '"Eliza, Queene of shepheardes" and the pastoral of power', *English Literary Renaissance*, 10 (1980), pp. 153–82.

18   On the ruler as hermaphrodite see Edgar Wind, *Pagan Mysteries in the Renaissance*, 2nd edn (London: Faber and Faber, 1968), p. 214. The Holy Roman Empire, and indirectly the emperor, had been depicted symbolically as an Amazon on a famous map of Europe reproduced in Schleiner, '*Divina Virago*', p. 166, from Sebastian Münster's *Cosmography* (Basel, 1588). For Elizabeth's male analogues, see Roy Strong, *The Cult of Elizabeth* (Wallop, Hampshire: Thames and Hudson, 1977), pp. 122–4; and his *Portraits of Queen Elizabeth I* (Oxford: Clarendon Press, 1963), pp. 68, 156–7; David Bevington, *Tudor Drama and Politics: A Critical Approach to Topical Meaning* (Cambridge, MA: Harvard University Press, 1968), p. 6; and Frances A. Yates, *Astraea: The Imperial Theme in the Sixteenth Century* (London: Routledge and Kegan Paul, 1975), pp. 42–51.

19   Johnson, *Elizabeth I*, pp. 195–6, 201; Lacey Baldwin Smith, *Treason in Tudor England: Politics and Paranoia* (Princeton, NJ: Princeton University Press, 1986), p. 13.

20   See, for example, her letter to Anjou in *Letters of Queen Elizabeth*, p. 145; and on the courtship in general, the detailed account in Martin Hume, *The Courtships of Queen Elizabeth*, rev. edn (London: E. Nash, 1904).

21   *Nugae Antiquae*, vol. 1, pp. 177–8.

22   William Camden, *Annales*, trans. R. N[orton], 3rd edn (London: for Benjamin Fisher, 1635), p. 469. (Like other contemporary writers, Camden also more than once alludes to the 'masculine' virtues by which Elizabeth exceeded her sex.) In '"Eliza, Queene of shepheardes"', Louis Montrose has noted the queen's 'paradoxical analogy' without attempting to explicate it. Her parliamentary speeches often seem deliberately to befuddle her gender identification in regard to the marriage issue. See Neale, *1559–1581*, p. 127.

23   See Carole Levin, 'Queens and claimants: political insecurity in sixteenth-century England', in *Gender, Ideology, and Action: Historical Perspectives on Women's Public Lives*, ed. Janet Sharistanian (New York: Greenwood Press, 1986), pp. 41–66. See also Hume, *Courtships of Queen Elizabeth*, pp. 334–61. Examples of the queen presented as the nation's mother are easy to come by. See Neale, *1584–1601*, p. 74; Montrose, 'Shaping fantasies'; and Heisch, 'Parliamentary rhetoric', p. 54.

24   See Juliet Dusinberre, *Shakespeare and the Nature of Women* (New York: Barnes and Noble, 1975), p. 95.

25   *Tudor Royal Proclamations*, vol. 1, p. 308. Of course, the issue of her princehood may have had important personal dimensions for her. To say that all those involved in her birth and upbringing had hoped for a boy would be to understate the matter.

26   Such separation is always, of course, a matter of degree. For discussion of non-Western analogues, see Sherry B. Ortner and Harriet Whitehead (eds), *Sexual Meanings: The Cultural Construction of Gender and Sexuality* (Cambridge: Cambridge University Press, 1981), especially the essays by Fitz John Porter Poole, pp. 116–65, and Ortner, pp. 359–409; Shirley Ardener (ed.), *Defining Females: The Nature of Women in Society* (New York: John Wiley, 1978), Introduction, pp. 41 and 47; and Kirsten Hastrup's essay, pp. 49–65. I am indebted to Judith Kegan Gardiner for suggesting both these references. A familiar if partial Western analogue is, of course, the Virgin Mary. See Geoffrey Ashe, *The Virgin* (London: Routledge and Kegan Paul, 1976). I am also indebted to William Blake Tyrrell's provocative analysis, *Amazons: A Study in Athenian Mythmaking* (Baltimore, MD: The Johns Hopkins University Press, 1984).

27   There is, by now, a fairly massive literature on the subject. See Natalie Zemon Davis, 'Women on top: symbolic sexual inversion and political disorder in early modern Europe', in *The Reversible World*, ed. Barbara A. Babcock (Ithaca: Cornell University Press, 1978), pp. 147–90, reprinted with minor revisions from Davis's book *Society and Culture in Early Modern France* (Stanford: Stanford University Press, 1975); David Underdown, *Revel, Riot, and Rebellion: Popular Politics and Culture in England 1603–1660* (Oxford: Clarendon Press, 1985), pp. 102–11; and Peter Stallybrass, '"Drunk with the cup of liberty": Robin Hood, the carnivalesque, and the rhetoric of violence in early modern England', *Semiotica*, 54 (1985), pp. 113–45.

28   Cited from Phillip Stubbes in Linda Woodbridge, *Women and the English Renaissance: Literature and the Nature of Womankind, 1590–1620* (Urbana: University of Illinois

Press, 1984), p. 139. As Woodbridge's discussion indicates (pp. 139–51), moralists linked the idea of women in masculine attire with the idea of male effeminacy.

29   See Schleiner's survey of Amazon portraits in '*Divina Virago*', and Strong, *Portraits of Queen Elizabeth I*. There is a painting of Elizabeth at Tilbury, believed to be contemporary, in St Faith's Church, Gaywood, King's Lynn, Norfolk, reproduced as the color frontispiece to A. M. Hadfield, *Time to Finish the Game: The English and the Armada* (London: Phoenix House, 1964), which shows Elizabeth surveying the troops. She appears to be carrying a sword, but not wearing a breastplate. Her head is surrounded with a ring rather like a halo. In addition to the foreign and post-Elizabethan depictions mentioned by Schleiner, Constance Jordan has argued for the Siena 'Sieve' portrait of Elizabeth as a study in royal androgyny in her 'The Siena portrait of Queen Elizabeth I and contemporary conceptions of women's rule', which she was kind enough to let me read in manuscript.

30   James Aske, *Elizabetha Triumphans* (London, 1588), cited from John Nichols's reprint in *The Progresses and Public Processions of Queen Elizabeth* (London: John Nichols, 1823), vol. 2, pp. 545–82.

31   *The Copie of a Letter sent out of England to Don Bernardin Mendosa, Ambassadour in France for the King of Spaine, declaring the State of England . . . found in the Chamber of Richard Leigh, a Seminarie Priest, who was lately executed for High Treason, committed in the time that the Spanish Armada was in the Seas* (London, 1588), reprinted in *The Harleian Miscellany*, ed. William Oldys and Thomas Park, vol. 1 (London: for John White and John Murray, 1808), pp. 142–60. Given the letter's purpose, which was to account for the failure of English Catholics to rise to the aid of the Spaniards, we should not perhaps expect the author to record anything but the strength of English patriotism. This account of Tilbury does not mention Amazonian attire – only that the queen marched 'curiously' to survey the troops with her sword carried before her. It does, however, give a paraphrase of the key part of her speech, p. 152.

32   Knox, *First Blast of the Trumpet*, pp. 12–13. I am not, of course, arguing that Knox's views were universally accepted, only that they expressed fears which many other people shared, at least partially and part of the time. As an antidote to Knox, see [John Aylmer,] *An Harborowe for Faithfvll and Trewe Svbiectes* (Strassburg, 1559), which includes a favorable comparison between Elizabeth and Joan of Arc. See also the discussion of other Amazon figures in popular materials from the 1570s and 1580s in Laura Caroline Stevenson, *Praise and Paradox: Merchants and Craftsmen in Elizabethan Popular Literature* (Cambridge: Cambridge University Press, 1984). In *Famous Victories of Henry V* (1586), for example, it is suggested that a cobbler's Amazonian wife would be a better soldier in France than he (pp. 167–8). This is very different from the marginalization of female power which we will briefly notice later on in Shakespeare's version of *Henry V*.

33   Aske is cited from John Nichols's reprint, *The Progresses and Public Processions of Queen Elizabeth*, vol. 2, p. 545. See also Woodbridge's survey of similar ideas in contemporary moralists, *Women and the English Renaissance*, pp. 139–41; and the brief survey of other poems in Leicester Bradner, 'Poems on the defeat of the

Spanish Armada', *Journal of English and Germanic Philology*, 43 (1944), pp. 447–8. Aske's comparison of himself as a writer to the 'mother' of his work is, of course, sixteenth-century commonplace, but suggestive of more than mere commonplace in combination with his earlier statement. On the parallel with Long Meg and the density of cultural preoccupation with the Amazon in the immediate post-Armada period, I am also indebted to Gabriele Bernhard Jackson's 'Topical ideology: witches, Amazons, and Shakespeare's Joan of Arc' [subsequently published in *English Literary Renaissance*, 18 (1988), pp. 40–65] which she has kindly sent me in manuscript. Working independently, she and I have arrived at remarkably similar conclusions about Joan and Elizabeth I.

34 For the purposes of this article, I use the First Folio (F1) text of the plays, quoting from Charles Hinman's facsimile edition, *The First Folio of Shakespeare* (New York, 1968). I have used Hinman's 'through line numbers' (TLNs) in giving references.

35 These are brought out with particular clarity in David Bevington's notes, *The Complete Works of Shakespeare*, ed. David Bevington, 3rd edn (Glenview, IL: Scott, Foresman, 1980), p. 560.

36 For elements of the controversy, see Woodbridge, *Women and the English Renaissance*, p. 139; and Stephen Greenblatt, 'Fiction and friction', in *Reconstructing Individualism: Autonomy, Individuality, and Self in Western Thought*, ed. David Wellbery and Thomas C. Heller (Stanford: Stanford University Press, 1986), pp. 30–52. The two accounts may appear contradictory, but Greenblatt is discussing physiology and Woodbridge, gender construction. It could be argued that sixteenth-century gender distinctions carried some of the cultural force they did because men and women were taken to be so physiologically homologous. In our own time, the opposite situation exists: men and women are perceived as quite distinct physiologically, and gender categories are much less clearly and rigidly defined.

37 There is one minor exception: Holinshed refers to a movement after Joan's death to rehabilitate her memory and associate her with 'Debora.' *Holinshed's Chronicles of England, Scotland, and Ireland*, vol. 3 (London: for J. Johnson et al., 1808), p. 172.

38 Doran, *Henry VI, Parts II and III*, pp. 57–9. Doran makes a strong case for the early quartos as good acting versions of Parts 2 and 3. At the time she made the argument, it was heresy; now more and more textual scholars are coming around to the same position. If *1 Henry VI* follows the pattern of these other plays, the figure of Joan would have carried most of her virulence in performance. It would have been structurally impossible to leave her out of the play altogether. Another possibility is that the references which link Joan most closely with Elizabeth were inserted later on. This strikes me as unlikely, but it cannot be ruled out altogether. The reading offered here is predicated on the assumption that Joan of Arc – in some form recognizably related to the version we have – was part of *1 Henry VI* in 1591–2 performance. That is when the figure would have had the most powerful 'local' significance.

39 Cited from Thomas Nashe, *A Countercuffe to Martin Junior* (1589), in Smith, *Treason in Tudor England*, p. 114.

40 *Shakespeare: The Complete Works*, ed. G. B. Harrison (1948; repr. New York: Harcourt, Brace and World, 1968), p. 116n.

41   See the sources cited above in notes 1, 3, and 4, especially John Dover Wilson's edition of *1 Henry VI*, which has elaborate textual notes surveying editorial opinion about the authorship of each scene. The quotation is from p. 165.

42   Cited from Levin, 'Queens and claimants', pp. 58–9; and F. G. Emmison, *Elizabethan Life: Disorder* (Chelmsford, Essex: County Council, 1970), pp. 42–3. On the ease with which such rumors were propagated, see Smith, *Treason in Tudor England*, pp. 136–7.

43   Emmison, *Elizabethan Life: Disorder*, p. 42. Emmison's evidence relates to Essex, but the suspension of earlier vigilance against treasonous remarks was a widespread phenomenon.

44   John Stubbs, *The Discoverie of a Gaping Gulf whereinto England is Like to be Swallowed* (n.p., 1579), sig. A4, B3, C2, and D3. Stubbs points out at some length that Elizabeth's marriage would plunge England into more civil wars like those of the reign of Henry VI. I am also indebted to Lloyd E. Berry, *John Stubbs' Gaping Gulf with Letters and Other Relevant Documents* (Charlottesville: University Press of Virginia, 1968).

45   Mendoza is quoted in Berry's preface to Stubbs, *Discoverie of a Gaping Gulf*, p. xxxiii. Camden is cited from his *Annales: The True and Royall History of the famous Empresse Elizabeth*, trans. Abraham Darcie (London, 1625), Book 3, pp. 16 and 67. Protestant fears were no doubt fueled by the fact that the very statute by which Elizabeth had Stubbs punished was one dating from the Catholic times of Philip and Mary.

46   See Berry's discussion in *Stubbs' Gaping Gulf*, pp. li–liv. Another example is *Willobie His Avisa* (1594), which is, whatever else it may be, a satire on the various suitors of Elizabeth. See the edition by G. B. Harrison (ed.), *Willobie His Avisa* (London: John Lane, 1926); and B. N. De Luna, *The Queen Declined: An Interpretation of Willobie His Avisa* (Oxford: Clarendon Press, 1970), which gets lost in detail but does point out the numerous parallels between the attributes of Avisa and Eliza. On the basis of the nexus of topical ideas discussed here, I would be willing to add another equally speculative possibility: the Willobie whom Avisa (Eliza) scorns might have reminded contemporaries of Lord Willoughby, whom Elizabeth had neglected to aid in France. The High Commission appears to have agreed that the work had dangerous political implications: it was ordered burned in the late 1590s.

47   Cited from the reprint of the proclamation in Berry's *Stubbs' Gaping Gulf*, pp. 150–1 (Appendix I). Stubbs's tract and the earl of Northampton's answer to it also mention the Wars of the Roses in connection with the royal marriage, Northampton claiming that the contention would indeed be 'set on foot again, if such usurpations of royal dignity continue.' See Berry's edition, p. 65 (Appendix II).

48   In the analogy, Anjou, of course, was the snake. Stubbs, *Discoverie of a Gaping Gulf*, A2r. It is tempting to speculate that Stubbs's emphasis on womanly weakness as something the queen must at all costs avoid, his subtle turning of the queen's own 'male' rhetoric against the proposed French match, may have been one of the things she found most intolerable about his tract.

49   The episode is, of course, borrowed from the chronicles; most of the other instances of inversion are not.

50 *State Papers Relating to the Defeat of the Spanish Armada*, ed. John Knox Laughton (London: Navy Records Society, 1894), vol. 2, p. 69. See also Hadfield, *Time to Finish the Game*, pp. 89–90 (on the queen's irresolution before the event) and pp. 152–74; Michael Lewis, *The Spanish Armada* (New York: Macmillan, 1960), pp. 175–83; Garrett Mattingly, *The Defeat of the Spanish Armada* (London: Jonathan Cape, 1959), pp. 285–97; and R. B. Wernham, *After the Armada: Elizabethan England and the Struggle for Western Europe 1588–1595* (Oxford: Clarendon Press, 1984), to which the following discussion is indebted. I am also indebted to the following topical studies which link the play to military events of the 1590s or more general anxieties of the period: Geoffrey Bullough, 'The uses of history', in *Shakespeare's World*, ed. James Sutherland and Joel Hurstfield (London: Edward Arnold, 1964), pp. 96–115; Bullough (ed.), *Narrative and Dramatic Sources of Shakespeare*, vol. 3 (New York: Columbia University Press, 1975), pp. 24–25; T. W. Baldwin, *On the Literary Genetics of Shakespeare's Plays 1592–1594* (Urbana: University of Illinois Press, 1959), pp. 333–4; John Dover Wilson's introduction to *Henry VI Part 1*; A. C. Hamilton, *The Early Shakespeare* (San Marino, CA: Huntington Library, 1967), pp. 14–15; Emrys Jones, *The Origins of Shakespeare* (1977; repr. Oxford: Clarendon Press, 1978), pp. 119–26 (Jones's is by far the most sensitive topical reading to date); Hereward T. Price, *Construction in Shakespeare*, University of Michigan Contributions in Modern Philology, no. 17 (Ann Arbor: University of Michigan Press, 1951), pp. 25–33 (one of the best general readings of the play); Ernest William Talbert, *Elizabethan Drama and Shakespeare's Early Plays: An Essay in Historical Criticism* (Chapel Hill, NC: University of North Carolina Press, 1963), pp. 163–4; and more generally, C. G. Thayer, *Shakespearean Politics: Government and Misgovernment in the Great Histories* (Athens: Ohio University Press, 1983), which argues that the problem of succession toward the end of Elizabeth's reign was one impetus behind Shakespeare's history plays.

51 As Emrys Jones has pointed out (*The Origins of Shakespeare*, pp. 120–1), Shrewsbury had been the longtime jailor of Mary Queen of Scots: he was in many ways strongly associated with the anti-Catholic cause. The assertion about Shrewsbury and Talbot at Tilbury comes from the letter to Mendoza (note 31 above), and is perhaps not trustworthy, but the general point about Shrewsbury's perceived public role remains valid. Shrewsbury himself was apparently not present at Tilbury, or was there only briefly, since Leicester sent him a letter describing the queen's visit.

52 See in particular Thomas Coningsby, *Journal of the Siege of Rouen, 1591*, ed. John Gough Nichols, *The Camden Miscellany, Volume the First* (n.p.: Camden Society, 1847); and John Dover Wilson's discussion in his introduction to *1 Henry VI*. Several of the discussions of topicality cited in note 49 also mention the similarities. See also Schrickx, 'Nashe, Greene and Shakespeare in 1592,' which points out parallels between contemporary pamphlet discussions of the French wars and Shakespeare's play, but uses them to argue against Shakespeare's authorship. Much ink has been spilt over whether or not the play makes use of the Rouen materials as an actual source. It is a crucial matter for dating the writing of Part 1, but not crucial in terms of audience perception of the plays in performance. Whether or not Shakespeare intended the details to recall specific episodes in France, they certainly would have been interpreted generally in terms of the French situation.

53 See the detailed discussion in Wernham, *After the Armada*, pp. 148–76. Direct quotations are from pp. 167 and 172.

54 Ibid., pp. 171, 174–5; for Stubbs's participation see also *Stubbs' Gaping Gulf*, ed. Berry, pp. xlii and xlvi.

55 There is a very helpful discussion of these plays in Bevington, *Tudor Drama and Politics*, pp. 187–211. He, however, portrays Shakespeare's *Henry* plays as moderate by the standards of other patriotic plays of the period. My reading of Joan will question that characterization.

56 See David Underdown's discussion in *Revel, Riot, and Rebellion*, pp. 38–40. On the dynamics of witchcraft beliefs more generally, see Mary Douglas, *Purity and Danger: An Analysis of Concepts of Pollution and Taboo* (London: Routledge and Kegan Paul, 1966), Introduction and pp. 98–107; Keith Thomas, *Religion and the Decline of Magic: Studies in Popular Beliefs in Sixteenth- and Seventeenth-century England* (1971; repr. Harmondsworth: Penguin, 1973), pp. 515–680; Michael MacDonald, *Mystical Bedlam: Madness, Anxiety, and Healing in Seventeenth-century England* (Cambridge: Cambridge University Press, 1981); and Alan MacFarlane, *Witchcraft in Tudor and Stuart England: A Regional and Comparative Study* (New York: Harper Torchbooks, 1970).

57 Witchcraft against Elizabeth is mentioned in James R. Siemon's excellent study, *Shakespearean Iconoclasm* (Berkeley, CA: University of California Press, 1985), p. 55. See also Strong, *Portraits of Queen Elizabeth I*, pp. 32, 40–1. For the queen's association with demonism, see Sir John Harington, *Nugae Antiquae*, vol. 1, p. 165; Paul Johnson, *Elizabeth I*, pp. 223–4; and Garrett Mattingly, *The Defeat of the Spanish Armada*, pp. 166–7. As Mattingly notes, there had been a series of well-known and alarming prophecies about a disaster which was to occur in the year 1588.

King John

Jean E. Howard and Phyllis Rackin

Howard and Rackin's account of King John *focuses on its characteristic divisions, and the way in which the female characters bear the ideological and narrative weight of this fractured play. As an explicit dramatization of contested regal legitimacy, the play's focus on maternity, on the Bastard Faulconbridge, and on genealogies of rule, is explicated and developed. Here Shakespeare pushes women to the centre of a decentred drama.*

Jean E. Howard and Phyllis Rackin, 'King John', in *Engendering a Nation: A Feminist Account of Shakespeare's English Histories* **(London: Routledge, 1997), pp. 119–33.**

Although there is no conclusive evidence for the date of *King John*'s first production (estimates range from 1591 to 1598), many scholars place it between the two tetralogies. It is tempting to accept that suggestion, because the play seems in many ways to have been conceived as an antithesis to – or perhaps a reaction against – *Richard III*. Of all Shakespeare's Elizabethan histories, *Richard III* is the one that brings the action closest to the present, and of all of them, it is most fully invested in the official Tudor version of England's medieval past, which claimed that only with the marriage of Henry Tudor and Elizabeth of York was England saved from a devastating civil war that had been God's punishment for the deposition of a legitimate king, Richard II. Looking backward to the preceding plays and forward to the Elizabethan present, *Richard III* retrospectively imposes a tidy ending on the first tetralogy: old crimes are punished, every chicken comes home to roost, and the moral account books are neatly balanced to provide a providential warrant for the accession of Henry VII. Separated from the temporal and genealogical chain that unites the two tetralogies, *King John* moves farthest back into the past, and the entire action seems designed to foreground every kind of moral and political and historiographic ambiguity. The providential justice that determines the outcome in *Richard III* is nowhere to be seen, and every attempt to resolve the action or make sense of it is immediately frustrated by the moral ambiguities of an episodic plot where success and failure ride on the shifting winds of chance. Whatever its date of composition, *King John* exposes the ideological faultlines that threatened to undermine the genealogical narratives that could make the marriage of Henry Tudor and Elizabeth of York seem a secure resolution to the civil strife which preceded it, the turning of brother against brother, father against son. If the play was produced between the two tetralogies, that may help to explain why the story of the loss and recuperation of royal authority and national integrity that ended so neatly in *Richard III* had to be restaged, but with much more difficulty and in a different way, in the second tetralogy.

In the plays of the first tetralogy, female characters fall neatly into gendered groups. Although Joan is a peasant and the Countess of Auvergne and Margaret of Anjou are aristocrats, all three are united in nationality and in their roles as enemies to the English, male protagonists' struggle to preserve the legacy of Henry V. In *Henry VI, Part II*, Margaret and Eleanor are bitter enemies, but Shakespeare characterizes them in similar terms and uses them for similar purposes: self-willed and ambitious, both women defy their husbands' authority and threaten the peace of the realm, exposing the weakness of patriarchal authority in an increasingly disordered world. In *Richard III*, Margaret is a vengeful Lancastrian widow and Elizabeth a Yorkist queen, but before the play ends they too are united with each other and with the Duchess of York in a chorus of distinctively female lamentation – all victimized and bereaved, all gifted with the power to prophesy and curse and articulate the will of Providence.

The *Henry VI* plays depict a world where male right is threatened by female wrong; in the wicked world ruled by Richard III, the women line up on the side of heaven and the Earl of Richmond. But no such simple moral equations are possible in *King John*. Its female characters will not reduce to a single class or category. Like the ambiguous ethos of the play itself, the female characters here are deeply divided, both in action and in characterization. Elinor is a soldier queen, a tough, Machiavellian dowager; Constance an outraged, lamenting mother; Blanch a compliant, helpless victim. Elinor and Constance back rival claimants for the English throne, and they wrangle openly on stage, adroitly subverting each other's claims and arguments (II. i. 120–94). Constance and Blanch are both depicted as suffering victims, but neither can be consoled without wronging the other, and when they kneel together before the Dolphin (III. i. 308–10) they do so to plead for opposite decisions.

In a well-ordered patriarchal world, women are silent or invisible. First as daughters, then as wives, they are subject to male control, and men speak and act on their behalf. But in *King John*, the fathers and husbands are dead, reduced to the status of names in history books, and the mothers survive on Shakespeare's stage to dispute the fathers' wills and threaten their patriarchal legacies. Elinor and Constance interrupt the parley between the two kings to accuse each other of adultery, each other's sons of bastardy (II. i. 120–33). Elinor impugns her grandson's birth in order to deny him the patriarchal right she knows is his (I. i. 39–43). Constance, in the name of that right, impugns the legitimacy of her husband, subverting the patriarchal lineage that authorizes her son's claim to the throne. She proposes an alternate, female genealogical chain, deriving from Elinor and conveying a heritage of sin and suffering: 'Thy sins are visited in this poor child,/ The canon of the law is laid on him,/ Being but the second generation/ Removed from thy sin-conceiving womb' (II. i. 179–82). And she refuses to hold her tongue, despite the men's commands. As Juliet Dusinberre points out, it 'is clear from reading the play – and Deborah Warner's 1988 production reinforced this impression – ... that up till the end of Act III the dramatic action is dominated by the women characters, and this is a cause of extreme embarrassment to the men on stage' (Dusinberre, 1990: 40).

Speaking with strong, irreverent voices, these women claim a place in the historical narrative and challenge the myths of patriarchal authority that the men invoke to justify their actions. When John answers the French threat with the conventional boast, 'Our strong possession and our right for us,' Elinor wittily and irreverently reminds him, 'Your strong possession much more than your right,/ Or else it must go wrong with you and me' (I. i. 39–41). When Pandulph claims that Constance lacks the 'law and warrant' that give him, the papal legate, the authority to curse John, Constance replies by challenging the law itself:

> when law can do no right,
> Let it be lawful that law bar no wrong;
> Law cannot give my child his kingdom here,
> For he that holds his kingdom holds the law;
> Therefore since law itself is perfect wrong,
> How can the law forbid my tongue to curse?
>
> (III. i. 185–90)

In *King John*, Shakespeare subjects masculine voices to skeptical feminine interrogation, and the history he represents becomes problematic, an arena for contending interests to compete and for unauthorized voices to be heard and to challenge the voices of patriarchal authority.

Like Margaret and Joan, the disorderly women in the first tetralogy, women in *King John* usurp masculine prerogatives. Elinor announces in the opening scene that she is 'a soldier' (I. i. 150), and her role is no anomaly in a play where 'ladies and pale-visag'd maids / Like Amazons come tripping after drums,' changing 'their thimbles into armed gauntlets ... their needl's to lances, and their gentle hearts / To fierce and bloody inclination' (V. ii. 154–8). Unlike Talbot, who found Joan's presence on the battlefield unnatural, the men in *King John* seem to accept the fact of warrior women, even though the presence of women seems to lead to gender blurring. The English soldiers, for example, are said to have both 'ladies' faces' and 'fierce dragons' spleens' (II. i. 68). When the Earl of Salisbury weeps, the Dolphin declares that he values those 'manly drops' above the 'lady's tears' that have melted his heart in the past (V. ii. 47–9). Both contenders for the English crown – the bold and warlike John no less than his infant rival – find their authority compromised by subjection to the domination of powerful, vociferous mothers, and the King of France bows to the threats of a mother church. Unwilling to break his truce with John lest they 'make ... unconstant children' of themselves (III. i. 243), he finally agrees to do both after Pandulph threatens that 'the Church, our mother, [will] breathe her curse, / A mother's curse, on her revolting son' (III. i. 256–7).

Blanch is the only woman in the play who is cast in the traditional feminine mold. Imported into the plot (as John, apparently, imports her into France) only for her ill-fated marriage to the Dolphin, she is placed in the archetypically feminine role of a medium of exchange between men. Blanch is perfectly docile: 'My uncle's will in this respect [i.e. the marriage] is mine. / If he see aught in you that makes him like, / That any thing he sees, which moves his liking, / I can with ease translate it to my will' (II. i. 510–13). With no will or agenda of her own, Blanch is ready to be used as an instrument of kinship arrangements, political alliance, and patriarchal succession. Perhaps taking his cue from the name of the historical character, Shakespeare depicts his Blanch as a blank page awaiting the inscription of masculine texts. To the Dolphin, Blanch is a 'table' where his own image is 'drawn' (II. i. 503). To the two kings, she is the medium in which they will write their peace treaty. And to all three men, she represents a site for the inscription of a patriarchal historical narrative.

Exercising a traditional patriarchal right by marrying his son to the blank and docile Blanch, the French king makes his strongest claim to leave a mark on history: 'The yearly course that brings this day about,' he declares, 'Shall never see it but a holy day' (III. i. 81–2). Like Elizabeth of York in *Richard III* and Katherine of France in *Henry V,* Blanch will serve as the inert female material of masculine history-making. But in *King John*, that female material also includes the recalcitrant and self-willed Elinor and Constance. Rejecting the French king's effort at prospective history-making, Constance demands,

> What hath this day deserv'd? what hath it done,
> That it in golden letters should be set
> Among the high tides in the calendar?
> Nay, rather turn this day out of the week,
> (III. i. 84–7)

And Constance's own appeal to the heavens – 'Let not the hours of this ungodly day / Wear out the [day] in peace; but ere sunset, / Set armed discord 'twixt these perjur'd kings!' (III. i. 109–11) – seems to be answered. Refusing to allow the marriage a place in the historical record, Constance rejects the news of it as a 'tale' 'misspoke, misheard' (III. i. 4–5) and later demands to have the day on which it took place removed from the calendar. Denying the men's story and demanding the literal erasure of the date, she speaks for the forces that make the writing of patriarchal history impossible in the world of this play.

Inverted by a world turned upside down, the traditional bases for order and unity become in *King John* sources of disorder and conflict. The bonds that unite mother and child serve to divide Elinor and Constance. The marriage of Blanch to the Dolphin, which momentarily promises to unite the rival forces after their inconclusive battle for Angiers, is immediately contravened by the intervention of the papal legate, Pandulph, a spokesman for a religious power as ambiguous as every other source of authority in this play; and Pandulph's intervention becomes a source of further conflict when the Dolphin uses it as an excuse to claim the English throne. Blanch, the conventional compliant woman, allows herself to be used as an instrument of kinship arrangements, political alliance, and patriarchal succession. But Constance's immediate, outraged rejection of the news of Blanch's marriage as a 'tale' 'misspoke, misheard' and her hyperbolic demand to have the day on which it took place removed from the calendar remind an audience that the political alliance the marriage is designed to effect would still leave Constance and Arthur and the hereditary rights they claim unincorporated and unappeased and that this marriage will have no impact upon history.

Failing in her traditional feminine role as a medium to unite the warring kings, Blanch becomes the embodiment of their divisions. Niece to the English king, wife to the French Dolphin, she pleads desperately for the peace her marriage was designed to secure. Having failed in her plea, she cries,

> Which is the side that I must go withal?
> I am with both, each army hath a hand,
> And in their rage, I having hold of both,
> They whirl asunder and dismember me.
> (III. i. 327–30)

This image of dismemberment makes Blanch the human embodiment of the many divisions that characterize this play – of the divisions among the female characters, of the division of the English throne between John's possession and Arthur's right, and especially of the divided allegiances that perplex the audience as they struggle with the ethical and political ambivalences that make *King John* the most disturbing of all Shakespeare's English histories. Geography and aggressive masculinity favor John against a youthful rival supported by foreign powers, and John's defiance of the papal legate – 'from the mouth of England/ ... no Italian priest/ Shall tithe or toll in our dominions' (III. i. 152–4) – must have evoked a sympathetic response from Shakespeare's audience; but John's claim to the crown is fatally compromised by his lack of genealogical authority.

Even the authority of history is compromised. In this play, it is not John but the King of France who values history and wants to write it. Philip appeals to historical genealogy to support Arthur's claim, describing him as a 'little abstract' of what 'died in' Arthur's father, which 'the hand of time/ Shall draw...into as huge a volume' (II. i. 101–3). He swears that he will put John down 'Or add a royal number to the dead, / Gracing the scroll that tells of this war's loss/ With slaughter coupled to the name of kings' (II. i. 347–9). But the historical scroll he foresees will never be written, for Philip, no less than his English enemy, lives in a world where the historical project is stalled in contradiction. No actions are conclusive, neither the wills of fathers, nor the marriages of children, nor the French king's repeated efforts at prospective history-making. John himself seems to have the last word on the subject on the one occasion – just before his death – that he associates himself with an historical text: the text he imagines is as fragile and mutable as he now sees his own life to be: 'a scribbled form, drawn with a pen/ Upon a parchment,' shrinking up against the fire that will destroy it (V. vii. 32–4).

The image of the burning parchment completes Shakespeare's picture of John's estrangement from the tradition of Tudor historiography. Tudor accounts of John's reign tended to emphasize his quarrel with the Pope, collapsing the distance between John's world and their own to depict John as a heroic prototype of Henry VIII, a patriotic English king defying the foreign power of the papacy. Compared to his predecessors, Shakespeare makes very little use of the anti-papal material, and his John is a much less sympathetic figure than theirs. Constructed in terms of difference and distance, Shakespeare's amoral portrait of John resists the patriotic appropriations of humanist historiography. Even in the twentieth century, the play has been called the 'most unhistorical' of Shakespeare's English histories (Honigmann, 1967: xxxi). John envisions his history as a fragile manuscript, the kind of text produced in his own time, not as the enduring monument that Renaissance humanists tried to create in the printed books they produced. Moreover, when John envisions the manuscript shrinking up in flames, he anticipates what would happen when the monasteries were destroyed in the time of Henry VIII, who becomes, in this construction, not the heir and fulfillment of John's historical legacy, but its destroyer.

King John has been called an 'incoherent patchwork' where 'the action is wandering and uncertain' (Honigmann, 1967: xxxi). This incoherence is moral as well as structural, and it relates closely to the crisis in patriarchal authority the play depicts. In *King John*, Shakespeare leaves his audience, like the Bastard, 'amaz'd' and lost 'among the thorns and dangers' of an incomprehensible world (IV. iii. 140–1), where every source of authority fails and legitimacy is reduced to a legal fiction. For the characters within the play, there is no clear royal authority. For the audience watching it, there is no unblemished cause and no unquestioned authority to claim their allegiance. None of these dilemmas is resolved until the end of the play when John's death ends the crisis of patriarchal authority and the Bastard adopts the idiom of historical faith and patriotic jingoism. The accession of Prince Henry, we are promised, will 'set a form upon that indigest / Which he [John] hath left so shapeless and so rude' (V. vii. 26–7). It is significant that before this reconstruction can take place, the women's voices must be stilled (Vaughan, 1989). Blanch is removed from the stage, reduced to a genealogical pretext for the Dolphin's claim to the English throne. Elinor and Constance die, offstage and unhistorically. Their deaths three days apart are reported in a single speech of six lines (IV. ii. 119–24) as if to suggest the containment of these bitter enemies within a single, gender-determined category, their reduction from vociferous actors to the silent objects of male narration. As Juliet Dusinberre has astutely observed, 'the play goes to pieces once the women leave the stage, or once the boys leave it ... and it never recovers the energy associated with the new world of the Bastard and the new generation: the boys. Or, in our terms, and certainly in Elizabethan terms, the women' (Dusinberre, 1990: 51–2).

As long as the women live and speak, they set the subversive keynote for the other characters. John and the French king trade charges of usurpation (II. i. 118–20), matching the women's mutual charges of adultery. Pandulph shares their distrustful vision of political process, embracing *realpolitik* with a cynicism that matches their own. The Bastard shares their iconoclastic idiom, satirizing the heroic language that 'talks as familiarly of roaring lions / As maids of thirteen do of puppy-dogs,' and linking it to the patriarchal authority it claims to represent when he protests, 'I was never so bethump'd with words / Since I first call'd my brother's father dad' (II. i. 459–67).

King John not only demystifies the past it represents; the Bastard's ironic soliloquies on the ways of 'worshipful society' (I. i. 184–216) and 'Commodity, the bias of the world' (II. i. 561–98) extend the critique to the time of the present theater audience; and the subversive vision implicit in the represented action also reaches back into its own prehistory to undermine the heroic image of Cordelion. Like *Henry VI, Part I*, *King John* looks back to a dead, heroic king, but while the legacy of Henry V was opposed and endangered in the world his infant son inherited but could not rule, it remained an intact and clearly defined, if increasingly remote, ideal. In *King John*, the legacy of the great Cordelion is problematized and dispersed. The audience sees his lion's skin adorning the back of the dishonorable Archduke of Austria, 'little valiant, great in villainy, / . . . ever strong upon the stronger side' (III. i. 116–17), and the same scene that describes his 'honor-giving hand' bestowing knighthood upon Robert Faulconbridge (I. i. 53) also reveals that he dishonored Faulconbridge by seducing his wife. Cordelion has left no clear successor. His only biological son is a bastard. His heir by law of primogeniture is his nephew Arthur. The Bastard has 'a trick of Cordelion's face' and 'the accent of his tongue' (I. i. 85–6), but Arthur, a dispossessed and defenseless child, has his lineal right to the throne. And John, who has neither, sits upon that throne.

The dispersion of Cordelion's legacy among three defective heirs makes it impossible even to know who is the rightful king of England, and it gives rise to the crucial issue in *King John* – the problem of legitimacy. As Herbert Lindenberger has pointed out, 'The action of historical drama is more precisely a struggle for legitimacy than a struggle for power as such. Dramas that depict a hereditary throne generally present sharply divergent readings of genealogies to justify the rights of various contenders for the throne' (Lindenberger, 1975: 160). Genealogical anxiety haunts Shakespeare's Lancastrian kings, and genealogical arguments rationalize the rebellions that plague them. *Richard III* follows what Robert Ornstein has called the 'time-honored custom for usurpers to bastardize those they overthrew' (Ornstein, 1972: 26n) when he orders Buckingham to 'infer [i.e. assert] the bastardy of Edward's children' (III. v. 75); and imputations of bastardy provide potent weapons in all the plays. In *Henry VI, Part I*, for instance, even the threat of being thought a bastard helps to persuade Burgundy to change sides in the middle of a war (*1 Henry VI*, III. iii. 60–1).

Although legitimacy is always an issue in Shakespeare's history plays, it is nowhere else so central as it is in *King John*. Failures of authority – problems of legitimacy – take a variety of forms in and around *King John*. For the characters within the play, these range from specific, literal accusations of bastardy (brought against Arthur and John as well as Philip Faulconbridge) to the general absence of any clear royal authority. For the audience watching the play, there is no unquestionably legitimate cause to claim their allegiance. For scholarly editors, the play has a problematic text and a clouded authorial genealogy. Not only does it include an abundance of fictional material not found in the historiographic sources; in addition, there is no way to know whether Shakespeare is the original author of that fictional material, since much of it is also found in a roughly contemporary play, *The Troublesome Raigne of Iohn King of England* (1591). No one has been able to determine which play was written first (although, of course, many arguments have been advanced on both sides of the question).

The entire action hangs on an unanswerable (and finally unanswered) question: 'who is the legitimate heir of Cordelion?'; and the presiding spirit of this play is not the king who gives it its name but the human embodiment of every kind of illegitimacy – the Bastard. The most powerful and dramatically compelling of the characters, the Bastard is also the one to whom John assigns 'the ordering of this present time' (V. i. 77), and the one to whom Shakespeare gives the last word in the play. The Bastard's literal illegitimacy characterizes the status of the king (who relies on 'strong possession' rather than 'right' for his throne), the problems the play explores, and the curious nature of Shakespeare's creation. The Bastard has no real place in history, neither in the chain of patriarchal succession, where he can never inherit his father's throne, nor in the historical record Shakespeare found in Holinshed. He dominates a play which is unique among Shakespeare's English histories for its own lack of historical authority. *King John* has the flimsiest of relationships to its historiographic sources, compressing and marginalizing John's dispute with Rome and the revolt of his nobles and centering instead on a historically insignificant character invented for the sixteenth-century stage.

Despite efforts to identify a historical prototype for the Bastard, the only undisputed historical source for the character is a single sentence in Holinshed on 'Philip bastard sonne to king Richard, to whom his father had given the castell and honor of Coinacke, [who] killed the vicount of Limoges, in revenge of his fathers death' (1587: II, 278). If the *Troublesome Raigne* was a source for Shakespeare's play, the Bastard has a dramatic source there, but whichever version came first, the Bastard's origins are theatrical. His role is empowered, like that of Falstaff in the Henry IV plays, not by any historical authority, but by the sheer theatrical energy of his characterization.

The fact that the Bastard is characterized in positive terms represents an important stage in the history plays' negotiations between historical authority and theatrical power. In the first tetralogy, bastardy is typically an attribute of unsympathetic characters, and theatricality is associated with subversion. The Bastard's most obvious theatrical predecessors – Joan, Jack Cade, and Richard III – are the most animated and distinctive characters in their respective plays, but they are all cast as antagonists to true royalty and the English state. The Bastard shares their vividly individualized speech, their theatrical energy, their irreverence and contempt for traditional pieties; but, unlike them, he is a loyal subject to English royalty, and an enthusiastic spokesman for English patriotism. As such, he prefigures the renegotiation of the relationship between historical authority and theatrical power that will take place in the second tetralogy. In the earlier plays, the emblematic flatness of the characters who act in the name of God and country and the uniformity of their language contrast with the vivid particularity of those who oppose providential order to pursue their own agendas. In the figure of the Bastard, the binary scheme that opposes theatrical character to historical plot breaks down, producing a character as riven by contradiction as the play he dominates. Moreover, as Peter Womack has suggested, that a bastard is the play's most vivid spokesman for 'England' and its most jingoistically patriotic figure anticipates the gradual process by which the idea of the nation became distinguishable from the idea of the monarch (Womack, 1992: 116–26). Significantly, it is during the crisis of royal legitimacy enacted in this play that an unauthorized spokesman such as the Bastard Faulconbridge can emerge both to speak for England and to become the most theatrically attractive figure in the play.

Despite the theatricality of the Bastard's characterization, the character himself is profoundly contemptuous of theatrical display and enthusiastic in his loyalty to the English crown and nation. He denounces the citizens of Angiers who watch the battle between rival kings for possession of their city by comparing them to a base-born audience 'in a theatre' who 'gape and point / At... industrious scenes and acts of death' performed by their betters (II. i. 373–6). He speaks reverently of 'the lineal state and glory of the land' (V. vii. 102) and he ends the play by swearing his 'faithful services / And true subjection everlastingly' (V. vii. 104–5) to the new king and proclaiming the jingoistic moral:

> This England never did, nor never shall,
> Lie at the proud foot of a conqueror,
> But when it first did help to wound itself.
>
> . . .
>
> Nought shall make us rue
> If England to itself do rest but true.
>
> (V. vii. 112–18)

As many critics have noted, these speeches seem inconsistent with the Bastard's earlier characterization, for just as his vivid dramatic presence implicitly betrays his origins in the theater he despises, the explicit representation within the play of his origin in bastardy inscribes him, along with the women, in the register of illicit sexuality that subverts the 'lineal state and glory of the land' to which he gives his allegiance.

These contradictions come to a head in the curious episode, which serves to introduce the Bastard, that takes up most of the first act in *King John* and exposes, like nothing else in any of Shakespeare's histories, the arbitrary and conjectural nature of patriarchal succession and the suppressed centrality of women to it. The Bastard – here called Philip Faulconbridge – and his younger brother Robert come before the king to dispute the Faulconbridge legacy, Robert claiming that his older brother is not really their father's son and should not inherit the Faulconbridge lands and title. The Faulconbridge quarrel, like the war between Arthur and John over the English throne, hinges on ambiguities and ruptures in the relationship between legal and biological inheritance. In both families – that of the king and that of the Faulconbridges – the patriarchal succession has been interrupted. John has taken the throne that belongs by law of primogeniture to Arthur, a fact that Shakespeare emphasizes by suppressing Holinshed's record of Richard I's bequest of the throne to John, by inventing Elinor's unequivocal assertion that John's claim is based on 'strong possession much more than . . . right,' and even by implying that Arthur is Cordelion's son (as he does by ambiguous wording in II. i. 2, when France describes Cordelion as the 'great forerunner' of Arthur's 'blood' and again in II. i. 177, when Constance tells Elinor that Arthur is her 'eldest son's son').

Like the controversy over the crown, the Faulconbridge controversy involves a disputed will and rival claimants to patriarchal succession, and both quarrels involve the mothers – but not the fathers – of the contending heirs. John's mother, Elinor, and Arthur's mother, Constance, play important roles in the historical contest between their sons, but neither is the chief actor. The fictional Faulconbridge quarrel, on the other hand, centers on a woman, for Lady Faulconbridge's infidelity has created the nightmare situation that haunts the patriarchal imagination – a son not of her husband's getting destined to inherit her husband's lands and title. The Faulconbridge episode makes explicit the ideological fault line that lies beneath the stridency of patriarchal claims and repressions – the repressed knowledge of women's power to subvert men's genealogical continuity and their genealogical claims.

John's attempt to arbitrate the Faulconbridge quarrel exposes a deep contradiction in patriarchal law. 'Sirrah,' he says to Robert, 'your brother is legitimate':

> Your father's wife did after wedlock bear him;
> And if she did play false, the fault was hers,
> Which fault lies on the hazards of all husbands
> That marry wives. Tell me, how if my brother,
> Who, as you say, took pains to get this son,
> Had of your father claim'd this son for his?
> In sooth, good friend, your father might have kept
> This calf, bred from his cow, from all the world;
> In sooth he might; then if he were my brother's,
> My brother might not claim him; nor your father,
> Being none of his, refuse him. This concludes:
> My mother's son did get your father's heir;
> Your father's heir must have your father's land.
>
> (I. i. 116–29)

According to the laws of patriarchy as expounded by John (and according to good English law in Shakespeare's time), a wife, like a cow, is mere chattel, the possession of her husband. All her actions, even an act so radical as betrayal of the marriage bond, are powerless to affect her son's name, possession, legal status, or identity. Only the man's entitlement has significance under law. Any child she bears is his, even if he is not the biological father. Thus, the very absoluteness of patriarchal right provides for its own subversion, since women can in actuality, though not in law, disrupt and subvert male genealogy.

By admitting that the relationship between father and son is finally no more than a legal fiction, John attacks the very basis of patriarchal thought. Relying on 'strong possession' rather than 'right' for his throne (I. i. 40), John opposes the patriarchal authority that would legitimate Arthur. Having himself crowned a second time, he denies the permanence and efficacy of the ritual that made him king (IV. ii. 1–34). Everything, even the unique ceremony by which monarchial authority is passed down in temporal succession from one male ruler to the next, now becomes repeatable and reversible. When the French king describes Arthur as a 'little abstract' of the 'volume' that 'died in' Arthur's father (II. i. 101–3), he grounds the historical record in nature. But John's verdict on the Faulconbridge controversy demythologizes that record, depriving it of the natural status implied by the French king's metaphor of man as volume and boy as abstract and exposing it as a social construct designed to shore up the flimsy and always necessarily putative connections between fathers and sons.

Elinor is the first to guess the Bastard's true paternity, for she can read the wordless text of his physical nature:

> He hath a trick of Cordelion's face;
> The accent of his tongue affecteth him.
> Do you not read some tokens of my son
> In the large composition of this man?
>
> (I. i. 85–8)

But without Lady Faulconbridge's testimony, the Bastard's paternity would remain conjectural, and his name and title would belie the biological truth of the paternity they purported to represent. It takes one woman to guess the truth and another to verify it. In Holinshed, Cordelion recognizes his bastard son, giving him 'the castell and honor of Coinacke.' In the *Troublesome Raigne*, the Bastard guesses his true paternity even before he asks his mother. In fact, he gets the news from Nature herself: 'Methinks I hear a hollow echo sound,' he says,

> That *Philip* is the son unto a King:
> The whistling leaves upon the trembling trees,
> Whistle in concert I am *Richard's* son;
> The bubbling murmur of the water's fall,
> Records *Phillipus Regis filius*;
> Birds in their flight make music with their wings,
> Filling the air with glory of my birth;
> Birds, bubbles, leaves and mountains, echo, all
> Ring in mine ears, that I am *Richard's* son.
> (*Troublesome Raigne* 1591: Part I: i. 242–51)

Only in Shakespeare is he required to receive his paternity from the hands of women.

Lady Faulconbridge is an unhistorical character, but she is the only one who knows the truth about the Bastard's paternity. The Bastard's words are significant: 'But for the certain knowledge of that truth / I put you o'er to heaven and to my mother' (I. i. 61–2). The Bastard's ironic coupling of his adulterous mother with heaven as the only sources of the elusive truth of paternity suggests an affinity between them as keepers of a knowledge never directly accessible to men. In *King John* Shakespeare goes as far as he will ever go in making women, women's skeptical voices, and women's truth central to the history he staged, leaving his sources behind and venturing into the realm of the unwritten and the conjectural, and into the inaccessible domain (the no man's land) where the secrets of paternity are kept.

References

Dusinberre, Juliet (1990) '*King John* and embarrassing women', *Shakespeare Survey*, 42: 37–52.

Honigmann, E. A. J. (ed.) (1967) *King John*. London: Methuen.

Lindenberger, H. (1975) *Historical Drama and the Relation of Literature and Reality*. Chicago: Chicago University Press.

Ornstein, Robert (1972) *A Kingdom for a Stage: The Achievement of Shakespeare's History Plays*. Cambridge, MA: Harvard University Press.

Vaughan, V. M. (1989) '*King John*: a study in subversion and containment', in *King John: New Perspectives*, ed. D. T. Curren-Aquino, pp. 62–75. Newark: University of Delaware Press.

Womack, Peter (1992) 'Imagining communities: theatres and the English nation in the sixteenth century', in *Culture and History 1350–1600: Essays on English Communities, Identities and Writing*, ed. David Aers, pp. 91–145. Detroit: Wayne State University Press.

5

History and Politics

Walter Cohen's essay on 'Political Criticism of Shakespeare' (1987) discusses the politicization of literary studies in North America during the 1980s. Cohen usefully identifies 'two main strategies in British Marxist studies of Shakespeare: a revisionist historical analysis of the plays in their own time and a radical account of their ideological function in the present' (Cohen, 1987: 27). It is a distinction which animates the broad topic of 'history and politics' in Shakespeare criticism: whose history and whose politics? In 1952, R. W. Babcock could write that 'probably the most important type of modern criticism is historical criticism' (Babcock, 1952: 6): 'Basically, historical criticism enhances the aesthetic value of a piece of early literary art by increasing its intellectual appeal' (1952: 8). Forty years later, Lisa Jardine argued for the importance of *Reading Shakespeare Historically* (1996) as a way of gaining 'a fresh understanding of the rootedness of our present uncertainties, derived by some kind of engaging dialogue with the textual residue of history' (Jardine, 1996: 1). For Babcock, historical criticism of Shakespeare is about the past; for Jardine, it is about the present, and this dual focus can be seen through the historical and political approaches to Shakespeare in the twentieth century. As Peter Brook puts it in his introduction to Polish theatre director Jan Kott's *Shakespeare, our Contemporary*, 'Shakespeare is a contemporary of Kott, Kott is a contemporary of Shakespeare' (Kott, 1967: x).

Kott's own view of the histories was pessimistic, stressing the circular repetition of disunity and violence: 'for Shakespeare history stands still. Every chapter opens and closes at the same point...when the new prince...assumes the crown he will be just as hated as his predecessor. He has killed enemies, now he will kill former allies. And a new pretender appears in the name of violated justice. The wheel has turned full circle. A new chapter opens. A new historical tragedy' (Kott, 1967: 6). The specifics of the individual reigns become blurred, as what emerges from the plays is 'the image of history itself. The image of the Grand Mechanism' (1967: 9), imagined as 'the grand staircase of history' (1967: 31).

Many critics have worked by historicizing Shakespeare's plays in more detail. Blair Worden's essay 'Shakespeare and Politics', in a volume of *Shakespeare Survey* devoted to the theme, argues that if Shakespeare's plays reveal little about their author, 'they leave little doubt about when they were written' (Worden, 1990: 9). The 'new historicism' associated with Stephen Greenblatt is discussed in Dutton and Wilson (1992) and in Veeser (1989, 1994). Greenblatt's own discussion of Shakespeare can be found in his *Renaissance Self-fashioning* (1980) and *Shakespearean Negotiations* (1988), where he argues for a 'study of the collective making of distinct cultural practices and inquiry into the relations among these practices – a poetics of culture' (Greenblatt, 1988: 5). Exemplary of this approach is his much anthologized essay 'Invisible Bullets', first published in *Shakespearean Negotiations*. In it, Greenblatt moves from an account of Thomas Harriot in Virginia to a discussion of 'the production and containment of subversion and disorder' in *1 Henry IV* (1988: 40), concluding that,

> Like Harriot in the New World, the Henry plays confirm the Machiavellian hypothesis that princely power originates in force and fraud even as they draw their audience towards an acceptance of that power. And we are free to locate and pay homage to the plays' doubts only because they no longer threaten us. There is subversion, no end of subversion, only not for us. (Greenblatt, 1988: 65)

Also pessimistic about the possibilities of political change is Richard Helgerson's *Forms of Nationhood* (1992). Helgerson takes Shakespeare's history plays, alongside Elizabethan cultural institutions of the law, mapping, the literature of discovery and trade, as extreme instances of a 'preeminently royal image of England' (Helgerson, 1992: 244), in which

> the exposure of kingship in a narrative and dramatic medium that not only displayed power but revealed the sometimes brutal and duplicitous strategies by which power maintained itself might be thought to subvert the structure of authority it ostensibly celebrated. But though the plays do bear a subversive potential, neither it nor their festive power of inversion have in fact made themselves felt in any historically disruptive way. (1992: 244)

These apparently quietist political interpretations have their radical counterparts: Jonathan Dollimore and Alan Sinfield's essay on 'History and Ideology: The Instance of *Henry V*' (1985) argues that the play's 'displaced, imaginary resolution of one of the state's most intractable problems' (1985: 225) – the war in Ireland – foregrounds conflict rather than resolution. Michael Neill's essay 'Broken English and Broken Irish: Nation, Language, and the Optic of Power in Shakespeare's Histories' (1994) also discusses the disruptive and unreconciled presence of Ireland in the history plays, a topic considered by Highley (1997) and by Andrew Murphy in his article reprinted below. Graham Holderness's *Shakespeare Recycled: The Making of Historical Drama* (1992) argues that the history plays are open to conservative readings but that they 'also contain the potentiality for radical and progressive reproduction, on account of their historical origins in a period before the shape of bourgeois culture was fully and definitely formed' (Holderness, 1992b: 232).

Leonard Tennenhouse discusses the way in which 'theatrical spectacles displayed the power of the state' in his *Power on Display: The Politics of Shakespeare's Genres* (1986: 72). Tennenhouse argues for the interplay of order and disorder as the history play attempts to stabilize 'the conflict among contradictory origins of power': power as 'the inevitable unfolding of order' versus the depiction of history as 'nothing else but the history of forms of disorder' (Tennenhouse, 1986: 82). He observes that 'it cannot be accidental that the *Henriad*, which produces Shakespeare's most accomplished Elizabethan monarch, should also produce his most memorable figure of misrule' – Falstaff (1986: 83). Phyllis Rackin also locates in Falstaff the history plays' resistance to authority: 'his uninvited, disruptive presence at the coronation and his refusal to stay banished insistently betray the taint of theatrical mediation and the scandal of anachronism that inevitably attend the scene of Shakespeare's historical representation' (Rackin, 1990: 145). Harold Bloom's collection *Falstaff* (1991) gathers a range of essays on the character.

In his *Shakespeare's Political Drama* (1988: ix), Alexander Leggatt discusses 'the ordering, and enforcing, the gaining and losing, of public power in the state', both English and Roman. Rather than seeing the plays in groups or as an extended sequence, he discusses each as 'a fresh experiment, so that what emerges is not a single, homogeneous view of Shakespearian politics but a series of explorations of differing material, asking the same questions but not always getting the same answers' (1988: x–xi). These questions focus around issues of realism and myth, and the relation of the medium of drama to the process and relation of history, and these Leggatt addresses through careful and engaged readings of each play. In a cautious and researched view of *Tudor Drama and Politics: A Critical Approach to Topical Meaning*, David Bevington (1968) compares Shakespeare's historical interests with those of contemporary plays, and finds that 'the topical force of Shakespeare's political portraiture is non-progressive. No matter how much in his later plays he analyses the defects of hierarchy, Shakespeare's constant motive is to preserve its true function as the only viable defense against social disintegration' (Bevington, 1968: 241). In *Shakespeare's Political Realism* (2001: 13), Tim Spiekerman argues 'that Shakespeare can indeed teach us something about politics' in general, rather than about the partisan sympathies of the author or his characters. Hugh Grady's *Shakespeare, Machiavelli and Montaigne* (2002) discusses these political philosophers as indirect influences on the history plays' composition and reception, and discusses the 'growing pessimism' of the 'trajectory of intertwined power and subjectivity' (2002: 27) between the 'fully fallen, Machiavellian – and to that extent "modern" – world' (2002: 67) of *Richard II* to the darker 'counter-narrative' of *Henry V* (2002: 225).

Many critics develop and qualify the insights of E. M. W. Tillyard (1944) in seeing the history plays as political documents of the 1590s. Lily Campbell (1947) links the plays to their immediate historical context to see them as 'political mirrors of history', teaching 'politics to the present' (1947: 125). Leah Marcus's historicist project of 'localization' – reading Shakespeare's plays within an immediate nexus of topical meanings – is developed in her *Puzzling Shakespeare: Local Reading and its Discontents* (1988): her chapter on *1 Henry VI* is reprinted on pp. 147–82. Annabel Patterson's *Shakespeare and the Popular Voice* (1989) also tries to recover Shakespeare's intersections with contemporary social and political events: her chapter on *Henry V* discusses the allusion to Essex in the chorus to Act 5 as an 'extreme form of topicality, a moment of historical expectation that can be dated with precision, and whose very poise, optimistic or pessimistic, on the edge of the unknown is central to the meaning of the artefact' (Patterson, 1989: 83). David Norbrook (1996) considers contemporary political doctrine on rebellion and *Richard II*. These indicative critics focus on the play in its immediate context: for others the resonances of the plays have been updated to their own period. Thus G. Wilson Knight's *The Sovereign Flower* (1958) follows his wartime *The Olive and the Sword* (1944) in praising Shakespeare as the poet of English national confidence, arguing that 'Shakespeare's royalist thinking is, for the most part, patriotic' (Knight, 1958: 13), and advising that 'often in reading Shakespeare we do well to expand the obvious content, to put modern nations, or parties, for separate persons, and world-affairs for the turbulencies of state. Well-known works will at once start up into relief with new, because contemporary, meanings' (1958: 14).

With a rather different political agenda, Terry Eagleton's conclusion to his 1986 book *William Shakespeare* delights in breaking the 'bad news' to Shakespeare: the fallibility of a liberal belief in 'a way of harnessing what is most productive about bourgeois transgression to the old polity, grafting upon that settled structure fertile strains of dynamic energy and individual self-development' (Eagleton, 1986: 99). He admits, though, that Shakespeare 'may well have suspected as much himself', as a man who seems, ironically, to have been 'almost certainly familiar with the writings of Hegel, Marx, Nietzsche, Freud, Wittgenstein and Derrida' (1986: ix–x). In their introduction to the volume *Political Shakespeare*, Jonathan Dollimore and Alan Sinfield claim cultural materialism's attentiveness to the political and ideological significance of all cultural productions. Rather than trying to mystify this dimension, 'it registers its commitment to the transformation of a social order which exploits people on the grounds of race, gender and class' (Dollimore and Sinfield, 1985: viii). Politically engaged criticism is collected by Holderness for his *Shakespeare's History Plays* collection (1992), which has a useful introduction outlining developments in approaches to the history plays since Tillyard.

The debates about these kinds of historicist readings were the subject of an issue of the journal *New Literary History* in 1990. Richard Levin's 'Unthinkable Thoughts in the New Historicizing of English Renaissance Drama' (1990: 433–47) develops some of the contentions of his *New Readings vs. Old Plays* (1979). His article indicts new historicist shibboleths about self-conscious theatre, about the constructedness of gender, about changing concepts of selfhood and subjectivity: 'they homogenize Renaissance thought' (Levin, 1990: 437). He also goes on to counter the claims with opposing evidence. A number of scholars replied in the journal. Catherine Belsey's 'Richard Levin and In-different Reading' (1990: 449–56) defends a criticism which 'deliberately seeks out the moments of difference within the text, looks out for the formal breaks and disruptions which draw attention to discontinuities of meaning' (1990: 455). Jonathan Dollimore's contribution, 'Shakespeare, Cultural Materialism, Feminism and Marxist Humanism' (1990: 471–93) stresses the specificity of materialist criticism through a critique of writing by Lynda E. Boose (1987), Carol Thomas Neely (1989) and Kiernan Ryan (1989). Another collection of essays, Ivo Kamps's *Shakespeare Left and Right* (1991), includes contributions by Levin and his critics, including Gayle Greene and Michael Bristol, and again makes explicit the ground of the debate about political or ideological approaches to Shakespeare. Graham Bradshaw's *Misrepresentations: Shakespeare and the Materialists* (1993) takes sustained issue with new historicism in a critical debate with Greenblatt (1980, 1988), Evans (1986), Hawkes (1986), and Sinfield (1992), among others. Bradshaw accuses his critical adversaries of a 'failure to engage seriously with Shakespeare's irreducibly complex designs' and consequently the failure 'to engage seriously with their professed belief... that values are culturally and historically specific' (Bradshaw, 1993: 18). He cites as fallacious the 'new historicist E-effect, or estrangement effect': 'whatever separates "us" from Shakespeare and the Renaissance is more important than what joins us, so that anybody who thinks Shakespeare is our contemporary is showing how little he or she understands' (1993: 28–9). 'As for the argument that there is no Shakespeare, only "Shakespeares", this book presents a lengthy reply', Bradshaw proposes. 'A short answer would be that "Shakespeares" is interesting but Shakespeare are better' (1993: 33).

References and Further Reading

Babcock, R. W. (1952) 'Historical criticism of Shakespeare', *Modern Language Quarterly*, 13: 6–20.

Belsey, Catherine (1990) 'Richard Levin and in-different reading', *New Literary History*, 21: 449–56.

Bevington, David (1968) *Tudor Drama and Politics: A Critical Approach to Topical Meaning*. Cambridge, MA: Harvard University Press.

Bloom, Harold (1991) *Falstaff.* New York: Chelsea House.

Boose, Lynda E. (1987) 'The family in Shakespeare studies; or – studies in the family of Shakespeareans; or – the politics of politics', *Renaissance Quarterly*, 40: 707–42.

Bradshaw, Graham (1993) *Misrepresentations: Shakespeare and the Materialists*. Ithaca, NY: Cornell University Press.

Campbell, Lily Bess (1947) *Shakespeare's 'Histories': Mirrors of Elizabethan Policy*. Huntington Library Publications. San Marino, CA: Huntington Library.

Cohen, Walter (1987) 'Political criticism of Shakespeare', in *Shakespeare Reproduced: The Text in History and Ideology*, ed. Jean E. Howard and Marion F. O'Connor. London: Methuen.

Dollimore, Jonathan (1990) 'Shakespeare, cultural materialism, feminism and Marxist humanism', *New Literary History*, 21: 471–93.

——and Sinfield, Alan (eds) (1985) *Political Shakespeare: New Essays in Cultural Materialism*. Manchester: Manchester University Press.

——and—— (eds) (1988) 'History and ideology: the instances of *Henry V*', in *Alternative Shakespeares*, ed. John Drakakis. London: Methuen.

Dutton, Richard and Wilson, Richard (1992) *New Historicism and Renaissance Drama*. Longman Critical Readers. London: Longman.

Eagleton, Terry (1986) *William Shakespeare*. Oxford: Blackwell.

Evans, Malcolm (1986) *Signifying Nothing: Truth's True Contents in Shakespeare's Text*. Brighton: Harvester Press.

Grady, Hugh (2002) *Shakespeare, Machiavelli and Montaigne: Power and Subjectivity from Richard II to Hamlet*. Oxford: Oxford University Press.

Greenblatt, Stephen (1980) *Renaissance Self-fashioning: From More to Shakespeare*. Chicago: University of Chicago Press.

——(1988) *Shakespearean Negotiations: The Circulation of Social Energy in Renaissance England*. Berkeley, CA: University of California Press.

Hawkes, Terence (1986) *That Shakespearian Rag: Essays on a Critical Process*. London: Methuen.

Helgerson, Richard (1992) *Forms of Nationhood: The Elizabethan Writing of England*. Chicago: University of Chicago Press.

Highley, Christopher (1997) *Shakespeare, Spenser, and the Crisis in Ireland*. Cambridge: Cambridge University Press.

Holderness, Graham (1992a) *Shakespeare's History Plays: Richard II to Henry V*. Basingstoke: Macmillan.

——(1992b) *Shakespeare Recycled: The Making of Historical Drama*. London: Harvester Wheatsheaf.

Howard, Jean E. and O'Connor, Marion F. (eds) (1987) *Shakespeare Reproduced: The Text in History and Ideology.* London: Methuen.

Jardine, Lisa (1983) *Still Harping on Daughters: Women and Drama in the Age of Shakespeare.* Brighton: Harvester.

——(1996) *Reading Shakespeare Historically.* London: Routledge.

Kamps, Ivo (ed.) (1991) *Shakespeare Left and Right.* London: Routledge.

Knight, George Wilson (1944) *The Olive and the Sword: A Study of England's Shakespeare.* Oxford: Oxford University Press.

——(1958) *The Sovereign Flower: On Shakespeare as the Poet of Royalism.* London: Methuen.

Kott, Jan (1967) *Shakespeare, our Contemporary,* 2nd edn. London: Routledge.

Leggatt, Andrew (1988) *Shakespeare's Political Drama: The History Plays and the Roman Plays.* London: Routledge.

Levin, Richard L. (1979) *New Readings vs. Old Plays: Recent Trends in the Reinterpretation of English Renaissance Drama.* Chicago: University of Chicago Press.

——(1990) 'Unthinkable thoughts in the new historicizing of English Renaissance drama', *New Literary History,* 21: 433–47.

Marcus, Leah S. (1988) *Puzzling Shakespeare: Local Reading and its Discontents.* Berkeley, CA: University of California Press.

Neely, Carol Thomas (1989) 'Constructing the subject: feminist practice and the new Renaissance discourses', *English Literary Renaissance,* 18: 5–18.

Neill, Michael (1994) 'Broken English and broken Irish: nation, language, and the optic of power in Shakespeare's histories', *Shakespeare Quarterly,* 45: 1–32.

Norbrook, David (1996) '"A liberal tongue": language and rebellion in *Richard II*', in *Shakespeare's Universe: Renaissance Ideas and Conventions,* ed. John Mucciolo et al. Hants: Scolar Press.

Patterson, Annabel M. (1989) *Shakespeare and the Popular Voice.* Oxford: Blackwell.

Rackin, Phyllis (1990) *Stages of History: Shakespeare's English Chronicles.* Ithaca, NY: Cornell University Press.

Ryan, Kiernan (1989) *Shakespeare.* London: Harvester Wheatsheaf.

Sinfield, Alan (1992) *Faultlines: Cultural Materialism and the Politics of Dissident Reading.* Oxford: Clarendon Press.

Spiekerman, Tim (2001) *Shakespeare's Political Realism: The English History Plays.* Albany, NY: State University of New York Press.

Tennenhouse, Leonard (1986) *Power on Display: The Politics of Shakespeare's Genres.* London: Methuen.

Tillyard, E. M. W. (1944) *Shakespeare's History Plays.* London: Chatto and Windus (rev. edn 1969).

Veeser, H. Aram (1989) *The New Historicism.* New York: Routledge.

——(1994) *The New Historicism Reader.* New York: Routledge.

Wilson, Richard (1993) *Will Power: Essays on Shakespearean Authority.* London: Harvester Wheatsheaf.

Worden, Blair (1990) 'Shakespeare and politics', *Shakespeare Survey,* 44: 1–15.

Shakespeare's Irish History

Andrew Murphy

Andrew Murphy discusses the traces in Shakespeare's histories of the war in Ireland which preoccupied the Elizabethan administration through the later 1590s. He amplifies their cumulative significance through an historically contextualized reading of relations between England, Wales, Scotland and Ireland. In re-siting the plays conclusively in their immediate historical moment, he focuses on textual and political specifics in a welcome corrective to over-general historical schema.

Andrew Murphy, 'Shakespeare's Irish History', *Literature and History*, 5 (1996), pp. 38–59.

I(i)

In an important and well-conceived article on *Henry V*, Michael Neill has observed that, 'with the notable exception of Spenser's "cloudily enwrapped" allegory' of *The Faerie Queene*,

> the English enterprise in Ireland seems, at first sight anyway, to have had remarkably little impact on imaginative literature. In the theater Shirley's *St Patrick for Ireland* (1639) carefully confined itself to the mythical past, and only in a few scenes of the anonymous *Famous History of Captain Thomas Stukely* (1605) were the Irish wars actually brought onto the stage – though they were given a sort of fantastical existence in the courtly fantasies of Jonson's *Irish Masque at Court*. Given the amount of political, military, and intellectual energy it absorbed, and the moneys it consumed, Ireland can seem to constitute . . . one of the great and unexplained lacunae in the drama of the period.[1]

What Neill points to here is a significant silence in the drama of the Renaissance period – a failure, or unwillingness, on the part of English dramatists to engage with one of the most urgent and important political crises of the close of the sixteenth century: the war in Ireland.

This 'Nine Years War' represented one of the greatest threats faced by Elizabeth's administration. For the first time since the original Anglo-Norman incursion into Ireland in 1167, England faced the prospect, in the closing decade of the sixteenth century, of losing control of the entire island of Ireland. Since the Irish were fighting with the backing of the Spanish crown, Irish 'independence' represented an enormous threat to English security, as the island could well serve as a launching point for a Spanish attack on the island of Britain itself. As Fynes Moryson noted, in his account of the Irish war, a phrase in common currency at the time was 'He that will England winne, must with Ireland first beginne.'[2]

And yet, as Michael Neill observes, this entire crisis of the century's end is largely unregistered in the imaginative literature of the period. The reasons for this 'lacuna' (as Neill terms it) are manifold and complex, and are, I would suggest, as much connected with English attempts to construct an English national identity as they are with English perceptions of Irish rebelliousness and the political threat which it represented. As Richard Helgerson has noted in *Forms of Nationhood*, in England in this period

> a unique set of conditions ... gave men of middling status and humanist education, men born at or shortly following the midcentury, the task of laying the discursive foundations both for the nation-state and for a whole array of more specialized communities that based their identity on their relation to the nation and the state.[3]

A number of commentators[4] have registered the way in which Ireland was deployed by English writers in this process of national self-construction. Most recently, Andrew Hadfield and Willy Maley, in their introduction to *Representing Ireland: Literature and the Origins of Conflict, 1534–1660*, have noted that

> one of the most important ways in which Ireland was read in this period was as a series of negative images of Englishness. Ireland, in this respect, as well as being a text, is a negative of a photograph of English identity which never comes into view; we have only the negative, not the original print.[5]

Hadfield and Maley's point is well made, but, in a sense, it serves to oversimplify the situation. English identity certainly was in large measure predicated upon a process of contradistinguishing a set of English national characteristics from a stereotype of the 'wild Irish',[6] but just as the Irish resisted English dominance militarily in this period, so they also presented to the English a resistance to the simple binary colonial stereotype through which the English would define both their neighbours and themselves. It is this resistance, I would suggest, that is partly responsible for the lacuna that Neill registers in the imaginative literature of the period.

I(ii)

In part the English experience of an Irish resistance to the standard tropes of colonialist discourse arose out of the structure and history of the Anglo-Irish situation. Where many historians and literary critics have sought to conflate Ireland's colonial history with that of other territories colonised from England,[7] it should be noted that Ireland's colonial experience is quite distinctive in a number of different ways, not least because of its extended history (Ireland has probably had the longest history of colonial relations) and because of the ethnic, cultural and geographical proximity of the Irish to the English. This latter element of multiple proximity has always troubled any simple application of the paradigm of colonial stereotyping to the Irish situation. For example, in one of the very earliest colonial texts written about Ireland – Gerald of Wales' *Expugnatio Hibernica* (*The Conquest of Ireland*) – the author finds himself being profoundly troubled by the relationship between the colonial project in Ireland and that other, greater colonial project then in progress: the third Crusade. Gerald was present at the English court when Henry II refused the request of Heraclius, the patriarch of Jerusalem, that he either lead a crusade to the Holy Land, or at least send one of his sons in his place. Henry's son Prince John offered to take up the command, but his father sent him to Ireland instead. Gerald traces all of Henry's subsequent misfortunes back to this decision:

> whereas his father the king should have responded to the powerful summons issued by the patriarch at this time ... by immediately embarking on the crusade in person, or at any rate by the prompt despatch of one of his sons to serve Christ in his place, at the very time when he received this summons, and in the very presence of the distinguished emissary who had come to proclaim this important message, he sent his son not to the East, but to the West, not against the Saracens, but against Christians[8] to pursue their own interests rather than Christ's interests.[9]

Gerald finds himself here, we might say, caught in the space between two kinds of Otherness: the cultural, ethnic and religious Otherness of the East and the imperfect Otherness of the Irish, England's Christian neighbours, who share so much history and culture in common with the English.

In the early modern period, we find this odd Irish liminality neatly focused in the figure of Hugh O'Neill, who served as leader of the Irish in the Nine Years War. O'Neill himself was a profoundly ambiguous character, having been born in Ireland of Gaelic parentage, but fostered as a child by an Anglo-Irish family, in the expectation that he would one day be inserted back into his native Ulster in order to assist his English patrons gain some purchase on that impenetrable Gaelic stronghold.[10]

In due course returned to Ulster, O'Neill was initially created Baron of Dungannon by the English and then elevated to the earldom of Tyrone. Initially, O'Neill appeared to be quite amenable to the role which the English had mapped out for him. As Margaret MacCurtain notes in *Tudor and Stuart Ireland*

> to all appearances he became English and he served under the queen's banner in the Irish wars ... He joined the earl of Essex in his futile effort to colonise

Antrim and Down in 1573 and when Sir Henry Sidney was [re]appointed
deputy in 1575, Hugh O'Neill hurried to the support of his patron.[11]

However, as time went by, O'Neill began to play a kind of dual game,
straddling the worlds of English and native Irish politics. Much against the
wishes of his English patrons, O'Neill contrived to add to his English
aristocratic titles the headship of the O'Neill sept, becoming known as 'The
O'Neill', a name 'in comparison whereof', William Camden tells us, 'the
very title of *Cæsar* is contemptible in *Ireland'*.[12]

While, initially, O'Neill succeeded in temporising with the crown as he
pursued his own agenda within both political realms, in time relations with
the English became more and more strained, leading eventually to open hos-
tilities. As relations deteriorated, O'Neill exploited his knowledge of the sign
system of English civility to his own advantage. Fynes Moryson tells us, for
instance, that on one occasion 'pretending to build a faire house (which our
State thinkes a tye of ciuilitie) he got license to transport to *Dungannon* a great
quantitie of lead to couer the Battlements of his house: but ere long imployed
the same only to make bullets for the warre.' We find here an instance of what
Jonathan Dollimore has called (in another context) 'transgressive reinscription'
– 'a *turning back* upon something and a perverting of it typically if not exclusively through inversion and displacement.'[13] O'Neill adopted this transgressive strategy in more obvious ways also once the war got underway, as he
trained, equipped and even dressed his army after the English fashion.[14] In
fighting O'Neill's army the English were placed in a similar troubling position
to that experienced by Gerald of Wales as he contemplates the twin colonial
projects in the distant east and the proximate west. Like Caesar's Anthony, the
English may have felt that they 'seeme to spend [their] Fury/Vpon [them-
selves]' (*Anthony and Cleopatra*, T L N 2588–9).[15] Or we might say, adapting
from Dollimore, that O'Neill prosecutes 'the most disturbing of all forms of
transgression, namely that whereby the outlaw turns up as inlaw.'[16]

What O'Neill's career – especially during the period of the Nine Years
War – served to do was both to focus the traditional problematics of applying the colonial paradigm to Ireland and to intensify the sense of uncertainty about the nature of Irish identity. This uncertainty necessarily in turn
served to call English identity into question since, as we have seen, the
positive construction of that identity was intimately bound up with the
negative constitution of a sense of Irishness.[17] This is one reason, I would
suggest, for the relative silence of English writers on the question of the war
in Ireland, registered by Michael Neill, since Ireland places under strain the
task of national imagining that Richard Helgerson considers as having been
the particular assignment of Shakespeare's generation. As Neill himself acknowledges, however, Ireland *is* present in the writing of the period – its
'shadowy presence', as he puts it, can be discerned in many places, not least

in Shakespeare's history plays. It is to these plays that I wish to direct my
attention in this article.

II(i)

We begin our analysis of the cycle of history plays with a text which, while
it does not include the greatest amount of material explicitly connected with
Ireland (it does not, for instance, like *Henry the Fift*, include an Irish character), nevertheless, does contain the greatest number of actual references to
'Ireland' and the 'Irish' of any Shakespeare play. This is the second play of
the first Henriad, known in its First Folio version as *The second Part of
Henry the Sixt*.

The exact year of composition of this play is uncertain, but it seems likely
that it was written sometime around 1591.[18] The play thus predates the
Nine Years War, being located within an Anglo-Irish decade during which,
as David Quinn has noted,

> a kind of peace was attained ... as Munster settled into a plantation and Con-
> nacht achieved an apparent equilibrium under a rationalized form of military
> taxation ... and while, too, Hugh O'Neill, before and after he attained the title
> of Earl of Tyrone in 1587, maintained a pacific policy behind which his effective
> strength grew.[19]

The relative stability of the English position in Ireland in this period is
reflected in the manner in which Ireland figures in the text of Shakespeare's
play. It is the Duke of Yorke who is most associated with Ireland in the text.
He has seen service there, and, in the play's opening scene, Salisbury, in
praising him, comments:

> ... Brother Yorke, thy acts in Ireland,
> In bringing them to ciuill Discipline:
> Thy late exploits done in the heart of France,
> When thou wert Regent for our Soueraigne,
> Haue made thee fear'd and honor'd of the people.
>
> (TLN 202–6)

Yorke himself claims in the same scene:

> Methinkes the Realmes of England, France, & Ireland,
> Beare that proportion to my flesh and blood,
> As did the fatall brand *Althæa* burnt,
> Vnto the Princes heart of *Calidon*.
>
> (TLN 244–7)

Later in the play, we learn of an Irish uprising and Yorke takes advantage of this turn of events to plot his attempt on the English throne. His Irish strategy is twofold: he will go there himself and use the occasion as an excuse to raise an army, but in his absence, he will employ Jack Cade 'to make Commotion' in England (TLN 1664). Though 'a head-strong Kentishman' (TLN 1662), Cade also has strong Irish connections, having served Yorke there. Cade is a multiply transgressive character in the play: a commoner who pretends to aristocratic parentage, but also an Englishman who is able to transform himself into a native Irishman. Yorke says of him:

> Full often, like a shag-hayr'd craftie Kerne,
> Hath he conuersed with the Enemie,
> And vndiscouer'd, come to me againe,
> And giuen me notice of their Villanies.
> (TLN 1673–6)

The composite presentation of Cade appears here much like the figure that Captain Thomas Lee (who was also much given to disguise) presents in his 1594 portrait by Marcus Gheeraedts the Younger.[20] As James P. Myers has noted of the portrait, Lee's 'pointed beard, his red military cape and white-and-delft-blue floral undergarment distinguish him readily as an Elizabethan; his high-peake morion, long spear, round shield strapped to his back, and his shoeless feet and hoseless legs mark him as an Irish chieftain.'[21]

What is striking about Shakespeare's Cade (and indeed about Lee also) is that not only is he presented as being able to assume, convincingly, an Irish appearance, adopting the 'shag-hayr' of the Irish 'glib' (a forward-combed hairstyle), but in the act of thus transforming himself, he deploys a strategy that English writers traditionally associated with the Irish themselves: the ability to shift into a different identity. This is one of the aspects of Irishness to which Spenser most vigorously objects in *A View of the Present State of Ireland* and which he delineates in Book V of the *Faerie Queene* in the figure of Malengin.[22] In the *View*, Spenser specifically links such mutability to the traditional Irish hairstyle, observing that when a thief

> hathe rune himself in to that perill of lawe that he will not be knowen he either Cuttethe of his glibbe quite by which he becommethe nothinge like himselfe, or pulleth it so lowe downe over his eyes that it is verye harde to discerne his thevishe Countenaunce.[23]

Cade's power, therefore, is presented as the power to forge (in every sense) an Irish strategy as a weapon against the Irish themselves. In the greater narrative of the play, Yorke also performs something like a version of this manoeuvre, in that he uses the realm of Ireland as a launching point for his own campaign in England. Thus the messenger registers his return from Ireland, at the head of a mixed army:

> The Duke of Yorke is newly come from Ireland,
> And with a puissant and a mighty power
> Of Gallow-glasses and stout Kernes
> Is marching hitherward in proud array.
>
> (TLN 2877–80)

Yorke himself proclaims, on entering with his army: 'From Ireland thus comes Yorke to claim his right, / And plucke the Crowne from feeble *Henries* head' (TLN 2991–2).

What is striking about this text, then, is the confidence which it projects in an English ability to penetrate, master, marshall, and control the Irish forces and the power which they represent. Indeed, we might say that this is a play in which Otherness of every kind is seen to be available to be recruited and subverted to serve the ends of a particular aristocratic class fraction: the text presents Yorke as commanding and deploying both the lower orders within English society and the native Irish to serve his military and political ambition.

II(ii)

Just prior to his departure for Ireland in *The second Part of Henry the Sixt*, Yorke observes

> Well, Nobles, well; 'tis politikely done,
> To send me packing with an Hoast of men:
> I feare me, you but warme the starued Snake,
> Who cherisht in your breasts, will sting your hearts,
> 'Twas men I lackt, and you will giue them me.
>
> (TLN 1647–51)

This same proverb of the frozen snake revived is also deployed by Spenser in his *View*, which was likely written in the mid-1590s. Spenser writes of Hugh O'Neill's early years:

> He was I assure youe the moste outcaste of all the Oneals then, and lifted vp by her maiestie out of the duste to that he nowe hathe wraughte himselfe vnto, And now he playeth like the frozen Snake whoe beinge for Compassion releiued by the husbandman sone after he was warme, begane to hisse and threaten daunger even to him and his.[24]

We notice a shift between these two deployments of the parable. In the play, Yorke sees *himself* as the snake, and the image is indicative of a certain English capacity for covert and measured action. Spenser's Irenius, by contrast, sees the Irish O'Neill as the snake, and, in a reversal of the image of the disguised Cade, he cautions that O'Neill has duplicitously penetrated the English realm and thus 'threaten[s] daunger'.

The shift in perspective registered by these different deployments of the proverb is perhaps indicative of the shift which occurred in Ireland in the years between the writing of Shakespeare's play and Spenser's tract. As we have already noted, in the likely year of composition of the second Henry VI play Hugh O'Neill was still more or less willing to act as agent for the crown. We might say that as an Irish ally he was available to be deployed by the English in much the same way as Irish power is available to be harnessed and directed by Yorke. By 1595, however, O'Neill was in open rebellion and was proclaimed a traitor by the queen. In February of that year his brother, Art, attacked and burnt the strategically important Blackwater Fort; Enniskillen was taken in mid-May; and the Irish inflicted a heavy defeat on the English at Clontibret in June. As O'Neill's novelist biographer, Seán Ó Faoláin, rather melodramatically puts it in describing the ongoing campaign: 'Cavan was burned flat. Louth was ravaged as far south as Drogheda. The colonists fled to their towns, and every gate and door was barred. After that there could be no retraction.'[25]

It was most likely in this same year of 1595 that Shakespeare wrote *The life and death of Richard the second* (to adopt again the First Folio title). In an odd way, the relationship between this play and its Henry VI predecessor is much the same as the relationship between the two versions of the parable of the frozen snake. Each play has its Irish dimension and the basic trajectory of the Irish material is much the same in each case. Ireland lies in the background of both plays as 'a world elsewhere' and it serves as convenient peripheral vehicle for manoeuverings within the realm of England itself – in Yorke's case, the raising of an army to support his attempt on the throne; in Richard's case, the appropriation of Gaunt's resources. As Richard comments, on hearing of Gaunt's death:

> Now for our Irish warres,
> We must supplant those rough rug-headed Kernes,
> Which liue like venom, where no venom else
> But onley they, haue priuiledge to liue.
> And for these great affayres do aske some charge
> Towards our assistance, we do seize to vs
> The plate, coine, reuennewes, and moueables,
> Whereof our Vncle *Gaunt* did stand possest.
>
> (TLN 802–9)

Both Yorke and Richard are absented from part of their respective plays as they conduct their Irish campaigns, and both finally return to Britain to face conflict there. However, again as in the case of the parable of the snake, when the story is told a second time, it has a different force and outcome. Where Yorke returns triumphant, at the head of an army which has incorporated elements of the Irish, Richard's return is, by contrast, signalled by a progressive depletion of his followers. As Salisbury informs Richard on his arrival on the shores of Britain:

> One day too late, I feare (my Noble Lord)
> Hath clouded all thy happie dayes on Earth:
> Oh call backe Yesterday, bid Time returne,
> And thou shalt haue twelue thousand fighting men.
>   (TLN 1423–6)

Richard loses his army before he even arrives back in Britain and then loses his crown in his Welsh confrontation with Henry.

Between the 1591 play and its 1595 successor, then, we get a shift in the way in which Ireland is presented on the Shakespearean stage. In the first instance, Ireland is a territory to be deployed as an English source of strength; in the second, it is associated with a catastrophic draining away of that strength, leading to Richard's loss of power, and ultimately to his death.

We have already noted that Richard's Irish venture is in part motivated by a desire to appropriate Gaunt's resources. As Richard's journey sets out an image of England's increasingly fraught relationship with Ireland, so Gaunt himself provides, before his death, an idealized image of the English national unit in his 'sceptred isle' speech (TLN 681–704). Philip Edwards was among the first to notice (in *Threshold of a Nation*) that Gaunt's reference to *England* as a sceptred *isle* is rather telling.[26] In Gaunt's image, England extends westward and northward, to obliterate Scotland and Wales, becoming an entire island unto itself, 'bound in with the triumphant sea' (TLN 702). In this account of the nation, the problematic territory of Ireland is essentially excluded, as if simply abandoned to its venomous kern, and the ethnic divisions within the island of Britain itself are simply written over: England's boundaries become coterminal with the shores of the island of Britain.

In the Henry IV plays, these elided British divisions return, as the stability of the national unit is threatened by a shifting alliance forged among the Welsh, the Scots, and certain elements of the English themselves. What we find in these plays is a profound engagement with the issue of the uncertainties and fragmentation of national identities. It is as if the failure to secure a stable positive English identity contradistinguished from a negative Irish identity – in Gaunt's terms, a sceptred isle securely distinguished from a land of venomous kern – has prompted a re-examination of the relationships among the populations of Britain itself, giving rise to a realisation that these relationships also cannot be securely distinguished and sustained.

In the first of the Henry IV plays, the source of the disruption within Britain is initially identified as being Wales and, specifically, the Welsh leader, Owen Glendower. Westmerland, briefing Henry on the Crusade preparations, informs him that the discussions were interrupted when

> all athwart there came
> A Post from Wales, loaden with heauy Newes;
> Whose worst was, That the Noble *Mortimer*,
> Leading the men of Herefordshire to fight
> Against the irregular and wilde *Glendower*,
> Was by the rude hands of that Welshman taken,
> And a thousand of his people butchered.
>
> (TLN 40–6)

Glendower and his Welsh allies appear here as alien forces stationed on the borders of the English state, threatening its integrity. The actions of the Welsh women in the wake of the battle serve to emphasise the barbaric Otherness of this people. As Westmerland's report continues, taking up the fate of the 'thousand . . . people butchered', we learn that:

> Vpon [their] dead corpses there was such misuse,
> Such beasstly, shamelesse transformation,
> By those Welshwomen done, as may not be
> (Without much shame) be told or spoken of.
>
> (TLN 47–50)

The implied sexual brutality of the Welsh women, transgressing codes of martial and gender roles and of bodily as well as national integrity, emphasises a multiple lack of civility on the part of the Welsh. And yet, as the play proceeds, these easy distinctions and dichotomies begin to fragment. In the first instance, Mortimer, having been despatched against Glendower and defeated by him, ultimately becomes Glendower's ally and his son-in-law. In this sense, the division between the civilised Self and the barbarian Other fails to be sustained in the text, as their forces and objectives combine, within the broader framework of a northern English / Welsh / Scottish coalition.

Mortimer might, of course, be seen simply as an early instance of the phenomenon of the colonist 'going native', seduced by Glendower's daughter, that 'faire Queene in a Summers Bowre' (TLN 1748). And, indeed, we might find here echoes of a certain 'fair[i]e Queene' and of another

'Summers Bowre'. In the play, Glendower, translating for Mortimer's wife, informs Mortimer that

> She bids you,
> On the wanton Rushes lay you downe,
> And rest your gentle Head vpon her Lappe
> And she will sing the Song that pleaseth you.
> (TLN 1753–6)

In a similar moment, in Book II of Spenser's poem, we find that 'the whiles some one did chaunt [a] louely lay',[27] Guyon and the Palmer seek and finally encounter Acrasia in the Bower of Bliss, keeping their way

> Through many couert groues, and thickets close,
> In which they creeping did at last display
> That wanton Ladie, with her louer lose,
> Whose sleepie head she in her lap did soft dispose.
> (II. xii. 76. 6–9)

Stephen Greenblatt has, of course, registered the colonial significance of the Bower of Bliss episode, reading it specifically in an Irish context, against the narrative of Spenser's *View*[28] and, indeed, at the conclusion of the episode, we discover exactly an analogue of the colonial defector, who refuses to return to the community to which he belongs. Grill, we are told, berates the Palmer for restoring him to human form, preferring to remain a hog, so that the Palmer responds: 'The donghill kind / Delights in filth and foule incontinence: / Let *Grill* be *Grill*, and haue his hoggish mind' (II. xii. 87. 6–8).

By contrast, however, the first Henry IV play presents a rather more complex picture than this. The Welsh bower does not simply evoke a decadent alien formation which proves attractive to the defecting Mortimer. In fact, even as, on the one hand, the scene registers a sharp division between the worlds of English and Welsh – literally, in its inclusion of both the Welsh and English languages in the script (or rather, on the stage, since the Welsh material is not included in the printed text of the play) – at the same time, these divisions are put into question in the scene, most notably in the figure of Glendower, who contrives to straddle both worlds.

Glendower is presented as moving fluently between the registers of English and Welsh. At a purely linguistic level, we see him act as translator, mediating between his daughter and her English husband. But Glendower himself also draws attention to the greater significance of his medial position and of his own cross-cultural history. When challenged by Percy during the dispute over the division of the kingdom, he proclaims

> I can speake English, Lord as well as you:
> For I was trayn'd vp in the English Court;
> Where, being but young, I framed to the Harpe
> Many an English Dittie, louely well,
> And gaue the Tongue a helpefull Ornament;
> A Vertue that was neuer seene in you.
>
> (TLN 1650–5)

Christopher Highley, in an article on 'Wales, Ireland, and *Henry IV*', has astutely noted how remarkably resonant this portrait of the early fifteenth century Glendower is with the contemporary image of the late sixteenth century Hugh O'Neill. As Highley observes, hearing this speech of Glendower's 'the play's first audiences could have recalled Tyrone's similar upbringing' and he goes on to note that

> Both Glendower and Tyrone had experienced the 'civilizing' effect of English culture and both had served English authority: Glendower as a follower of Henry Bolingbroke, Tyrone as an ally of Elizabeth. With both men, though, familiarity with English ways had only bred a latent resentment, and upon returning to their respective homes they had rebelled against their former English benefactors and masters.[29]

Highley further draws our attention to the various ways in which the connection between O'Neill and Glendower was indeed made by many of Shakespeare's contemporaries. He directs us, for instance, to a text included among the Irish state papers for 1598, entitled a 'Report by divers Welshmen concerning the Earl of Tyrone', which includes the following observation:

> That he was proclaimed King of Ireland, and that he was called 'Earl Terowyne, which is a word of Welsh, which is in English, the Earl of Owen's land', also that 'he descended of Owyne Clyne Dore, who had interest both in Ireland and Wales', and 'that there was a prophecy the Earl of Tyrone should prevail against the Engllish nation'. Further, that he was proclaimed Prince of Wales, and that he had friends in Wales that looked for him, as he was both favourable and bountiful to Welshmen.[30]

On the basis of the connections established by Christopher Highley, then, we might say that Ireland, though it doesn't figure explicitly in the text of the Henry IV plays, nevertheless, has an odd kind of dual presence in the narrative. On the one hand, I have been suggesting that the contemporary situation in Ireland, which disrupts the process of establishing any stable sense of an easy binary relationship between England and Ireland, prompts a reconsideration of the broader issue of how national identity is constituted within the island of Britain itself. On the other hand, we might say that we can see adumbrated within the figure of Glendower the image of Hugh O'Neill, emerging again, we might say, as a figure of liminal disruption, serving to interrogate the easy tropes of national self-imagining. We find these issues focused with particular clarity in the final play of the second Henriad: *Henry the Fift*.

III

The second of the Henry IV plays was most likely written in 1598. In August of that year, the northern Irish forces secured their greatest victory over the English, at the battle of the Yellow Ford. Before the year was out, they had swept southward, destroying the Munster plantation, and driving the colonists (including Spenser and his family) from the land.[31] Fynes Moryson, in his memoir of the Nine Years War, wrote that the year 1598, together with 'the next following, became so disasterous to the English, and successfull in action to the Irish, as they shaked the English gouernement in this kingdome, till it tottered, and wanted little of fatall ruine.'[32] In 1599, despite some opposition in the Privy Council, Robert Devereux, the second Earl of Essex, won the commission for Ireland and set off declaring 'I have beaten Knollys and Montjoye in the councele, and by G–d I will beat Tyr-Owen in the feilde.'[33] For the purpose of the campaign, 'he had', Moryson informs us, 'an Army assigned him, as great as himselfe required, and such for number and strength, as *Ireland* had neuer yet seene.'[34] Essex's departure was much heralded[35] and his triumphant return much anticipated. We find this anticipation registered, of course, in the text of the Folio version of *Henry the Fift*,[36] when the chorus to Act V, in imagining Henry's triumphant return to London, proclaims: 'But now behold',

> How London doth powre out her Citizens,
> . . .
> As by a lower, but by louing likelyhood,
> Were now the Generall of our gracious Empresse,
> As in good time he may, from Ireland comming,
> Bringing Rebellion broached on his Sword;
> How many would the peacefull Citie quit,
> To welcome him?
>
> (TLN 2872–84)

The text of *Henry the Fift* extends the engagement with the issue of national identities and of the relations among the various communities within the

British isles initiated in the Henry IV plays. The second scene of the play touches on the adversarial relationship that exists between England and its northern neighbour, as Henry warns his council

> We must not onely arme t'inuade the French,
> But lay downe our proportions, to defend
> Against the Scot, who will make roade vpon vs,
> With all aduantages.
>
> (TLN 283–6)

Canterbury and Exeter seek to reassure Henry that the Scots present no real threat to the integrity of England, that his northern English loyalists 'Shall be a Wall sufficient to defend / Our in-land from the pilfering Borderers' (TLN 288–9). We get a sense here of England's being drawn in behind its northern borders, which are marked now not by 'the triumphant sea, / Whose rocky shore beates backe the enuious siedge / Of watery Neptune', but rather by a Hadrianesque defensive wall which serves to keep the alien element at bay (as if Gaunt's English island has now shrunk to Canterbury's 'in-land' England). Canterbury concludes with a piece of confident advice:

> Diuide your happy England into foure,
> Whereof, take you one quarter into France,
> And you withall shall make all Gallia shake.
> If we with thrice such powers left at home,
> Cannot defend our owne doores from the dogge,
> Let vs be worried, and our Nation lose
> The name of hardinesse and policie.
>
> (TLN 361–7)

The play is finally, however, unwilling to settle for such ceding of territory as this and such retrenchment upon firmer ground. Where Canterbury calls on Henry to 'diuide [his] happy England into foure', the play as a whole shows a willingness to explore the fact that the monarch's realm is *already* divided into four distinct units and the play struggles to make sense of the relationship that exists among the four elements.

These issues are brought sharply into focus in the 'four captains' scene of the play, where we are presented with an English army that is, as David Cairns and Shaun Richards have noted, paradigmatic of the nation as a whole, as its membership is shown to include English, Welsh, Scots, and Irish representatives.[37] Cairns and Richards conceive of this scene as ultimately figuring a bogus vision of unity within the British realm, with the playwright taking great care to include markers of *exclusion* in his characterisation of the three Celtic captains, even as they are incorporated into the larger institution of the English army. They argue that while the three Celts 'are united in their service to the English Crown', their

> use of the English language . . . reveals that 'service' is the operative word, for in rank, in dramatic importance, and in linguistic competence, they are comical second-order citizens. They are, moreover, disputatious, and the argument between Fluellen and Macmorris, which is resolved by Gower's admonition, is further dramatic evidence of the harmony which England has brought to the fractious occupants of the Celtic fringe.[38]

Cairns and Richards's point is well made, but it fails to attend, I would argue, to the complexities of the Irish situation as they are written through this scene.

Discussions of the Irish dimension of the scene have tended to centre on the figure of the Irish captain Mackmorrice, specifically on his explosive outburst when his Welsh counterpart, Fluellen, begins to talk about the Irishman's 'nation':

> *Welch*: Captain *Mackmorrice*, I thinke, looke you, vnder your correction, there is not many of your Nation.
>
> *Irish*: Of my Nation? What ish my Nation? Ish a Villaine, and a Basterd, and a Knaue, and a Rascall. What ish my Nation? Who talkes of my Nation? (TLN 1237–42)

Mackmorrice's response is obscure and has given rise to a number of different interpretations. In an influential commentary on the passage, Philip Edwards has suggested that

> The paraphrase should run something like this. 'What is this separate race you're implying by using the phrase "your nation"? Who are you, a Welshman, to talk of the Irish as though they were a separate nation from you? I belong in this family as much as you do'. This is the essence of it − indignation that a Welshman should think of Ireland as a separate nation from the great (British) nation to which the Welshman apparently thought he belonged.[39]

Most subsequent critics have adopted Edwards's interpretation of the exchange, with Gary Taylor, for instance, quoting Edwards's proffered paraphrase as his gloss on the line 'What ish my nation?' in his Oxford edition of the play.

One of the problems with Edwards's interpretation is that it seeks to produce a single meaning from what is, in fact, a profoundly ambiguous passage. In the process, Edwards misses the deeper resonances of Mackmorrice's response. In addition we should note that Edwards essentially treats the Irish

captain's interrogative not as a question but as a statement – 'a furious repudiation of difference', as he calls it.[40] But in so doing, he disregards the possibility that Mackmorrice's question may be just that – a genuine question: 'What
ish my nation?'

Taken as a question, Mackmorrice's interrogative opens up a variety of
issues pertinent to the play in the context of the particular historical
moment in which it was written. In the first instance, we note that Mackmorrice's remark can be seen as resonating with a general English anxiety
regarding the project of establishing a coherent sense of Irish identity. In
this sense, his question appears in the text as a challenge, throwing into
doubt the issue of how the Irish can properly be classified and identified.
'What ish my nation?' is a blunt expression of this uncertainty, an interrogation of what *constitutes* the Irish nation.

We can see the extent to which this challenge to the construction of
stable identities is encoded in the text if we recall the particularities of
Mackmorrice's positioning in the play. Like O'Neill, Mackmorrice is himself
an oddly ambiguous figure. Appearing here as virtually the first 'stage
Irishman',[41] his speech betokens a stereotypical Irish identity, yet he nevertheless takes his place within the English army, fighting for the English
imperial cause. And like O'Neill's own soldiers, he appears, we presume, as
an Irishman garbed in the redcoated uniform of an English soldier. To the
extent, then, that Mackmorrice is, like O'Neill himself, ambiguously and
mercurially aligned with both an Irish and an English identity, the question
'What ish my nation?' may emerge as being directed both at and from that
very condition of liminal uncertainty itself. In this sense we might say that
Edwards's assessment of the passage as 'a furious repudiation of difference' is
exactly right, at least in the sense that what Mackmorrice's questioning
serves to effect is an interrogation of difference itself – of the bases on
which difference is erected and achieved. As David Baker has astutely observed of this exchange in general: 'MacMorrice's questions have the effect
of preventing any final meaning – any discursive end "point" – from
emerging at all. Here, the voicing of imperial power gives way to a discursive heterogeneity, interrogates itself, and finds itself unable to sustain the
distinctions on which it rests.'[42]

We find this failure to sustain distinctions at play later in the text also, as
the play draws on toward its conclusion in Frye's 'happy rustle of bridal
gowns and banknotes'. In the final scene, the conflict between England and
France has been resolved and the royal parties of French and English come
together in an effort to secure the peace. The scene is the occasion for what
Gary Taylor has termed as a 'Freudian slip' in the F1 text of the play.[43] As
the scene opens, Henry extends a welcome to the French party and his
courtesy is returned by the French king, Charles:

> Right ioyous are we to behold your face,
> Most worthy brother England, fairely met.
> So are you, Princes (English) euery one.
>
> (TLN 2996–8)

Queen Isabel then moves to second her husband's sentiment, but, addressing Henry, she makes a revealing substitution. 'So happy be the Issue Brother *Ireland*' (TLN 2999), she greets him, rather than, as we might expect, 'So happy be the issue brother *England*'.[44]

This error in the text could be recruited in support of the view of the ending of *Henry the Fift* put forward by Sinfield and Dollimore. Taking their cue from Edwards, they 'see the attempt to conquer France and the union in peace at the end of the play as a re-presentation of the attempt to conquer Ireland and the hoped-for unity of Britain... The play offers a displaced, imaginary resolution of one of the state's most intractable problems.'[45] It should be noted, however, that it is not the conquered France that gets confused with Ireland but rather the conquering England. Again, this overlapping seems to point less to what Sinfield and Dollimore have traced in the play as 'the ideal subservience' of Ireland to England, than to the deep interconnectedness of the two national groups and to the intense difficulty of the task of distinguishing discrete, coherent (and hierarchically organised) separate national identities from among them.

Henry the Fift appears to end in a grand gesture of unity, as Henry, in wooing Katherine, tells her that 'England is thine, Ireland is thine, France is thine, and *Henry Plantaginet* is thine' (TLN 3226–8), holding out the possibility of a great union of thrones, nations, and bodies. Seen in this light, Cairns and Richards may well be right when they see the play as presenting 'a piece of dramatic wish-fulfilment: that a contemporary cause of discord, namely Ireland, should come to [a] satisfactory conclusion'.[46] For all that, however, we must also say that the play finally fails to effect its ambitious project of maintaining a certain Gauntean sense of a coherent England, while somehow simultaneously (through the attempted incorporation / subordination / unification of the diverse national elements within the realm) accommodating to that sense of England the very boundaries and differences that Gaunt ignored. Ireland is crucially at the centre of that failure, as it raises issues of equivalence, proximity, and identity which the play is finally unable to assimilate to its grand unifying ambition.

IV

Essex did not succeed in his grand ambition of 'beat[ing] Tyr-Owen in the feilde'. He proved unequal to the task of managing O'Neill's transgressive liminality. In a half hour meeting with the Lord Lieutenant, O'Neill succeeded in wresting from him a truce that was greatly to the advantage of the Irish, leading to Essex's disgrace and, ultimately, to his execution.[47] Essex was succeeded in Ireland by Charles Blount, Lord Mountjoy. The style of Mountjoy's departure from England was in marked contrast to that of his predecessor: 'without any publique ostentation, or great attendancy, in the month of February 1600. he tooke his iourney toward *Ireland*'.[48] Mountjoy inflicted a decisive defeat on O'Neill at Kinsale in 1601 and finally accepted his surrender at Mellifont on 30th March 1603.

The date of O'Neill's surrender is, of course, significant, as it came just six days after the death of Elizabeth (a fact which Mountjoy concealed from O'Neill until after he had made his surrender). With the accession of James VI as king of Scotland, England, Wales, and an Ireland that had, for the first time ever, been brought into complete submission, the way seemed open for a new imagining of the national unit and the relations between its constituent parts. James certainly pushed for such a reimagining, as he sought to enact a grand project that would unite his territories into a single realm.

With the exception of *Henry VIII*, the Shakespeare canon after *Henry the Fift* confines itself to the mythical historiographic tradition where Britain is concerned. As Leah Marcus has shown in *Puzzling Shakespeare*, however, this mythic history is also deeply enmeshed in contemporary history and politics, with the Lear plays and *Cymbeline* taking up issues of union and disunity. In *Cymbeline*, we encounter a series of disjunctions, both domestic and political, which the play resolves in its conclusion, as lovers are reunited, lost children are restored to their inheritance, and the nation is connected with its imperial destiny. We might say of the play that it seeks to return us to the world of *The second Part of Henry the Sixt*, which sees a variety of different communities as being readily available for the service of a particular aristocratic fraction within the state. The confidence of the play's vision of union resonates with the confidence expressed just a couple of years later in John Davies' *Discouerie of the Trve Cavses why Ireland was neuer Entirely Subdued* (1612), in which Davies charts the success of his colonial project of integrating Ireland into the British legal realm. What both *Cymbeline* and the *Discouerie* neglect in their respective accounts of union, however, is the fact that the grand union scheme of the early seventeenth century was entirely notional: James failed to secure the necessary backing for the proposals in the English parliament and, in addition, Ireland's place within the scheme was never exactly clear.[49] In Britain, differences between England and Scotland would contribute to the eruption of the Civil War; in Ireland, Davies's imperial legal policy would play a part not just in the Irish uprising of 1641 (sensationally chronicled in John Temple's *The Irish Rebellion* of 1646), but would also serve to intensify the Anglo-Irish conflict by introducing an entrenched group of Scottish Protestant settlers into Ulster.

Despite the apparent confidence of *Cymbeline's* mythic pastoralism, then, and the triumph of Mountjoy's having succeeded (where Essex failed) in 'Bringing Rebellion broached on his Sword', what persisted (and persists) in the Irish situation, long after the deaths of both Shakespeare and O'Neill in 1616, is the confusion and anxiety registered in the plays written during the course of the Nine Years War. What *Cymbeline* neglects, finally, we might say, is Shakespeare's own Irish history.

Notes

1 Michael Neill, 'Broken English and broken Irish: nation, language, and the optic of power in Shakespeare's histories', *Shakespeare Quarterly*, 45: 1 (Spring 1994), p. 11.

2 Fynes Moryson, *An Itinerary* (London, 1617), vol. II, p. 3.

3 Richard Helgerson, *Forms of Nationhood: The Elizabethan Writing of England* (Chicago, 1992), p. 209.

4 Though not Helgerson himself, whose otherwise engaging and impressive book is surprisingly (and disappointingly) silent on the subject of Ireland.

5 Andrew Hadfield and Willy Maley, 'Introduction: Irish representations and English alternatives', in Brendan Bradshaw, Andrew Hadfield and Willy Maley, *Representing Ireland: Literature and the Origins of Conflict, 1534–1660* (Cambridge, 1993), p. 7.

6 A point which Michael Neill, 'Broken English', also makes: 'Ireland played [a] crucial part in the determination of English identity, functioning as the indispensable anvil upon which the notion of Englishness was violently hammered out' (p. 3).

7 See, in particular, the work of historians Nicholas Canny and David Beers Quinn and literary critical work such as David Cairns and Shaun Richards, *Writing Ireland: Colonialism, Nationalism and Culture* (Manchester, 1988); Patricia Coughlan (ed.), *Spenser and Ireland: An Interdisciplinary Perspective* (Cork, 1989), and also Bradshaw et al., *Representing Ireland*.

8 In the original: 'hunc filium suum non in orientem sed in occidentem, non in Saracenos sed in Christianos . . . transmisit' (*Expugnatio Hibernica: The Conquest of Ireland*).

9 Gerald of Wales, *Expugnatio Hibernica: The Conquest of Ireland*, parallel text, trans. A. B. Scott (Dublin, 1978), p. 237.

10 For the most recent work on O'Neill, see Hiram Morgan, *Tyrone's Rebellion: The Outbreak of the Nine Years War in Tudor Ireland* (Woodbridge, 1993). No adequate scholarly biography of O'Neill is currently available, though the Irish novelist Seán Ó Faoláin's *The Great O'Neill* (London, 1942) is still of interest. Though the book lacks documentation, Ó Faoláin does draw heavily on contemporary sources and records. See also Nicholas Canny, 'The Treaty of Mellifont and the re-organisation of Ulster, 1603', *The Irish Sword*, 9: 37 (Winter 1970), pp. 249–62, and 'Hugh O'Neill, Earl of Tyrone, and the changing face of Gaelic Ulster', *Studia Hibernica*, 10 (1970), pp. 7–35. For an interesting fictional treatment of O'Neill's life, see Brian Friel's *Making History* (London, 1989). For a near

contemporary account of O'Neill's career, see Thomas Gainsford, *The True and Exemplary and Remarkable History of the Earle of Tirone* (London, 1619).

11   Margaret MacCurtain, *Tudor and Stuart Ireland* (Dublin, 1972), p. 83.

12   William Camden's *Annales* was published in an English translation by R. Norton in 1630 under the title *The Historie of the Most Renowned and Victorious Princess Elizabeth*...This quotation is taken from vol. IV, p. 54.

13   Jonathan Dollimore, *Sexual Dissidence: Augustine to Wilde, Freud to Foucault* (Oxford, 1991), p. 323. For further instances of such 'transgressive reinscription', see the present writer's 'Gold lace and a frozen snake: Donne, Wotton and the Nine Years War', *Irish Studies Review*, 8 (Autumn 1994), which provides details of an encounter between O'Neill and John Harington, during which O'Neill prevailed upon Harington to read aloud parts of his translation of Ariosto's *Orlando Furioso*. Harington was much taken aback by the reception he received from O'Neill.

14   See G. A. Hayes-McCoy, 'The army of Ulster, 1593–1601', *The Irish Sword: The Journal of the Military History Society of Ireland*, 1 (1949–53): 'When Hugh O'Neill, Earl of Tyrone, won his first victory at Clontibret in 1595 he astonished his opponents by bringing a force of musketeers clad "in red coats like English soldiers" into action against them. In the days of his seeming loyalty he had secured the services of six English captains to train six companies of Tyrone men for action, as was supposed, against the Queen's enemies in the north' (p. 105).

15   For the purposes of this article, I use the First Folio (F1) text of the plays, quoting from Charlton Hinman's facsimile edition, *The First Folio of Shakespeare* (New York, 1968). I have used Hinman's 'through line numbers' (TLNs) in giving references. In using F1, I am following the insight offered by Leah Marcus that, in pursuing certain kinds of historicist analysis (what Marcus has termed 'local reading'), 'we need to use texts that are close to the period of production we are studying – not because those texts are more "valid" than others, but because their language and shaping of events may reverberate with immediately contemporary ideas in subtle ways that later texts do not' (*Puzzling Shakespeare: Local Reading and its Discontents* [Berkeley, 1988], p. 45). This observation is particularly relevant to the much edited Shakespeare canon. A number of the plays examined here were also published in quarto editions which differ significantly from the F1 text (they are traditionally included among the so-called 'bad' quartos). For an extremely useful example of a historicist reading of the differences between two such texts, see Annabel Patterson's analysis of Q1 and F1 *Henry the Fift* in *Shakespeare and the Popular Voice* (Oxford, 1989). A more extended treatment of the relationship between the chronology of these texts, their various versions, and their historical context would make for a very interesting project, but lies outside the scope of the present study.

16   Dollimore, *Sexual Dissidence*, p. 15.

17   Ann Rosalind Jones offers a somewhat similar argument in relation to John Webster's treatment of Ireland and Italy in *The White Devil*: '"Englishness" required its supplements, its sinister outsiders and sites of banishment for threats to the imperialist policy that consolidated, from the center, the self-representations of that "green and pleasant" land. But at the same time, those supplements threatened,

at least in the work of Webster, to throw off balance the concepts of legitimacy and self-identity which nationalist discourse sought to establish'. 'Italians and Others: *The White Devil* (1612)', in *Staging the Renaissance: Reinterpretations of Elizabethan and Jacobean Drama*, ed. David Scott Kastan and Peter Stallybrass (London, 1991), p. 260.

18 For the dating of the plays, I rely on Stanley Wells and Gary Taylor with John Jowett and William Montgomery, *William Shakespeare: A Textual Companion* (Oxford, 1987). For *2 Henry VI*, see pp. 111–12, under the play's quarto title *The First Part of the Contention*.

19 David Beers Quinn, *The Elizabethans and the Irish* (Ithaca, 1986), p. 133.

20 Both Cade and Lee eventually suffered the same fate, in that involvement with aristocratic conspiracies brought them finally to their deaths: Cade is killed when the rebellion which he is prompted to by Yorke fails and Lee is executed as a traitor at Tyburn, following his involvement with the abortive Essex rebellion.

21 James P. Myers, 'Early English colonial experiences in Ireland: Captain Thomas Lee and Sir John Davies', *Eire-Ireland*, 23: 1 (Spring 1988), p. 11. See also Brian de Breffny, 'An Elizabethan political painting', *Irish Arts Review*, 1: 1 (Spring 1984) and Hiram Morgan, 'Tom Lee: the posing peacemaker', in Bradshaw et al., *Representing Ireland*.

22 See *Faerie Queene*, Book V, canto ix. It is no coincidence that the first fragment of the poem – the 'Two Cantos of Mvtabilitie' – should be set in Ireland.

23 *A View of the Present State of Ireland*, in *The Works of Edmund Spenser: A Variorum Edition*, ed. Rudolf Gottfried (Baltimore, 1949), p. 102.

24 Ibid., p. 168.

25 Ó Faoláin, *The Great O'Neill*, p. 195. In fact, Ó Faoláin overstates the case here: the defining characteristic of O'Neill's career was his ability to temporise with the English authorities – strategic retraction and submission came as easily to him as rebellion and he contrived to secure a pardon from the Queen more than once during the course of the Nine Years War.

26 Philip Edwards, *Threshold of a Nation: A Study in English and Irish Drama* (Cambridge, 1979), p. 74. On Gaunt's speech, see also Graham Holderness, '"What ish my nation?": Shakespeare and national identities', *Textual Practice*, 5: 1 (1991), pp. 80–99.

27 Edmund Spenser, *The Faerie Queene*, edited by Thomas P. Roche and C. Patrick O'Donnell (New Haven, 1981), II. xii. 74. 1.

28 See 'To fashion a gentleman: Spenser and the destruction of the Bower of Bliss', in *Renaissance Self-fashioning: From More to Shakespeare* (Chicago, 1980).

29 Christopher Highley, 'Wales, Ireland, and *Henry IV*', *Renaissance Drama*, n.s. 21 (1990), p. 94.

30 *Calendar of State Papers Ireland 1598–9*, pp. 461–2.

31 A contemporary account of the Munster campaign, possibly written by Spenser himself, describes the overwhelming of the settlements: 'There came vpp latelie of the Rebells not past 2000. being sent by the said Traitour E: of Tyreone vpon whose ariveall all the Irish rose vpp in Armes against the english which were lately planted theire...And going straight vppon the English as they dwelt disparsed before they could assemble themselues spoiled them all, their howses sacked and

them selues forced to flie away for safetye' – included in *The Works of Edmund Spenser*, ed. Gottfried, p. 238.

32 Moryson, vol. II, p. 24.

33 Quoted from a letter from Essex to John Harington; see the collection of Harington's miscellaneous prose included in *Nugae Antiquae* (London, 1804), p. 246.

34 Moryson, vol. II, p. 27.

35 From Camden we learn that he departed 'out of *London* accompanied with a gallant traine of the flower of the Nobility, and saluted by the people with ioyfull acclamations', *Annales*, in Norton's *Historie*, IV, p. 139.

36 Almost all of the Irish references are lacking from the Quarto version of the play, published in 1600. See Annabel Patterson's reading of the differences between the two texts in *Shakespeare and the Popular Voice*. For a facsimile of the Quarto text, see Michael Allen and Kenneth Muir (eds), *Shakespeare's Plays in Quarto* (Berkeley, 1981). For a diplomatically edited version of the text, see *The Cronicle History of Henry the Fift*, ed. Graham Holderness and Bryan Loughrey (Hemel Hempstead, 1993).

37 Cairns and Richards, *Writing Ireland*, p. 12.

38 Ibid., p. 10. See also Jonathan Dollimore and Alan Sinfield's analysis of the play in 'History and ideology: the instances of *Henry V*', in John Drakakis (ed.), *Alternative Shakespeares* (London, 1988). Of this scene Dollimore and Sinfield observe: 'the Irish, Welsh and Scottish soldiers manifest not their countries' centrifugal relationship to England but an ideal subservience of margin to centre' (p. 217).

39 Edwards, *Threshold of a Nation*, pp. 75–6.

40 Ibid., p. 76.

41 For a useful 'historical study of the earliest Irish, Welsh and Scottish characters in English plays', see J. O. Bartley, *Teague, Shenkin and Sawney* (Cork, 1954). Bartley discusses 'Shakespeare's Irish Soldier' at pp. 16–17.

42 David J. Baker, '"Wildehirissheman": colonialist representation in Shakespeare's *Henry V*', *English Literary Renaissance*, 22 (1992), p. 46.

43 See his single volume edition of the play in the Oxford series (Oxford, 1982), p. 18.

44 In common with most other editors, Taylor emends 'Ireland' to 'England' here. Michael Neill's edition of the play in the Folger Shakespeare series retains 'Ireland' on the basis that it represents a deliberate attempt to foreground the play's Irish concerns.

45 Dollimore and Sinfield, 'History and ideology', p. 225.

46 Cairns and Richards, *Writing Ireland*, p. 9.

47 Thomas Gainsford in his *History of the Earle of Tirone*, in a single paragraph-long sentence, details item by item Essex's progress from his 'priuate parley with *Tyrone*' to 'how his fortunes and Life ended' (p. 24). On Essex's encounter with O'Neill, see the 'Journall of the L. Lieutenants procedinges from the xxviijth Aug. tyll the viijth of Sept. 1599' included with John Harington's various writings in *Nugae Antiquae* and John Dymmock, *A Treatise of Ireland*, included in *Tracts Relating to Ireland*, ed. Richard Butler (Dublin, 1843). Both accounts present O'Neill as offering Essex virtually a parody of English courtly behaviour in the

encounter (Dymmock writes: 'before the Lord Lieutenant was fully aryved...
Tyrone tooke of his hatt and enclyninge his body did his duty unto his Lordship
with very humble ceremony, contynewynge the same observancy the whole tyme
of the parlye' [p. 50]) – an instance, again, I would suggest, of 'transgressive reinscription'.

48   Gainsford, *History of the Earle of Tirone*, p. 28.
49   Most of the texts produced in support of the union cause – for example, the
     pamphlets written by Francis Bacon, John Hayward, John Thornborough, John
     Skynner, William Cornwallys and John Gordon, or the literary texts produced by,
     among others, Samuel Daniel, John Ford and Ben Jonson – focused on the union
     of the island of Britain, to the exclusion of the realm of Ireland. James himself, in
     his first speech to the English parliament, imagined the union in terms of a
     marriage between himself and Britain: 'What God hath conioyned then, let no
     man separate. I am the Husband, and all the whole Isle is my lawfull Wife'. He
     goes on to hope that 'no man will be so vnreasonable as to thinke that I that am a
     Christian King vnder the Gospel, should be a Polygamist and husband to two
     wiues'. *The Political Works of James I*, ed. Charles Howard McIlwain (Cambridge,
     MA, 1918), p. 272.

Shakespeare and National Identities

Graham Holderness

*Holderness's challenging article considers the continuing appropriation
of Shakespeare's history plays to different political agendas and historical
circumstance. Much of his argument focuses on an analysis and contextualization of two iconic films of* Henry V: *Laurence Olivier's of 1944
and Kenneth Branagh's of 1989. This engaged materialist investigation
of the texts' operation in different cultures effectively interrogates the
nineteenth-century identification of the particular patriotism of the
genre.*

Graham Holderness, '"What ish my nation?": Shakespeare and National
Identities', *Textual Practice*, 5 (1991), pp. 74–93.

I

Offhand I can't remember a day when it seemed so marvellous or mad to be
English. Suddenly the chronic inconvenience of London's transport strike
and the continuing horrors of the mining dispute were put into the merciful
perspective of history.

    It began in Westminster Abbey where I sat close to the Queen Mother and
watched her fight back tears and surrender to smiles with a packed congregation

as the funniest hours of her reign were celebrated in the familiar words and music of Sir Noel Coward.

And it ended here at Stratford, with a young, brave and poetic Henry bridging the centuries between by reminding us of the unlikely spirit which won Agincourt. Nothing much seemed so very different...

What links the vision of young Mr Kenneth Branagh, making his Royal Shakespeare debut as a raw, stocky warrior, with Coward's latterday musings, is the patriotic poet which lurked beneath these different facades...

To hear Mr Branagh wonder incredulously at the valour of his rag-tag-and-bobtail troops was to hear echoes of Derek Jacobi reading the moving war diaries of Coward at the unveiling of his memorial stone.

And when Branagh squats among his men, blackened with the efforts of the war, and urges them once more into the breach – well – we had heard that sentiment back in the Abbey when Penelope Keith set the sea of handkerchiefs dabbing at moist eyes...

I won't press the coincidence. Suffice to say that neither the service at the Abbey nor Adrian Noble's spare, bare production at Stratford were mere tub-thumping exercises in mindless nationalism.

There was pain, irony, wit and humanity in both. As Ian McDairmid's conversational chorus informs us: Henry had a kingdom for a stage. Which of course was like Coward turning his stage into a kingdom. Both, in their way make a little thing like a transport shutdown seem irrelevant. All this from old masters and new blood. Between Harry's Harfleur spirit and Coward's London Pride, it did not, after all, seem improbable that there are still good reasons to be in England now that April's almost here.

Jack Tinker (*Daily Mail*, 29 March 1984)[1]

The distinction here between 'patriotism' (of the handkerchief-dabbing type) and 'nationalism' (of the tub-thumping variety) is a reasonable starting-point for the following explorations of British patriotic and national identities, as they appear mediated through the cultural reproduction of Shakespearean drama, and in particular through Kenneth Branagh's widely celebrated film adaptation of *Henry V*, itself based on the 1984 Royal Shakespeare Company stage production eulogized in Jack Tinker's review.[2] To have a forceful and vigorous ideology of nationalism, you have to have a forceful and vigorous nation to enact and substantiate it. If the 'nation' in question happens, like Britain, to be an eclipsed world power – no longer a great imperial aggressor, no longer a significant colonial leader, no longer a dominant industrial or economic force – then what basis remains for a particular, quantifiable 'national' consciousness? If the political and economic character of the 'nation' owes more to its participation in larger political and economic units – the EEC, NATO, American foreign policy, the multinational capitalist economy, the International Monetary Fund – then what sense does it make to continue talking about a specific, isolable 'national' identity?

All that seems left to the disappointed or reformed British nationalist is an emotion of 'patriotism', which can evidently be distinguished from the politics of nationalism, and is capable of surviving such losses and transformations as the demise of Empire and the descent from world eminence relatively undamaged and unscathed. Patriotism is associated with 'poetry', with emotion, with the heart, with tears; 'nationalism' with 'mindless' aggression, with 'tub-thumping' jingoistic assertiveness. In a review of the subsequent film version of *Henry V*, Tom Hutchinson in *The Mail on Sunday* later proposed the same distinction: 'the film ... touches the heart of emotion rather than the instinct for patriotism.'[3] But in the earlier review of the stage production, patriotism is indissolubly linked with the past. The plangency of patriotic feeling here derives from what Tom Nairn calls 'the glamour of backwardness': a nostalgia, a craving, unappeasable hunger for that which is irretrievably lost. Yet that loss may be regarded also as neither complete nor inconsolable, since the utterances of a 'patriotic poet' such as William Shakespeare (or Noel Coward) can transcend the absence and negation of history, and suffuse the soul with – not exactly a new fulfilment, but at least a new longing, a new mixing of memory and desire. Militaristic violence, inseparable from the historical actuality of nationalism, is strangely appeased in this flood of remembrance,[4] strangely pacified by 'the merciful perspective of history'. The British patriot, now no longer a nationalist, looks back regretfully, with resigned sadness, to his 'finest hour' in 1940, or the 'unlikely' victory of his ancestors at Agincourt; but, as re-awakened memories, these scenes of historical violence, recollected in tranquillity, acquire a power to comfort and console.

The patriotic emotion is anchored in the past. Inspired by the 'valour', 'gallantry' and 'courage' displayed by the manly deeds of a warrior race and immortalized in the words of the 'old masters' (represented here by the in-this-context-unfortunately-named 'Shake-spear' and 'Coward'), patriotism paradoxically expresses itself in gestures of weakness, in a 'surrender' to tears. The binary polarization of gender implicit in this construction is evident in the femininity shared by those cast, respectively, as tear-jerker and tear-jerked (Penelope Keith and the Queen Mother); and the contradictory quality of the patriotic emotion itself manifested in the male observer's luxurious relishing of a weakness discovered in the contemplation of strength – like D. H. Lawrence, the writer here enjoys feeling his 'manhood cast / Down in the flood of remembrance' as he 'weeps like a child for the past.'[5]

The patriotic emotion is anchored in the past, and besieged, embattled in the present. The England that surrounds Jack Tinker gives him no cause for patriotic celebration: it is rather a scene of bitter social conflict and class-antagonism, an England of transport and coalfield strikes. The English patriot doesn't see his emotional conviction rooted in the actuality of the nation that surrounds him, which seems systematically to negate his ideal national image. The patriotic emotion searches past and future for a habitable space, nostalgically embracing the glamour of backwardness, and optimistically extrapolating a projected landscape of hope. Elsewhere in the review Tinker quotes some lines from Noel Coward's *Cavalcade*, which exactly encapsulate that contradictory emotion: 'Let's drink to the spirit of gallantry and courage that made a strange Heaven out of unbelievable Hell, and let's drink to the Hope, that one day this country of ours, which we love so much, will find dignity and greatness and peace again.'

II

The authentic accent of what might anachronistically be described as a 'postmodern' patriotism can in fact be located in what we think of as the very heart of the traditional discourse of British nationalism: it is even there in that notorious speech attributed to John of Gaunt in Shakespeare's *Richard II*, which in turn provided subsequent ages with a basic vocabulary of patriotic rhetoric.

> This royal throne of kings, this sceptred isle,
> This earth of majesty, this seat of Mars,
> This other Eden, demi-paradise,
> This fortress built by Nature for herself
> Against infection and the hand of war,
> This happy breed of men, this little world,
> This precious stone set in a silver sea
> Which serves it in the office of a wall
> Or as a moat defensive to a house
> Against the envy of less happier lands,
> This blessed plot, this earth, this realm, this England...
>   (*Richard II*, II. i. 40–50)

It is natural to think of this fictionalized John of Gaunt as a great supporter of monarchical prerogative and royal power: certainly outside the play his famous patriotic speech has invariably been employed to endorse absolute authority, to support the autocratic will of many subsequent British kings and governments. Within the play of course this speech actually functions as a diatribe of criticism against the ruling monarch: Gaunt is not even depicting the England of the present, but expressing a nostalgic regret for an England which has long since vanished into the historical past. It is precisely because the England he sees before him – Richard's England – falls so far short of his idealized vision of what he believes England once was, that his poetic vision of national glory is so brightly and vividly imagined.

The realm of England is here defined largely in terms of its monarchy, its history distinguished by the quality of its kings: but the monarchs Gaunt idealizes are not like Richard. They are the warlike, crusading, feudal kings of the early Middle Ages: so Gaunt's speech is after all no panegyric of royal absolutism, but a lament for the passing of a feudal kingdom in which king and nobility were united by a natural balance of forces into a united 'happy breed of men'. Gaunt's speech is not merely an appeal for strong leadership in the king, and it is certainly not a defence of the Renaissance doctrine of divine right and absolute royal authority. On the contrary, he imagines royal authority as inseparable from the power of the nobility; the golden age he longs for and regrets is that of a feudalism held together by the authority of a strong king *and* by the power of a strong aristocracy. Gaunt's attack on Richard's style of government concentrates on the fact that Richard has replaced the feudal bonds of 'fealty' – the system of reciprocal obligations which bind lord and subject in a feudal polity – with economic contracts:

> England, bound in with the triumphant sea...
> ...is now bound in with shame,
> With inky blots and rotten parchment bonds
> (II. i. 63–4)

Richard is now a mere 'landlord' of England, rather than a king; he has sought to dispense with the loyal co-operation of the nobility, and to rule with the assistance of an upstart bureaucracy of 'favourites'. Determined to shake off the influence of the barons, he has introduced radical economic policies to raise revenue without reliance on the great land-holders. The unacceptability of Richard's kingship consists, in Gaunt's eyes, in his modernizing programme of de-feudalization, and his consequent slighting of the traditional aristocracy. It is ironic that so many subsequent appeals to English patriotism have been mounted on the basis of this elegant and barbaric statement of baronial self-interest and celebration of a class that has scarcely earned the unqualified admiration of even the most conservative of thinkers. But as we shall see, the hypostatization of a sectional class-interest as the ideology of a 'nation' is a symptomatic element in the history of British patriotism.

When the patriotic rhetoric of this speech is imitated, Gaunt's investment in the glamour of backwardness is often incorporated along with the imperious vigour of his nationalistic vision. Some years ago the Department of the Environment produced a television advertisement as part of an anti-litter campaign. A succession of visual images depict urban squalor, industrial detritus and general untidiness – a river seeping oil and tar; empty streets blowing with waste paper like tumbleweed in a Western ghost-town; a cat snarling in a filthy gutter outside the open, flapping doors of a pub. The images were accompanied by those famous and familiar Shakespearean lines, spoken in voice-over commentary. Lines we are accustomed to hear uttered with a hush of reverence and breathless adoration, and with a musical effect akin to the sound of the last post being played at sunset across some colonial parade-ground in the Far East, were here intoned harshly, with an accent of resentment, bitterness, and dissatisfaction. Gaunt's patriotic speech was made to operate as an aggrieved, harshly ironic commentary on the scene of depressing untidiness. At some time, the voice implied, things have been different; Britain was once a proud (and tidy) nation; this royal throne of Kings has not always been so besmirched and soiled by – litter; there was a time when the seat of Mars was cleaned regularly, and where this other Eden was genuinely fit for human habitation.

A moment's consideration of the standards of civic hygiene prevailing in the 1590s would provoke some scepticism about this implicit charge. The advertisement however had little use for authentic historical deference, being concerned only to construct, through the language of Shakespeare, an ideal type of 'the English nation', against which images of the shortcomings of the present might be measured. Its persuasive discontent was no simple reproof, admonishment, or rational appeal, but rather a paternalistic rebuke, a constituting of the untidy British subject as a violator of purity and innocence, guilty of profaning an idealized image of what the nation once was, and might be again. Think, intones the Shakespearean voice, think of the august and distinguished company of ancestral illuminati, ancient and modern, you are offending by your anti-social behaviour: those celebrated knights of the theatre like Sir Laurence Olivier and Sir John Gielgud, with whom such speeches are customarily associated; their great chivalric grandsires, that earlier generation of militaristic rather than histrionic knights, such as John of Gaunt; various kings and queens, ancient and modern, sometime rulers of 'this sceptred isle'; and above all their heir, the modern custodian of this precious stone, set in a silver sea – (Mrs) Thatcher, the national housekeeper Herself. Thus a text which was originally the expression of an incomparable nostalgia for another time, is mobilized as an authoritative voice enjoining on us all an active commitment to the glamour of backwardness. The nostalgic lament for a vanished Elizabethan age takes us spiraling vertiginously down the intertextual labyrinths of quotation, with no terminus in sight, this side of Paradise, other than a fourth term of Tory government.

III

We began in Westminster Abbey, that focal point of traditional 'British' culture where the institutions of church, monarchy, and democratic constitution (in Philip Larkin's words) 'meet, blend and are robed as destinies'.[6] With imagined wing our swift scene now flies, via John of Gaunt's image of England as a 'precious stone set in a silver sea', to a margin, an edge, a border; to the south coast of Britain, and specifically to those white cliffs of Dover, over which, in Vera Lynn's wartime song, 'there will be blue-birds' – 'tomorrow, just you wait and see'. What more lyrical expression could there be of the patriotic hunger for an endlessly deferred fulfilment than that poignant expression of elegaic existentialism which, like John of Gaunt's speech, and Noel Coward's *Cavalcade*, attaches its emotion to the past and future as a way of confronting the absence and pain of the present? The iconic image that goes with the song is of course the famous white cliffs themselves, that long chalk escarpment which offers to the envy of less happier lands so characteristically 'English' a seascape.

'Wherefore to Dover?' my reader might well enquire, echoing the accumulating incredulities of Regan and Cornwall in *King Lear*: 'Wherefore to *Dover*?'. The seaport of Dover, those famous white cliffs, and more generally the stretch of coastline from Southampton to the Thames estuary, occupy a peculiar and privileged place in the iconography and mythology of British nationalism. My initial reference to Vera Lynn invokes the Second World War, and specifically the period 1940–4 when France was under German occupation, and Britain in constant fear of an invasion. That 'rump' of England then felt (not for the first time) the vulnerability of exposure to another land-mass, the threatening point of France that pokes aggressively towards southern Britain, intimately close in space (narrow enough to swim across) yet always mistrusted, perpetually perceived as alien, frequently feared. Of course in a war of aerial transport, long-range heavy bombers, guided missiles, that part of England was (though subject to shelling from the French coast) in many ways no more vulnerable than any other, its borders capable of being breached at any point. But it is those cliffs of the south coast that provide us with our most characteristic national image of vulnerability, exposure, openness to the peril of foreign invasion.

The mythological status of the white cliffs of Dover is far more ancient than 1940. In those legendary and mythological narratives that preceded the advent of modern historiography, Dover was actually what the anthropologist Malinowski called a 'spot of origins', a particular geographical location regarded by tradition as the source of a nation's genesis. Anthropologists have identified in the proliferation of such narratives a structural form which they term the 'myth of origin', a narrative which purports to explain the process of a nation's appearance in history. Medieval historians traced the ancestry of their various national populations and monarchies to the dispersal of the Trojan princes after the fall of Troy: Geoffrey of Monmouth claimed that the English were descended from Brutus, allegedly a descendant of Aeneas. In Holinshed there is a narrative describing the conquest of

what was to become Britain by Brutus, whose companion Corineus succeeded in overthrowing the giant Gogmagog, the island's original inhabitant
– 'by reason whereof the place was named long after, *The Fall or leape of
Gogmagog*, but afterwards it was called *The Fall of Dover*'.[7] As John Turner
has shown, such pseudo-historical narratives were retold in the Renaissance
as morality fables, calculated to guide political conduct; but they were also
retold as myths, designed to legitimize power: 'The black holes in time were
to be occluded, the dangerous discontinuities of history papered over with
myths that would confirm authority and marginalize the claims of political
opposition.'[8] When James I in 1604 had himself proclaimed King of 'Great
Britain', he was deliberately re-introducing an antiquarian geographical term
in order to establish 'one single rule' over England and Scotland. The name
itself was falsely derived from Brutus, and in 1605 James was celebrated in
the Lord Mayor's show as the second Brutus who, in fulfilment of Merlin's
ancient prophecy, would 'reunite what the original Brutus had put asunder'.[9]

The narratives of this 'mythical charter' enact a sequence of invasion,
conquest, colonization and fragmenting. Dover is the point of entry, the
aperture through which a new force of domination can enter the territory,
settle it, and then – in a tragic political error – part it asunder. Reading
through the political to the sexual, Britain is the female body, invaded by
the colonizing male; the appropriate feminine resistance is overthrown, and
the country planted with fertile seed. The inevitable result of this process is
however not unity, but parturition, splitting, division; not the formation of a
single unified whole, but the multiplying of centrifugal energies. The myth
imagines national origin as a cyclical process of invasion, unification, plantation, and division.

Precisely because in this myth Dover is the source of national identity, it is
also the weakest point of the territory's physical defences. What one male can
do to a female body, what one conqueror can do to a territory, another male,
another conqueror, can repeat; and in every repetition the action is (in an
important sense) identical. The fundamentally unitary nature of conquest/
intercourse cuts sharply across powerful taboos based on binary oppositions of
difference (legitimate/illegitimate, married/un-married, pure/contaminated,
good/evil); and thereby forms the basis of that male sexual jealousy which in
turn butts onto xenophobic nationalism: that point where the linked elements
of 'father' and 'fatherland' in the word 'patriotism' meet. Along the south
coast England presents her white, chaste purity to the potential invader as a
defensive repellent, but also as a temptation. 'Succeed where Napolean failed'
urges an advertisement for the local South-East England tourist industry, the
words emblazoned across an aerial photograph of the familiar iconic escarpment: 'spend a day in White Cliffs country'. The point where the nation's
identity begins is also the point where it could most easily be violated or re-
conquered.[10]

IV

A key scene of Shakespeare's *Henry V* (Act II, scene 2) is set on that coastline, historically at Southampton (though usefully, for my purposes, the Folio text of the play misprints Southampton as 'Dover'). Henry and his nobles have here reached the 'extreme verge' of their territorial confine, a point of no return. Everything has been staked on the success of the French adventure; at the end of the scene Henry affirms, rhetorically but accurately, that his authority as monarch depends on victory: 'No King of England, if not King of France.' At this margin of the kingdom, which has the perilous quality of all territorial borders, the riskiest, most dangerous aspect of the whole enterprise – more subversive than the uneven odds at Agincourt – is encountered: internal dissension, mutiny within the ranks, self-betrayal. The periphery of England, that no-man's-land between England and France, marked by the sharp dividing line of the white cliffs, sanctified by the legendary myth of origins, is the point chosen for the enactment of a particular ritual: the cleansing of the English body politic by a sacrificial execution.

In the play-text Exeter defines the treachery of the conspirators simply as a hired murder, a contract killing undertaken for a French purse. On discovery however one of them, the Earl of Cambridge, hints at an ulterior motive:

> For me, the gold of France did not seduce,
> Although I did admit it as a motive
> The sooner to effect what I intended.
>
> (II. ii. 151–3)

In fact of course the three men arraigned here historically represented the cause of the deposed Richard II; the Earl of Cambridge's ulterior motive was that of re-establishing the legitimate dynasty toppled by the Lancastrians' usurpation. Ultimately they succeeded in forming the Yorkist power in the Wars of the Roses, in murdering Henry's son and in putting three kings on the English throne. The narrowing-down of this complex constitutional problem to a simple focus on the question of political loyalty is a characteristic achievement of Henry's style of government, and of course a familiar mechanism of ideological coercion in times of war. Political dissent becomes treachery: internal difference is forced to collapse under the moral and ideological pressures of international conflict.[11]

Kenneth Branagh placed particular emphasis on his decision to reinstate sections of the play-text omitted from Laurence Olivier's film version, and in particular the whole of Act II, scene 2:

I decided on including some significant scenes that Olivier's film, for obvious reasons, had left out: in particular, the conspirators' scene where Henry stage-manages a public cashiering of the bosom friends who have been revealed as traitors. The violence and extremism of Henry's behaviour and its effect on a volatile war cabinet were elements that the Olivier version was not likely to spotlight.[12]

The general line of comparison here is that Olivier's film treatment was severely constrained by its wartime context of production: as a patriotic celebration of Britain's military strength and resolve, sponsored by the Ministry of Information, indissolubly linked both psychologically and strategically with the projected (and of course successful) Allied invasion of occupied France, the film was unlikely to place any emphasis on internal treachery, or to foreground qualities in Henry's character and behaviour that might be read as unpleasantly 'violent' or 'extreme'.

Both film versions establish this scene by adapting the device of Shakespeare's Chorus. In the Olivier version, a painting of the white cliffs of Southampton/Dover frames an unmistakably theatrical set, the prow of a stage ship where Henry and his nobles receive the sacrament before embarking. The overtly theatrical quality of the scene relates it closely to the reconstructed Elizabethan stage on which all the earlier scenes have been played. In the Branagh version Derek Jacobi as Chorus appears on a cliff-top (white, of course) from which he delivers the prologue to Act II. The sequence of directions reads:[13]

> The Chorus is standing on a grassy cliff edge, looking out to sea. He turns to look at the camera.

> > *Chorus*:   The French, advised by good intelligence
> >   Of this most 'dreadful' preparation . . .

> He turns to look towards the cliff top and we cut closer to the traitors who have now appeared, passing through frame as their names are mentioned.

> > *Chorus*:   One, Richard Earl of Cambridge . . .

> As he walks away along the cliff edge, wrapping his scarf around him against the cold sea air, beyond him we see the dramatic white cliffs of the English coastline.

Once the dramatic action is resumed, the Chorus disappears (though in the original theatrical production he frequently remained on stage), and the 'traitor scene' is established firmly in a naturalistic 'hostelry' (p. 36). The action is also played naturalistically, with a consistent emphasis on individual emotion. The key issue here is personal rather than political; the key emphasis falls on the shocking treachery of Henry's friends, particularly his 'bed-fellow' the Earl of Cambridge. At one point Henry throws Cambridge over a table with an almost sexual intensity, violently enacting the pain of personal betrayal (s.d. p. 40, illustration p. 41). The conspirators confess only their guilt: Cambridge's lines about an alternative motive are cut.

The main interest of the scene as presented here consists in a dramatization of the psychological stresses and strains of such a critical situation, as experienced in Henry's character. The dominant device of close-up is used here, as throughout the film, to register the psychological costs of authority. Branagh's intention may have been to foreground the violence and extremism of Henry's behaviour: but the naturalistic medium ensures that the nature of the spectator's engagement with the action is one of individual identification. Branagh's use, in the quotation on p. 88, of theatrical metaphors – 'stage-manages', 'spotlight' – actually draws attention to the *anti-theatrical* medium of filmic naturalism, in which very little space is left for the spectator to reflect on the nature of the dramatic medium itself. No one could gather from this scene, any more than from Olivier's version of the same scene, that there is implicit in the dramatic text a subtext related to the critical question of legitimacy. Branagh has conspired with the character of Henry himself to obliterate the play's momentary exposure of a stress-point in the unity of the commonwealth. In this way the possibility of political dissent can be completely occluded, both within and through the text, since all political opposition is converted on this ideological terrain to civil treachery and personal betrayal.

The key difference between the two film versions seems to me to reside in their respective adaptations of Shakespeare's Chorus. I have argued elsewhere[14] that Olivier's adaptation of the Chorus, and his initial setting of the production-text within a reconstructed Elizabethan theatre, put into circulation some of the 'radical and subversive potentiality of Shakespeare's play...to foreground the artificiality of its dramatic devices'. Branagh's adaptation of the Chorus is equally inventive and in many ways effective. The device of beginning with the Chorus in an empty film studio, and opening set doors on to the dramatic action, is an ingenious updating of Olivier's mock Globe theatre. Though the Chorus is sometimes shown to be involved in the action (e.g. at the siege of Harfleur), he more characteristically appears as an alienation-effect, emerging surprisingly from behind a tree after the execution of Bardolph, or appearing to block out the final scene of diplomatic reconciliation in the French court, where he delivers that sharply undercutting prophecy which calls into question Henry's political achievement. But the radical departure from Olivier's use of this device rests in the fact that although the Chorus becomes involved in the action, the action never strays on to the territory of the Chorus. At one point in the original Royal Shakespeare Company stage production, Henry and the

Chorus, in a brilliant *coup de théâtre*, almost bumped into one another, miming a surprised double-take of near-recognition: with a shock of delight we saw the fictional world of the dramatic action suddenly enter the fictionalizing activity of the Chorus. But in the film the naturalism of the action itself is never compromised in this way, despite the self-reflexive interventions of the intrusive choric witness.

It is abundantly clear, despite its radical features, in what relation Olivier's film stood to the nationalistic ideology of its time. But where does the Branagh film stand in relation to contemporary patriotic and nationalist ideologies? The original (1984) stage production, directed by Adrian Noble, and in which Branagh played the king, became known as the 'post-Falklands' *Henry V*. That suggests of course a prevailing mood of revulsion against war, against imperialistic shows of strength, against militaristic patriotism. The film can easily be read in line with this view: it was 'made for a generation with the Indo-China war and the Falklands behind it and is wary of calls to arms', according to Philip French.[15] Branagh has 'stripped the veneer of jingoism from the play and shown war in its true horror';[16] the film 'emphasises the horror and futility of battle'.[17]

But the term 'post-Falklands' may not be quite as simple as that. 'Post' (as in 'postmodernism') does not always translate easily as 'anti' or 'counter': and it could well be that along with the obvious political advantages accruing to the power victorious in a military conflict ('no Prime Minister of Britain, if not Empress of South Georgia'), the Falklands war bequeathed to British culture a decidedly ambiguous interest in war, not entirely unconnected with the characteristic emotions of patriotism. Certainly many of the post-Falklands cultural productions, such as Charles Wood's play *Tumbledown*,[18] betray a fascination with the experience of combat, with soldierly camaraderie, with the anguish of extreme suffering, with the psychological stresses of military leadership. Branagh's approach to the character of Henry V[19] was certainly to some degree founded on exactly such a fascination with the moral and emotional complexities made available in the theatre of war. His notorious consultation of Prince Charles,[20] by way of research into the isolation of office and the loneliness of command, indicates a readiness to refer directly and to attend sympathetically to the contemporary experience of monarchical power. In the stage production he played the character of Henry so as to disclose those emotional complexities, to reveal weakness as well as strength, self-suppression as well as self-aggrandisement, personal loss as well as national victory. In that production the Brechtian device of the Chorus was able to offer a counterpoise to this open though ambivalent admiration for the heroic individual: in the relatively naturalistic medium of the film, and of course under Branagh's own direction, there is no such system of checks and balances to subvert the invitation to empathic identification with the psychology of power.

Again, if we compare the very different social roles of Olivier and Branagh, we would expect very different perspectives on the play to emerge. The one was almost a natural product of the English *ancien régime*, his manly shoulders practically designed for the touch of the regal sword; the other aggressively constructs his own social persona as the tough and ambitious boy from working-class Belfast, determined to make it in the competitive market-place of the British theatre, as impatient with traditional institutions and fossilized establishments as the young shock-troops of the Thatcherite Stock Exchange. Now it is quite evident that Branagh's studious and systematic campaign of self-publicity, a strategy he obviously considers necessary to the fulfilment of his artistic ambitions, engages with the naturalistic medium of the film to provoke a structural parallelism between actor and hero.[21] This theme runs through all the reviews of the film. In deciding to make it, Branagh 'took on much the same odds as Henry did at Agincourt';[22] he 'has marshalled his forces as well as Henry led his army'.[23] 'Clearly he has some sort of affinity with the part of King Henry, but it doesn't seem an actorly affinity. Branagh too talks like a winner, and *Henry V* offers him better than any other play in the repertoire what might be called a yuppy dynamic, a mythology of success and self-definition rather than struggle.'[24]

A structural parallel is also perceived between the 'band of brothers' with whose help Henry achieves such extraordinary success, and the team of actors assembled by Branagh to make the film. Here in the reviews we encounter a series of metaphors which oddly and unselfconsciously link theatrical and militaristic vocabularies. 'Before shooting started, Branagh, like Henry, addressed his troops, his happy few, saying he wanted to make it a "company picture"'.[25] 'There is already something of the spirit of Henry's happy few in the cast and crew behind the camera ... every member of this film unit would go to the wall for Kenneth Branagh.'[26] 'The actors ... beamed like the happy few, ready to cry God for Kenneth.'[27]

Even odder is a tendency, quite in the spirit of that great tradition of public school patriotism which identified hand grenades with cricket balls, to express the relationship between theatre and heroic combat in metaphors of sport. Branagh himself dubbed his team 'the English all-stars', and several critics quipped along the same hearty and sporting lines: 'Branagh has fielded the first XV.'[28] 'This is how Englishmen play their football, so it seems a perfectly natural style in which to wage their wars.'[29] 'The English take Harfleur with the help of one horse and the first XI.'[30] Alexander Walker described Branagh as resembling 'a rugby forward who collects a bloody nose on the battlefield'.[31] We don't have to search for long among these testaments of reception to observe the blessed spirit of patriotic emotion returning in these attenuated forms.

Lastly there is the crucial relationship between this film as a cultural product and the kind of cultural pattern being forged by Branagh in his entrepreneurial interventions into the theatrical economy. He stands for a reaction against the established national institutions of theatre, such as the Royal Shakespeare Company, and for the development of a privatized theatrical economy, with organizations like his own Renaissance Theatre Company supported by private and corporate sponsorship. Those who also approve of such developments are filled with passions of admiration when they contemplate Branagh's audacity, energy, ambition, nerve, determination, etc., etc., right through the whole vocabulary of self-help and entrepreneurial capitalism. 'Branagh's blitzkrieg left the profession breathless at his nerve, his energy and his disregard for the obstacles.'[32] 'The cream of our classical talent and an army of extras, horses and stunt-men...was in itself a saga of nail-biting crises surmounted by his calm certainty of what he wants to do, and unshakeable confidence in being able to do it.'[33] Emma Thompson, who is married to Branagh and who plays Katherine in the film, embraces the same free-market vocabulary of risk and initiative, linked with the heroic language of war: 'These are the warrior years. These are the times to take the risks and do the big things we might not have the courage or energy for later on.'[34] Some critics offered a clearer-sighted analysis, whether prompted by enthusiasm or reservation: Richard Corliss in *The Times* called Branagh 'an icon of Thatcherite initiative', and Adam Mars-Jones in *The Independent* proposed an exact model for the cultural dialectics involved: 'The real chemistry is not between actor and part, but between the idea of the star as entrepreneur and the idea of the king as a self-made man.'[35] Clearly the myth enacted in this film is capable of signifying at this level, perhaps even more readily than at the level of national culture and politics.

I still of course haven't answered the question posed in my title: 'What ish my nation?', as the Irishman Macmorris belligerently inquires of the Welshman Fluellen in *Henry V* (III. ii. 125). The answer will lie, I think, in a recognition that the emotion of patriotism and the politics of nationalism always involve, in any given historical situation, attachment to a particular sectional group, or class, or 'team', or army, which can be seen as bearing or leading the national destiny. At the same time in every historical situation there is a larger, more pluralistic and multiple, more complex and contradictory national collective which any sectarian nationalist ideology must ignore, deny, or suppress. The most natural context for this operation to be successfully conducted is that of war: and we have seen in the dramatization of Henry V's policy how it can be done. We also know from our own experience of the Falklands war that it is possible for a government voted into power by 40 per cent of the population, and an army voted into power by nobody, to become self-appointed bearers of the entire nation's moral consciousness.

Raphael Samuel suggests that in contemporary Britain patriotic and nationalist feeling has sought and found a new home in the concept of the individual.[36]

Orwell wrote in 1940 that the 'privateness' of English life was one of the secrets of its strength ... his account anticipates some major themes in post-war British life, in particular the break-up, or erosion, of corporate loyalties, and the increasingly home-centred character of British social life. Patriotism, on the face of it, is one of the victims of those developments. Yet it may be that, denied expression in the public sphere, it is finding subliminal support in the semiotics of everyday life.

... Individualism also has more solid material supports. The spread of home ownership, the sale of council houses, and the inflation of house prices has renewed the importance of family wealth and given a whole new terrain to Lockean notions of private property. The revival of small businesses – a feature of British as of other post-industrial societies – is multiplying the number of home-based or family-run concerns, while the dispersal of employment shows signs of reunifying work and home. Ideologically, public spirit is much less highly regarded than it was in the 1930s and 1940s. On both Left and Right of the political spectrum, self-expression is treated as the highest good, individual rights as sacrosanct, and the enlargement of personal freedom – or its protection – the ideal object of policy. Government, for its part, has built a whole platform out of freedom of choice, making, or attempting to make, health, insurance, pensions, and schooling matters of individual responsibility, and turning non-intervention into the highest of statesmanly tasks. As Margaret Thatcher put it in one of her best-remembered maxims: 'There is no society, only men and women and families.'

Branagh's film version of *Henry V* is very clearly a product of this new age of individualism, and it is in this respect that it differs so sharply from the play-text of the 1590s and the Olivier film of the 1940s. Denied a home in nationalist politics, the emotional resources of patriotism gravitate inexorably towards their true heartland in the individualism of the new entrepreneur, whose conquest of new economic and artistic worlds continually endorses the cultural and ideological power of the old.

Kenneth Branagh did not, however, become constituted as such an individual subject, this 'icon of Thatcherite initiative', without a complex process of cultural negotiation. The film also has another history, through which can be traced the possibilities of its being read otherwise. Branagh is himself, of course, as a product of working-class Protestant Belfast, a compatriot of Captain MacMorris, as well as a fellow-countryman of William Shakespeare, heir to the mantle of Lord Olivier, and a loyal subject of Prince Charles's mother. The question 'What ish my nation?' would at certain stages of his life, if now no longer, have been capable of provoking in him an existential anxiety parallel to the confused and exasperated anger voiced by Shakespeare's Captain MacMorris. When in 1970 his family, horrified by the growth of political violence in the province, moved permanently to England (where his father had already been working for some years) Branagh felt, according to the testimony of his 'autobiography', 'like a stranger...in a very strange land'.[37] This initial condition of alienation was resolved only by the assumption of 'dual nationality' in a divided self: 'After a year or so I'd managed to become English at school and Irish at home' (p. 23). He lived, he acknowledges, a 'double life' (p. 24), perpetually conscious of a deep cultural difference masked by apparent assimilation and ethnic homogeneity.

Branagh's formative childhood experience was thus enacted on a highly significant marginal space of 'British' culture, close to another of those territorial borders on which the contradictions of a nationalist ideology become acutely visible. Born a British citizen, within the borders of the 'United' Kingdom, Branagh inherited a particular Irish sub-culture, that of a large working-class extended family on the edge of the Belfast docks. He was also heir, however, to the questionable advantages of that 'British' culture of self-improvement and meritocratic social mobility which took him eventually to RADA, the RSC and Kensington Palace. These social contradictions of divided culture and fragmented nationality can be read immediately from the brash, ambitious, self-mocking, self-important, painfully unstable discourse of Branagh's premature 'autobiography', a project in itself designed to consolidate a coherent social identity out of a fissured and contradictory social experience. They can also be read from the film, which, despite its totalizing attempt to relocate the problems of national identity and international conflict within the charismatic individual, occasionally uncovers and discloses surprising depths of cultural anxiety.

This anxiety can be traced in a symptomatic moment of textual 'excess', a point where the filmic narrative discloses an ideological 'stress-point' by delivering an emotional affect which remains unexplained by the contingent dramatic circumstances. As the miraculous victory of Agincourt becomes apparent, Captain Fluellen (played by Ian Holm) reminds Henry of the heroic deeds of his ancestor Edward, 'the Black Prince of Wales'. Fluellen offers a Celtic rereading of Anglo-Norman history, celebrating the heroic deeds of Welsh men-at-arms at Crecy, and appropriating Edward himself as an honorary Welshman. Branagh's screenplay interprets this exchange as follows:[38]

Fluellen :   ...I do believe your Majesty takes no scorn to wear the leek upon Saint Davy's day.

The power of the Welshman's simple feeling is too much for the King who speaks the following through tears which he cannot prevent. He is near collapse.

Henry V: I wear it for a memorable honour;
For I am Welsh, you know, good countryman.

The King breaks down, and the two men hug each other.

Such cinematic surges of emotional intensity are of course ambiguous in their effects, and can be read in many ways. Here there are readily available psychological explanations: this is the bitter price of heroism and military success; the post-orgasmic melancholy of the victor, satiated on violence; or the human cost of successful rule. Branagh's Henry also sheds tears at the hanging of Bardolph, the screenplay emphasizing the 'enormous cost' to the king of this necessary exercise of impartial justice (pp. 71–4). More generally, the film's capacity to reduce its participants and observers to tears is frequently cited as a measure of its authenticity: after the shooting of Agincourt, Branagh 'went home exhausted and somehow defeated, and for no good reason burst into tears';[39] and Prince Charles is reputed to have been similarly 'reduced to tears' at a special preview.[40] The demonstrative parading of open grief may at first sight appear subversive of the values of tough masculinity, the rigid suppression of emotion required for the serious business of warfare. But it should be clear from the sodden royal handkerchief with which we began, that these tears are closer to those rituals of mourning (such as the militaristic memorial service of 'Remembrance Day'), which are rather a liturgical collusion with the ideology of patriotic war than an emotional interrogation of its values.

The moment in the film of extreme emotional exchange between Fluellen and Henry is in fact quite different from these examples. Neither the film-text nor the screenplay can adequately explain its intensity, its excessive super-abundance of significance. And that leaking out of embarrassingly public grief seems to me to locate a fault-line in the film's hegemony: for the sudden burst of reciprocal grief is linked by the dialogue with questions of national identity. As we observe the dramatization of an English king and a Welsh soldier plangently embracing in a symbolic ritual of national unity, we also catch a momentary glimpse of an Irishman and a Scot weeping over the historical devastations of British imperialism. Can we not then read through the film's imagery of post-Agincourt 'carnage and wreckage' (p. 113) the smoking ruins of that battlefield that is Ulster? And can we not catch in those verminous men and women 'pillaging the bodies of the dead' (p. 113) a fleeting glimpse of the young Kenneth Branagh, joining in the looting of a bombed-out Belfast supermarket?[41] The iconic image of the dead boy carried by Henry throughout this sequence, in turn carries in this respect richer and deeper psychological reverberations than I have space to explore.

One of the most interesting details of Branagh's *Henry V* does not appear in the film (and is not therefore in the published screenplay, which is a record of the final edited version, not the screenplay from which the film was developed). When shooting the scene where the Chorus strides the white cliffs of Southampton/Dover (filmed in fact at Beachy Head, which is of course exactly midway between the two), Branagh tried to use the same location for another sequence:[42]

> We tried unsuccessfully to get another shot which I had felt at one stage could open the movie – a pan across the French coastline eventually taking in the white cliffs of England and ending on the contemplative face of yours truly. The whole thing was accompanied by the hollow crown soliloquy from *Richard II*, which seemed to express something of the message of our *Henry V.* The shot did not work, and I decided to drop the Richard anyway. It simply didn't belong.

Who, in that strangely elliptical and impersonal phrase, is 'yours truly'? The actor or the role? English Harry or Irish Ken? The doubling of identities is paralleled by a corresponding spatial ambivalence: that camera-pan simultaneously offers a depiction of the point-of-view of King Henry, firmly established on his own territory, contemplatively surveying the enemy coast; and delivers an external view of the 'English' coast as it would be seen by an enemy, an invader – or an immigrant. Prompted by the echoing words of Richard II, a king ousted from his own territory by the usurper whose heir now literally occupies its commanding heights, and by the semiotic value latent in Branagh's 'dual identity', the spectator presented with this filmic moment would have had ample opportunity to appreciate the position of an internal *émigré*, whose status within the nation is in some way questionable; the paradox of belonging and alienation, the cultural anxiety of the internal *émigré* about to establish his own territorial rights by violently overthrowing another's.

What would this sequence, if included in the film, have signified; and what are the underlying reasons for its exclusion? The speech in question from *Richard II* (III. ii. 144–77) is a penetrating interrogation of the realities of power. The state is about to fall into the hands of Bolingbroke, Henry V's father, and Richard's imagination is released to a vivid realization of the difference between effective power and mere legitimacy. Richard has no property in the realm to bequeath to his heirs, only the experience of royal tragedy – 'sad stories of the deaths of kings'. The imagery of hollowness runs throughout the speech, taking in the hollow grave, the hollow crown, and the 'wall of flesh' encircling the mortal life, which seems impregnable as a castle, yet contains only a vulnerable, isolated life. If the king's body is mortal, then sovereignty is a mere pageant, a stage performance, and the real sovereign of the royal court is death, the 'antic' who parodies and mocks all seriousness. The awareness of royal tragedy expressed here is nothing less than the Divine Right of Kings inverted, hollowed out to disclose the true nature of power.[43]

In the projected additional scene of Branagh's film, Richard's challenging interrogation is placed exactly on the sharp white line of a territorial border. Located there, the insistent questioning of the speech goes beyond an expression of melancholy resignation at the emptiness of power (the kind of thing calculated to set Prince Charles clutching for the royal nose-rag), to an earnest meditation on the nature of the peripheral delineations by which such spaces of hollowness are bound and contained. If we read that border as simultaneously the south coast of England, and the border between Ulster and Eire, we can grasp simultaneously the paradox of definition and arbitrariness, of clear geographical division and constructed geopolitical disposition, which belongs to all territorial borders, especially those between an imperialist and a colonized nation. Travelling back to that mythical spot of origins, which is simultaneously a possible point of exit (Beachy Head is a favourite haunt of suicides), some of the fundamental questions of British national identity can at last be posed. Does a geographical boundary such as the English Channel prescribe mutual hostility and reciprocal violence between the neighbouring nations?

> the contending kingdoms
> Of France and England, whose very shores look pale
> With envy of each other's happiness,
> May cease their hatred
> (*Henry V*, V. ii. 377–9)

The inclusion of that speech from *Richard II*, significantly poised on the edge of England, could have hollowed out an illuminating space between actor and character: a disclosure which could have expressed these cultural contradictions even more eloquently, if the film had found a means of including Shakespeare's reference to Essex, returning from Ireland, 'bringing Rebellion broached on his sword'. Meanwhile, as the film cameras whirred on the summit of Beachy Head, constructing a sequence destined to become a hollow absence in the film-text, far below and out to sea, other kinds of machinery were simultaneously hollowing out a link between 'the contending kingdoms', that 'Chunnel' which when completed will rob the white cliffs of much of their centuries-old symbolism. For once Britain is physically a part of Europe, the ideological stress on ancient national mythologies will be enormously intensified. The interesting combination, on the part of Britain's Tory government, of pro-European commitment and chauvinistic resistance to European union, testifies to the problems facing British national ideology. The government's insistence on the private funding of what is self-evidently a public construction project (leading to an endless series of financial crises), and the anxieties frequently expressed about what kinds of contamination may enter the realm once a major transport artery is plugged deep into its vitals (those who applaud the demolition of the Berlin Wall tend, when contemplating the Chunnel, towards extravagant fantasies of invasion by terrorists and rabid animals), indicate deep ideological ambivalences towards the destruction of a 'natural' boundary. Some residual reverence for the acculturated sanctity of the south coast even underlies reasonable conservationist anxieties about the fate of the white cliffs themselves; focusing as they do in particular on a spot some distance from the site of the tunnel itself, but legitimated by its very name as a space of that England (of which, according to the words of another popular wartime song, there will always be one) to be conserved: Shakespeare Cliff, near Dover.

Notes

1 Reprinted in *London Theatre Record*, 4: 7 (1984), p. 270.
2 *Henry V*, directed by Kenneth Branagh, produced by Bruce Sharman (1989); based on a 1984 production of the Royal Shakespeare Company, directed by Adrian Noble. My description 'widely celebrated' can be measured in the press reviews quoted later in this paper; and see also the *Shakespeare on Film Newsletter*, 14: 2, which cites in support of Robert F. Wilson's positive evaluation ('*Henry V*/ Branagh's and Olivier's Choruses') a celebratory 'Chorus of critics' (pp. 1–2). Branagh received Academy Award nominations as best actor and best director.
3 Tom Hutchinson, *The Mail on Sunday*, 8 October 1989.
4 The phrase derives of course from D. H. Lawrence's poem 'Piano' (see note 5), but occurs in the stage directions of Branagh's *Henry V* screenplay: see K. Branagh, *Henry V by William Shakespeare: A Screen Adaptation* (London: Chatto and Windus, 1989), p. 32.
5 D. H. Lawrence, 'Piano', in *Selected Poems of D. H. Lawrence*, ed. K. Sagar (Harmondsworth: Penguin, 1972), p. 21.
6 Philip Larkin, 'Church going', *The Less Deceived* (London: Faber and Faber, 1957).
7 Holinshed's *Chronicles*, vol. I, p. 443.
8 J. Turner, '*King Lear*', in G. Holderness, N. Potter and J. Turner, *Shakespeare: The Play of History* (London: Macmillan, 1988), p. 92. See also T. Hawkes, 'Lear's map: a general survey', *Deutsche Shakespeare-Gesellschaft West Jahrbuch* (1989), pp. 36–7.
9 Turner, in Holderness et al., *The Play of History*, p. 93.
10 Cf. Seamus Heaney's poem 'Act of Union', where a sexual relationship is linked metaphorically with the political connection of Britain and Ireland, colonizer and colonized: 'I grow older / Conceding your half-independent shore / Within whose borders now my legacy / Culminates inexorably.'
11 See K. P. Wentersdorf, 'The conspiracy of silence in *Henry V*', *Shakespeare Quarterly*, 27 (1976), and G. Holderness, '*Henry V*', in Holderness et al., *The Play of History*, pp. 70–2.
12 Branagh, *Henry V*, p. 12.
13 Ibid., pp. 35–6.
14 See G. Holderness, 'Agincourt 1944: readings in the Shakespeare myth', *Literature and History*, 10: 1 (1984), pp. 31–4; *Shakespeare's History* (Dublin: Gill and Macmillan, 1985), pp. 184–91; and Holderness et al., *The Play of History*, pp. 72–9.
15 P. French, in *The Observer*, 8 October 1989.

16 A. Mars-Jones, in *The Independent*, 5 October 1989.

17 C. Tookey, in *The Sunday Telegraph*, 8 October 1989.

18 Charles Wood, *Tumbledown* (Harmondsworth: Penguin, 1987).

19 Kenneth Branagh discusses his approach to the stage role of Henry V in *Players of Shakespeare*, ed. Philip Brockbank (Cambridge: Cambridge University Press, 1985), and in his own autobiography, *Beginning* (London: Chatto and Windus, 1989), pp. 137–9.

20 See Branagh, *Beginning*, pp. 141–4.

21 See Michael Quinn, 'Celebrity and the semiotics of acting', *New Theatre Quarterly*, 6: 22 (1990).

22 P. Lewis, *The Sunday Times*, 10 September 1989.

23 P. French, *The Observer*, 8 October 1989.

24 A. Mars-Jones, *The Independent*, 5 October 1989.

25 P. Lewis, *The Sunday Telegraph*, 24–30 September 1989.

26 B. Bamigboye, *The Daily Mail*, 18 November 1989.

27 P. Lewis, *The Sunday Times*, 10 September 1989.

28 Ian Johnstone, *The Sunday Times*, 8 October 1989.

29 A. Lane, *The Independent*, 30 September 1989.

30 A. Bilson, *Sunday Correspondent*, 8 October 1989.

31 A. Walker, in the *London Evening Standard*, 25 May 1989. Branagh himself ironically traced the roots of his career to a conjuncture of drama and sport: at school he was made captain of both rugby and football teams, 'I suspect for my innate sense of drama – I loved shouting theatrically butch encouragement to "my lads"' (Branagh, *Beginning*, p. 28).

32 P. Lewis, *The Sunday Times*, 10 September 1989.

33 P. Lewis, *The Sunday Telegraph*, 24–30 September 1989.

34 Quoted by P. Lewis, *The Sunday Telegraph*, 24–30 September 1989.

35 R. Corliss, *The Times*, 13 November 1989, and A. Mars-Jones, *The Independent*, 5 October 1989.

36 Raphael Samuel, 'Introduction: exciting to be English', in *Patriotism: The Making and Unmaking of National Identity*, vol. 1, *History and Politics*, ed. Raphael Samuel (London: Routledge, 1989), pp. xli–xlii, xxxix–xl.

37 Branagh, *Beginning*, p. 22.

38 Branagh, *Henry V*, p. 111.

39 Quoted by P. Lewis, *The Sunday Times*, 10 September 1989.

40 H. Davenport, *The Daily Telegraph*, 5 October 1989.

41 See Branagh, *Beginning*, p. 20.

42 Ibid., p. 239.

43 See Holderness, *Shakespeare's History*, pp. 59–61.

6

Performance

The history of modern performance criticism is usually traced to the work of Arthur Colby Sprague. In his *Shakespeare and the Actors* (1944), Sprague traced the accumulated stage business of the plays' theatrical history from the Restoration to the beginning of the nineteenth century, arguing that 'Shakespeare's plays were written for performance, and surely, through performance, light has been shed on many dark places in them' (Sprague, 1944: xxv). Sprague's methodology is exhibited at length in his *Shakespeare's Histories: Plays for the Stage* (1964), which engages with eighteenth- and nineteenth-century staging as well as more recent production history. Since Sprague, approaches to Shakespeare in performance have diverged to include accounts by theatre practitioners, theoretical discussions of the dynamics of theatre and, latterly, film, stage histories showing how individual plays have changed over a long period of productions, reviews and interpretations of current individual performances or productions, reconstructions of the contexts of historical productions, speculative accounts of theatrical possibilities, and theories of intention and reception. There is as much fruitful debate in this as in any other approach to Shakespeare.

In *Moment by Moment by Shakespeare* (1985), Gary Taylor attempts to analyse Shakespeare in performance from the perspective of the spectator and to investigate the pleasure of theatre-going through a sophisticated 'study of response' (Taylor, 1985: 3). Taylor argues that plays in performance unfold as a series of moments, not a static whole. One of his extended examples is from *Henry V*, and Taylor concludes his study:

> The dramatist's manipulation of emphasis might therefore be described in terms of his control of the direction, distance, velocity, mass, and impact of a hypothesis moving through a very particular kind of space. At least, any adequate description of how an audience responds to particular moments in that

movement must take account of all these factors, and must at the same time resist all of the associated occupational prejudices of the academic reader. I believe that anyone who could achieve such a description would indeed have succeeded in catching Shakespeare 'in the act of greatness'. (Taylor, 1985: 236)

In *The Shakespeare Revolution* – the title refers to his argument that 'the initiative in recovering Shakespeare has shifted to the theatre' (Styan, 1977: 232) – J. L. Styan argues that both page and stage are needed for the fullest appreciation: 'the scholar will modify the actor's illumination, the actor will modify the scholar's, a process of infinite adjustment' (1977: 237). The book discusses different eras in twentieth-century Shakespearean production. In his *Perspectives on Shakespeare in Performance* (2000), however, Styan proposes a more antithetical relationship between criticism and theatre:

> Criticism is inevitably a generalizing activity, whereas the theatre experience is always particular; criticism is reflective and docile, whereas perceptions in the theatre are wild and immediate and alive. Yet by performance, notions and theories can at least be tested, and the ultimate question can be asked – 'Does it work?' (Styan, 2000: 5–6)

H. R. Coursen's *Shakespearean Performance as Interpretation* (1992) sides with this approach:

> A Shakespearean script exists only in performance. Period. Performance sharpens 'the text' necessarily in this or that direction. We are free to debate or enjoy the choices a director and his actors make. But the debate has relevancy only as it responds to performance. Otherwise, 'the text' becomes a spaceship filled with tinkerers and dial-watchers, but with no destination. (Coursen, 1992: 15)

Harry Berger's *Imaginary Audition: Shakespeare on Stage and Page* (1989) takes issue with the proponents of what he dubs 'New Histrionicism': 'that reading is irresponsible unless it imitates playgoing' (Berger, 1989: xii). Instead, through a critique of the limited methodology of current performance criticism, including Styan (1977) and Taylor (1985), he proposes the practice of 'imaginary audition' as:

> an attempt to reconstruct text-centered reading in a way that incorporates the perspective of imaginary audition and playgoing; an attempt to put into play an approach that remains text-centered but focuses on the interlocutionary politics and theatrical features of performed drama so as to make them impinge at every point on the most suspicious and antitheatrical of readings. (Berger, 1989: xiv)

Richard Levin's 'Performance-critics vs Close Readers in the Study of English Renaissance Drama' (1986) also proposes that both schools of criticism can learn from each other:

one of the most valuable contributions that performance-criticism might make would be to curb the excesses of the close readers of the thematic and ironic schools, whose interpretations of the plays of this period are often so far removed from theatrical experience that they could not be conveyed in any performance...Once we acknowledge that the plays of Shakespeare and his fellow dramatists were written for the stage, then it necessarily follows that any interpretation of them that cannot be conveyed on the stage could not have been intended by the author and so must be rejected. (Levin, 1986: 545, 547)

Opposed to such deference to the theatre, Martin Buzacott, in his *The Death of the Actor*, questions the 'current social and aesthetic supremacy of *actors* in general' (1991: 7). Following Barthes's proleptic declaration of 'the death of the author', Buzacott announces the death of the actor as 'a body devoid of any cultural authority', instead arguing that 'Shakespearean texts speak regardless of the individual who presumes to be their mouthpiece' (Buzacott, 1991: 142). *Shakespeare Quarterly*, volume 36 (1985) includes a special issue 'Reviewing Shakespeare', with essays by Cary Mazer, Alan Dessen, Robert Speaight and H. R. Coursen. Thompson and Thompson (1989) gather a collection of essays on performance criticism which review its methodology and practice, including a useful bibliography (1989: 252–6). W. B. Worthen's (1989) discussion of performance criticism usefully reviews a number of different positions, arguing for the need to locate the claims of these approaches as criticism, and to integrate performance with other theoretical and methodological enquiries.

Alan Sinfield's essay in Dollimore and Sinfield's *Political Shakespeare: New Essays in Cultural Materialism* (1985/1994) offers one example of this integration: in 'Royal Shakespeare: Theatre and the Making of Ideology' Sinfield discusses the ideological work of the Royal Shakespeare Company (RSC) in Britain since the 1960s and argues for a more incisive critique of that '*Shakespeare* – the whole aura of elusive genius and institutionalised profundity' (Dollimore and Sinfield, 1985: 178) which is sustained through theatrical means. This politicized account of the RSC is developed in Robert Shaughnessy's *Representing Shakespeare: England, History and the RSC* (1994); Peter Holland's *English Shakespeares* (1997) takes a less polemical stance to Shakespearian performances from the late 1980s onwards. In 'Thatcher's Shakespeare?' (1989), Isobel Armstrong extends Sinfield's analysis in her discussion of the relationship between 'radical academic critique and the performing arts', and in his Afterword to *The Shakespeare Myth*, edited by Holderness (1988) Terry Eagleton criticizes the theatre practitioners represented in the volume, including Jonathan Miller and Sam Wanamaker, for failing to take up the challenge of radical Shakespeare critics: their 'bland Hampstead bohemianism' promotes 'depressing' 'liberal pluralism' and 'depoliticising eclecticism', and their 'dismally regressive opinions' are at odds with avant-garde political scholarship (Holderness, 1988: 206–7). Other essays on the theory of performance criticism are gathered in James C. Bulman's *Shakespeare, Theory, and Performance* (1996); *The Cambridge Companion to Shakespeare on Stage*, edited by Stanley Wells and Sarah Stanton (2002) offers historical and cross-cultural perspectives.

A recent growth in performance criticism has been in published diary accounts by actors of particular roles or productions, giving the practitioners' perspective. Michael Bogdanov and Michael Pennington's account of *The English Shakespeare Company: The Story of the 'Wars of the Roses' 1986–1989* (1990) covers the mounting of this ambitious and controversial series. Sally Beauman (1976) discusses in detail Terry Hands's production of *Henry V* at the RSC. The *Players of Shakespeare* series offers commentary by Royal Shakespeare Company actors. Volume 2 (Jackson and Smallwood, 1988) includes Kenneth Branagh's account of his stage performance of Henry V; volume 3 (Jackson and Smallwood, 1993) sees Ralph Fiennes, Penny Downie and Anton Lesser discuss roles in *Henry VI* and *Richard III*; and there are reflections on productions of *King Henry VIII* and *Richard III* in volume 4 (Smallwood, 1998). Barton's volume *Playing Shakespeare* (1984) reports on workshops in which actors discuss and experiment with different readings of Shakespeare's language. Ralph Berry's *Shakespeare in Performance* (1993) includes a chapter on 'Laughter in *Richard II*: The Subplot of Mood'. In H. R. Coursen's *Shakespeare in Production: Whose History?* (1996), productions of the history plays on stage and screen during the 1990s are discussed. Other recommended interventions into the field of performance criticism are Worthen (2003) and, for a historical perspective, Wells (1997).

Several series take individual plays and discuss their stage histories. Titles in the 'Text and Performance' series include Malcolm Page on *Richard II* (1987) and T. F. Wharton's *Henry the Fourth, Parts 1 and 2* (1983), and Emma Smith's *King Henry V* in the 'Shakespeare in Production' series (2002) offers a text of the play alongside a specific performance history introduction and commentary. The 'Shakespeare in Performance' series includes Scott McMillin's *Henry IV, Part 1* (1991), Margaret Shewring's *King Richard II* (1996), of which a chapter is reprinted below, and James Loehlin's account of *Henry V* (1996), which develops the idea of a 'secret play within the official one' (1996: 1) in relation to twentieth-century stage and film performance. Hugh Richmond's *King Henry VIII* (1994) discusses a play which has a more continuous performance tradition than a critical one, and Geraldine Cousin's *King John* (1994) focuses particularly on performances from the 1970s and 1980s. Dennis Kennedy's *Looking at Shakespeare: A Visual History of Twentieth-century Performance* (1993) combines methodological and descriptive commentary, and the contributions to his collection *Foreign*

Shakespeare: Contemporary Performance (1993) shift the focus away from British theatre.

By contrast with these studies, which usually favour culturally central productions in Stratford-upon-Avon, London and Hollywood, John Russell Brown's polemic *Free Shakespeare* (1997) argues that 'seeing the usual kinds of Shakespeare production will not help the reader to advance further' (Brown, 1997: 3). Brown suggests that directors may impose 'a confinement, a cutting down of a work founded on something other than an intellectual idea' (1997: 14), and advocates 'radical experiment', much of it based on Elizabethan staging practices such as cue-scripts for actors, the same lighting for stage and audience, and stressing 'the explorative and fluid engagement for which they were written' (1997: 83, 82). The most developed account of recreated Elizabethan staging is Pauline Kiernan's *Staging Shakespeare at the New Globe* (1999), which reflects on the early findings of the rebuilt Globe theatre on London's Bankside, drawing heavily on the insights derived from its first full 'original-style' production of *Henry V*. Standard works on the Shakespearian theatre are by Gurr (1992) and Thomson (1992). Gurr's work on *Playgoing in Shakespeare's London* (1996) and *The Shakespearian Playing Companies* (1996) develop this field.

The discussion of Shakespeare in recent performance has flourished in the area of film and television productions of the plays. Pioneering studies by Manvell (1971) and Hamilton Ball (1968) on silent versions were followed by Jorgens (1979), who usefully divided Shakespearian film into the 'theatrical', in which film is used to record a performance designed for theatrical representation; the 'realist', which uses film's mimetic qualities to situate the play in a realist context; and the 'filmic', where the director is a 'film poet, whose works bear the same relation to the surfaces of reality as poems do to ordinary conversation' (Jorgens, 1979: 10). *Watching Shakespeare on Television* (1993) by H. R. Coursen develops some of the specifics and the implications of the reduced format of Shakespearian film on video and small screen. Susan Willis (1991) discusses the BBC television Shakespeare series. Kenneth Branagh comments on his film of *Henry V* in a screenplay published in 1989, and the film is discussed by Deborah Cartmell in her *Interpreting Shakespeare on Screen* (2000). Samuel Crowl also considers Branagh's film in his *Shakespeare Observed* (1992), and gives a stimulating reading of the series of history plays performed under Michael Bogdanov's direction as 'The Wars of the Roses'. Ace Pilkington's *Screening Shakespeare from Richard II to Henry V* (1991) analyses the BBC series, Olivier's *Henry V* (1944) and Welles's *Chimes at Midnight* (1966). Contributors to *The Cambridge Companion to Shakespeare on Film* (Jackson, 2000) consider specific genres and plays, including Barbara Freedman and H. R. Coursen on *Richard III*.

Performance 251

References and Further Reading

Armstrong, Isobel (1989) 'Thatcher's Shakespeare?', *Textual Practice*, 3: 1–14.
Ball, Robert Hamilton (1968) *Shakespeare on Silent Film: A Strange Eventful History*. London: Allen and Unwin.
Barton, John (1984) *Playing Shakespeare*. London: Methuen.
Beauman, Sally (1976) *The Royal Shakespeare Company's Production of Henry V*. Oxford: Pergamon Press.
Berger, Harry (1989) *Imaginary Audition: Shakespeare on Stage and Page*. Berkeley, CA: University of California Press.
Berry, Ralph (1989) *On Directing Shakespeare: Interviews with Contemporary Directors*. London: Hamish Hamilton.
——(1993) *Shakespeare in Performance: Castings and Metamorphoses*. Basingstoke: Macmillan.
Bogdanov, Michael and Pennington, Michael (1990) *The English Shakespeare Company: The Story of 'The Wars of the Roses', 1986–1989*. London: Hern.
Branagh, Kenneth (1989) *Henry V by William Shakespeare: A Screen Adaptation*. London: Chatto and Windus.
Brockbank, Philip, et al. (1985) *Players of Shakespeare: Essays in Shakespearian Performance by Players with the Royal Shakespeare Company*. Cambridge: Cambridge University Press.
Brown, John Russell (1966) *Shakespeare's Plays in Performance*. London: Edward Arnold.
——(1997) *Free Shakespeare*, new and expanded edn. London: Applause.
Buchman, Lorne M. (1991) *Still in Movement: Shakespeare on Screen*. Oxford: Oxford University Press.
Bulman, James C. (ed.) (1996) *Shakespeare, Theory, and Performance*. London: Routledge.
Buzacott, Martin (1991) *The Death of the Actor: Shakespeare on Page and Stage*. London: Routledge.
Cartmell, Deborah (2000) *Interpreting Shakespeare on Screen*. Basingstoke: Macmillan.
Collick, John (1989) *Shakespeare, Cinema and Society*. Manchester: Manchester University Press.
Coursen, Herbert R. (1992) *Shakespearean Performance as Interpretation*. Newark: University of Delaware Press.
——(1993) *Watching Shakespeare on Television*. Rutherford: Farleigh Dickinson University Press.
——(1996) *Shakespeare in Production: Whose History?* Athens: Ohio University Press.
——(1999) *Shakespeare: The Two Traditions*. Madison, NJ: Associated University Presses.
Cousin, Geraldine (1994) *King John* (Shakespeare in Performance). Manchester: Manchester University Press.
Crowl, Samuel (1992) *Shakespeare Observed: Studies in Performance on Stage and Screen*. Athens: Ohio University Press.
Dawson, Anthony B. (1988) *Watching Shakespeare: A Playgoers' Guide*. Basingstoke: Macmillan.

Dollimore, Jonathan and Sinfield, Alan (1985) *Political Shakespeare: New Essays in Cultural Materialism*. Manchester: Manchester University Press, 2nd edn 1994.

Gurr, Andrew (1992) *The Shakespearean Stage 1574–1642*, 3rd edn. Cambridge: Cambridge University Press.

—— (1996a) *Playgoing in Shakespeare's London*, 2nd edn. Cambridge: Cambridge University Press.

—— (1996b) *The Shakespearian Playing Companies*. Oxford: Clarendon Press.

Holderness, Graham (ed.) (1988) *The Shakespeare Myth*. Manchester: Manchester University Press.

Holland, Peter (1997) *English Shakespeares: Shakespeare on the English Stage in the 1990s*. Cambridge: Cambridge University Press.

Jackson, Russell (ed.) (2000) *The Cambridge Companion to Shakespeare on Film*. Cambridge: Cambridge University Press.

—— and Smallwood, R. L. (1988) *Players of Shakespeare 2: Further Essays in Shakespearian Performance*. Cambridge: Cambridge University Press.

—— and —— (1993) *Players of Shakespeare 3: Further Essays in Shakespearian Performance*. Cambridge: Cambridge University Press.

Jorgens, Jack J. (1979) *Shakespeare on Film*. Bloomington, IN: Indiana University Press.

Kennedy, Dennis (ed.) (1993a) *Foreign Shakespeare: Contemporary Performance*. Cambridge: Cambridge University Press.

—— (1993b) *Looking at Shakespeare: A Visual History of Twentieth-century Performance*. Cambridge: Cambridge University Press.

Kiernan, Pauline (1999) *Staging Shakespeare at the New Globe*. Basingstoke: Macmillan.

Levin, Richard (1986) 'Performance-critics vs close readers in the study of English Renaissance drama', *Modern Language Review*, 81: 545–59.

Loehlin, James N. (1996) *Henry V* (Shakespeare in Performance). Manchester: Manchester University Press.

McKernan, Luke and Terris, Olwen (1994) *Walking Shadows: Shakespeare in the National Film and Television Archive*. London: British Film Institute.

McMillin, Scott (1991) *Henry IV, Part 1* (Shakespeare in Performance). Manchester: Manchester University Press.

Manvell, Roger (1971) *Shakespeare and the Film*. London: Dent.

Page, Malcolm (1987) *Richard II* (Text and Performance). Basingstoke: Macmillan.

Pilkington, Ace G. (1991) *Screening Shakespeare from Richard II to Henry V*. Newark: University of Delaware Press.

Richmond, Hugh M. (1994) *King Henry VIII* (Shakespeare in Performance). Manchester: Manchester University Press.

Shaughnessy, Robert (1994) *Representing Shakespeare: England, History and the RSC*. London: Harvester Wheatsheaf.

—— (1998) *Shakespeare on Film* (New Casebooks). Basingstoke: Macmillan.

—— (2000) *Shakespeare in Performance* (New Casebooks). Basingstoke: Macmillan.

Shewring, Margaret (1996) *King Richard II* (Shakespeare in Performance). Manchester: Manchester University Press.

Smallwood, R. L. (1998) *Players of Shakespeare 4: Further Essays in Shakespearian Performance*. Cambridge: Cambridge University Press.

Smith, Emma (2002) *King Henry V* (Shakespeare in Production). Cambridge: Cambridge University Press.

Sprague, Arthur Colby (1944) *Shakespeare and the Actors: The Stage Business in his Plays (1660–1905)*. Cambridge, MA: Harvard University Press.

—— (1964) *Shakespeare's Histories: Plays for the Stage*. London: Society for Theatre Research.

Styan, J. L. (1977) *The Shakespeare Revolution: Criticism and Performance in the Twentieth Century*. Cambridge: Cambridge University Press.

—— (2000) *Perspectives on Shakespeare in Performance*. New York: P. Lang.

Taylor, Gary (1985) *Moment by Moment by Shakespeare*. London: Macmillan.

Thompson, Marvin and Thompson, Ruth (eds) (1989) *Shakespeare and the Sense of Performance: Essays in the Tradition of Performance Criticism in Honor of Bernard Beckerman*. Newark: University of Delaware Press.

Thomson, Peter (1992) *Shakespeare's Theatre*, 2nd edn (Theatre Production Studies). London: Routledge.

Wells, Stanley (1997) *Shakespeare in the Theatre: An Anthology of Criticism*. Oxford: Oxford University Press.

—— and Stanton, Sarah (2002) *The Cambridge Companion to Shakespeare on Stage*. Cambridge: Cambridge University Press.

Wharton, T. F. (1983) *Henry the Fourth, Parts 1 and 2* (Text and Performance). Basingstoke: Macmillan.

Willis, Susan (1991) *The BBC Shakespeare Plays: Making the Televised Canon*. Chapel Hill, NC: University of North Carolina Press.

Worthen, W. B. (1989) 'Deeper meanings and theatrical technique: the rhetoric of performance criticism', *Shakespeare Quarterly*, 40: 441–55.

—— (2003) *Shakespeare and the Force of Modern Performance*. Cambridge: Cambridge University Press.

In the Context of English History

Margaret Shewring

Margaret Shewring's careful account of twentieth-century stagings of Richard II as part of a sequence of history plays shows that performance offers insights into the particular interconnectedness of the tetralogy. Drawing on information about the productions and their reception, she shows how the productions operated within specific historical and theatrical frameworks.

Margaret Shewring, 'In the Context of English History', in *King Richard II* (Shakespeare in Performance) (Manchester: Manchester University Press, 1996), pp. 91–116.

Frank Benson was the first to mount a professional production of *Richard II* on the English stage alongside productions of other Shakespearian English history plays. In 1901 he presented a 'Week of Kings' at the Shakespeare Memorial Theatre in Stratford-upon-Avon, drawing together a series of his most remarkable productions, and remarkable personal performances, which he had developed with his company over more than a decade. The 'Week of Kings' brought together *King John, Richard II, 2 Henry IV, Henry V, 2 Henry VI* and *Richard III* with Benson playing his favourite role, Richard II, on Shakespeare's birthday. The time was ripe for such a venture. It chimed well with the national fervour and pride being expressed in England as a whole in the context of the Boer War, as well as with the more local sense of festival in the commemoration of Shakespeare's birthday in Stratford. W. B. Yeats responded warmly to the special nature of the occasion. His experience of English theatre was limited, but in Stratford he found himself delighted with the quasi-medieval location in which 'the theatre was charming in red-brick Gothic' and was so full that 'they had to get him a kitchen chair as no other seat was vacant' (Trewin, 1960: 127, citing the contents of Yeats's letter to Lady Gregory at Coole). This sense of festival was, for Yeats, further intensified by Benson's decision to stage a 'Week of Kings': 'Partly because of the spirit in the place, and partly because of the way play supports play the theatre has moved me as it has never done before' (Trewin, 1960: 142–3).

Yeats's appreciation of 'the way play supports play' was not that of Dowden, who argued for a gradual cumulative knowledge and understanding in the study, but that of a theatre practitioner responding with heightened awareness to the full range of performance languages being employed by the Bensonians. He had a special personal and professional interest in the company's verse-speaking and presentational skills, for Benson was to stage *Diarmuid and Grania*, a play by Yeats and George Moore, in Dublin, in autumn 1901. 'He talked also of events that were in the Warwickshire winds: the chance of a school of acting, a hope that the chief players of the time would be engaged for Stratford, the thought that this Festival might become "with favouring chance the supreme dramatic event of the world"' (Trewin, 1960: 127).

Staging a group of related plays makes demands both on the company of players involved and on their audiences, as players and audiences alike need to devote two or three evenings (or, perhaps, one full day) to experience the plays as a group in the theatre. It also generates a special energy; an energy Yeats equates with Festival Theatre. Benson's innovative 'Week of Kings' derived much of its strength from its ability to draw on a group of successful productions already well established in the company's repertoire. It seems that he made no significant changes in the scope or structure of individual plays in order to shape them into one large narrative of epic proportions. It was not until fifty years later that any professional company in Britain was to follow Benson's initiative and develop it into the staging of a full, connected cycle of plays telling a continuous narrative. Then, in 1951, another company based at the Memorial Theatre in Stratford-upon-Avon took up the challenge.

This chapter concentrates on the place of *Richard II* in three major professional productions of cycles of Shakespeare's history plays: Anthony Quayle's staging of the tetralogy in 1951, the Royal Shakespeare Company's *The Wars of the Roses* in 1963–4, and the English Shakespeare Company's *The Wars of the Roses*, 1986–9. The place of *1 Henry IV* and *2 Henry IV* in these cycles is discussed by Scott McMillin (1991) and Barbara Hodgdon (1993) in their volumes in this Shakespeare in Performance Series. The following discussion of *Richard II* would benefit from being read in the context of their analyses.

Directorial approaches to any individual history play differ when that play is presented as part of a trilogy (or tetralogy) or in the wider context of the full cycle of Shakespeare's English histories as they depict the consequences of Carlisle's prophecy (*Richard II*, IV. i. 133–49) of the Wars of the Roses. The full narrative dramatises the fate of the English Crown from the reign of Richard II to that of Richard III. Individual characters no longer dominate. Rather, each play takes its place in a complex discussion rooted in power politics, and individual characters are seen in relation to their ability to seize or to retain power. This, in turn, influences casting. It is usual, for example, in productions of *Richard II* which contribute to the staging of a larger cycle, for the casting of Bolingbroke to be at least as significant as that of King Richard. It is, after all, Bolingbroke whose ability to rule is a dominant issue in both parts of *Henry IV*. Similarly, the role of Prince Hal develops naturally into that of Henry V. Cycle productions inevitably demand a strong controlling voice. It is therefore not surprising that such enterprises were not undertaken before the position of the director in the twentieth-century theatre was fully established as someone whose concept could dominate the shape of a production. Equally significant is the growing importance of the designer. Whereas the Victorian actor-managers drew on a range of specialist advisers in order to research and develop appropriate settings, the place of a single designer, working closely with a director, has since then become increasingly influential. Certainly the contribution of the designer to the staging of cycles is crucial, for it is the designer who creates the visual unity that is necessary to complement the narrative as it is carried through several individual plays. Above all, the staging of a major cycle demands a large company. This, in turn, has meant that such an undertaking has been limited almost exclusively to major companies with the commercial basis and backstage support to make the enterprise viable.

Anthony Quayle Directs the Tetralogy, 1951

In 1951, to commemorate the Festival of Britain, Anthony Quayle directed the tetralogy from *Richard II* to *Henry V* at the Shakespeare Memorial Theatre in Stratford-upon-Avon, enabling Stratford to make a significant contribution to the nationwide celebrations. Journalists flocked to report the Festival events, and their reports reveal an awareness of both regional and national pride. For example, we find Alan Fairclough in the *Daily Mirror* extolling the fact that 'Every Briton can be proud of the way the Festival of Greater Britain, not just of London, has opened here [in Stratford-upon-Avon]. This is the first of twenty-three local Festivals all over the country' (26 March 1951). The special nature of the occasion was emphasised further by the presence of television cameras in the foyer on the opening night of the first play (*Richard II*). Anthony Quayle, in his curtain speech to mark the opening of the Shakespeare Season, described the four plays in the repertoire as an 'epic of England'. So they are, and, as Alan Dent remarks, 'it seems very odd that they do not seem to have been acted consecutively before, here or anywhere else' (*News Chronicle*, 26 March 1951).

The tetralogy marked an extensive refurbishment of Stratford's theatre which included new interior decoration for the auditorium, the installation of a new lighting system and an extension of the stage out over the orchestra pit. For the 1951 season this structure was further enhanced to suggest the close actor–audience relationship of the Elizabethan playhouse. *The Sunday Times* described Tanya Moiseiwitsch's set as:

> a wooden structure with stairs at each side leading to a gallery at the centre over massive gates. It appears rough and unfinished as if it had been quickly put together by the players of the period and the grey of the unpainted, weathered timber offsets the rich colour of the costumes. The illusion of the Elizabethan stage is also enhanced by a canopy-like background to suggest the interior of a large tent. (18 March 1951)

No front curtain was used, and the basic set remained constant throughout the season.

The appropriateness of staging the plays together was explained in the programme insert for *Richard II*:

> It is generally agreed that the four plays of this season's historical cycle form a tetralogy and were planned by Shakespeare as one great play. They present not only a living epic of England through the reigns of the three kings, but are also a profound commentary on Kingship.

By no means all the critics were happy with this perception. The *Birmingham Gazette* was not alone in seeing at least the first play as 'a botched job' which denied Richard's status as 'an independent tragic figure'. Indeed, 'for the sake of Prince Hal, who is yet to come, he [Richard] bends himself too plastically to his non-heroic role in the cycle.' For this critic, at least, Michael Redgrave's performance as Richard lacked 'not only the power of an uncompromisingly tragic emotion, but power of personality' (26 March 1951). Indeed many of the reviewers in 1951 found themselves trying to assess Redgrave's perform-ance in terms more appropriate to the accumulated theatrical tradition rooted in the cult of personality epitomised by Benson and Gielgud than to the role as conceived within the logic of the full tetralogy. So Redgrave's interpret-ation of Richard was criticised for concentrating too much on the presenta-tion 'of an effeminate, irresolute, capricious fop' (*Birmingham Gazette*, 26 March 1951). A similar unease was voiced by Alan Dent in the *News Chron-icle*: 'Mr Redgrave plays the King in a flamboyant, honey-sweet way that matches his sartorial splendour. In the first act he draws the scornful, mocking and spoilt young King – the royal playboy surrounded by his flatter-ing yes-men – with a brilliant certainty...In the later acts he seemed oddly deficient in pathos'. For the critic in the *Manchester Guardian*,

> Michael Redgrave, in effect, plays two kings. One, dressed in what fashion writers call pastel shades, shrugs and turns his head and gives slashing feminine glances with his pale blue eyes as he fingers a weak chin and hopelessly tries to keep order among his squabbling courtiers. The second speaks and carries himself more manfully and dresses more soberly. The white character, as Mr Redgrave sees it, is a nervous emotional incompetent who undervalues his crown while he wears it, gives it up without a fight when Bolingbroke raises his voice, and then bitterly regrets his weakness. (24 March 1951)

Redgrave was clearly aware of the tension between Richard's capricious incompetence and the need to win sympathy and pity in his deposition and subsequent death. Claude Westell, too, felt the conflict:

> As shown to us by Mr Redgrave, one could despise the languid, haughty popinjay of the early scenes: the pale-faced aesthete of the fluttering eyelids, the pursed lips and the mincing gait. One could shut out completely all sympathy for the cynic who so heartlessly mocked the dying John of Gaunt. Yet so delicately pitched was this characterisation that when it came to Flint castle and the monarch's descent to receive the Judas-like salutation of Boling-broke, one's sympathies swung like a weather vane at a change of wind. (*Birmingham Mail*, 26 March 1951)

As the play unfolded, critics began to discover that Redgrave had 'taken command of the self-absorbed, self-pitying and fickle royal butterfly' and 'endowed him with a voice of lyrical beauty' (*Coventry Evening Telegraph*, 26 March 1951). For Harold Hobson, Redgrave's voice lent itself to the play's 'luxuriously grief-stricken speeches, and he spoke them with a fine music, at the same time establishing the irresponsibility of the unhappy king' (*The Sunday Times*, 25 March 1951). This production confirmed Shakespeare's wisdom in writing into the Queen's part more of Anne of Bohemia than Isabel the child bride. So

> the parting with the Queen ... [was] a scene beautifully enacted, with Heather Stannard, all melting tenderness and compassion, as the Queen ... Richard, on his way to prison, is walking with head bent intent on telling his rosary. The Queen, waiting to snatch her moment with him, moves forward, but he does not see her until a priest touches his arm and points to her. Then the King moves towards her with a look of infinite tenderness and sadness in his eyes.
> (Claude L. Westell, *Birmingham Mail*, 26 March 1951)

Such scenes seem to give the lie to Olivier's memory of Redgrave's Richard as 'an out-and-out pussy queer' (Rossi, 1977: 97). Indeed Richard Findlater put the overt homosexuality in context, as Malcolm Page notes: 'Instead of Gielgud's kindly, lyrical victim, Redgrave presented a harsh, unsentimentalized portrait, sharp with cruelty, spite and envy; yet the feline homosexual of the early scenes was, for all his malicious weakness, a right royal Plantagenet' (Page, 1987: 252). Richard David, while appreciating the skill in Redgrave's performance, was less convinced of this sense of royalty – 'as a portrait of a wayward weakling, it was superb; but it lacked a quality essential to Shakespeare's Richard – kingliness' (David, 1953: 134).

The sense of unease expressed by these reviewers points as much to the strength of the performance in the context of the first play of a sequence as to what the critics perceived as its weaknesses. For the production focused on *Richard II* as a study not in personal tragedy but in the nature of kingship itself. In place of the tragedy of Richard the audience was offered the rise to power of a strong, ambitious Bolingbroke. As Dent recalls, 'we found ourselves watching the excellent Bolingbroke (Harry Andrews) instead of the King, for in this Bolingbroke's eyes lurked an infinity of contemptuous patience while he heeded Richard's elaborately fanciful speeches' (*News Chronicle*, 26 March 1951). This Bolingbroke was 'a magnificiently turbulent and unruly figure' (Hobson, *The Sunday Times*, 25 March 1951), played 'from first to last finely complementary to Mr Redgrave' (*The Times*, 26 March 1951), a Bolingbroke who 'by sheer force of suggestion contributes, as he sits silent and formidable on the throne he has usurped, to Richard's moral triumph' (*The Times*, 26 March 1951). Harry Andrews's 'unbending, authoritative Bolingbroke' (*Birmingham Gazette*, 26 March 1951) was to continue as King Henry IV, while a new, young, Welsh actor joined the company as Prince Hal – Richard Burton.

It was Richard Burton's *Henry V* which would carry the achievement and focus of Quayle's staging of the tetralogy. Indeed, for Quayle, the key to interpreting the tetralogy was to be found in this role, for Henry V 'personified, to the people of Shakespeare's England, the ideal King: brave, warlike, generous, just, and – it must be added – loving humour' (programme, 1951). In this context, and 'to off set this hero', 'the tragic *Richard the Second*, who would seem to have all the defects of Prince Hal's virtues, is not only historically, but dramatically, the perfect counterpoise and prologue' (programme).

The RSC's *The Wars of the Roses*

Not until 1964 did the Royal Shakespeare Company stage the full cycle of Shakespeare's seven English history plays, which collectively tell the full story of the Wars of the Roses. Under the direction of Peter Hall, John Barton and Clifford Williams the RSC in 1963 began this concentration on the cycle of history plays, staging the three parts of Shakespeare's *Henry VI* in a two-part adaptation, *Henry VI* and *Edward IV*, followed by *Richard III*. The tetralogy of *Richard II*, the two parts of *Henry IV* and *Henry V*, was added in 1964 to mark the Company's contribution to the quatercentenary celebrations of Shakespeare's birth alongside a season of festival events, a major exhibition and the opening of the Shakespeare Centre (adjacent to the Birthplace in Henley Street and one of the properties of the Shakespeare Birthplace Trust). The 1964 season opened on 15 April with a performance of *Richard II*.

That the 1964 tetralogy was conceived as an extension of the 1963 Wars of the Roses trilogy is clear from the continuity in set design. John Bury's stage picture provided a sustained visual image. *Richard II* was 'played on the same metallic stage and before the same studded walls as were used for last year's brilliant "Wars of the Roses" trilogy' (*Nottingham Guardian*, 16 April 1964). 'In colour the set had small variations of a basic brown, black and grey, and simple sharp contrasts for costume and properties' (Brown, 1966: 195). The reviewer for the *Nottingham Guardian* noted that John Bury added to his 'Roses' set 'where the play [*Richard II*] demanded new items, and he has touched up the grey with gold, which is repeated on the throne and on the costumes' (16 April 1964). So the critic for the *Liverpool Post* records 'settings, which have the subdued gleam of dull gold' (16 April 1964). The stage offered a variable, flexible space, sometimes empty and unlocalised, at other times using a few large items of scenery. Much of the responsibility for creating the imaginative location fell to the cast. 'Two triangular constructions upstage revolve between scenes to become parts of castle, forest, garden, dungeon, etc., and props such as the throne are rolled smoothly on or deftly carried into position by members of the cast. The table in the throne room rises from the floor' (*Worcester Evening News*, 16 April 1964).

Crucial to any understanding of the direction of the full cycle, and of the place of *Richard II* in that cycle, is the extent to which this great undertaking marked a celebration of the concept of 'Company'. How better to celebrate the achievements of the Royal Shakespeare Company than the production of seven plays from the late sixteenth century in a cultural and performance context which demonstrated their broad relevance to the 1960s? As John Russell Brown (1966) stresses, there can be no doubt that the cycle of English history plays offered Peter Hall and his colleagues an opportunity to illustrate all the skills that could be demonstrated by a company trained meticulously to work *together* – a company which, on the whole, ignored the 'star' system in favour of a sense of shared purpose. So, 'for battles, group entries or other spectacular opportunities (take the lists at Coventry in *Richard II* or the embarkation of Henry V at Southampton) the stage is filled with nimble and well-drilled supernumeraries giving, by action, costume, properties and make-up, an extraordinarily complete attempt at verisimilitude' (Brown, 1966: 195). And, for Brown, the precision of the company work and the level of co-operation and inventiveness can best, perhaps, be captured in what was, for him, 'a representative image' of the project as a whole – a scene change:

> There is music and a slow, purposeful filing off-stage, nicely judged to illustrate the political factions and the concerns of the characters. The lights change and two large, dark, triangular-based structures turn before a dark trellised background. And the stage is now a battlefield, with instruments of war, care worn soldiers, and the slow yet alert tempo of battle. (Brown, 1966: 195)

In 1963 the young David Warner was cast as the weak Henry VI. The year 1964 saw him playing Richard II in a way which 'expressed every aspect of Richard's complex personality: the posing, the play acting, the apparent effeminacy, the sudden outbursts of pettish temperament. To these he adds a pathetic dignity and a remarkable ability to express a wide range of emotion. If, occasionally, he gets weighed down by the appalling length of the speeches, so from time to time do the rest of the cast' (*The Liverpool Post*, 16 April 1964). *The Evening Standard* described him as 'looking like one of Dostoievski's Christ-like martyrs' – weak and ineffectual, indeed 'about as bloodless as a vegetarian dinner' (16 April 1964). Certainly Warner 'used nervous smiles and a loose-limbed awkwardness to suggest anxious timidity' in both *Henry VI* and *Richard II*, while 'Richard's commands were underplayed so that even these gave an impression of weakness' (Brown, 1966: 198). Such a reading could be accommodated in *Richard II* played as part of a full cycle, but would, perhaps, have been less appropriate had the play stood on its own. As in 1951, the role of Bolingbroke was played with considerable strength and theatrical presence: the casting of Eric Porter was important as a foil to Warner's Richard. Porter had already played Boling- broke in 1952/3, to Paul Scofield's Richard, for Tennent Production Ltd: a performance directed by John Gielgud and staged at the Shakespeare Memorial Theatre prior to a London season. In 1964 Porter projected a 'kind of violence, particularly at the start of the play. But unlike the inter- mittent cloud bursts of Richard's ill temper, this [was] a controlled and directed violence' (*The Liverpool Post*, 16 April 1964).

Violence, controlled and uncontrolled, offered the key to any interpret- ation of the 1964 *The Wars of the Roses*. Hall and his collaborators presented Shakespeare's histories in a context in which the national crisis triggered by the deposition of Richard II pervaded all the plays in the cycle. But that crisis was presented not in terms of *who* ruled, but *how* they ruled and how the consequences of that political control affected the social and economic health of the nation. Such an interpretation contrasted sharply with Quayle's celebratory, patriotic 1951 tetralogy.

This change in emphasis mirrored the changes both in critical interpret- ation and in theatrical conditions. Arguably the 1951 tetralogy owed its em- phasis to a school of thought much influenced by E. M. W. Tillyard (1944). This stressed the place of monarchy in a series of hierarchical relationships. The tetralogy's medieval and early Tudor world, mediated through an Eliza- bethan playwright's eyes, was presented on a set with clear visual allusions to the Elizabethan stage and to a world-view that accepted the place of monarchy. The play centred on the tension between a king's 'two bodies' – the person and the office of a king. But even within that 'safe' context, the 1951 production reflected, too, a growing awareness that the underlying issue of the cycle was not only the celebration of nationalism in a patriotic narrative but the analysis of influential political figures as they negotiated for power within a changing world order. This shift in emphasis to the political rather than the tragic and purely historical structure of the plays was evident within Moiseiwitsch's set. For, although this clearly alluded to the Elizabethan stage, it positioned the throne downstage right. The effect was not to reinforce the focus on 'state' and kingship but to open a central area of the performance space to a flexible blocking which put the focal emphasis on the changing pattern of relationships within that space, a space that marked the way across the stage to and from the throne.

By 1964 attitudes to Shakespeare's histories had changed decisively. Scholars came to stress the interpretation of the cycle of history plays as one unified narrative conceived and written to raise crucial issues relating to government and its consequences. It may be more than coincidence that one of the most astute academic contributions to the criticism of Shakespeare's

history plays as an interconnected cycle was published by the Society for Theatre Research in 1964: Arthur Colby Sprague's study of *Shakespeare's Histories: Plays for the Stage*. Like Sprague, Hall embraced the notion of the overall unity of the cycle, both in scholarly and theatrical terms, but laid greater stress than Sprague on the narrative of the histories not as a grand design but as the exploration of a crisis – the crisis in which the nation finds itself as power changes hands. For Hall, *The Wars of the Roses* did not offer an answer. What was offered was a demonstration of a problem.

This approach was timely in the 1960s. It accorded well with the current trend for the questioning of accepted world-views in the spirit of contemporary politics, epitomised by the writing of Jan Kott in *Shakespeare Our Contemporary* (1967). In the theatre this questioning was much influenced by the work of Bertolt Brecht, both in general terms and in the context of the English theatre since 1956. There can be little doubt that the company work of the Berliner Ensemble, and their political emphasis, when they toured to England in the late 1950s was taken, if not as a model, at least as a challenge to reconsider the accumulated stage traditions of centuries. In the case of *Richard II* this led to a rethinking of the place of the King in a wider context of political relevance (rather than to an opportunity for great actors to indulge themselves in the personality cult of the eponymous role). Such a shift in perception did not come overnight. It was part of a much wider cultural shift in audience expectation and audience demands, a shift acknowledged by the programme for the full cycle of history plays for the 1964 season, which sets out the Royal Shakespeare Company's aims for this production in the guise of a conversation between directors. In this they note that 'Richard has built an island of indulgence, art, fashion, elegance . . . an elaborate artifice for the satisfaction of his own personality and which does not cater for the needs of the country as a whole', thus setting a context in which 'Bolingbroke, the new man, the caring man, the man of integrity, becomes a rebel, almost against his will' (RSC programme, 1964). *Richard II* is seen as 'strongly medieval in character, an extended ritual', but a very fragile one. 'When Richard is deposed and his world breaks up, the language of the play begins to change radically.' And so, after the deposition, Bolingbroke 'moves steadily towards a more concise and realistic utterance' (RSC programme, 1964). Above all, throughout the full cycle of plays 'the directors . . . made Shakespeare persistently anti-heroic and deflationary' (Brown, 1966: 198). In this context, the inclusion of the Aumerle episodes undercut rather than reinforced any sense of true loyalty. So 'multiple throwing down of gages before Aumerle . . . quickly deflated the pretensions of the newly-loyal nobles' (Brown, 1966: 197–8), while Patience Collier as the Duchess of York played 'frankly . . . for laughs' (*Liverpool Post*, 16 April 1964).

Richard II was not, in this production, so much a dramatisation of an old order as a seedbed of potential violence, violence that became overt in scenes of battle and the destruction of civil war in the later plays in the series. But even in the more formal verse structure of *Richard II* the violence was never far below the surface. Sometimes it was made visually explicit. The reviewer for the *Birmingham Mail* was struck by the 'fearsomely realistic equipment for the lists at Coventry' (W.H.W., 16 April 1964), while John Russell Brown noted the emotional moment turning to physical pain when Richard 'smashed the looking glass...with his bare fist and so inflicted pain upon himself' (1966: 196). 'In prison he [Richard] was tethered by a huge, noisy chain that had to be flung aside to allow movement...the sound and apparent weight of that chain may well have been the domineering impression given by the Prison Scene' (1966: 196). Perhaps the most shocking moment in which the violence broke through and became actual is indicated clearly in a relatively clean prompt copy (archive of the RSC at the Shakespeare Centre) and noted by Brown: 'Richard II struck the dying Gaunt with a whip repeatedly' (1966: 196). Collectively

> the plays became a high-class cartoon, a relentless horror comic. An elevated tone was sustained by restrained colour in the setting, slow tempo and deliberate utterance...horror and violence were presented by liberal splashes of blood, and by inventive business that elaborated every opportunity for the exhibition of cruelty and pain that the text suggested, and more that were foisted on the text. (Brown, 1966: 196)

For Brown all this was part of the season's 'continuous emphasis of violence and of the shallowness of politicians' pretensions' (1966: 196). Much of this was gratuitous in the context of *Richard II*, although among the most 'interesting achievements' of this production was the violence that accompanied Bolingbroke's judgement on Bushy and Green, 'building that into a scene of general social interest rather than a further revelation of the emergent ruler' and so serving 'to accentuate one vein in the text...that has often been obscured by a picturesque accentuation of pageantry and royal panoply' (1966: 197). Certainly there was little trace of the conventional elements of national and imperial splendour to accompany the season as a whole.

The choice of John Bury as set designer in itself reinforced the directors' approach. Bury's harsh set, with its clanging metallic surfaces (including the stage floor), was the work not of a designer trained in conventional techniques but one whose experience in theatre was working with Joan Littlewood's Theatre Workshop in Stratford East, London, for whom he had designed *Richard II* in 1955. The small cast and low budget of the Theatre Workshop, coupled with a sense of struggle, both practical and political, that motivated Joan Littlewood's work, inevitably influenced Bury's concept of the place of design in the theatre. He offered not a decorative stage picture but an environment to complement the issues raised within the plays, as his work with Peter Hall for the RSC's *Hamlet* in 1964 made plain. As in *The Wars of the Roses*, the stage picture for *Hamlet* offered a visual development of the production's dominant concept.

In 1963/4, for *The Wars of the Roses*, the directors' overriding concern was to look again at the full cycle of history plays in the context of a debate about power at all social levels. So one of the effects of coupling *Richard II* with the rest of Shakespeare's six-part *Henriad* was to see the play, arguably for the first time in England, as a genuinely timeless political piece – political in the sense in which Brecht and the Berliner Ensemble would have understood the term.

The English Shakespeare Company's *The Wars of the Roses*

When the English Shakespeare Company presented *Richard II* in December 1987, in the Theatre Royal, Bath, the play was added to an already devised English history cycle from *1 Henry IV* to *Henry VI*. Indeed, it is this decision to *add Richard II* which is the key to an understanding of the ESC's approach to the script. This decision must be seen, too, in the light of the aims and ambitions of the Company.

In *The English Shakespeare Company: The Story of 'The Wars of the Roses' 1986–1989*, Michael Bogdanov and Michael Pennington (1990) document their formation of the English Shakespeare Company, their struggle for funding and their passionate belief in taking Shakespeare – in full, epic scale – out of the established, metropolitan, national theatres and carrying his plays to the people as a whole. Their record contains all the frustrations, pettiness – and idealism – of those intent on changing the way in which the majority of people conceive a night in the theatre, by demonstrating the immediate relevance of Shakespeare's plays to the present and attempting to use those plays as part of a contemporary social and political agenda. Guided by Jodi Myers and Fleur Selby (on behalf of the Touring Department of the Arts Council of Great Britain), Pennington and Bogdanov were encouraged to think not of a small-scale studio venture but of a 'product big enough to revitalise the old "Number One" circuit':

> We had been invited to think large. Nothing is larger in Shakespeare than the epic sequence of Histories that runs over eight plays from the Deposition of Richard II in 1399 to the founding of the Tudor dynasty by Henry VII on Bosworth Field in 1485. (Bogdanov and Pennington, 1990: 5)

So Pennington and Bogdanov began work on the *Henriad*. They were in no doubt that the story of the trilogy – and on into the *Henry VI* plays – was worth telling. To quote Michael Pennington:

Shakespeare's way with history was rather casual, to say the least. By compressing it, imagining it and twisting it around, he insisted on his right as a teller of stories to make an alternative version of events that would still be true to the spirit of the past. (ESC programme)

The trilogy of the *Henriad* opened at the Theatre Royal, Plymouth. The last weeks of rehearsals in November 1986 took place in a 'gigantic disused hangar on the sea front' (Bogdanov and Pennington, 1990: 56). At this point Bogdanov realised that the audience would need to know the story of *Richard II* in order to explain the historical context of the *Henriad*, and so it was decided to tell that story, in popular folk-ballad form, as a Prologue. Bogdanov notes:

> Taking as its title Hal's name for himself when disguised in *Henry V*... 'Harry Le Roy' was launched on the world and I chose the most junior member of the company to sing it: an Acting Assistant Stage Manager, who had the responsibility of leading the company out and introducing the whole cycle. (Bogdanov and Pennington, 1990: 56–7)

It was not long before the ballad (with its music composed by Terry Mortimer) was seen to be no real substitute for the full story, and *Richard II* was incorporated into the repertoire. The idea of completing the story on stage appealed to Pennington and Bogdanov. The full cycle had not been staged since the RSC's *Wars of the Roses* (1964) and was 'certainly never seen on tour before' (Bogdanov and Pennington, 1990: 68). So the notion of adding *Richard II* to an existing cycle, a cycle designed to tour, took hold. It would need to make use of the same permanent set as devised by Chris Dyer (although by the summer of 1987 'Chris had virtually abandoned the set and props, leaving the re-drawing in the hands of a young assistant, Colin Peters' (1990: 102)). Above all it would need to fit into the existing cycle in terms of period choice, costumes and casting.

The Company wanted to demonstrate the plays' immediacy by seeking out their implications for an audience in the 1980s. They believed that audience would be conscious of the apparent unfairness of authority, the haphazard (rather than the idealist) approach to war – at least on the part of the majority of the troops – and the enormous, overriding sense of guilt and waste whether in relation to Vietnam or to English policy in the Falklands. For Michael Bogdanov '*The Henrys* were plays for today, the lessons of history, unlearnt ... We were in the era of New Brutalism where a supposed return to Victorian values under the guise of initiative and incentive masked the true goal of greed, avarice, exploitation and self' (1990: 24).

In keeping with this perception of the immediacy of the issues explored in the play, coupled with an overriding sense of metatheatre, the Company's intention was to allow the periods within which the plays were presented (in terms of costumes, cultural signs, manners, etc.) to move from the second half of the nineteenth century for *Henry IV* to the second half of the twentieth century by the end of the performance of the final play in the cycle. The resulting anachronisms were seen, for the most part, as constructive rather than perplexing. Interestingly, when Bogdanov expressed that sense of immediacy, he did so in terms which included a quotation from the dying John of Gaunt:

> Westminster Rule. Centralisation. Censorship. Power to the City. Bleed the rest of the country dry. Bolingbroke / Boadicea / Britannia was in the saddle. The 'rotten parchment bonds' of the fourteenth century were being drawn up again as Britain went into hock, selling herself to any and all who had the money to buy a stake in her and fill the coffers of the fortunate few.
> This land...
> Is now leased out...
> Like to a tenement or pelting farm:
> That [*sic*] England, that was wont to conquer others,
> Hath made a shameful conquest of itself. (*Richard II*, II. 1)
>
> A conspiracy of silence and complicity surrounded shuffles, resignations, rise and fall, crash and takeover – the desperate feeling of manipulation and manoeuvre in the air...How could the plays *not* be understood in a contemporary context? (Bogdanov and Pennington, 1990: 24)

Given the choice of 'period' for the staging of the two parts of *Henry IV*, *Richard II* could not, logically, be presented in a medieval context. The choice of costumes in the rest of the cycle had begun eclectically, responsive only to the twin demands of contemporary relevance and touring, although there was 'a sort of chronology to be found' (1990: 103). Eventually Stephanie Howard suggested setting *Richard II* in the Regency period. This, as Pennington writes, 'would then allow us, with the advent of Bolingbroke as King Henry IV, to *retain* our Victorian frock coats and scarlet tunics for *his* court' (1990: 103; my italics) in marked contrast to 'the Regency officers and lounge lizards of Richard II's lotus-eating court' (1990: 139). Eventually Bogdanov came to believe that the choice of period was not an altogether happy one. Reminiscing about the decision, he is practical – even pragmatic. The Regency style, Beau Brummell dandyism 'suited our purposes; a profligate, dilettante Richard. I suspect that were we to embark on a one-off production of the play this is not the period we would ideally choose' (1990: 107).

Talking through the same problem in interview, Michael Pennington saw both advantages and disadvantages in a Regency-style *Richard*. One strength which emerged was its relevance to the theme of social inequality which surfaces more strongly later in the cycle:

there's kind of extreme contrast between the highly liberal, highly extravagant, highly aesthetic part, at the top end of society and exceptional poverty and exceptional unhappiness underneath it, more extreme than many other periods in history – 'George spent more in an evening than a working man had in a year at his disposal' – it seemed to me exactly like Richard.

And so, even if the choice of period created some problems in terms of establishing the late medieval code of belief in royal divinity, it did enable a sense of extravagance to be conveyed. As Pennington went on to elaborate, 'This Richard is an aesthete.' Favourites are part of his artistic circle, 'at least they drink good claret, and at least their dinner parties are where the conversation is good – it's witty even if it is cruel.' In the context of the production of the full cycle of history plays, *Richard II* emphasised a period of decadence and misrule (rather than the personal problems of a tragic king). Yet it made its own mark so that, later in the cycle, the audience missed 'the style of Richard's court, the sheer glamour of it – the sheer inspiration – the sheer temperament/personality of it'.

Creating the sense of Regency luxury posed its own problems. It was not just the overall feel for an updated cycle with its rather eclectic approach to costuming which restricted the interpretation of *Richard II*. Bogdanov freely admits that 'attempting a setting for this sumptuous scenario within the framework of our steely black structure was a poser' (Bogdanov and Pennington, 1990: 107):

> I added three sets of net curtains – all we could afford – sprayed the back set purple and left the two front sets white. We 'rouched' them. This allowed for a certain amount of softness when properly arranged, but did not quite match the velveteened volumes of the imagination, great swathes of silk and satin festooned liberally in the great hall surrounded by gilded oils and Louis Quinze. What we *did* have was our (my) bits of chenille tablecloth, that we had used to drape the tavern in the Boar's Head. They would have to do. I draped the throne (symbol of misuse), an easel, the card table, three chairs and a cushion. (Later we bought a few off-cuts of velvet.) It did. Just. (1990: 107–8)

The evocation of period made use, too, of music and of the sense of grand sets which needed time to move and arrange. The concept of company as established by the ESC (that is, a group of participants in which each member did anything and everything that was required) meant that actors, as well as stage crew, were used to shift scenery – and that the rather long scene changes were integrated into the rhythm of this rather formal play:

> There was quite a lot of shifting about to do for the lists and for the castle – there was a big, big flying piece that had to be got in, placed properly and locked on, and there were towers and staircases which came right up against it; there was also a

big sliding panel and gates at the back that we used . . . it all took time and it was accompanied by Schubert and various other musical interludes from all periods, particularly from the Georgian period. (Pennington in interview)

On its opening night all this attention to scenery, particularly to the *very* steep staircase, slowed the rhythm, making the show run for three and a half hours. The sense of flagging energy was compounded by lighting problems. Lighting that had worked in the context of rehearsal was inadequate and over-subtle in a large stage space. This became particularly important in the prison scene, which was confined in a small area defined only by light:

I mean the stage was open right up to the back but it was dark and there was a working area which ran from the bed on one side . . . to the bucket on the other – and the equivalent depth to that width. I had wanted it to seem to be even smaller . . . with light coming through a very high window as in a medieval prison . . . but the practicalities of getting killed and all the rest of it, the traffic through the scene, meant that you needed a bit more space – although still very confined. (interview)

The casting for *Richard II* needed to fit logically into a pattern of overall continuity and development. It seemed appropriate for Pennington to take on the role of Richard. (Indeed, one of the accidents that had led to the foundation of the ESC was the RSC's failure to employ Pennington in 1986/7, the season in which Jeremy Irons was eventually cast as Richard II.) Discussing his approach to the part, Pennington mentioned his long-standing wish to play Richard, 'originally because I thought it was a great romantic role full of the most glorious language' (interview). Indeed, he had previously read the play in traditional terms – 'a splendid romantic heroic tragedy, with minimal politics' (interview). But Bolingbroke was soon to be seen as Henry IV and it would not be appropriate to present him as the villainous usurper with Richard as the tragic victim.

Pennington *was* well cast as Richard II. Interestingly, some of the reviews seem to echo an approach more fitting to 'a play of personality' than to a dramatisation of the nature of authority, revealing it in all its messiness. Like McKellen, Pennington sought ways to give life to the curiously enigmatic figure whose rule was guaranteed by Divine Right. Both actors found in the script the clues for a self-indulgent, vain figurehead who used ceremony and ritual to bolster his own self-confidence in the face of bickering, niggling politicians – a star personality, establishing his own flamboyant court in the face of increasing moral reproof (not for sexual liberty, but for sheer thought-less extravagance). The image created by Pennington's Richard was reminis-cent of that of the French aristocracy in the years leading to the Revolution, an analogy evoked by the dandy image often associated with the Scarlet Pimpernel. The opening stage picture offered a view of an aesthete's court

– the dandified Richard lounging on a chaise longue while the throne was shrouded in darkness at the rear of the stage. The fabrics were velour, with white soft-linen ruffs and a richly patterned knee-length frockcoat for Richard, and Henry Hereford already contrasted in a high-necked, royal blue uniform – with red, high-buttoned collar, gold buttons and epaulettes. His beard was precisely cut, to echo his stiff image. Richard was not so much relaxed as enjoying being 'on show' – cynical, cold, flippant and affected. A range of costumes was used in this opening sequence – more or less lush dependent upon the personal and ideological allegiance of the participants. So Mowbray was more the courtier than the military man – suggested by his large green artist's cravat, and yet his awkward posture in such elegant clothes suggested an over-dressed thug – of the King's party, yet not born to a courtly life. The awkwardness was conveyed through his rather harsh verse-speaking, too. Certainly he was agitated when the Duke of Gloucester was mentioned; and this, coupled with the King's nervousness, underlined Richard's implicit guilt over the murder. Richard resorted to his customary glib, shallow cynicism only to discover that such a weak 'cover-up' would not do. Bogdanov pays tribute, in *The English Shakespeare Company*, to Pennington's portrayal of Richard. He highlights, in particular, Pennington's skill in the deposition scene:

> He played with Bolingbroke as a cat with a mouse. The crown was dangled like a carrot, it was held high, gently offered, snatched away, the anguish of the virgin, refusing yet knowing ultimately the prize would have to be given away, determined to tease and frustrate, delaying the moment as long as possible. And the language to match. I wanted to keep it all, every intricate, exquisite moment, but time was to pare this sequence down to a spare minimum. (1990: 106–7)

For Pennington it was the stage picture with its strong blocking that dominated this scene. For, unusually, the ESC staged the deposition 'with Bolingbroke very much in a position of power and Richard very much disadvantaged by this staging – rather than with the star in the middle'. Pennington recalls the various actors who played Bolingbroke during the production's life responding differently to this staging:

> I remember Michael [Cronin] wanting Bolingbroke to come and join Richard and to have a closer exchange with him towards the end, after the mirror has been broken, because Bolingbroke actually enters into Richard's rhyming, riddling world and plays the game with him, rather generously, rather kindly – plays the game. And that was something that was Michael's invention and discovery. I think John [Castle], who first played Bolingbroke, kept his distance. (interview)

Pennington found that he enjoyed the deposition scene most in those performances in which it raised laughs:

It always worked best when he [Richard] was fighting back. His wit was the only weapon he had – and had predominantly – more than anyone else. It's his skill – 'say that again'... 'that's good'... 'let me think about that' – the whole 'put down' of Bolingbroke. The audience loves that because they sort of want Richard to fight back and here he can only fight back with just the lines. It was good when it all turned into wit. You know he's in deep distress but, like all scenes of high emotion, it's not the extremity of the emotion but the measures that the character takes to fight against the emotion that are most telling.

Towards the end of the play, in the prison sequence, what we see is not a king whose identity depends on a God-given Right to Rule, but 'a man reinventing his own language, reinventing himself' (interview).

In *The English Shakespeare Company*, Pennington is self-critical as he tries to assess his portrayal of Richard:

In the end...I think I failed...I was sad about it, because I had loved the part since I was a teenager. The problem was partly the context of the show and partly a miscalculation of my own. It was important, in the opening movement of a seven-play sequence, to emphasise Richard's disastrous qualities as a king and, in his egotism, indulgence and greed, how much he is slashing the fabric of his society. Bolingbroke's *putsch* is urgently needed: Richard is, publicly and personally, a sort of monster. (Bogdanov and Pennington, 1990: 107)

In interview Pennington recalled this need, imposed by the play in the cycle context, to 'establish what you might call the moral subtext of the play'. And so Richard's actions all have to be seen 'from a political point of view in order to justify Bolingbroke's rebellion'. Richard is a petty tyrant in the early scenes, but it is, Pennington believes, important to encourage some sympathy for the King once he is deposed: 'Your moral judgement criticises him but your instinctive human sympathy goes out to him...which is exactly the sort of ambiguity you get in all Shakespeare' (interview).

One of the consequences of the English Shakespeare Company's efforts to record their interpretation of the full cycle of plays for television was a reduction in the ambiguity of approach to *Richard II* invited, as Pennington realises, by Shakespeare's script. One of the casualties of a busy shooting schedule at The Swansea Grand, coupled with the need to play the complete cycle at least once for the Swansea audience, was that when *Richard II* was prepared by the English Shakespeare Company for International Television Enterprises Ltd in 1989, the majority of scenes with the loyal Aumerle had to be cut owing to lack of time, as did the scene between York and the Duchess of Gloucester (Act I, scene 2). Tim Milsom, the independent television producer entrusted with the filming process, ensured that four separate versions of a single performance were recorded from different angles. Nevertheless the performances had been conceived for the stage, and the television version has a restlessness born of the process of the recording, coupled with the omission, throughout the cycle, of the range of – sometimes quite lengthy and elaborate – scene changes. Also, there was no time for connection – there was only one day of shooting time allotted to each individual play in the cycle. All the editing process was completed subsequently.

And the editing process itself went further to underline the contemporary relevance of Shakespeare's history of England. At the beginning of the tape, while the credits are running, a series of images – of violence, of war, of characters from the cycle (their faces, superimposed on battle standards, waving in the wind) – run as news footage accompanied by ominous music and the hideous sounds of war:

> Philip Owens came up with a waving flag concept, and spent a weekend filming images from the plays projected onto a moving sheet. Brin McCue finally cut the sequence together a week before the market. We then, of course, realised we had a mute sequence, but Windmill Lane, who seem to have the resources to rise to any occasion, pulled one of their resident composers, Dennis Woods, out of the hat. Two days later we had title music. (John Paul, in Bogdanov and Pennington, 1990: 232)

Used originally for *Henry V*, *1 Henry VI* and *Richard III*, all these images of violence preceded and ran into the opening scene of Richard II's court when *Richard II* was added to the series.

The ability to direct the audience's response allows video to be more didactic than any stage performance. The employment of images of battle influences our reading of the ESC's *Richard II*, while the use of close-ups focuses attention on individual characters in a way that is not possible in live theatre. So the camera can highlight Richard's nervousness as Mowbray's challenge to Bolingbroke threatens to betray his own implication in Gloucester's murder, thus removing the ambiguity possible on stage. Equally, close-up can ensure that certain actors dominate the narrative or speak 'set speeches' *directly* to the audience. This is particularly evident in the way Gaunt's dying declarations to the Duke of York are given clear focus.

Of *Richard II* as a whole, 'the traditional one in our quiver', Pennington concluded in interview: 'It's a very formal piece of music, isn't it? There it is – and actually the best service you can do it is to get out of its way and let it be.'

References

Bogdanov, Michael and Pennington, Michael (1990) *The English Shakespeare Company: The Story of 'The Wars of the Roses', 1986–1989*. London: Hern.

Brown, John Russell (1966) *Shakespeare's Plays in Performance*. London: Edward Arnold.

David, Richard (1953) 'Shakespeare's history plays: epic or drama?', *Shakespeare Survey*, 6: 129–39.

Hodgdon, Barbara (1993) *Henry IV, Part 2* (Shakespeare in Performance). Manchester: Manchester University Press.

Kott, Jan (1967) *Shakespeare, our Contemporary*, 2nd edn. London: Routledge.

McMillin, Scott (1991) *Henry IV, Part 1* (Shakespeare in Performance). Manchester: Manchester University Press.

Page, Malcolm (1987) *Richard II* (Text and Performance). Basingstoke: Macmillan.

Rossi, Alfred (ed.) (1977) *Astonish Us in the Morning*. London: Hutchinson.

Sprague, Arthur Colby (1964) *Shakespeare's Histories: Plays for the Stage*. London: Society for Theatre Research.

Tillyard, E. M. W. (1944) *Shakespeare's History Plays*. London: Chatto and Windus (rev. edn, 1969).

Trewin, J. C. (1960) *Benson and the Bensonians*. London.

Stagecraft and Imagery in Shakespeare's *Henry VI*

Alan C. Dessen

Alan Dessen uses productions of Henry VI *as exemplary instances of the plays' textual and interpretative mobility. Discussing visual and verbal imagery, and the theatrical deployment of the chair-as-throne, he opens up questions about the extent to which theatre practitioners do and should reshape and reform the plays through performance. By thinking with the texts' stage directions and with analogous examples from the Elizabethan theatre, Dessen challenges some of the assumptions and practices of modern directors, and combines the dramatic with close linguistic attention.*

Alan C. Dessen, 'Stagecraft and Imagery in Shakespeare's *Henry VI*', in *The Yearbook of English Studies*, 23 (1993), pp. 65–79.

When dealing with Shakespeare's *Henry VI* on the page or on the stage, a critic, an editor, or a director immediately confronts the question of the integrity of the three plays as they have survived in the two quartos (among the earliest of Shakespeare's works to appear in print) and the First Folio (where Part One first appears). Since the eighteenth century, scholars and theatrical professionals have shown little confidence in or enthusiasm for these histories as intact entities, worthy of analysis as discrete units, but rather have either lumped them together as one item that can be dealt with summarily or raided them so as to appropriate detachable elements that suit the interpreter's agendas. For example, directors often graft Richard of

Gloucester's speeches from Part Three on to *Richard III* (the Olivier movie is the best known but by no means the only instance); several recent scholars have written tellingly about Joan de Pucelle;[1] and other distinctive parts have been singled out for attention or analysis, with one line ('The first thing we do, let's kill all the lawyers', *2 Henry VI*, IV. ii. 70)[2] achieving a cult status. Admittedly, starting in the 1960s and 1970s a few academic critics have argued forcefully on behalf of thematic or imagist integrity;[3] at least two directors (Terry Hands, Jane Howell) have treated the scripts with respect. But for the most part both scholars and theatrical professionals (weaned on standards and assumptions derived from subsequent plays in the canon) have only intermittent interest in this trilogy other than as context for *Richard III*.

The reasons for such neglect or atomization are no secret. For the academic critic, the interpretative tools that for generations have worked well for later Shakespeare plays, whether for analysis of 'character', imagery, or structure, do not provide satisfying results when applied to *Henry VI*. As to the latter, the Elizabethan fondness for episodic structure or multiple unity here collides with a post-Elizabethan prizing of concentration and subordination of elements (as seen also in comparable discomfort among critics with the rebel scenes in *2 Henry IV* or the Aumerle rebellion in *Richard II*). Despite a long series of apologias (starting in the early 1950s with H. T. Price),[4] interpreters have therefore sensed formlessness rather than coherence in this trilogy (a problem only 'solved' with the emergence of Richard of Gloucester as a focal figure).

Such an introduction, as a reader of scholarly essays will recognize, is a prelude to The Answer, a formulation that will set the record straight now and forever so that The Problem will no longer bother future readers. Sadly (for I would be delighted to set things aright), such is not the case, for I lack the insights that would enable me to descend from Mount Sinai to deliver the reader of these plays to the promised land. Rather, I offer a paradox linked to a closed loop, a version of the infamous hermeneutic circle. Thus, perhaps more than with any other group of Shakespeare plays, the key to each of the three parts of *Henry VI* as a discrete unit, a play with its own distinctive shape and rationale (regardless of the interpretation eventually to be drawn from that shape and rationale), lies in the play as an onstage event, the play as seen-heard rather than the play-as-read (and few will quarrel with the limitations of this trilogy as plays-to-be-read). Such a claim, in turn, usually leads to a paeon on behalf of performance-oriented interpretation. That approach, however (although now much in fashion), is keyed to often unexamined assumptions drawn from twentieth-century theatre, whereas the rationale behind Elizabethan staging (especially in the early 1590s when that rationale was still taking shape) can be different, in ways both subtle and obvious, from what we take for granted today. In my terms, Shakespeare, his fellow players, and his playgoers shared a theatrical vocabulary accessible, even obvious, then but easily blurred or eclipsed today.

Paradoxically, one consequence of this situation is that the staging of these three plays in our theatres rather than helping to bridge this gap in our understanding can instead widen it (so as to become part of the problem rather than part of the solution). When treating these plays as playscripts to be enacted by modern actors before today's audiences, theatrical professionals inevitably make many adjustments that in turn eliminate or blur elements important for the original strategy. My point is not to fault actors and directors (who to survive must take into account the theatrical vocabulary they share with their paying customers and whose negative attitude towards these plays has been heavily conditioned by critics, scholars, and editors) but rather to lament that what can be a valuable tool for investigating other scripts (seeing the play-on-the-page come to life on the stage) is often denied the would-be interpreter of *Henry VI*.

Two recent and highly visible productions can serve as instructive paradigms. Both Michael Bogdanov (English Shakespeare Company 1987–8) and Adrian Noble (Royal Shakespeare Company 1988–9) elected to present the first tetralogy to their audiences by condensing four plays into three, with *Richard III* standing alone and the three parts of *Henry VI* compressed into two plays (the ESC's plays were entitled *The House of Lancaster* and *The House of York*, the RSC's *Henry VI* and *The Rise of Edward IV*). The choices necessitated when setting up such compressed versions of event-filled history plays can then be instructive (e.g., what is deemed essential versus what is treated as disposable), especially in the context of the commercial and artistic success of the RSC's 1977–8 Terry Hands *Henry VI* trilogy (played 'warts and all' with few cuts) and the significant achievement of Jane Howell's first tetralogy for the BBC's 'The Shakespeare Plays' (one of the strongest items in that series). The plays *are* do-able, as demonstrated by Hands (along with Alan Howard, Helen Mirren, Emrys James, Peter McEnery, Julian Glover, and others),[5] Howell, and Pat Patton (whose Part Three in 1977 was one of the strongest shows I have seen in fifteen years of playgoing at the Oregon Shakespeare Festival).

As experienced directors, both Bogdanov and Noble were much concerned with the commercial as well as the artistic advantages of presenting three rather than four plays, so the choice to streamline the received script came easily. Some of Noble's rationale is set forth in the preface to the printed edition of his script where he describes himself as continuing a process started by Shakespeare. For example, Shakespeare saw 'the dramatic advantages of shape and focus achieved by running several events into one', a process, Noble observes, 'which we have taken further'. In his conclusion, moreover, he notes: 'We all had to learn to value narrative over "character moments" and to value storytelling over psychology."[6] Clearly, a different rationale is at work behind these plays, one that demands some adjustments from both the modern theatrical professional and the playgoer. Moreover, any compression of three event-filled plays into two is going to necessitate major omissions and adjustments ('running several events into one').

Both adaptations of the *Henry VI* material, in turn, followed the same general pattern. The material from Part One was allotted roughly ninety minutes so as to be completed by the first interval; the second half of the first play then contained the first three acts of Part Two; the last two acts of Part Two and the first two acts of Part Three (with much restitching of elements) occupied the pre-interval section of play number two; the remaining three acts of Part Three then finished the job.

Given such a master plan, certain problems emerge, problems that, in turn, can provide some insights into distinctive features of the three plays. First, the structural integrity of Shakespeare's Part Two was undermined. For example, the prophecies of Act I, scene 4 were not fulfilled. Both directors cut the references to Walter-water; indeed, Noble cut the entire scene (Act IV, scene 1), so that even though Suffolk's head did appear in Margaret's hands, the playgoer has no clue as to how he died (the plot summary in the programme informed the reader that Suffolk 'is murdered aboard ship as he leaves England'). Somerset, moreover, died in the next play (with no reference to castles or ale-house signs). The kind of implicit structure provided by the working out of prophecies or riddles (best seen in *Macbeth*) was therefore gone.

The same was true for the genesis of the Cade rebellion. Noble provided a powerful image to open *Edward IV*, with the Cade supporters rising from grated traps and filling the stage, but this subterranean emergence meant something very different at the outset of a new play as opposed to being experienced in Act IV, scene 2 of a continuum. Similarly, Bogdanov began his second play with a train station scene to show York's return from Ireland (Act V, scene 1), then switched to a Cade meeting hall rally (Act IV, scene 2). Gone therefore from both productions was any link between this new force unleashed upon England and the deaths of Gloucester, the Cardinal, and Suffolk or the earlier machinations of York; gone as well was any analogy to *Julius Caesar* where again a major political murder at the centre of the play comparable to the assassination of Gloucester opens the way to violence and war. To look closely at such compressions is therefore to bring into focus Shakespeare's sense of structure or cause and effect.

Both the RSC and ESC versions economized upon battle scenes in the second play so as to combine the first battle of St Albans (that ends Shakespeare's Part Two) with the battles that begin Part Three (and this alteration necessitated a host of other significant changes).[7] The most telling consequence of this compression was that a high percentage of the violence in Shakespeare's Parts Two and Three was now concentrated in the ninety-minute segment that begins the second play, for this stretch contained all the violence of Part Two (e.g., the Cade scenes, done by Noble with many onstage decapitations and a host of severed heads on poles, York versus Clifford, Richard versus Somerset) and then most of the violence in Part Three (the battles of Acts I and II, the murders of Rutland and York, the death of young Clifford). At the interval of Noble's production, one observer (who did not know Shakespeare's script) asked me: 'What are we watching – a Renaissance *Full Metal Jacket?*' Controlled use of onstage violence in the original scripts has (in this segment) yielded to theatrical overkill.

Of the many changes and elisions, I shall consider several small choices that had a disproportionately large impact. Thus, Bogdanov pared down considerably the 'common man' scenes from the first two acts of Part Two (although, unlike Noble, he did retain the Simpcox episode), so that Peter and his master Horner disappeared from view. No charge of treason was therefore brought against York by means of Horner's reported comments, so that, in turn, no particular reason remained for choosing Somerset over York as Regent of France (Gloucester recommends to the king that Somerset get the regency 'because in York this breeds suspicion' (I. iii. 203–4)). Bogdanov's King Henry, moreover, not Gloucester, provided 'this doom' (l. 202). Although on the surface only an innocuous series of cuts and changes, such giving of the decision to Henry had a significant effect upon the portrayal of three major figures. First, Henry appears much more decisive as a politician than is the case anywhere else, a shift that sets up a very different progression to his one strong moment when, after recovering from his swoon at the news of Gloucester's death, he banishes Suffolk in Act III, scene 2. Secondly, Gloucester loses one of his two highly visible judgements (the other coming with Simpcox) and hence some of his special stature, a diminution that contributed to one of the weak spots in this production. Thirdly, an insight into the danger posed by York is eliminated, as was also true in some other cuts made by Bogdanov (most notably the elimination of York's speech that ends Act I, scene 1 and the paring down of Gloucester's final speech in Act III, scene 1, including his reference to 'dogged York, that reaches at the moon, / Whose overweening arm I have plucked back' (ll. 158–9)). Having Henry deliver the 'doom' therefore has a significant impact upon three of the key figures in this play and upon the dynamics of Part Two as a whole.

Comparable small but telling changes can be noted in Noble's production. In both Shakespeare's Part Three (IV. viii. 38–50) and Noble's adaptation, Henry VI has a speech in which he naïvely concludes that, because he has been mild and merciful, the people will support him rather than Edward in the coming conflict. In Noble's version, Henry exits after this speech (so some playgoers were surprised to see him turn up in prison a few scenes later); in Shakespeare's scene, however, he is immediately confronted and arrested by the Yorkists (whom the people *have* supported) so that the speech serves as the first half of a one-two punch, with the second element, the deflation, gone from Noble's version. Similarly, in Shakespeare's Part Three, a Henry VI anxious to relinquish kingly power gives over his political authority to both Warwick and Clarence (Act IV, scene 6), but in Noble's version only Warwick is so designated. Shortly thereafter (Act V, scene 1) Clarence arrives at Coventry (where his brothers are besieging Warwick) and decides to change sides, forsaking Warwick in favour of the Yorkist cause. Does it not make a difference to our understanding why Clarence makes this switch whether he is or is not a sharer in kingly power? At the least, a figure who has left his brothers in order to gain half a kingdom (however provisionally) is not faced with the same choice as a figure who has played second fiddle to an older brother and now is to be second again to Warwick (as in Noble's stripped down version).

Such choices and resulting problems are (perhaps) inevitable given the squeezing of three plays into two, but that three-into-two choice is itself a product of a series of assumptions (both aesthetic and commercial) about the dramaturgy and coherence of these early Shakespeare plays. What if, in contrast, these histories do have a distinctive theatrical shape or logic (as suggested above in my account of the prophecies and the role of Gloucester's assassination in Part Two), albeit one not as accessible today as that found in later comparable plays?

To pursue such a defence of the integrity of these plays I will focus upon a few distinctive and revealing configurations. My emphasis will be upon scenes and images that, although easily blurred for a reader today, would be hard for a playgoer in the 1590s to miss; that depend more upon visual-theatrical than upon poetic-verbal effects (or are underdeveloped in poetic-verbal terms); and that were omitted or blurred significantly in the RSC and ESC productions (and, in a few instances, were realized meaningfully in other productions).

Let me start with one of the least discussed moments in the most maligned of the three plays, *1 Henry VI*. At the nadir of her fortunes, just before her capture by York, Joan de Pucelle appeals for help to a group of onstage '*Fiends*' (V. iii. 7. s.d.), but in response these fiends, according to the Folio stage directions, '*walk, and speak not*', '*hang their heads*', '*shake their heads*', and finally '*depart*' (s.ds at ll. 12, 17, 19, 23). This exchange has not fared well on the page or on the stage, for to deal with this script is inevitably to run foul of this scene and this appeal-rejection that in several ways tests the reflexes of today's interpreters. The Folio's call for fiends and for specific reactions is unusually clear (and presumably would have posed few problems in the 1590s for play-goers attuned to *Doctor Faustus*), but Elizabethan onstage presentation of the supernatural repeatedly strains 'our' paradigms of credibility (and canons of taste), with this moment a particular challenge.

Directors have therefore tinkered with the Folio signals. In Howell's rendition for television, Joan speaks her lines while staring at the camera so that no supernatural entities are in sight to walk, refuse to speak, hang their heads, and eventually depart. In Noble's rendition, various onstage corpses from the previous battle rose as if animated to provide an onstage audience but without the reactions to Joan's pleas specified in the Folio. In the Hands production, amid the onstage cannons that dominated the battle-field set, Joan offered herself to the fiends who appeared suddenly 'looking like gas-masked soldiers from the French trenches of the First World War'.[8] Bogdanov cut the fiends and altered the text, so that, alone on stage and looking at the audience, his Joan directed her appeal not to any diabolic entities but rather to the Virgin Mary, a change that eliminated any infernal climax for this sequence.[9] In contrast, in his 1975 Oregon Shakespeare Festival production, Will Huddleston introduced his fiends earlier (thinly disguised as Joan's followers, later her torturers) and then did stage the rejection; at the close of the play, moreover, the fiends make a final appearance above (with midnight tolling in the background) to snarl at the playgoers.

Even to a casual reader the interaction between Joan and the fiends leaps off the page in vivid (and, to many, offensive) fashion: a good example of what I term theatrical *italics*. To explore the potential in this moment, consider Joan and her devils not as a one-shot effect but as the climactic example of a larger progression of images and moments that starts in Act II. From her first appearance Joan has claimed supernatural powers (see I. ii. 72–92), a claim tested in the first meeting between Joan and Talbot that results in a stand-off; still, Joan scorns his strength (I. v. 15) and leads her troops to victory at Orleans. Moments later, Talbot, aided by Bedford and Burgundy, scales the walls and regains the town, so that a united English force wins back what had just been lost. The three leaders working together therefore accomplish what Talbot, facing Joan alone, could not.

Shakespeare then provides a gloss on both this victory and the larger problem of unity–disunity by means of Talbot's interview with the Countess of Auvergne. Her trap for Talbot fails, as he points out, because she has only caught 'Talbot's shadow', not his substance. The set of terms is repeated throughout the remainder of the scene (e.g., 'No, no, I am but shadow of myself. / You are deceived, my substance is not here') and is explained by the appearance of his soldiers, at which point he observes:

> Are you now persuaded
> That Talbot is but a shadow of himself?
> These are his substance, sinews, arms, and strength,
> With which he yoketh your rebellious necks.
>
> (II. iii. 45)

The individual standing alone, no matter how heroic (one thinks of Coriolanus), is but a shadow without the substance of his supporters, his army, his country.[10]

This play, however (as two generations of critics have reminded us), is about division, not unity, a division that has already been displayed in the split between Winchester and Gloucester and that widens in the Temple Garden scene (immediately following Talbot's lecture to the countess), with its symbolic plucking of red and white roses. The figures who had joined Talbot in the victory at Orleans, moreover, soon disappear (Bedford dies, Burgundy changes sides). Factionalism thrives, to the extent that the division between York and Somerset (unhistorically) undoes Talbot himself who, in the terms of Act II, scene 3, is denied his substance and must face death (along with his son) as a shadow of his heroic self. Sir William Lucy's listing of Talbot's titles (IV. vii. 60–71) can then be mocked by Joan as 'a silly stately style indeed', for 'him that thou magnifi'st with all these titles, / Stinking and flyblown lies here at our feet' (ll. 72, 75–6).

Joan's scene with her devils follows less than a hundred lines after her exchange with Lucy. With the French forces fleeing the conquering York, all Joan can do is call upon her 'speedy helpers' or 'familiar spirits' to help with their 'accustomed diligence', but neither the offer of her blood, with which she has fed them in the past, a member lopped off, her body, or even her soul will gain the needed support. She therefore concludes:

> My ancient incantations are too weak,
> And hell too strong for me to buckle with.
> Now, France, thy glory droopeth to the dust.
> (V. iii. 1)

No one makes grandiose claims for the imagery of this sprawling play. But a verbal patterning involving shadow and substance is clearly set forth in Act II and echoed thereafter (see Alencon's speech, V. iv. 133–7); moreover, Talbot eventually falls (and France ultimately is lost to England) because of divisions whereby 'substance' is denied and the hero must stand alone as shadow of himself. In her scene with the fiends, Joan too is deserted, denied by those who formerly supported her. Like Talbot, her heroic status cannot exist alone, so she becomes a mere shepherd's daughter, not the figure who raised the siege at Orleans and was a match for Talbot in battle. The denial by the fiends is here equivalent to the squabble between York and Somerset that undoes Talbot, a link that can be reinforced through the staging. For example, what if the fiends' scripted reactions to Joan's offer echo similar walking apart, hanging and shaking of heads, and departures by York and Somerset in Act IV, scene 3 and Act IV, scene 4 in response to Lucy's pleas on behalf of Talbot? If so, the playgoer would see two or three parallel failures by first Lucy and then Joan, rejections that visibly set up the deaths of the two previously unbeatable or 'heroic' figures. Just as Lucy fails to get the necessary support, a failure that means Talbot must give way to the new factions, so Joan fails to get the support that she too desperately needs and must give way to the third Frenchwoman, Margaret (who appears immediately upon Joan's exit with York). However interpreted in theological or political terms, these highly visible fiends can function as part of an ongoing pattern of images or configurations linked to the central themes of the play.

Of the three plays, Part One has been the most disparaged, but in both the Bogdanov and Noble three-into-two adjustments Part Two suffered the greatest damage because its elements were split into two separate plays. As noted earlier, such a split calls attention to the different kinds of through-lines or pay-offs set up in earlier scenes and realized later (as is most obvious with the prophecies). Other cuts and changes made by the two directors call attention to comparable links and images. For example, Noble manufactured a fresh image in Act IV, scene 2, for his Cade not only knighted himself (ll. 107–8) but also knighted Dick the Butcher, underscoring even further the indictment of titles and hierarchy. As part of his streamlining of Act V of Part Two, however, Noble cut Henry VI's knighting of Alexander Iden (V. i. 78); in the first play he had also cut Henry's grant of a dukedom to a kneeling Suffolk as a reward for bringing Margaret as bride (Part Two, I. i. 61–3). Shakespeare's own sequence of giving new titles to kneeling figures was therefore gone, with two instances of number two in the series but no number one and no number three.

All three plays but particularly Part Two gain much of their distinctive shape from such visible repetitions, but with many of these elements eliminated, transposed, or located in two different plays (and hence two different evenings) much of that rationale was gone. For example, Gloucester tells his wife that 'I must offend before I be attainted', for his foes, no matter how powerful, 'could not procure me any scathe / So long as I am loyal, true, and crimeless' (II. iv. 59, 62–3). Two acts later, Lord Say tells the king and Buckingham: 'The trust I have is in mine innocence, / And therefore am I bold and resolute' (IV. iv. 59–60). At their next appearances, however, both figures are accused and swiftly convicted by their enemies and are murdered shortly thereafter (with Gloucester's body and Say's head subsequently brought onstage). If such elements, however, are pared down or cut completely and placed in two separate plays, no such analogy or structural link is available (whatever interpretive spin one chooses to place upon it).

Part Three suffered the least from adaptation and compression, for several clearly linked moments were retained and were in the same play. Thus, in Shakespeare's Act I the Lancastrians led by young Clifford kill a Yorkist child (Rutland) and the symbol of the Yorkist cause (Richard); in Act V, the

Lancastrians do the same: the three brothers kill Prince Edward, and in the following scene Richard of Gloucester murders Henry VI in the Tower. In Patton's Oregon production a highly visible detail added to this patterning, for Margaret's taunting of York with the napkin bearing Rutland's blood left blood on Richard's face. Such a bloody face was then seen again on the father contemplating the son he has killed (Act II, scene 5) and most tellingly on Margaret herself after she had kissed her murdered son Edward (Act V, scene 5).

The streamlining occasioned by making three plays into two, however, did take its toll. Indeed, what may seem to the adapter redundancies and hence cuttable episodes looked at another way can add up to a distinctive feature of this play. For example, in his speech to his captors in Act III, scene 1 (pared down in both versions) Henry VI first raises questions about oaths and obedience but then laments the frailty of human nature:

> Look, as I blow this feather from my face
> And as the air blows it to me again,
> Obeying with my wind when I do blow
> And yielding to another when it blows,
> Commanded always by the greater gust –
> Such is the lightness of you common men.
> But do not break your oaths
>
> (III. i. 84)

Many disparate episodes in the next two acts provide demonstrations of this thesis: that, regardless of their pretensions about oaths and principles, feather-like men and women are 'commanded always by the greater gust'. In the next scene (Act III, scene 2) that greater gust is King Edward's lust for the beautiful widow that takes precedence over political allegiances, most notably his bond with Warwick; that turnabout is quickly paralleled in Warwick's rapid switch in reaction to this disgrace in which he tells his hated enemy Queen Margaret 'let former grudges pass, / And henceforth I am thy true servitor' and she responds: 'Warwick, these words have turned my hate to love / And I forgive and quite forget old faults' (III. iii. 195–201). The most obvious example comes when Clarence, who marches in ready to fight against his own brothers on behalf of Warwick, with little ado throws his red rose at his former ally and rejoins the Yorkists (eliciting Richard's delicious line: 'Welcome, good Clarence. This is brotherlike' [V. i. 105]).

Easily lost in this sequence of events, however, is Act IV, scene 7, a scene omitted from the two streamlined versions (and also from Patton's Oregon production) but one of the gems of Howell's rendition. Here Edward gains access to the city of York by vowing that he has come as duke, not as a would-be king ('I challenge nothing but my dukedom, / As being well content with that alone' (ll. 23–4)), but the arrival and threatened departure of Sir John Montgomery ('Then fare you well, for I will hence again./I came to serve a king and not a duke' (ll. 48–9)) puts Edward on the spot (in a manner that closely parallels the dilemma faced by Edward's father in Act I, scene 2: whether to keep his bargain with Henry VI or seek the crown now). In the spirit of 'like father, like son' Edward quickly caves in to the urgings of Richard and Hastings, so that, in Howell's rendition, with drums sounding in the background, the Mayor (rather than a soldier) shakily reads the proclamation of Edward's kingship and Montgomery, visibly itching for action, stands by impatiently, snatches away the paper, and offers his open challenge to single combat. The rapidity of Edward's switch in his professed intentions yields both dark comedy and a telling insight into the value of oaths and protestations in this political jungle.

In the spirit of Henry's speech on 'the greater gust', the sequence of turnabouts by key figures such as Edward, Warwick, and Clarence heightens the uncertainties and lack of any firm principles or beliefs in this Darwinian society and, if played in full, helps to explain the rise of Gloucester and the genesis of Richard III and *Richard III* (the first, longest, and most famous of Gloucester's speeches is positioned just after Edward's decision to marry his widow in Act III, scene 2). The streamlined versions tell the same story (often with considerable panache), but the repeated betrayals or apostasies (like the recapitulation in Act V of the brutal killings of Act I) are the bones and sinews from which this play takes its distinctive shape. To cut the Countess of Auvergne, Peter Horner, and Sir John Montgomery is to economize on time and personnel so as to enhance the narrative pace, but the price-tag involves the elimination of paradigms that, if attended to, can call attention to central themes and images. Whether with shadow-substance in Part One, the many analogous situations in Part Two, or the action following Henry's feather speech in Part Three, the repetitions, even apparent redundancies (according to today's sensibilities), *are* the essence of the plays.[11]

In calling attention to such losses, my goal is to bring into focus a broader and deeper interpretative problem. The stage directions for the fiends' reactions to Joan's pleas are unusually explicit, but the absence of any comparable signals for the reactions of York and Somerset to Lucy's pleas for help makes any claims about linkage between the two moments conjectural. Such lack of specific signals, however, is the norm in the extant playscripts, for in most cases clear indications of stage business or properties have not survived. Such gaps in our knowledge of what may have been obvious in the 1590s are compounded by the changes in theatrical vocabulary between then and now, for inevitably our inferences about how an Elizabethan company would have staged X are heavily conditioned by how *we* would stage X.

As a particularly useful example, consider the moment in Part Three when Edward IV, having been surprised and captured by Warwick and Clarence, is carried onstage '*in his gown, sitting in a chair*' (IV. iii. 27. s.d.). In the Howell television rendition, Edward is bound to his chair so that the image for the spectator is that of a prisoner (comparable to Gloucester in the blinding scene of *King Lear*). Howell's choice makes immediate sense to a viewer today, but it may also blur a distinctive effect keyed to the original stage conventions.

For what we today do not recognize is that, in the age of Shakespeare, bringing a figure onstage in a chair was the primary way of signalling '*enter sick*' or '*as if sick*'. To cite only a few of the many examples, in *Westward Ho* Mistress Tenterhook, pretending to be sick, calls for 'a chaire, a chaire'; a companion says 'shees sicke and taken with an Agony'. In *Othello*, after 'finding' the wounded Cassio, Iago cries 'O for a chair / To bear him easily hence' (V. i. 82–3) and mentions the chair twice more (ll. 96, 98); when the chair arrives, he adds: 'Some good man bear him carefully from hence. / I'll fetch the general's surgeon' (ll. 99–100) and 'O, bear him out o'th' air' (l. 104); the 1622 Quarto (but not the Folio) then directs Cassio in the next scene to be brought in '*in a Chaire*' (N1ʳ). Elsewhere in Shakespeare's plays, chairs are specified for sick and dying figures in *1 Henry VI* (II. v. 0. s.d., III. ii. 40. s.d.), *2 Henry VI* (II. i. 66. s.d.), and *King Lear* (IV. vii. 20. s.d., TLN 2771). Examples are also plentiful in the plays of Fletcher and Brome and can be found as well in Peele, Chapman, Dekker, Heywood, Marston, Massinger, Markham, Haughton, and Ford and in many anonymous plays.[12]

To return to the scene in Part Three, when Edward is carried onstage '*in his gown, sitting in a chair*', the initial signal for the original spectator would have been that this figure is entering '*sick*' or '*as sick*'. In this instance, however, the signals would be misleading, for Edward is embarrassed and vulnerable but not sick. But keep in mind that this play starts and ends with throne scenes, with that royal seat a symbol of the disorder in a kingdom in which three different figures are seen sitting upon the English throne. Indeed, in the opening scene the titular king, Henry VI, comes onstage to discover Richard of York seated upon his throne, an initial usurpation that typifies what is to follow. The presence of a king (or pseudo-king) brought onstage in what appears initially to be a sick-chair is therefore more than a momentary trick played upon the spectator. Rather, that initial confusion of throne-chair and sick-chair calls attention to an important set of associations that links disease to kings and power-brokers, associations reinforced by the unkinging, rekinging, and unkinging of Henry VI in the last three acts. Memories of both the opening confusion about the throne and the momentary sick-chair image of Act IV, scene 3 should then inform the final moments, where the surface order assumed by Edward ('Now am I seated as my soul delights,/Having my country's peace and brothers' loves' [V. vii. 35–6]) is undercut by a continuing sense of the kingdom's diseases, as typified in Richard's asides (e.g., 'I'll blast his harvest' [l. 21]). The momentary effect with Edward in his chair therefore reinforces a potentially meaningful iterative pattern that links disease imagery to the throne and to the larger political concerns of the play.

Nor is this sick chair/royal chair image limited to Part Three. Squabbles in the presence of Henry and his throne are a major symptom of what is wrong in Part One, so that in Howell's production Exeter delivers his choric speech on 'this base and envious discord' (and recalls the prophecy 'that Henry born at Monmouth should win all/And Henry born at Windsor should lose all') while pointing to the empty throne (III. i. 186–200). The scenes that precede and follow this chaotic activity around the boy-king seated on his throne are instructive. First, Shakespeare presents the plucking of red and white roses by Suffolk and York in the Temple Garden scene (II. iv.), a symbolic beginning to the divisions to come. Moments later, Mortimer, who is '*brought in a chair*' by his jailers (II. v. 0. s. d.), provides a long disquisition to Richard about the Yorkist claim to the throne. This claim, passed from this dying figure to the up-and-coming Richard, is linked visually to a figure in a sick-chair. Mortimer's ominous laying on of hands (see lines 37–8) is immediately followed by our first view of the young Henry VI, presumably on his throne, who is unable to control the squabble between Gloucester and Winchester or the fight, offstage and then onstage, between their servingmen. The one action this vulnerable king does take, however, is to restore Richard to his dukedom, so that the figure bequeathed a claim to the throne in the previous scene by a figure in a sick-chair is now given status and power by a demonstrably weak occupant of the royal seat. This sequence is then extended in the next scene where, during the loss and recapture of Rouen, the dying Bedford is '*brought in sick in a chair*' (III. ii. 40. s. d.) to witness Falstaff's cowardice and then the English victory. At the climax of this action, '*Bedford dies and is carried in by two in his chair*' (l. 114. s. d.).

Throughout the play, Henry's 'throne scenes' act out his inability to control internal divisions and, hence, England's diseases, but his first appearance in Act III, scene 1, sandwiched between scenes displaying figures dying in their sick-chairs, neatly sums up the problems linked both to the Yorkists' claim to the throne (symbolized by Mortimer) and the dying off of that loyal older generation devoted to the good of the country rather than factional interests (symbolized by Bedford). As with Joan's fiends and Talbot's shadow versus substance, much of the theatrical coherence of this episodic play arises from such linked images and configurations. If the final scene also has an onstage throne (as in Part Three), Suffolk's convincing the king to take Margaret as his bride (made ominous by Suffolk's closing reference to Paris and the implicit analogy between Margaret–Helen and England–Troy) enacts a climactic link between the royal chair and potential diseases to come. Again, even in this early play, a set of associations made accessible by conventional theatrical practice (*enter sick*) can be used to italicize important meanings and effects.

In Part Two, such chair–throne patterning is present but less emphatic, for Shakespeare uses violent deaths and the Cade rebellion to highlight the kingdom's diseases. The dead or dying Gloucester and Winchester are displayed onstage but (apparently) in sick-beds rather than sick-chairs. The impostor Simpcox, however, enters '*between two in a chair*' (II. i. 66. s.d.) in front of a weak king who, early in the same scene, is unable to control the quarrel between Gloucester and Winchester. Humphrey's uncovering of Simpcox's fraud acts out his important role in keeping some semblance of order in England, but, owing to Elinor's disgrace and his own naïvete, Humphrey's position is soon undermined. Simpcox in his chair therefore prepares us for a hapless Henry on his throne who is unable to protect Humphrey or Lord Say (the latter linked to the palsy and 'full of sickness and diseases' (IV. vii. 81, 85)); this king is therefore vulnerable to an obvious fraud (Cade) in Act IV and defenceless against a formidable opponent (York) in Act V (so, as a result, Henry finds York seated on his throne in the first scene of Part Three). When the inevitable confrontation does come, York's critique pinpoints the vulnerability of Henry as possessor of the royal seat, for he begins 'No! thou art not king', then cites the attributes of kingship ('That head of thine doth not become a crown;/Thy hand is made to grasp a palmer's staff/And not to grace an awful princely sceptre'), and concludes: 'Give place. By heaven, thou shalt rule no more/O'er him whom heaven created for thy ruler' (V. i. 93, 96–8, 104–5). As in the other two plays, such powerful accusations are enhanced by a subliminal memory of the purportedly lame Simpcox exposed as a fraud and forced to 'give place' from *his* chair (and leap over a stool) by the beadle. The whole may be greater than the sum of its parts, but first an interpreter must have all the parts and some sense of how they might work.

The productions cited in this essay provided a great deal of narrative excitement so as to engage and entertain playgoers (and television viewers) unfamiliar with the scripts. The many cuts and transpositions (along with the telescoping of disparate figures into one to economize on personnel) could be seen as the price-tag for mounting *Henry VI* at all (although the 1977–8 Hands trilogy provides testimony that three-into-two is not the only available route). In singling out some representative choices, my purpose therefore has not been to mount an indictment of the director-as-vandal. Rather, I have sought to bring into focus both the assets and liabilities of such modern onstage interpretations as a tool for understanding the original dramaturgy, theatrical vocabulary, and potential meanings. For the theatrical historicist, the changes made by Bogdanov and Noble can be especially revealing when the original onstage logic (whether linked to analogical thinking, distinctive images, or signifiers in a lost vocabulary) is no longer seen or appreciated, so that directoral adjustments serve as signposts that point to differing notions of how a play works or how that play is (or should be) put together. Such signposts can be particularly revealing in productions of *Henry VI* where the overall shape (or sense of organization) may be more in tune with Spenser's *The Faerie Queene* or Sidney's *Arcadia* than with *Henry V* or *Hamlet*.

The changes made by Bogdanov and Noble can therefore serve as a useful window into an Elizabethan theatrical logic (linked to a 1590s' sense of analogy, imagery, and onstage story-telling) that is difficult (at times impossible) to recapture today. Some directoral decisions or adjustments can produce considerable theatrical excitement (and in this area I have not done justice to any of the productions). Other changes, however, fail to achieve the intended goal (a graceful elision of three long, ungainly plays) but rather constitute radical surgery or, for a different metaphor, provide not an adaptation but a translation into a new and different theatrical language. Both Talbot's lecture on shadow versus substance and Henry VI's lament about the feather commanded by the greater gust should serve as chastening thoughts for interpreters of this trilogy on the stage or on the page.

Notes

1   See Leah Marcus, *Puzzling Shakespeare* (Berkeley, CA: University of California Press, 1988), pp. 51–96; Gabriele Bernhard Jackson, 'Topical ideology: witches, Amazons, and Shakespeare's Joan of Arc', *English Literary Renaissance*, 18 (1988), pp. 40–65; Nancy A. Gutierrez, 'Gender and value in *1 Henry VI*: the role of Joan de Pucelle', *Theatre Journal*, 42 (1990), pp. 183–93. For a recent provocative interpretation of one episode in *2 Henry VI*, see Craig A. Bernthal, 'Treason in the family: the trial of Thumpe v. Horner', *Shakespeare Quarterly*, 42 (1991), pp. 44–54.

2   Citations from Shakespeare are from *The Complete Pelican Shakespeare*, general ed. Alfred Harbage (Baltimore, MD: Penguin, 1969).

3   See in particular J. P. Brockbank, 'The frame of disorder: *Henry VI*', in *Early Shakespeare*, ed. J. R. Brown and Bernard Harris, Stratford-upon-Avon Studies 3 (1961), pp. 72–99; David Riggs, *Shakespeare's Heroical Histories: 'Henry VI' and its Literary Tradition* (Cambridge, MA: Harvard University Press, 1971); and Edward Berry, *Patterns of Decay: Shakespeare's Early Histories* (Charlottesville: University Press of Virginia, 1975).

4   Hereward T. Price, 'Construction in Shakespeare', *University of Michigan Contributions in Modern Philology*, 17 (1951), pp. 1–42 (pp. 24–37).

5   For accounts of this production see Homer D. Swander, 'The rediscovery of *Henry VI*', *Shakespeare Quarterly*, 29 (1978), pp. 146–63; David Daniell, 'Opening up the text: Shakespeare's *Henry VI* plays in performance', *Themes in Drama*, 1 (1979), pp. 247–77; G. K. Hunter, 'The Royal Shakespeare Company plays *Henry VI*', *Renaissance Drama*, 9 (1978), pp. 91–108.

6   Adrian Noble, *The Plantagenets* (London: Faber, 1989), pp. vii, xiv.

7   For example, owing to the transposition of elements young Clifford presented his angry speeches from the beginning of Part Three (e.g., I. i. 159–60) *before* the death of his father at the end of Part Two, the event that occasioned his pronouncement that 'my heart is turned to stone' (V. ii. 50). Some of the elements from Part Two, Act V, scene 1 were retained, but moving and reshaping them eliminated the climactic position of the first confrontation between the parties of York and Lancaster (and one potentially telling element, the choice by Salisbury not to kneel to Henry VI, was gone). To the degree that the sequence of elements is an integral part of theatrical 'meaning' and effect, the treatment of the end of Part Two and the beginning of Part Three by both Bogdanov and Noble was a translation rather than an interpretation.

8   Daniell, 'Opening up the text', p. 257.

9   Bogdanov did some radical surgery here by transposing the beginning of Act V, scene 3 to Act V, scene 4 so that one sustained sequence involving Joan followed the Suffolk–Margaret part of Act V, scene 3. The juxtaposition of the two French women remained, but the value of that link was changed (e.g., Joan's capture by York was not immediately followed by Suffolk's capture of Margaret). Bogdanov also cut Joan's shepherd father. His Joan, moreover, had her own distinctive music, but without the Folio fiends as a final comment this production offered no clear signal as to whether that music (and the auspices for her final moments) was holy or witchly. Here, as elsewhere, Bogdanov provided an engaging story, but the original punchline as set up in the Folio had been drastically changed.

10 For treatments of Act II, scene 3, see especially Daniel C. Gerould, 'Principles of dramatic structure in *Henry VI*', *Educational Theatre Journal*, 20 (1968), pp. 376–88 (pp. 379–80); Berry, *Patterns of Decay*, pp. 1–28; James A. Riddell, 'Talbot and the Countess of Auvergne', *Shakespeare Quarterly*, 28 (1977), pp. 51–7; Alexander Leggatt, *Shakespeare's Political Drama* (London: Routledge, 1988), pp. 1–8.

11 As shrewd, experienced directors, both Bogdanov and Noble were well aware of the opportunities for strong visual links between episodes. For example, Noble had Margery Jourdain's death at the stake (in his first play) repeat the fate of Joan (events divided between Shakespeare's Parts One and Two); also in his first play, the first meeting of Margaret and Suffolk (just before the interval) was echoed in the play's final moments when Margaret cradled Suffolk's severed head. Twice, moreover, Noble found strong images (albeit in two different plays) to convey the price-tag for the power associated with the throne. First, the dead Mortimer (at the end of Shakespeare's Part One, II. v) descended in his cage-prison, an object then replaced with Henry VI's golden throne (a disturbing and effective juxtaposition). Then, at the end of the second play the body of the murdered Henry VI descended in a similar fashion, to be replaced by a throne inhabited by Edward. In both instances, the image of a body under the throne was strong and meaningful.

12 Thomas Dekker, *Westward Ho*, V. i. 196–201 in *The Dramatic Works*, ed. by Fredson Bowers, 4 vols (Cambridge: Cambridge University Press, 1953–61), vol. II, p. 379 (for another example from the Dekker canon, see vol. I, p. 374). For examples roughly contemporary with *Henry VI*, see George Peele, *The Battle of Alcazar*, ed. W. E. Greg, Malone Society (Oxford, 1906), l. 1302; Peele,

Edward I, ed. W. W. Greg, Malone Society (Oxford, 1911), ll. 48–9 and *Locrine*, ed. Ronald B. McKerrow, Malone Society (Oxford, 1908), l. 33. For a further sampling of the evidence, see *The Works of Francis Beaumont and John Fletcher*, ed. Arnold Glover and A. R. Waller, 10 vols (Cambridge: Cambridge University Press, 1905–12), vol. I, pp. 374, 378; vol. IV, p. 76; vol. VI, p. 254; vol. ix, p. 375; Richard Brome, *The Dramatic Works*, 3 vols (London: Pearson, 1873), vol. I, pp. 218, 257; vol. II, p. 127 (*The Queen and Concubine*); vol. III, pp. 180, 263, 546; George Chapman, *The Gentleman Usher*, ed. John Hazel Smith (Lincoln, NE: University of Nebraska Press, 1970), IV. iii. 0. s. d., V. iv. 39. s. d.; Thomas Heywood, *The Dramatic Works*, 6 vols (London: Pearson, 1874), vol. I, p. 155; Philip Massinger, *The Plays and Poems*, ed. Philip Edwards and Colin Gibson, 5 vols (Oxford: Oxford University Press, 1976), vol. III, p. 461; Gervaise Markham and William Sampson, *Herod and Antipater* (1622), H3^r, 12^v; William Haughton, *Englishmen for My Money*, ed. W. W. Greg, Malone Society (Oxford, 1913), l. 2434; *A Yorkshire Tragedy*, ed. Sylvia D. Feldman, Malone Society (Oxford, 1973), l. 720. Sick-chairs are also to be found in plays as diverse as Marston's *Sophonisba*, Middleton's *Hengist King of Kent*, Jonson's *The Magnetic Lady*, Ford's *The Broken Heart*, May's *The Old Couple*, Drue's *The Duchess of Suffolk*, *A Warning For Fair Women*, *The Second Maiden's Tragedy*, *The Soddered Citizen*, and *The Telltale*.

Index

All's Well That Ends Well 120
Andrews, Harry 258–9
antitheatricality 107
Armada 150, 151, 160, 168, 171, 172
Armstrong, Isobel 248
Arnold, Matthew 25
As You Like It 62
Aske, James 158–9, 160, 173, 178–9
authority, resistance to 198

Babcock, W. R. 196
Bacon, Francis 54–5
Baker, David 218
Baker, Houston A., Jr 56
Bamber, Linda 144
Bell, John 15–16
Belsey, Catherine 200
Benson, Frank 254
Berger, Harry 103–23, 247
Berry, Ralph 99, 139, 249
Bethell, S. L. 37
Betterton, Thomas 9
Bevington, David 198
Blanpied, John 39–40
Bogdanov, Michael 249, 264, 265, 266,
    274, 275, 276, 278, 286, 287
Boose, Lynda 144
Bradley, A. C. 31, 98
Bradshaw, Graham 200
Branagh, Kenneth 226, 233–4, 236,
    237–8, 239–40, 249, 250
    see also Henry V (films)

Brecht, Bertolt 262
Bristol, Michael D. 125
Brook, Peter 196
Brooke, Nicholas 37
Brown, John Russell 250, 260, 263
Burton, Richard 259
Bury, John 263–4
Buzacott, Martin 248

Cairns, David 216–17, 219
Calderwood, James 39, 99, 124, 126, 138
Caliban 56
Camden, William 165, 177, 206, 222
Campbell, Lily 35, 199
Capell, Edward 13
Carlyle, Thomas 24
Catholicism 161, 165, 166, 168, 188
Cavendish, Margaret 5
Champion, Larry 36
character study 17–18, 19, 23–4
Charlton, H. B. 37
Cibber, Colley 9–10
Cibber, Theophilus 10
Clark, Sandra 15
Clemen, Wolfgang 98
Cohen, Ted 124
Cohen, Walter 196
Coleridge, Samuel Taylor 20–1
Comedy of Errors 43
Condell, Henry 2–3, 148
Coursen, H. R. 126, 247, 249, 250
Coward, Noel 225, 228

cross-dressing 157, 160, 161
Crowne, John 9
Culler, Jonathan 50
Cymbeline 220, 221

Davies, John 220
Dee, John 172
deformity
  Bacon on 54–5
  Caliban 56
  Johnson on 55
  Richard III 44, 45, 46, 47–50, 52–3,
    55, 56, 57, 58, 63
Dennis, John 4
Dessen, Alan C. 126–7, 272–88
Dobson, Michael 4
Dollimore, Jonathan 142, 197, 199–200,
  206, 219
Dorius, R. J. 140
Dowden, Edward 27–8
Driver, Tom 39
Dryden, John 5–6
Dusinberre, Juliet 143, 184, 188

Eagleton, Terry 100–1, 199, 248–9
Edwards, Philip 211, 217–18
Elizabeth, Queen 149–82, 220
  and continental campaigns 168–70, 171
  Joan of Arc association 149, 160–2,
    163, 164, 166, 168, 171–2, 173
  male body politic 149–53, 157–8, 166
  marriage negotiations 154–5, 162,
    164–5
  sexual rumours 156, 163–4
  succession problem 155–6
  Tilbury speech 150–1, 159, 175
  witchcraft associations 171–3
Elizabethan staging 250
Elizabethan world view 34, 261
English Shakespeare Company 255,
  264, 270
Erickson, Peter 145

Falstaff 6, 7, 17, 21–2, 31, 73–4, 81–3,
  84–5, 124, 136, 198
family/state analogy 145
feminism 143–5
film and television productions 250,
  270–1, 283
  see also Henry V (films)
First Folio 2, 148

Fischer, Sandra K. 123–42
Foakes, R. A. 99–100
Forker, Charles 37, 38
French, Marilyn 144
Freud, Sigmund 47
Frye, Northrop 37
Fuller, Thomas 5
Furnivall, F. J. 25

Garber, Marjorie 42–66
Garrick, David 15
gender 143–5
genre 2, 7, 9
  critical studies 34–40
Gentleman, Francis 10
Gerald of Wales 205, 206
Gervinus, G. G. 25–6
Gildon, Charles 8–9
Ginzburg, Carlo 90
Girard, René 45, 121
Goethe, Johann Wolfgang von 18–19,
  61
Grady, Hugh 199
Greenblatt, Stephen 197, 213
Greene, Robert 1
Griffith, Elizabeth 17
Grillparzer, Franz 61

Hadfield, Andrew 204
Hall, Edward 52
Hall, Peter 259, 260, 262
Hammond, Antony 54
Hands, Terry 273, 274
Hanmer, Thomas 13
Hapgood, Robert 139–40
Harington, Sir John 155, 222
Harrison, G. B. 162
Hawkes, Terence 124
Hawkins, William 4
Hazlitt, William 21–2, 23
Helgerson, Richard 197, 204, 206
Heminges, John 2–3, 148
Henry IV of France 169, 171
1 Henry IV 38, 72–81
  counterfeiting metaphors 135, 136
  critical history 16, 17, 24, 28
  destabilization 68–71
  econo-contractual metaphors 131–2,
    134–6
  Glendower/O'Neill association
    214–15

historiographical perspective 68–9
misrule and rebellion 74, 78–9, 80
performance history 249
redemption ethos 135
tavern scenes 76–8
time and space 71, 72–80, 81, 92
Welsh dimension 212–14
2 Henry IV 38, 81–91, 105, 215
critical history 17
econo-contractual metaphors 132–3,
136–7
misrule and rebellion 82, 86, 87, 89
performance history 249
sickness and decay imagery 81–2, 84,
86, 87
tavern scenes 83–5
time and space 71, 81, 87–91, 92
Henry V 10, 35, 36, 39, 197, 199, 233–4
contractual metaphors 137
critical history 7, 8, 14, 16, 20, 22,
29, 30
father/son relations 145
four captains scene 216–18
Irish dimension 215–19
national identity construction
215–18, 219
performance history 249, 259
wooing scene 137, 219
Henry V (films)
Kenneth Branagh 226–30, 233–5,
236, 237–8, 239, 240–3, 250
Laurence Olivier 10, 234, 235–6,
250
1 Henry VI 9, 24, 28, 30, 72–81, 144,
145, 148–9
carnivalesque inversions 166–8
contemporaneity 148, 162, 163,
168–70
critical history 1, 16
female dominance and misrule 160,
161, 166–8
Joan/Elizabeth association 149, 160–2,
163, 164, 166, 168, 171–2, 173
performance history 277–80, 284–5
Rouen episode 169–70, 181, 284
2 Henry VI 9, 10, 46, 183, 207–15, 220
Irish dimension 207–10
performance history 280, 285
3 Henry VI 9, 46, 53, 58
critical history 1
performance history 283–4

Henry VIII 36, 249
Highley, Christopher 214
Hill, Aaron 10
historical criticism 196–200
historiographical practice 71, 90–1,
220
history
deconstruction 59
deformation 42, 43, 50, 52, 57, 67
monumental 57
multiplicities 40
providential 39, 59
Shakespeare's interrogation of 39–40,
42, 44, 67
history plays
adaptations and rewritings 9–10, 15
critical history 1–31
generic issues 2, 7, 9, 21, 34–40, 60
providentialism 36, 39
see also individual plays
Holderness, Graham 35, 198, 200,
225–45
Holinshed, Raphael 127, 128, 130, 190,
194, 231–2
homosexuality 145, 258
Howard, Jean 144, 182–94
Howell, Jane 273, 274, 278, 283, 284
Hunt, Leigh 23
Hunter, G. K. 38

Inchbald, Elizabeth 24
individualism 238–9
Ireland 197–8, 203–25
and English national self-
construction 204, 206, 211, 214–15
Essex expedition 215, 219–20, 224–5
Nine Years War 203, 206, 207, 215

Jacobi, Derek 226, 234
James I 156, 220, 225, 232
Basilikon Doron 42
Jameson, Anna 23–4
Jardine, Lisa 196
Jenkins, Harold 68
Johnson, Samuel 13–14, 17–18, 55,
123
Jones, Ann Rosalind 222–3
Jones, Robert 40
Jonson, Ben 2, 3–4, 5, 6
Jorgens, Jack J. 250
Jorgensen, Paul 139

Kahn, Coppélia 145
Kamps, Ivo 200
Kastan, David Scott 39, 127
Kean, Edmund 23
Kelly, Henry 36
Kemble, John 23
Kemble, Stephen 23
Kennedy, Dennis 249–50
Kermode, Frank 18, 98
Kernan, Alvin 38
Kiernan, Pauline 250
King John 36, 98, 182–94
  critical history 20, 22, 23, 28, 29
  Faulconbridge controversy 192–4
  female characters and narrative
    weight 182, 184–6, 188–9, 194
  genealogies of rule 182, 187, 189,
    193
  legitimacy crisis 189–90, 191
  maternal focus 182, 192, 194
  moral and structural incoherence 188
  patriarchal subversion 184, 185, 186,
    188
  performance history 23, 249
kingship 197, 229, 258
  doctrine of the king's two bodies 86,
    150, 152
  royal androgyny 154, 156–7, 159
Knight, G. Wilson 97, 199
Knights, L. C. 97
Knox, John 152, 159, 167, 176
Kolin, Philip 143
Kott, Jan 196, 262

Lacan, Jacques 48–9
Lamb, Charles 23
language
  and characterization 98–9
  critical studies 97–101
  metaphor 98, 99, 100, 123, 124–5,
    126, 135, 139
  puns 100–1, 115
  rhetoric and control 125
  vocabulary of economics 124, 126,
    127–37
Lawrence, D. H. 97, 227
Lee, Sidney 30
Leggatt, Alexander 37, 198
legitimacy 189–90, 191, 235
Leicester, earl of 156, 163, 164, 168,
  175

Levin, Richard 200, 247–8
Lewis, C. S. 97–8
Lindenberger, Herbert 189
localization 148, 162, 163, 168–70, 199
Long Meg of Westminster 160
Lyly, John 171

MacCurtain, Margaret 205–6
Macdonald, Ronald R. 125–6
Machiavellianism 199
Mahood, M. M. 99
Maley, Willy 204
Malone, Edmund 148
Manningham, John 43
Marcus, Leah S. 147–82, 199, 220
Mary Queen of Scots 152, 156, 166, 172
masculinity and male identity 145
Meres, Francis 1–2
metaphor 98, 99, 100, 123, 124–5, 126,
  135, 139
mimesis 104–5, 106, 107
misrule and rebellion 67, 71, 78–9, 80,
  82, 84, 87, 89, 196, 198
Molloy, Charles 10
Montagu, Elizabeth 16–17
More, Thomas 45, 46, 53
Morgann, Maurice 17
Moryson, Fynes 203–4, 206, 215
Much Ado About Nothing 49–50
Muir, Kenneth 98, 139
Murphy, Andrew 203–25

Nashe, Thomas 1, 148, 163, 174
national identity construction 204, 206,
  211, 214–18, 219, 225–44
nationalism 226, 228, 232, 238
Neill, Michael 197–8, 203, 204, 206–7
new historicism 197, 200
New Shakspere Society 25, 29
Nider, Johannes 127
Nietzsche, Friedrich 56–7, 60–1, 62
Noble, Adrian 236, 274–5, 276–7, 278,
  280, 286, 287
Norbrook, David 199
Norton, Thomas 54

Olivier, Laurence 230, 234, 237, 258, 273
O'Neill, Hugh 205–6, 209, 210, 214,
  215, 218, 219–20, 221–2, 223,
  224–5
Ornstein, Robert 37

Parker, Patricia 18, 101
Parry, Dr William 154
paternal ideology 105, 106, 108, 118
patriarchy 103–6, 107, 114, 145, 184,
  186, 192, 193
patriotism 21, 26, 30, 148, 151, 191,
  226, 227–8, 230, 232, 237, 238,
  239
Patterson, Annabel 199
Pennington, Michael 249, 264–5,
  266–8, 269–70, 271
performance histories 246–88
  critical studies 246–50
  cycle productions 254–5, 256–71, 274
  film and television 250, 270–1, 283
  set design 255, 256, 259–60, 263–4,
    267–8
Philips, Ambrose 10
Pierce, Robert B. 145
politicization of literary studies
  196–200
Pope, Alexander 10–11, 12
Porter, Eric 261
Porter, Joseph 99, 125
primogeniture 104, 122
Prior, Moody 38–9
providentialism 36, 59, 183
psychoanalytic criticism 103–23
Pugliatti, Paola 40, 66–96
puns 100–1, 115

Quayle, Anthony 256

Rabkin, Norman 40
Rackin, Phyllis 35, 144, 182–94, 198
Redgrave, Michael 257–8
Ribner, Irving 36–7
Richard II 98–9, 107–23, 199, 242
  adaptations 9, 10
  critical history 18, 20, 21, 28, 29, 35
  deposition scene 9, 115, 269–70
  econo-contractual metaphors 127,
    129–30, 131, 229
  father/son interactions 107, 108, 114,
    118, 119, 121
  Gaunt/Bolingbroke relations 108,
    110, 111, 114, 117, 119
  genealogical mimesis 104–5
  Irish dimension 210–11
  language 98–9, 125, 131
  patriotic rhetoric 228–9, 230

performance history 249, 253–61,
  262–3, 266–70, 271
Richard III 42–66, 98, 99, 144, 183
  adaptations 9, 22
  birth narratives 45, 46, 58
  critical history 15–16, 20, 23, 28, 34
  deformity 44, 45, 46, 47–50, 52–3,
    55, 56, 57, 58, 63
  doubling and displacement 50–2
  female characters 183–4
  Freudian reading 47–8
  the historical Richard 44, 45–6, 49
  performance history 23, 30–1
  Richard as monster 45, 46, 49
  sources 54–5
  wooing scene 53, 61–2
Richards, I. A. 19
Richards, Shaun 216–17, 219
Richardson, William 18
riot and disorder 157, 166–7, 186
Ross, A. Elizabeth 38
Ross, Charles 44
Rossiter, A. P. 40
Rous, John 45
Rowe, Nicholas 6–8
Royal Shakespeare Company 248, 255,
  259, 260, 262
Rymer, Thomas 11

Saccio, Peter 49
Samuel, Raphael 238–9
Schlegel, August von 19–20
Seager, Francis 54
sexual inversion and political
  disorder 157, 166, 167, 177
Shakespearean criticism
  character study 17–18, 19, 23–4
  contemporary opinions 1–4
  eighteenth-century 10–18
  Johnsonian 13–14
  neoclassical 5, 10, 13
  post-Restoration 4–10
  psychoanalytic criticism 103–23
  Romantic 17, 18–24
  twentieth-century 29–31
  Victorian 24–9
  women readers and audiences 16–17
Shaw, George Bernard 24, 30–1, 175
Shewring, Margaret 253–64
Sidney, Sir Philip 59, 60
Siegel, Paul N. 36

294   *Index*

Sinfield, Alan 197, 200, 219, 248
Smidt, Kristian 39
Smith, Bruce R. 145
Smith, Emma 249
Spenser, Edmund 165, 208, 209, 210, 213
Spiekerman, Tim 198–9
Sprague, Arthur Colby 246, 262
Spurgeon, Caroline 18, 98
Stubbs, John 164–5, 166, 170, 180
Styan, J. L. 247
Swinburne, A. C. 28–9

Tate, Nahum 9
Taylor, Gary 217, 218, 246–7
The Tempest 56
Tennenhouse, Leonard 198
Theobald, Lewis 11–13
Thompson, Emma 238
Tillyard, E. M. W. 34–5, 54, 199, 261
Tinker, Jack 224–5, 227, 228
Titus Adronicus 57
Traversi, Derek 35
Turner, John 232

Velz, John 38
Vergil, Polydore 45
Vickers, Brian 99, 144–5
Von Hartmann, Eduard 62

Waller, Lewis 30
Walsingham, Francis 168
Warburton, William 12
Warner, David 260
Wars of the Roses 165, 233, 255
Wars of the Roses (performance cycle) 259–71
Watson, Donald 38
Webber, Joan 125
Weimann, Robert 100
Wells, Robin Headlam 145
Whately, Thomas 18
White, Hayden 60
Whiter, Walter 18
Wilders, John 35–6
Wilhelm II of Prussia 48
Willbern, David 101
Wilson, John Dover 38
Wilson, Robert 171
witchcraft 171–3
women readers and audiences 16–17
Worden, Blair 197
Worthen, W. B. 248

xenophobic drama 171

Yachnin, Paul 66–7, 68, 90
Yeats, W. B. 29–30, 254